WOODROW WILSON:
A MEDICAL AND
PSYCHOLOGICAL BIOGRAPHY

Woodrow Wilson:
A Medical and
Psychological Biography

EDWIN A. WEINSTEIN

Princeton University Press
Princeton, New Jersey

FOR
ANNE

CONTENTS

LIST OF ILLUSTRATIONS

All photographs except 16 are from collections in the Princeton University Library or Archives (*Following page 210*).

PREFACE

WOODROW WILSON in his private and public life coped with stresses which few other Presidents have encountered. Along with the pressures of war, revolution, and peace-making, he suffered from a variety of neurological, medical, and psychologically induced illnesses. These included dyslexia as a child, and depressions, psychosomatic complaints, and progressive cerebral vascular disease as an adult. He experienced the first of a series of strokes at the age of thirty-nine, when he was a professor at Princeton. Ten years later, in 1906, while president of the university, he had a vascular occlusion which deprived him of most of the sight of his left eye. Minor episodes occurred during his terms as Governor of New Jersey and President of the United States. In April 1919, at the Paris Peace Conference, he developed a generalized viral illness which, superimposed upon prior brain damage, resulted in transient disturbances of behavior. In October 1919, he sustained a massive stroke which paralyzed the left side of his body, robbed him of much of his remaining vision, and caused enduring mental changes.

This volume deals with Wilson's health and personality and considers the impact of his illnesses on affairs at Princeton and on later national and international events. To these ends, I have studied the growth of his personality in the context of family relationships and the broader socio-cultural milieu. I have reviewed his religious beliefs, not only because of their role in the formation of his character, but because they were important in shaping his conception of disease. Wilson's developmental dyslexia has been considered in terms of its effects on his relationship with his parents and on the development of his thought and language. I have evaluated Wilson's depressions and their psychosomatic expressions from the standpoint of the stresses involved in fulfilling parental expectations and transcending the bounds of a narrow early environment. As Wilson's writings and political utterances were, to a remarkable degree, symbolic representations of his illnesses and other personal problems, I have considered their content in some detail.

The scope of the study is limited by my lack of contact with my "patient," by the medical knowledge and customs of the time, and by circumstances connected with the unique office of President of the United States. Following his devastating stroke, for example, Wilson was not hospitalized and case records were not kept (or they were kept and have subsequently been destroyed). Accurate information about Wilson's illness was not issued, and subsequent accounts are biased for personal and political reasons. On the other hand, I have had the advantage of hindsight, which has enabled me to supplement incomplete data with clinical judgment.

Wilson himself was a prolific letter writer and, in his earlier years, he described his symptoms in detail in his correspondence with his parents, his first wife, and his friend Mary Allen Peck. Unlike other Presidents, he composed his own speeches: most of his addresses were extemporaneous. I have been greatly aided by the unpublished diary of Wilson's personal physician, Dr. Cary T. Grayson, and the unpublished memoir of his brother-in-law and close friend, Stockton Axson.

Readers should know that, in reproducing the text of quoted material, I have not corrected misspellings or used the editorial *sic* unless necessary for clarity. Thus what might strike the reader as a typographical error is most likely not one.

I owe much to my intimate association over the past ten years with the editors of *The Papers of Woodrow Wilson*. Arthur S. Link, who made this study possible, shared his unparalleled knowledge of Wilson's background and career with me, and his criticisms and suggestions have greatly improved the text. David W. Hirst gave me much valuable information, and our many discussions have helped to clarify my thinking. I appreciate the interest of John E. Little and former Associate Editor John Wells Davidson. I am honored that this book should appear as a supplementary volume of *The Papers of Woodrow Wilson*. It is with pleasure that I express my thanks to the Board of Trustees of the Woodrow Wilson Foundation for my appointment as the first Woodrow Wilson Foundation Fellow.

I am grateful to Professor Link for offering me the use of the Axson memoir and to Cary T. Grayson, Jr., for permission to examine and quote from his father's diary. I am indebted to my medical consultants: Dr. Robert A. Newburger, Dr. Milton Mendlowitz, Dr. Henry Spector, Dr. Abraham Kornzweig, Dr. Hobart A. Reimann, Dr. Lawrence D. McHenry, Jr., Dr. Martha Bridge Denckla, and Dr. J.D.W. Pearce. Dr. Edward S. Gifford kindly provided me with a report of Dr. George de Schweinitz's ophthalmological examination of Wilson.

I am pleased to acknowledge the assistance of Ms. Judith A. Schiff, Head, Manuscripts Division, Yale University Library; Ms. Helen W. Slotkin, Archivist of the Massachusetts Institute of Technology; Ms. E. Gvora, Reference Librarian of the Thunder Bay (Ontario) Public Library; and Ms. Thelma Van Norte, Director of Medical Record

Services, Central State Hospital, Milledgeville, Georgia. The Woodrow Wilson House of the National Trust for Historic Preservation permitted the examination of Wilson's eyeglasses. The staff of the Manuscripts Department of the Firestone Library of Princeton University has been most helpful.

Dr. Pendleton Herring, Dr. David McK. Rioch, and Lucy and Paul Haagen read chapters of the manuscript. The editing of Mrs. Margaret Douglas Link has added notably to the book's literary quality. William A. Link and Susannah Jones gave indispensable editorial assistance. I am deeply indebted to my friend, Ms. Violet Waddell, for typing portions of the manuscript and to my wife, Anne, for her many labors of love. I owe my final debts to R. Miriam Brokaw, my helpful editor at Princeton University Press, and to Phyllis Marchand, who prepared the comprehensive index.

EDWIN A. WEINSTEIN
Bethesda, Md.
April 15, 1980

CHRONOLOGY OF WOODROW WILSON'S
MAJOR ILLNESSES

May 1896	Initial stroke causing marked weakness of right upper extremity (RUE) and sensory disturbances in fingers, misdiagnosed as neuritis. Unable to write normally for almost a year.
June 1904	Stroke causing weakness of RUE persisting for several months.
May 28, 1906	Stroke manifested by sudden loss of vision in left eye which persisted and weakness of RUE.
Nov. 1907	Attack of weakness and numbness of fingers of RUE of several months duration.
July 1908	Two attacks of "neuritis" affecting RUE.
Dec. 1910	Transitory weakness of right hand.
April 1913	Attack of "neuritis" involving left upper extremity.
May 1914	Vascular pathology in retinal arteries noted.
1915-1919	Bouts of severe headache lasting several days, perhaps associated with hypertension.
May-Sept. 1915	Transient episodes of weakness of right hand.
Apr. 3-7, 1919	Influenza at Paris Peace Conference with manifestations of brain and cardiac involvement.
Sept. 1919	Severe headaches, diplopia, and signs of cardiac decompensation.
Sept. 25, 1919	Transitory left hemiplegia.
Oct. 3, 1919	Massive stroke resulting in permanent left hemiplegia, severely restricted vision, and mental impairment.
1923-1924	Further loss of vision.
Feb. 3, 1924	Died.

WOODROW WILSON:
A MEDICAL AND
PSYCHOLOGICAL BIOGRAPHY

CHAPTER I

Family and Boyhood

WOODROW WILSON'S FAMILY had its roots in Scotland and northern Ireland. His father, Joseph Ruggles Wilson, was born in Steubenville, Ohio, in 1822. He was the youngest of the seven sons of James Wilson (there were also three daughters), an immigrant from Ulster, who became a printer and newspaper editor in Philadelphia and went on to an active career as an editor, publisher, businessman, and judge in Ohio. A Jeffersonian Republican and then a Whig, James Wilson took part in many bitter political struggles and indulged in the colorful rhetoric of the day. He supported the candidacy of William Henry Harrison in 1840 and attacked the incumbent Democrats as "Goths & Vandals" who had to be pulled down from their high places.[1] Judge Wilson, after a term in the Ohio legislature in 1816 and a long career as a Whig partisan, tried to set up his sons in business and find political positions for them. To his regret, he was unable to provide for his youngest boys.[2]

Joseph Ruggles Wilson learned his father's printer's trade and then taught school briefly. He attended Jefferson (now Washington and Jefferson) College and then studied for the ministry at Western Theological Seminary in Pittsburgh and Princeton Theological Seminary. One of Wilson's teachers at Princeton was the physicist Joseph Henry, later the first director of the Smithsonian Institution. Wilson was ordained by Ohio Presbytery in 1849. In the same year he married Janet Woodrow, daughter of a Presbyterian minister. Joseph R. Wilson successively served two small congregations and eked out a living by teaching rhetoric at Jefferson College and natural science at Hampden-Sydney College. In 1855, he accepted a call from the Presbyterian Church of Staunton, Virginia. Marion Wilson, the first child, was born on October 20, 1851; Annie Josephine Wilson, on September 8, 1853. Thomas Woodrow Wilson was born in Staunton on December 29, 1856.[3]

[1] James Wilson to Elisha Whittlesey, March 26, 1836, quoted in Francis P. Weisenburger, "The Middle Western Antecedents of Woodrow Wilson," *Mississippi Valley Historical Review,* XXIII (December 1936), 382.

[2] *Ibid.,* pp. 376, 385-87.

[3] Although Wilson was called "Tommy" as a child and was known as such to close friends to the end of his life, I will refer to him as "Woodrow" throughout this book.

From the Staunton pastorate, Joseph R. Wilson rose rapidly in the Presbyterian ministry. In 1858, the family moved to Augusta, Georgia, where Wilson occupied one of the most important pulpits in the South. In the same year, he received the degree of Doctor of Divinity from Oglethorpe University. Other honors and offices followed. After the sectional split in the Presbyterian Church in 1861, Dr. Wilson was one of the founders of the southern church and was elected permanent clerk of its General Assembly. In 1865, he became stated clerk, the denomination's chief executive officer, a post he held until 1898. In 1870, he was elected Professor of Evangelical Theology and Sacred Rhetoric at the Columbia (South Carolina) Theological Seminary; at the same time, he became stated supply (temporary minister) of the First Presbyterian Church of Columbia. In 1874, he moved to the First Presbyterian Church of Wilmington, North Carolina, where he served for fourteen years.

While nothing is known of James Wilson's ancestry, Woodrow Wilson's maternal grandfather, the Rev. Mr. Thomas Woodrow, came from a long line of Scottish Presbyterian ministers. He was a graduate of Glasgow University and went from Scotland to a church in Carlisle, England, where he served for fifteen years. Woodrow Wilson's mother, Janet (always called Jessie or Jeanie), was born in Carlisle in 1830, the fifth of eight children. In 1835, the family emigrated to America, where Jessie's mother died soon after their arrival. The children were cared for by their mother's sister, Isabella Williamson, whom Thomas Woodrow soon married. Despite his scholarly background and education, Woodrow did not have a distinguished career in America. He preached first in Poughkeepsie, New York, then in Brockville, Ontario, and, in 1837, became pastor of the First Presbyterian Church of Chillicothe, Ohio. The Presbyterian Church was rent by conflicts over doctrinal standards and slavery, and Woodrow resigned in 1848, giving ill health as the reason.[4] The remainder of his career he spent in small country churches. Woodrow Wilson remembered his Grandfather Woodrow, who preached once in his father's church, a patriarch with a strong Scots accent, who balanced a pair of borrowed glasses on his nose and never paused in his swift-flowing discourse.[5] He died in 1877.

An important influence on Woodrow Wilson was James Woodrow, a maternal uncle. He was a distinguished scientist who became Professor of Natural Science in Connection with Revelation at the Co-

---

[4] Weisenburger, p. 388.
[5] Ray Stannard Baker, *Woodrow Wilson: Life and Letters,* 8 vols. (Garden City, N.Y., 1927-1939), I, 19.

lumbia Theological Seminary. James Woodrow had studied under Louis Agassiz at Harvard and received the Ph.D. degree from Heidelberg. *Who's Who in America* for 1906-1907 lists him as an associate of the Victoria Institute of London and of Isis of Dresden, and as a fellow of the American Association for the Advancement of Science and of the International Congress of Geologists. Dr. Woodrow was a strong supporter of the theory of evolution; he believed that science was a means of revealing God's truth. During the Civil War he served as the chief of the chemical laboratory of the Confederate Army. After the war, he opened a printing office for books, lawyers' briefs, college catalogues, and church papers; he also edited and published two Presbyterian journals. Among other church offices, he served as moderator of the synods of Georgia and South Carolina and was executive officer of the southern Presbyterian General Assembly's Foreign Mission Board. Because of his teaching of evolution, he was tried for heresy (though never convicted) and dismissed from the Columbia Theological Seminary. Afterward he became president both of a bank and of South Carolina College (now the University of South Carolina). He died in 1907.[6]

Woodrow Wilson was extremely proud of his Scots Presbyterian ancestry. At Bryn Mawr College, he boasted to students that anyone who had amounted to anything in American politics was of Scotch-

---

[6] A contemporary described James Woodrow as follows: "I first knew James Woodrow . . . in his early thirties. . . . I took a law brief to his office. He had a reputation among lawyers all over the State for proof-reading. I found that he did it all himself. He looked up, personally, even the lawyer's citations in his law-books. . . . When he got the State printing, his competitors gleefully declared that the good Presbyterian would have to do Sunday work to keep up the legislative Record. But every Saturday night at midnight he would go down to the office, put the men out, and lock up. Then at midnight Monday morning, he would go down to the office, unlock, and let the men in and put them to work at a minute past twelve. He delegated nothing. He read his own proof; unlocked his own office; taught his own classes; and kept his own missionary books. In his fights for the evolutionary theory, he fought a lone fight . . . and he never compromised. . . . And here's an odd thing. He lived here [Columbia] for nearly fifty years, but I doubt if he had a close friend in town. He was too busy for the soft amenities of friendship . . . he just did not mix with the crowd. He was the most punctual man I ever knew. He never was a minute early or late in keeping an appointment. He lived his life by rule. You never saw such a dauntless fighter in causes which he loved. But he fought straight and scorned to win crookedly. In reconstruction days, when the blacks were in the South Carolina State House piling up taxes on us, we considered for a time defeating them by tampering with ballots. But Dr. Woodrow said at the meeting: 'I am willing to take a gun and help to drive them out, but if you use these tissue ballots I shall make public protest.' " Washington A. Clark to William Allen White, quoted in William Allen White, *Woodrow Wilson: The Man, His Times, and His Task* (Boston and New York, 1924), pp. 22-23.

Irish descent.[7] Perhaps jokingly, he told a group of New Englanders that every line of strength in the history of the world was one colored by Scotch-Irish blood.[8] Wilson gloried in the Scottish Presbyterians' fight for religious liberty and was fond of evoking the picture of the signing of the Covenant on a tombstone in Greyfriars Church in Edinburgh. During his presidency, he declared: "The stern Covenanter tradition that is behind me sends many an echo down the years."[9]

Joseph Ruggles Wilson was an orthodox Calvinist who believed in an ordered universe, ruled by a God who had established a covenant of grace with his people, in which forgiveness of sins was exchanged for submission to His will. God used men for His purposes and presided over all things. The key to happiness and success lay in the sense of personal worth gained from ethical and moral achievement in God's service. The good Christian was a busy one, and success, or lack of it, was a matter of one's own responsibility, regardless of extrapersonal social and economic forces. In carrying out God's plan, one could strive for high goals, assume leadership, and face crises with supreme confidence. "From such beliefs," in the words of Arthur S. Link, "came a sure sense of destiny and a feeling of intimate connection with the sources of power."[10] His son, Woodrow, never deviated from his father's faith in an omnipotent God and a universe governed by natural and moral law.

Dr. Wilson was a powerful and erudite preacher in an age in which eloquence and the propounding of great principles were paths to success in the ministry, law, and politics. Religion and politics were closely entwined, and sermons and political addresses, alike, produced great rhetoric before large audiences. Passages were memorized and discussed in homes and places of business. Dr. Wilson never forgot the thrill of seeing Daniel Webster standing in front of the Capitol on a blazing hot day, extending his hand toward the sun and opening his speech with the salutation, "Hail, Thou Sun of Liberty." "And do you know," Dr. Wilson would say as he told the story with characteristic

[7] Lucy Maynard Salmon to Ray Stannard Baker, January 6, 1926, the Papers of Ray Stannard Baker, Library of Congress; hereinafter cited as the Baker Papers.

[8] An after-dinner speech to the New England Society in the City of New York, December 22, 1900, in Arthur S. Link, David W. Hirst, John E. Little et al., eds., The Papers of Woodrow Wilson, 38 vols. to date (Princeton, N.J., 1966-   ), Vol. 12, pp. 52-53; hereinafter cited as PWW.

[9] Address at a luncheon given at the Mansion House, London, December 18, 1918, in Ray Stannard Baker and William E. Dodds, eds., The Public Papers of Woodrow Wilson, 6 vols. (New York and London, 1925-1927), V, 346.

[10] Arthur S. Link, Wilson, 5 vols. to date (Princeton, N.J., 1947-   ), II, 64.

humor, "I thought the sun winked back at him."[11] Dr. Wilson's sermons were dramatic and colorful and filled with brilliant figures of speech. For example: "Sow yourselves . . . in its [the world's] every field of influence. Knead yourselves into its every possible loaf of soul-nourishing bread. Be vitalizing wheat, indeed, in all that the word implies."[12] For Dr. Wilson, oratory was not only a form of literature; it was also the divinely inspired art of persuasion by which God's truth could enter into men's hearts and uplift their spirits.

Southern Presbyterianism was a religion of the gentry and the educated, prosperous middle class, and enjoyed a prestige out of all proportion to the number of its adherents. As members of the social elite, the Wilsons lived comfortably, with servants. In Columbia, they purchased a lot, and Mrs. Wilson supervised the building of a large house. Dr. Wilson was a vigorous community leader and had large congregations in Augusta and Columbia, and a wealthy one in Wilmington. He was also active in church and sectional politics and shared the sentiments of the community on the burning issues of slavery and secession. From his pulpit in Augusta, he justified the institution of slavery on moral and scriptural grounds.[13] He invited the first General Assembly of the southern Presbyterian Church to meet in his church in Augusta and served for a summer as a chaplain in the Confederate Army.

Joseph R. Wilson saw himself primarily as an educator and much preferred the pulpit and the classroom to pastoral routine. He left his post in Augusta to join the faculty of the Columbia Theological Seminary at a financial loss. Fortunately, he was able to supplement his income by serving as stated supply of the First Presbyterian Church of Columbia. However, the congregation in 1873 expressed a desire for a full-time minister to be a real pastor to them. Upon the installation of the new minister, Dr. Wilson lost his pulpit. With the support of his brother-in-law, James Woodrow, and another colleague at the seminary, he then led a movement in the faculty for compulsory attendance at the seminary chapel by the students. The time chosen coincided exactly with the hour of services at the First Church. The students objected vigorously to the decree because it interfered with their right

[11] Stockton Axson, Memoir of Woodrow Wilson, unpublished MS. in the possession of Arthur S. Link; hereinafter cited as Axson Memoir.

[12] John M. Mulder, *Woodrow Wilson: The Years of Preparation* (Princeton, N.J., 1978), p. 20.

[13] See his sermon, *Mutual Relation of Masters and Slaves as Taught in the Bible* . . . (Augusta, Ga., 1861).

to freedom of worship. Thirteen of them were suspended for refusal to attend services at the chapel. The board of the seminary supported Wilson, but the students appealed its ruling to the General Assembly. To bolster his position, Dr. Wilson ran for election as commissioner to the General Assembly in 1874, but he was badly defeated. After bitter debate, the Assembly voted a compromise solution: it affirmed confidence in the faculty but recommended that attendance at services be made voluntary. Dr. Wilson felt that he was being asked to assume responsibility for the education of the students without the power to fulfill it and resigned. He then accepted the lucrative $4,000-a-year post as pastor of the First Presbyterian Church of Wilmington.[14] Ten years later, Woodrow Wilson told his fiancée, Ellen Louise Axson, that his father had left the seminary, not because of dissatisfaction with his work, but because the General Assembly had "sustained the self-will of the students."[15]

To most Wilson biographers, Joseph Ruggles Wilson has appeared as a dominating, confident, outgoing, and highly opinionated figure. The youngest member of a striving, competitive family—two of his brothers became generals in the Civil War, and they and others were successful in business—he made his own way in the world. His industry and aggressiveness brought success, but his outspoken approach also made enemies. A well-built, handsome man, he was especially popular with the ladies of his congregations. While religious, he was not pious or ascetic; he smoked a pipe incessantly and was known to take a drink of "Presbyterian Scotch."[16] From the time that Woodrow was in his teens, his father took regular summer vacations alone at Saratoga, a favorite watering place for ministers, while Mrs. Wilson and the children visited relatives or went off on their own. Dr. Wilson's principal avocation, as well as vocation, was talking. He was conversant with a broad range of topics which he loved to discuss at length. Well-grounded in the classics, he was fond of weaving Latin quotations into his speech and in tracing a word back to its Latin or Greek root.[17] Quick at repartee, Dr. Wilson took especial delight in jokes, puns, and humorous anecdotes. According to Stockton Axson, who spent many hours with Dr. Wilson, he never forgot a joke, never wearied of repeating the ones he liked (often to the same person), and rarely missed an opportunity to pun. He was also fond of horseplay, sometimes to the embarrassment of his more dignified son. A favorite antic was to

[14] For a detailed account of the controversy, see Mulder, *Wilson: The Years of Preparation,* pp. 12-17.

[15] WW to Ellen Louise Axson, October 12, 1884, *PWW,* Vol. 3, p. 349.

[16] White, *Wilson,* p. 16.   [17] Axson Memoir.

hand his ticket to a railway conductor with the request that he wanted
"a little punch." His wit also ran to teasing younger members of the
family. Toward the end of his life, when he suffered from cerebral
arteriosclerosis, he became gruff and irascible, but, in his younger
days, his humor was not bitter or malicious except when directed
against his enemies.[18]

Another side of the personality of Joseph Ruggles Wilson is revealed
in the letters to his son and in the recollections of Stockton Axson.
All of his life, Dr. Wilson said, he had been troubled by feelings of
inferiority, and had had to fight the agonies of shyness and the torments
of self-consciousness.[19] He was disturbed by feelings of self-doubt and
a habit of morbid introspection—apparently an occupational disease
of Presbyterian ministers.[20] Woodrow Wilson thought that his father
underestimated his own capabilities.[21] In his later years, Dr. Wilson's
career ran into difficulties, and he was subject to spells of the "blues";
much of his advice to his son concerned conquering self-consciousness
and depression. In retrospect, Dr. Wilson's compulsive punning and
clowning may be interpreted as antidotes to shyness and self-consciousness and as ways to control situations. Combinations of shyness
and vanity, self-depreciation, and high ambition are not at all unusual
in the lives of achieving people.

The content of Dr. Wilson's jokes and anecdotes was often a symbolic representation of some specific problem, particularly with his
colleagues and congregations. Once, when he was having trouble
making ends meet because the congregation in Wilmington was delinquent in paying his salary, he met a parishioner who commented
that his horse looked better groomed than himself. It was so, Dr.
Wilson replied, because he cared for his horse, while his congregation
took care of him. He liked to reminisce about the way he had practiced
oratory as a young man in his father's barn. He said that a cow,
placidly chewing her cud, made as intelligent an audience as some of
his congregations.

The theme of good looks was prominent in Dr. Wilson's remarks
and anecdotes. He once spoke of one of his enemies, Thomas Alexander Hoyt, who was Ellen Axson Wilson's uncle, pastor of a fashionable Philadelphia church, and married to a rich wife. Dr. Wilson

---

[18] *Ibid.*

[19] *Ibid.*; see also Joseph Ruggles Wilson to WW, January 25, 1878, *PWW*, Vol. 1, p. 346.

[20] Ellen Axson, for example, referred to the "duty of *self-examination*" of "our good Presbyterian ancestors." ELA to WW, February 4, 1884, *ibid.*, Vol. 3, p. 7.

[21] WW to ELA, April 13, 1884, *ibid.*, p. 127.

said that, while the Rev. Dr. Hoyt was the handsomest man he knew, he was "a wolf in sheep's clothing."[22]

Dr. Wilson had a strong dislike for Ralph Waldo Emerson, because Emerson was a liberal Unitarian and syncretist in religion. Dr. Wilson once saw the Sage of Concord asleep in a railway carriage. His head was thrown back, and he snored with his mouth open. "It was," Dr. Wilson reported, "the biggest mouth I ever looked into."[23] Speaking of Benjamin Morgan Palmer of New Orleans, one of the most distinguished preachers in the South, Wilson said that, when he got up to speak, he looked like a gorilla, but when he finished he looked like a god.

Despite his extraordinary good looks, Dr. Wilson was conscious of his long nose and enormous ears and feet. One of his stories concerned a Dr. MacFarland, a Presbyterian minister with a particularly long nose. Finding himself in the minority on a question put by the presiding officer at a church meeting, Dr. MacFarland sprang to his feet and excitedly shouted several times, "No! no!" Whereupon the moderator declared: "The motion is carried, notwithstanding Dr. MacFarland's nose." Dr. Wilson doted on stories about the General Assembly. Probably the wittiest of all of his comments came in response to the Assembly's declaration that the theory of evolution was heresy: "Oh, the ears of the Presbyterian jackass, they extend to the ends of the earth."[24]

Whatever the reason for Joseph R. Wilson's preoccupation with looks—he may have been teased by his brothers—and his use of the theme in his metaphors, it greatly affected Woodrow, who grew up acutely conscious of his facial features. He believed that his homeliness made him unattractive to women. He told his first love, his cousin, Harriet Woodrow, that if he had his father's face and figure it would not matter what he said.[25] One of his favorite limericks ran:

> For beauty, I'm not a star.
> There are others more handsome by far.
> But my face, I don't mind it,
> You see, I'm behind it.
> It's the people in front that I jar.

Jessie Wilson has been described as quiet, gentle, shy, reserved, highly principled, and intensely devoted to her family. Although she

---

[22] The Hoyts later visited the Woodrow Wilsons when Wilson was president of Princeton University. Hoyt placed his boots outside his room at night, and Wilson polished them. Margaret Axson Elliott, *My Aunt Louisa and Woodrow Wilson* (Chapel Hill, N.C., 1944), pp. 119, 127.

[23] Axson Memoir.   [24] *Ibid.*   [25] Baker, *Wilson*, I, 31.

enjoyed the affection and admiration of her husband and son, she was often unhappy in her relationships outside the home. She had a great sense of status and personal dignity, and some of Dr. Wilson's parishioners thought that she felt superior and was cold and standoffish. In Augusta, she did not belong to any of the various societies or auxiliary associations of the church.[26] Ray Stannard Baker relates that, when the Wilsons came to Augusta, some of the ladies, with characteristic helpfulness, delivered little presents of fruit and preserves. They soon realized that this sort of thing hurt Mrs. Wilson's pride.[27] She was similarly upset when, on a boat excursion near Wilmington, she was offered some cake. Everyone except the Wilsons was eating, but Mrs. Wilson replied: "No, no, thank you. I couldn't eat it for anything—not here on the deck!"[28] She also had trouble keeping servants.[29] Even by the standards of the day, she was prudish. Once when she was ill, Woodrow and a neighbor, Ellen Bellamy, sat through the night at her bedside. Dr. Wilson was sleeping in the study, and the Wilson girls were married and living away. When Mrs. Wilson recovered, she was so embarrassed because an unmarried woman had spent a night in her home that she never invited the girl back into the house.[30] She was kind to people in want, by whom she could feel appreciated. The Wilson's handyman in Wilmington, David Bryant, recalled that she never turned a tramp—black or white—away from the door.[31] During the Civil War, she converted Dr. Wilson's church into a hospital for sick and wounded northern and southern soldiers. Among her social equals, however, she had few friends. When Woodrow Wilson was President of the United States, he wrote tactfully of his mother: "She was so reserved that only those of her household knew how steadfast and loyal she was."[32]

Jessie Wilson's temperament contrasted sharply with that of her garrulous, sociable husband. She differed most markedly in her utter seriousness and lack of joyfulness. Like her brother, James, she had no sense of humor and rarely joked.[33] She was fiercely loyal to her family and expressed strongly partisan views about the church con-

[26] Pleasant A. Stovall to RSB, June 8, 1925, Baker Papers.

[27] Baker, *Wilson*, I, 33.

[28] White, *Woodrow Wilson*, p. 60.

[29] WW to EAW, August 17, 1886, *PWW*, Vol. 5, p. 322.

[30] White, *Woodrow Wilson*, p. 60.

[31] *Ibid.*, p. 59.

[32] WW to William J. Hampton, September 13, 1917, Woodrow Wilson Collection, Firestone Library, Princeton University; hereinafter cited as the Wilson Collection.

[33] White, *Woodrow Wilson*, p. 24; Edith Gittings Reid, *Woodrow Wilson: The Caricature, the Myth, and the Man* (London, 1934), p. 6.

troversies in which her husband and brother were so often engaged. She always defended and supported them completely and accused their opponents of insolence, ignorance, spite, and malice. From the time (1874) for which family records are available, she was chronically ill and depressed. No organic cause was ever found for her symptoms of nervousness, headache, and other pains, and their nature suggests that they were of psychosomatic origin. She also worried a great deal about the health and safety of her family.

Mrs. Wilson's extremely strong feeling for her family and her probably emotionally caused illnesses may have had a connection with deprivation in her youth. As has been noted, her mother died shortly after she came to America. Jessie retained a frightening memory of a long, rough sea voyage in winter, of being swept overboard, and of saving herself by grasping a rope, with what Woodrow Wilson called "true Scottish pluck." She grew up with a dread of storms and a fear of the water. (Probably as a result of his mother's phobia, Woodrow Wilson never learned to swim.) After her father remarried, he seemed to lose interest in the children of his first marriage; he mentioned none of them in his will. Jessie remained very close to her brothers and a sister, Marion (she lived with Marion prior to her marriage to Joseph R. Wilson). Thomas Woodrow, Jr., after whom Woodrow was named,[34] provided the money to send Jessie to a girls' academy in Chillicothe. Except for the letter announcing Woodrow's birth, no correspondence between Janet Wilson and her father has been found; it may be significant that the letter was not written until the baby was four months old.[35] Also Jessie Wilson made only a single brief reference to her father in her letters to Woodrow.

Woodrow Wilson gave William Bayard Hale and his authorized biographer, Ray Stannard Baker, the impression that his grandfather had been a distinguished preacher. Baker states that Thomas Woodrow was "so notable a success as a pulpit orator, and his reputation for learning was so great, that he was called to the pastorate of the Hogg Presbyterian Church of Columbus, Ohio, where he remained until his death."[36] However, when Francis P. Weisenburger consulted church records, he found that there was no church of that name, and that Thomas Woodrow spent the remainder of his career ministering to poor small-town congregations of less than fifty members after leaving Chillicothe.[37]

[34] WW to Robert Bridges, March 15, 1882, PWW, Vol. 2, p. 107.
[35] Janet Woodrow Wilson to Thomas Woodrow, April 27, 1857, ibid., Vol. 1, p. 7.
[36] Baker, Wilson, I, 18-19.
[37] Weisenburger, p. 389. The fact that Thomas Woodrow twice gave ill health as the

Children who feel abandoned may compensate by fantasizing about, or exaggerating the importance of, their ancestors. The Woodrows believed that their line extended back to Patrik Wodro, who crossed the English Channel with William the Conqueror, not as an ordinary priest, but in the retinue of a high churchman.[38] By emphasizing the tradition of their distinguished ancestry, Wilson's mother contributed greatly to the enormous pride that Woodrow Wilson took in his Scottish descent.[39] It is likely that Jessie Wilson looked to her husband and son to restore the family's prestige. Although there is no evidence to prove it, one might guess that her health was better in Woodrow's earliest years, when she could always be close to him and when her husband's star was in the ascendancy.

The Wilson household was like that of most other Presbyterian preachers of that day. Sundays were strictly observed. Daily prayers and Bible readings took place, conducted by Dr. Wilson when he was home and by Mrs. Wilson when he was away. Mrs. Wilson and Woodrow's sisters played the melodion, and the family sang hymns and Scottish ballads. The Wilsons were very much closer to the Woodrow family than to Dr. Wilson's, and Woodrow relatives made frequent and lengthy visits. Woodrow was particularly fond of his Aunt Marion Woodrow Bones, and played a great deal with his girl cousins. As has been mentioned, Dr. Wilson was not in the least austere and kept up a lively family atmosphere. Card playing and games of chance were not permitted, but when Woodrow was old enough, he and his father played billiards and chess. The study in which Dr. Wilson wrote his sermons was a *sanctum sanctorum* to which entry was prohibited, except when he was away and his wife could get in to clean out the smell of tobacco smoke. The Wilsons were great readers. They subscribed to both English and American periodicals, and they enjoyed reading aloud from the novels of Sir Walter Scott and Charles Dickens and the essays of Charles Lamb. Even though Dr. Wilson preached that women were by their nature too lovingly tender and too weak to withstand the strains of higher education, he believed that they should be able to participate in the family circle and to impart the principles of religion to their children. Mrs. Wilson, to judge by her letters, was highly intelligent and literate. Wilson's elder and favorite

---

reason for resigning from his pastorate suggests that emotional illness may have been a factor in his disappointing career.

[38] James Wilson Woodrow to RSB, January 27, 1926, Baker Papers.

[39] Wilson admitted in 1912 that, in eulogizing the Scots and Scotch-Irish, he was eulogizing himself. See his talk to the editors of foreign-language newspapers, September 4, 1912, *PWW*, Vol. 25, p. 97.

sister, Marion, had a fine linguistic talent and worked after the Civil War as a translator of manuscripts for a Boston publishing house.[40]

Woodrow, for ten years the youngest child, was the favorite, and he grew up enjoying the complete loyalty and devotion of his parents and sisters. The Wilson correspondence, like so many family letters of the time, was filled with fervent expressions of affection. Even when Woodrow was a man, Dr. Wilson habitually addressed him as "My darling son" or "My precious son," and Jessie Wilson's letters contained strong sentiments of love and longing. There was a complete absence of any overt expressions of anger or resentment. Woodrow's mother was wholly approving and uncritical; when Wilson's father reproached him or pointed out his faults, he did so in the context of Christian love, duty, and morality.[41] Woodrow Wilson had a great sense of family responsibility, not only for his parents, but for the numerous relatives whom he took into his home and helped to support.

Dr. Wilson believed passionately that the objectives of education were the development of mind and character and the cultivation of clear thinking and expression. In his view, orderly speech came only from orderly thought, and the rules of expression depended on a knowledge of Latin and English grammar. Woodrow Wilson regarded his father as his greatest teacher and, as an adult, he liked to say that his own clear precise speech was the result of his father's insistence that he be able to say exactly what he meant. He also liked to recall that he and Dr. Wilson would go over the speeches of Daniel Webster to see if they could find words in which Webster's thoughts could be better expressed, but they could never improve on Daniel. Another one of Woodrow's memories was that of his father taking him to visit mills and factories. Dr. Wilson explained to his son the principles of chemistry and physics by which the raw materials were converted into finished products and thus entered into the streams of trade. When they returned home, Woodrow would describe what he had seen; and his father would insist that the boy put his observations and impressions into perfect English. Dr. Wilson was also a stickler for proper enunciation. When someone in the family spoke hurriedly, he would look at the offender, smile, and say "ar-tic-u-la-tion."[42]

The most remarkable feature of Wilson's childhood was that he had not learned his letters until he was nine years old and could not read until he was twelve. Although the Civil War disrupted schooling in

[40] Elliott, *My Aunt Louisa*, p. 107.

[41] See, for example, JRW to WW, March 27, 1877 and January 25, 1878; JWW to WW, October 6, 1879, *PWW*, Vol. 1, pp. 254-55, 345-46, 575.

[42] Axson Memoir.

the South, the boy did not lack for instruction at home. In addition to his father, his mother, sisters, and Aunt Marion all tried to teach him.[43] Even as determined a pedagogue as Dr. James Woodrow resigned himself to the situation, saying that if the family could not make a scholar out of the boy, they could at least make him a gentleman. At thirteen, he was a very slow reader and did badly at Major Joseph T. Derry's "select classical institution" in Columbia. Wilson's difficulties, Derry later recalled, occurred, not because he was not bright enough, but because "he was apparently not interested."[44] Yet Woodrow loved to have his parents and sisters read to him, and one of his most cherished memories was of listening in rapture to the tales of Scott, Dickens, and James Fenimore Cooper and to the stories of the Scottish Covenanters.[45]

Woodrow Wilson and his biographers have given various explanations for his slowness in reading. Wilson, in a conversation with Dr. Cary T. Grayson, his White House physician, said that he had been a "lazy boy."[46] In 1912, he told William Bayard Hale the unlikely story that he had not been taught to read because his mother had unfortunate memories of having been forced to learn Latin in her sixth year. He also gave Hale the equally implausible reason that his father was averse to having his son get his first glimpses of the world of knowledge other than through his father.[47] Another unlikely explanation is that given by Alexander and Juliette George in their biography, *Woodrow Wilson and Colonel House: A Personality Study*.[48] They say that Dr. Wilson was a frightening father—a tyrant and a martinet who destroyed his son's self-esteem and left him with a permanent sense of inadequacy and personal worthlessness. Woodrow, according to the Georges, was filled with hostility which, out of fear, he could not express openly. He manifested his resentment in a refusal to learn to read. Thus, the boy foiled his father's perfectionistic demands.

In light of the evidence and of the research of the past twenty years, it is much more likely that Woodrow Wilson had *developmental* dyslexia. The term dyslexia, derived from *dys* and the Greek *lexicis*, "pertaining to words," simply means difficulty in reading. The des-

[43] Jessie Bones Brower to RSB, November 5, 1925, Baker Papers.

[44] Baker, *Wilson*, I, 42.

[45] Memorandum of interviews with Cary T. Grayson, February 18 and 19, 1926, Baker Papers.

[46] *Ibid.*

[47] William Bayard Hale, *Woodrow Wilson* (New York, 1912), pp. 36-37.

[48] (New York, 1956.)

ignation itself is nonspecific as to cause. Dyslexia may be a result of brain damage, of low intelligence, of an impoverished social environment, and, occasionally, of emotional factors. *Developmental* dyslexia refers to reading difficulty in a child of normal intelligence who is free of brain damage and comes from a socially advantaged home in which there has been ample opportunity to learn. The condition, undiagnosed in Wilson's youth, was first described definitively in the 1890s under the term "congenital word blindness." This designation indicates the genetic aspects of the condition and has nothing to do with visual acuity[49] *per se*, but relates specifically to the recognition of words and letters. In the United States, developmental dyslexia, or specific reading disability, occurs in about ten percent of the school population[50] and is about five times more frequent in boys than in girls. It appears mainly with phonetically coded orthographies such as English, and does not interfere with the ability to learn the rules of grammar and the acquisition of a vocabulary, even a large one. The condition is often associated with defects in spelling and calculation. Most children learn to read in a few years, and remedial teaching may help.

Current views, derived from new methods of study, are that developmental dyslexia is caused by delay in the establishment of the specialized dominance of the left cerebral hemisphere of the brain for certain features of language. Anatomical and functional differences between the two halves of the brain exist at birth and, with growth, the asymmetry becomes more marked, and the hemispheres are increasingly specialized. The left hemisphere is popularly known as the language hemisphere and the right as the one specialized for tasks of visual-spatial organization. Actually, each hemisphere is specialized for language in a different way. The left hemisphere is dominant for the phonetic, sequential, syntactic, and referential,[51] or denotative,

[49] Wilson's dyslexia may have been the reason why he was given eyeglasses as a child, presumably on the assumption that he was nearsighted. A recent examination of the glasses that he used when he was President indicates a moderate farsightedness, making it improbable that he was ever nearsighted. I am indebted to Dr. Albert Kornzweig, Clinical Professor Emeritus of Ophthalmology, and Dr. Arnold Prywes, both of the Mount Sinai Medical School, for the examination.

[50] Sam D. Clements, *Minimal Brain Dysfunction in Children: Terminology and Identification* (Washington, 1966).

[51] Two modes of symbolism are generally recognized: referential, or denotative, and experiential, or connotative. In referential symbolism, a universally constant relationship exists between the word (or gesture) and its referent, between say, the word "chair" and the object "chair." Examples of purely referential symbols are the Morse Code, flag signaling devices, and alphabetical and mathematical notations. Experiential symbols express feelings, and their meaning depends more on context, emotions, and social

aspects of language, while the right is more specialized for the affective or emotional and the experiential or connotative features.[52]

One theory of developmental dyslexia is that, with the maturational delay in the establishment of these different strategies of language and cognition, there is competition between the two hemispheres for control of the same function, such as reading, and thus performance suffers. Dominance has a correlation with handedness: right-handed children almost always have left hemisphere dominance for the structural, phonetic, and sequential features of language, while left-handers are more apt to have mixed dominance or bilateral representation of the same function. A considerable number of dyslexic children are either left-handed or have a family history of left-handedness.[53] They often attempt to use a right hemisphere approach, that is, they try to visualize the whole word or sequence rather than piecing it together phonetically. Poor readers thus make more phonetic than optical errors.

The evidence that Wilson was a dyslexic child can be summed up in three main groups of facts. First (by his own repeated admissions), he was a very slow reader in adult life.[54] The bane of his work in graduate school at Johns Hopkins was the amount of reading required for his assignments. "Steady reading," he told his fiancée, "always demands of me more expenditure of resolution and dogged energy than any other sort of work: and it, consequently, tells upon me sooner."[55] As a professor at Princeton, he found the correction of examination papers an extremely tedious task.[56] Along with his trou-

---

relationships. The American flag is referential in the sense that it denotes territorial sovereignty and experiential in the sense that it expresses feelings of patriotism and national identity. The letter "A" in the referential function is the first letter of the alphabet, but the Scarlet Letter which Hester Prynne embroidered on the front of her dress derived meaning from the values of Puritan society.

[52] Eran Zaidel, "Lexical Organization in the Right Hemisphere," in Pierre A. Buser and Arlette Rougeu-Buser, eds., *Cerebral Correlates of Conscious Experience: Proceedings of an International Symposium on Cerebral Correlates of Conscious Experience, Held in Senanque Abbey, France on 2-8 August 1977* (Amsterdam, 1978), pp. 177-97; E. A. Weinstein and R. P. Friedland, "Behavioral Disorders Associated with Hemi-inattention," in Weinstein and Friedland, eds., *Hemi-inattention and Hemisphere Specialization* (New York, 1977).

[53] Wilson was right-handed, but one of his daughters was left-handed.

[54] Wilson diary, June 10 and November 7, 1876, *PWW*, Vol. 1, pp. 137, 222.

[55] WW to ELA, November 29, 1884, *ibid.*, Vol. 3, p. 496.

[56] Interview with Winthrop More Daniels, March 30, 1940, in the Henry Wilkinson Bradgon Collection, Firestone Library, Princeton University; hereinafter cited as the Bragdon Collection.

bles in reading in English, Wilson, despite years of effort, could translate from German and French only with the aid of a dictionary, and he was never able to speak either language.[57]

Second, Wilson was only a fair speller and was poor in arithmetic. Eleanor, his youngest daughter, described how he "frowned at the prospect of adding even a short column of figures, and sometimes called to us from the next room, 'Children, what is seven times eight?' " He disliked anything to do with handling personal finances, and his wife managed all household money matters.[58] When the Wilsons were about to build their house in Princeton, he made an error in figuring the interest on a prospective loan, a mistake that greatly distressed him. He was less sensitive in later years: he joked in a speech about how he had "an infirmity" which prevented him from remembering figures.[59]

Third, strong evidence that Wilson had the mixed cerebral dominance and the bilateral representation for language, associated with childhood dyslexia, came in 1896, after his first known stroke. His right hand suddenly became so paralyzed that he was unable to use it to write. In a few days, with little practice, he was able to write left-handed with complete legibility and perfectly formed characters.[60]

One can assume that the boy's reading disability had a profound effect on his family. In their ignorance of its cause, Wilson's parents could attribute the condition only to lack of interest or willfulness. His mother probably became more apprehensive and his father more insistent on drilling his "lazy" son. Failure to read for himself made the boy more dependent on his parents, who were his main sources of information about the outside world; and he may have felt guilty about disappointing them. Not least, it deprived him of the thrill of discovery and mastery that a child gets from the acquisition of knowledge on his own. This may have made him feel inferior to boys of his own age. He also wore glasses, which may have hampered his play.

On the positive side, the type of cerebral organization associated with dyslexia and Wilson's adaptation to it may have contributed to his use of auditory and visual imagery in his imaginative play as a child, and to his cognitive, linguistic style as an adult. As a young

[57] *Ibid.*; WW to ELA, April 27, 1885, *PWW*, Vol. 4, p. 532; WW to Edwin R. A. Seligman, April 19, 1886, *ibid.*, Vol. 5, p. 163.

[58] Eleanor Wilson McAdoo, *The Woodrow Wilsons* (New York, 1937), p. 12.

[59] "The Banker and the Nation," an address in Denver to the American Bankers' Association, September 30, 1908, *PWW*, Vol. 18, p. 430.

[60] About this stroke and Wilson's ability to write with his left hand and its importance in confirming the diagnosis of developmental dyslexia, see pp. 141-42.

child, Woodrow would act out James Fenimore Cooper's Leather-stocking tales, which had been read to him by his mother. He and his younger cousin, Jessie Bones, painted their faces with berry juice, brandished tomahawks, and tied their helpless victims to the stake. Dressed in mail made from raveled carpet, Woodrow was a Crusader knight who rode forth on a broomstick to rescue Christian maidens imprisoned in Saracen castles. In his teens, he created another imaginary world and lived many hours as Vice Admiral Thomas W. Wilson, Duke of Eagleton, commander in chief of Her Majesty's "Flying Squadron." "Admiral Wilson" wrote daily reports to the Navy Department, and his main achievement was the discovery and destruction of a nest of pirates in the Pacific Ocean. While the boy's main interest was in naval affairs, "Lord Thomas W. Wilson" also found time to command the Royal Lance Guards. Wilson got his materials from Cooper's sea tales, from Frederick Marryat's stories, and from illustrations of ships clipped from the newspapers and magazines to which his family subscribed. Even though Woodrow had never seen a ship, or even the ocean, he learned every class or type of sailing ship, its name and home port, and the proper use of every sail, shroud, and spar.[61] His drawings were amazingly accurate. Wilson spent a remarkably long time in his imaginary world. As late as the summer of 1874, when he was seventeen, he was writing the rules and regulations of the Royal United Kingdom Yacht Club, Commodore Lord Thomas W. Wilson, Duke of Carlton, Admiral of the white, Royal Navy, &c. &c.[62]

Such worlds of fantasy are, of course, normal features of intellectual growth. They also provide an escape from the pressures of the real world and involve the adoption by the child of an identity removed from the family. Imaginative play may also be a means of overcoming specific fears: Wilson's occupation with naval affairs may possibly have had some connection with the fear of the water inculcated by his mother.[63] The remarkably accurate portrayal of Wilson's naval establishments forecasts his signal ability vividly to describe places like the Houses of Parliament and events like the Battle of Princeton, which he had never seen.

Wilson's difficulty in learning to read, and probably to spell, undoubtedly motivated him to take up the study of shorthand. In 1872, at the age of fifteen, he became interested in the system devised by

[61] Hale, *Woodrow Wilson*, p. 46.

[62] Wilson notebook, c. July 1, 1874, *PWW*, Vol. 1, pp. 54-55.

[63] As President of the United States, Wilson had an interest in fighting ships and was fonder of the navy than of the army.

Andrew J. Graham, a modification of the phonetic system of Sir Isaac Pitman. Wilson worked seriously but, despite his eagerness and diligence, learned slowly. He continued to practice during his freshman year at Davidson College (1873-1874) and, in the spring of 1875, after working at home, asked Graham for private lessons. Graham refused, but Wilson remained enthusiastic, carried on a correspondence with Graham, and tried to convert his friends to the system. Eventually he became highly proficient.

Contrary to what many of his biographers have said, Wilson was an active and healthy boy. He rode horseback, played for the Lightfoot Baseball Club, and was chosen its leader, not for his athletic skill, but because of his knowledge of parliamentary procedure. There is no evidence of any illness in childhood and no record of any behavior that would indicate that he was frail or sickly. Even someone as health-conscious as his mother could recall no illness or "weakness of any kind" in his childhood.[64] The misconception was created by Wilson's illnesses of later life and statements by Wilson himself to his biographers. These were offered by way of explanation of events about which Wilson felt guilty or ashamed. As will be described, he left Davidson College after his freshman year, not because he was physically ill, but because he was depressed, homesick, and lonely. However, he gave Baker and Hale the impression that he had been in poor physical health, and he told Stockton Axson that he had left because he had scarlet fever.[65] According to Dr. Grayson, he had had an attack of measles that permanently weakened his physique.[66] Later biographers took their cue from Hale, Baker, and Grayson. They were particularly influenced by Dr. Grayson's statement that Wilson was not constitutionally strong.

The medical climate of the time also influenced Dr. Grayson's opinion. The Doctor did not meet his patient until Wilson was President of the United States and had had intermittent symptoms of cerebral vascular disease for sixteen years. At the turn of the century, it was believed that diseases, even infectious ones like tuberculosis, had an underlying diathesis, or constitutional predisposition. Another factor in the impression of Wilson's poor health as a child was the misconception that intellectually brilliant people were physically frail. This myth was not dispelled until Lewis Terman's study of gifted children was published in the 1930s. Actually, Wilson must have had an ex-

[64] JWW to WW, December 9, 1880, *PWW*, Vol. 1, p. 700.

[65] Hale, *Woodrow Wilson*, p. 51; Baker, *Wilson*, I, 77; Axson Memoir.

[66] Cary T. Grayson, *Woodrow Wilson: An Intimate Memoir* (New York, 1960), p. 80.

ceptionally strong constitution to withstand the ravages of cerebral vascular disease for as long as he did. However, once the notion of Wilson's weak constitution became established, it served as a metaphorical representation of his dislike of physical force and opposition to war, and was used by his political enemies to depict him as unvirile and cowardly.

Woodrow Wilson entered Davidson College, a small Presbyterian institution near Charlotte, North Carolina, when he was sixteen years old. It was the first time that he had been away from his family. Eleven years later, on the occasion of escorting his younger brother, Josie (Joseph R. Wilson, Jr., born in 1867) to school, he recalled the pain of his separation from his mother.[67] At college, he was homesick, and one of the first entries in the notebook he kept was a long, gloomy prayer, telling of the "rough" and "dark" road that one had to take to "heaven's gate."[68] Wilson, poorly prepared academically, was placed on probation in mathematics and Greek and conditioned in ancient geography and Latin. His grades for the first semester were fairly good; his lowest mark was 74 in mathematics. He joined a debating group, the Eumenean Society, and copied out its constitution. He had a congenial roommate, played on the freshman baseball team, and spent much time alone reading.[69] One classmate recalled that he was "witty, genial, superior, but languid."[70]

The reasons for the "languid" behavior may be found in his journal and in the letters that he received from his mother. On May 3, 1874, he noted: "I am now in my seventeenth[71] year and it is sad, when looking over my past life to see how few of those seventeen years I have spent in the fear of God, and how much time I have spent in the service of the Devil. Although having professed Christ's name some time ago,[72] I have increased very little in grace and have done almost nothing for the Savior's Cause here below. O, how hard it is to do that which ought to be my greatest delight! *If God will give me the grace I will try to serve him from this time on, and will endeavour to attain nearer and nearer to perfection.*" He then quotes a minister's advice:

"Make your complaint, tell him how obscure everything still looks

[67] WW to ELA, July 28, 1884, *PWW*, Vol. 3, p. 262.

[68] Wilson notebook, November 6, 1873, *ibid.*, Vol. 1, pp. 33-34.

[69] Hale, *Woodrow Wilson*, pp. 49-50.

[70] The Rev. Dr. A. M. Fraser, quoted in Baker, *Wilson*, I, 74.

[71] Actually, he was in his eighteenth year.

[72] Wilson had been received into the membership of the First Presbyterian Church of Columbia on July 5, 1873.

to you, and beg Him to complete your cure. He may see fit to try your faith and patience by delaying this completion; but meanwhile you are safe in his presence, and, while led by his hand, he will excuse the mistakes you make, and pity your faults. He has a reason for everything he does. Having been pardoned by your God and Savior, the next thing you have to do is to show your gratitude for this infinite favor by consecrating yourself entirely to him, body, soul, and spirit."[73]

Wilson goes on to admonish himself to choose devout and holy associates, to read books for stimulation of his Christian life rather than for amusement, to settle down to a few favorite authors, and to read their works over and over again until their thoughts became his own. He closes by citing advice to spend more time in prayer, "to prefer a religion of principle to one of mere feeling," and to study and imitate the life of Christ.[74] Wilson does not specify what his sin, faults, and mistakes were, nor does he explain what services he had rendered the Devil, but he does appear to have been feeling guilty and troubled. Probably, he had had sexual stirrings.

At about the same time, Wilson developed a cold and a cough which greatly distressed his family. His mother wrote on May 20, 1874:

"My darling Boy, I am so anxious about that cold of yours. How did you take it? Surely you have not laid aside your winter-clothing? Another danger is in sitting without fire these cool nights. Do be careful, my dear boy, for my sake. You seem depressed—but that is because you are not well. You need not imagine that you are not a favorite. *Everybody* here likes and admires you. I could not begin to tell you the kind and flattering things that are said about you, by everybody that knows you. Yes, you will have no lack of friends in Wilmington—of the warmest sort. There seem to be an unusual number of young people about your age there—and of a superior kind— and they are prepared to take an unusual interest in you particularly. Why my darling, nobody could *help* loving you, if they were to try!

"I have a bad head-ache this morning dear—and wont attempt to write you a letter. My chief object in writing is to tell you that I love my absent boy—oh *so* dearly—and to enclose $5.00 If that is not enough be sure and let me know, dear.

"Josie was delighted at the receipt of your letter last night. He joins me in warmest love to dearest brother[.]

"May God bless you, my sweet boy. Your own Mother."[75]

Wilson's reply has not been preserved, but he must have had barely

---

[73] Wilson journal, May 3, 1874, *PWW*, addenda to Vol. 6, p. 693.
[74] *Ibid.*, p. 694.
[75] JWW to WW, May 20, 1874, *ibid.*, Vol. 1, p. 50.

time to answer before he received another letter from his mother. She complained that the house girl had been ill and had left her alone in the house so that she and Josie (age six) had to spend their nights at her daughter's home. Dr. Wilson was away at the General Assembly, and Mrs. Wilson told of her concern about his pending resignation from the Columbia Theological Seminary. She emphasized her worry about Woodrow's cold and told him that he would have to come home if it continued.[76]

Throughout his life, Wilson had many "colds," of which the symptoms were rarely specified. Mainly, they seem to have consisted of feelings of tiredness, lassitude, and thickheadedness. In this instance, even though he may actually have had a spring cold, the outstanding features are those of depression. In view of the boy's religious training and orientation, it is not surprising that he should have structured his feelings in a religious context. Mrs. Wilson's letters indicate that she worried about Woodrow's health, and that she felt lonely when he and Dr. Wilson were away. It is likely that Woodrow was extremely concerned about his mother's illness and felt guilty about leaving her "alone." On completing the school year, he went home and occupied himself again in the affairs of the Royal United Kingdom Yacht Club and Commodore Lord Thomas W. Wilson.[77]

Wilson intended to return to Davidson for his second year. He had accepted the office of corresponding secretary of the Eumenean Society for 1874-1875 and had begun to keep a journal of correspondence. There is also an entry in his notebook on about June 1 about asking his parents to permit him to attend business college after he had completed his college course.[78] Curiously, he wrote of leaving Davidson in 1879, although he was in the class of 1877. The slip may be meaningless or it may have been a manifestation of inner doubt. In either case, he did not return to Davidson in the autumn and spent the next year with his parents in Wilmington. Baker states that Wilson remained in Wilmington for reasons of his health, and because he was not academically prepared for Princeton.[79] Actually, Wilson was quite well and had made excellent grades during his second semester at Davidson; he even raised his mathematics mark to 88. He simply was not emotionally prepared to leave home.

Wilson told Hale that he "took it easy" over the year,[80] but he seems

---

[76] JWW to WW, May 26, 1874, *ibid.*, addenda to Vol. 6, pp. 694-95.
[77] Wilson notebook, c. July 1, 1874, *ibid.*, Vol. 1, pp. 54-55.
[78] Wilson notebook, c. June 1, 1874, *ibid.*, p. 53.
[79] Baker, *Wilson*, I, 77.
[80] Hale, *Woodrow Wilson*, p. 51.

to have accomplished a good deal. He studied Greek, practiced his
shorthand, and became interested in a project to translate the New
Testament into Graham. In contrast to drab, war-ravaged Columbia,
Wilmington was an historic and thriving seaport. It had been a headquarters for Lord Cornwallis in the Revolutionary War and a leading
port for blockade runners during the Civil War. Despite his mother's
fears, Wilson took the opportunity to explore the docks, talk to men
who had served on blockade runners, climb aboard the ships, and
take trips down the Cape Fear River. He considered going to sea, but
was talked out of it by his mother. His social life was limited; he said
later that he looked too old and dignified to be invited out with young
people,[81] but he made the acquaintance of John Bellamy, a recent
Davidson graduate. He and Bellamy read books such as Scott's *The
Pirate* aloud to each other and discussed plots and characters. He was
too shy to approach girls with any intensity, but he did meet a few.
When a friend warned him that he was like "a miserable moth flut-
tering around the flame of beauty" and that he would get his "wings
scorched," he replied that the infrequency of his visits to the "fair sex"
made this unlikely.[82]

By the time that Wilson entered Princeton in 1875, he had given up
whatever ideas he may have had of entering the ministry. He may
have made the decision during his emotional crisis at Davidson. Although his father later commented that Woodrow would have made
a wonderful preacher, there is no evidence of any parental pressure
upon him to enter the ministry. Wilson thought of Princeton as a place
of preparation for a political or literary career. As a boy, he had joked
about entering the United States Senate and had daydreamed about
emulating the Christian statesman, William E. Gladstone. But his first
systematic planning began about April 1875. Stimulated by Andrew
J. Graham's article in *The Student's Journal*, Wilson began to collect
quotations and ideas on political and biographical matters for an *Index
Rerum* (index of subjects).[83] The Index, actually begun in February
1876, contains mainly items from and about British statesmen, historians and literary figures. The longest item is an account of Edmund
Burke from the *American Cyclopaedia*. There are also quotations on
bad habits, eloquence, and heroism—all indicative of Wilson's conviction that the development of one's character was part of the training

[81] WW to Harriet Augusta Woodrow, January 15, 1881, *PWW*, Vol. 2, p. 14.

[82] John William Leckie to WW, May 7, 1875; WW to Leckie, draft of a letter, May
28, 1875, *ibid.*, Vol. 1, pp. 63, 65.

[83] WW to Andrew Jackson Graham, c. April 24, 1875, *ibid.*, p. 62.

of a statesman. Included, also, was a passage from Lord Macaulay, the historian, who became one of Wilson's early models. Macaulay attributes his accuracy in facts to his love of castle building and the way he could construct the past into a romance.[84]

[84] Index Rerum, *ibid.*, p. 108.

CHAPTER II

Princeton Student

THE COLLEGE OF NEW JERSEY at Princeton in 1875 was an institution (nondenominational in name but in fact under strong Presbyterian control) of about 400 students and 30 faculty members. It had only recently begun to recover from the effects of the Civil War and to emerge from the narrow sectarianism that had hindered its intellectual development. The election, in 1868, of a new president, James McCosh, signaled the beginning of great change. McCosh was a graduate of the University of Edinburgh and a founder of the Free Church of Scotland, which had broken away from the formality of the established Presbyterian church. He had come to Princeton from the Professorship of Logic and Metaphysics at Queen's College, Belfast. McCosh, bred in the school of Scottish empiricism, believed that the purposes of education were the training of the faculties of the mind,[1] the inculcation of habits of discipline, and the maintenance of moral standards. While McCosh disapproved (at times violently so) of the radical curricular changes introduced by President Charles William Eliot at Harvard,[2] he adopted a limited elective system for juniors and seniors, the first change in the Princeton curriculum in fifty years. Like Dr. Wilson and James Woodrow, Dr. McCosh accepted the theory of evolution and believed that scientific discoveries would prove the truth of divine moral and natural law. In fact, he was probably the leading clerical reconciler between revealed religion and Darwinism of his time. Restlessly ambitious, McCosh wanted to make Princeton a great university that would rival Harvard intellectually, but that would also preserve its own religious values. Often opposed by the clerically dominated board of trustees, he tried to select professors on the basis of ability rather than of orthodoxy. In 1876, on the occasion of proposing an Episcopalian as head of the new engineering school, he told the

[1] The mind was regarded as made up of such faculties as the senses, memory, feelings, imagination, will, and judgment. Belief in the evidence of the sense and the power of reasoning were matters of common sense and divine inspiration.

[2] James McCosh, *The New Departure in College Education: Being a Reply to President Eliot's Defence of It in New York, February 24, 1885* (New York, 1885), pp. 4, 12, 22.

board: "When I came here . . . I found the College a profoundly religious one, and I have labored to keep it so. But I reckon it perfectly consistent with this, that we should take at times an instructor belonging to another evangelical denomination, provided he is very eminent in his department. This will not impair but rather strengthen our Presbyterianism. Of the thirty officers of the College, twenty-eight are at the present time Presbyterians, and a good number, perhaps too many, are Presbyterian ministers."[3]

President McCosh was the intellectual as well as the religious leader of the college. He organized meetings in his own library, where upperclassman, graduates, and faculty members could hear and discuss papers. When he arrived at Princeton, he found that the volumes of the library were kept under lock and key and dispensed grudgingly by the professor of Greek, Henry Clay Cameron, on only one day a week. McCosh built a new library with easier access to books and hired a professional librarian. He promoted scholarships and fellowships, built new classrooms and dormitories, and established schools of science and engineering. Instruction of freshman had been carried out mainly by tutors, resident in the dormitories—duties which were additional to the chores of taking attendance in chapel and monitoring students' behavior. The tutors were poorly paid young men, just out of college, waiting to choose a career or enter a theological seminary. McCosh believed that the freshmen, many of them sixteen and seventeen years old, needed instruction and he turned over more of the teaching to professors. McCosh's first building was a gymnasium—he was fascinated by gymnastics and regarded exercise as necessary for the proper functioning of the mind. This gymnasium was the first building on the Princeton campus to have running water.

Such projects required money, and McCosh was an able fund raiser. He traveled about lecturing and seeing alumni; and, during his twenty-year term of office, the enrollment of the college doubled and its endowment trebled. Along with the economic and cultural growth of the country in the 1870s and 1880s, there developed a change in the composition of the student body. Formerly, a college education had not been thought necessary, or even desirable, for a business career, and the great majority of students who had come to Princeton did so to prepare for the pulpit, the bar, medicine, or teaching. This was no longer true by the 1870s. Well over half of Wilson's class of 1879 went into business, and only 18 percent entered the ministry. Along

[3] Kenneth H. Condit, *A History of the Engineering School of Princeton University, 1875-1955* (Princeton, N.J., 1962), pp. 9-10.

with this trend occurred a sharp decline in the proportion of Presbyterians among the student body.

Dr. McCosh, or "Jimmy" as he was called, took a great personal interest in students. He and his wife, Isabella, regularly visited boys who were sick.[4] Dr. McCosh was a familiar figure on the campus as he took his daily walk and was often seen carrying cuttings and plantings to beautify the grounds. Over the strong opposition of the alumni, McCosh maintained the policy of his predecessors of banning fraternities. He disliked the political maneuvering of the Greeks and believed that they distracted the boys from study and encouraged dissipation. Wilson and the other students laughed at and mimicked McCosh's many idiosyncrasies—his heavy Scottish burr, his peculiarly rapid, head down, dog-trotting gait, and his mannerism of passing his hand from the top of his bald head down across his forehead to the tip of his nose. Once he tried to catch a robin which had flown into his classroom, all the while admonishing the class to stop laughing and warning them that levity was a sin. Yet they appreciated his affection for them and respected his integrity and devotion to Princeton. The personality of James McCosh had an influence on Wilson second only to that of his parents. From McCosh, Wilson gained renewed assurance of the superiority of the Scots' character, a tradition of nonsectarianism in education, a model of leadership, and a desire to make Princeton the greatest university in the country.

Princeton still had an intensely religious atmosphere in the 1870s. Attendance at chapel services was compulsory, and there were daily prayer meetings and frequent religious revivals. In 1876, one revival lasted for four weeks and resulted in 115 conversions. Also, student behavior was often such as to lend support to the belief in natural depravity. Freshmen were hazed severely, and unpopular professors and tutors were subject to pranks, sometimes even the exploding of firecrackers, or even bombs, in rooms and classes. In the annual cane spree, sophomores attacked any freshman holding a cane. On a horn spree, students paraded through town to the accompaniment of tin horns. They then collected fences, wooden outhouses, and sidewalk planks for a huge bonfire.[5] On one occasion, stone throwing led to a battle between students and members of a traveling Wild West circus.

[4] In fact, the infirmary at Princeton is named The Isabella McCosh Infirmary.

[5] There is no evidence that Wilson was involved in hazing. He did participate in a hoax in which he and several classmates, posing as instructors, gave "examinations" to unsuspecting candidates for entrance into the class of 1880. Wilson diary, June 15 and 16, 1876, *PWW*, Vol. 1, pp. 141, 142.

The administration sought to curb such behavior by imposing strict disciplinary measures. Card playing and horn blowing were prohibited, and students were not allowed to leave town without permission. In particular, they were forbidden to go to Trenton, which President McCosh thought was the graveyard of purity.

Ritualized violence and organized religious excitement provide communal bonds, and conditions at Princeton produced an intense class spirit. Aside from "natural depravity," this development can be attributed to the rural location and social isolation of the college, the paternalistic attitudes of the administration, the absence of general student self-government, and the relative paucity and lack of diversity of extracurricular activities.

Almost all these activities were centered in the literary debating clubs, the American Whig Society, known as Whig, and the Cliosophic Society, or Clio. Whig and Clio, rivals since their founding in colonial times, included more than half of the student body in their memberships. The societies had their own adjoining halls and governments— a senate composed of graduate members and a house of undergraduates who elected their speakers and other officers. Only the senate could amend the constitution and expel members. The halls held oratorical contests and debates. Competition was keen for selection of the commencement Latin salutatory, English salutatory, and valedictory speakers. Beginning in 1876, teams from Whig and Clio competed in debate for the coveted Lynde Prize and generated an excitement aroused in later years only by intercollegiate football. In contrast to the dullness of the regular curriculum, the halls stimulated thought and discussion and kept students in contact with the events of the outside world. Any prominent political or literary figure could be elected a member. Southerners had usually joined Whig and Northerners Clio, and many, if not most, of the debates were on political subjects. The subject of the first Lynde contest was "Resolved, that it would be advantageous to the United States to abolish universal suffrage."

The halls had extensive libraries. In Wilson's time, Whig had eight thousand books (many of them not in the college library) and subscribed to many current British and American periodicals. There was a great rivalry between the societies, and members swore never to give away their secrets. The "secrets" included the interior arrangement of the building, the names of the offices and officers, and the fact that "Brother" was a title of address. A Princeton historian has stated that observation of the oath of secrecy "exalted the dignity of the Hall, stimulated loyalty and rivalry and furnished a test of character in holding before the members the high duty of observing their plighted word."[6]

President McCosh strongly favored the halls in the belief that they prepared students for public service in the church, the courts, and legislative assemblies. The existence and influence of the societies were probably the reasons why fraternities never established themselves to any extent at Princeton.[7]

Like most serious students at Princeton, Wilson was less interested in the formal curriculum than he was in his own reading, the activities of the debating societies, and the recently established college newspaper, *The Princetonian*. He read extensively in political and literary biography. In his freshman year, he became entranced with the romantic, colorful style of Lord Macaulay's *History of England*. In his sophomore year, he discovered in *The Gentleman's Magazine* descriptions of the picturesque styles of the great parliamentary orators—Pitt, Bright, Gladstone, and Disraeli. Later, Wilson told William Bayard Hale that no one circumstance had done more to determine the first cast of his political ideas than the accounts of the debates in Parliament by the "Member for Chiltern Hundreds," that is, Edmund Burke.[8]

Wilson joined Whig, and his first presentation was a paper, "Rome was not built in a day." That he was uncertain of its quality is suggested by the fact that he was fined twenty-five cents for not submitting it to the subcommittee for criticism.[9] In January 1877 he won second prize in the sophomore oratorical contest for "The Ideal Statesman."[10] In this speech, Wilson emphasized hard work, adherence to principle, unselfishness, and the soul and skills of an orator as the requirements for political leadership. In his junior year he wrote essays on Thomas Carlyle, Otto von Bismarck, and William Pitt, Earl of Chatham. Wilson's most remarkable achievement as a college student came in his

[6] Jacob N. Beam, *The American Whig Society of Princeton University* (Princeton, N.J., 1933), p. 155.

[7] This account of Princeton during the McCosh era is based mainly on the following works: Thomas Jefferson Wertenbaker, *Princeton 1746-1896* (Princeton, N.J., 1946); Varnum Lansing Collins, *Princeton* (New York, 1914); Beam, *The American Whig Society*; Charles Richard Williams, *The Cliosophic Society of Princeton University* (Princeton, N.J., 1916); Frederic Rudolph, *The American College and University* (New York, 1962); Henry W. Bragdon, *Woodrow Wilson: The Academic Years* (Cambridge, Mass., 1967), pp. 15-18; and Edwin M. Norris, *The Story of Princeton* (Boston, 1917).

[8] Hale, *Woodrow Wilson*, p. 63.

[9] Beam, *The American Whig Society*, p. 188.

[10] "The Ideal Statesman," January 30, 1877, *PWW*, Vol. 1, pp. 241-45.

senior year, when his essay, "Cabinet Government in the United States," was accepted for publication in a national journal, *The International Review* of Boston.

Wilson took part in a number of debates and literary contests, but on the whole he was more successful in the political and business affairs of Whig than he was as an orator and debater on set topics.[11] He spoke often and effectively on politics and procedures and served on the most important committees. He was chosen as one of the three historians of the society and was elected speaker in his junior year. One member of Whig recalled him as a firm and decisive presiding officer.[12]

Early in 1877 Wilson also organized and wrote the constitution for the Liberal Debating Club. Membership in this club was limited to the Class of 1879. The Liberal Debating Club was governed by a president and a secretary of state appointed by the president, and was modeled on the British Parliament. Contemporary political issues were the subjects of bills introduced by the secretary of state and the members—the gentlemen from New Jersey, Virginia, North Carolina, etc. If the majority of the members voted against the secretary of state, it was his duty to resign. According to the constitution, the club was to be a brotherhood founded on the "principles of Justice, Morality and Friendship"; and its members were "to assist and encourage each other in every possible way." This ideal was apparently realized as the members met regularly on Saturday nights until their graduation in 1879. Seven of the eight members—Wilson, Hiram Woods, Jr., Robert Harris McCarter, Charles Andrew Talcott, Harold Godwin, James Edwin Webster, and Edward Wright Sheldon—remained close friends for the rest of their lives.[13] The organization and success of the Liberal Debating Club illustrates Wilson's political interests, his love of parliamentary procedure and language, and his ability to evoke in others enthusiastic support of projects in which he was interested.

Wilson's standing as a campus leader was recognized when, in his junior year, he was elected managing editor of *The Princetonian*. He wrote most of the paper's editorials; his varied topics included proposals for improvement of the halls, proper behavior and work habits, criticism of too scanty gym clothing, reviews of books and plays, the frequency of prayer meetings, improvement of sanitary facilities and

[11] Henry W. Bragdon suggests that Wilson did not shine because the halls fostered an ornate, pompous style of oratory, which contrasted with his controlled delivery. See Bragdon, *Wilson*, pp. 32-33.

[12] Edward E. Worl to Henry W. Bragdon, January 20, 1942, Bragdon Collection.

[13] See the Constitution of the Liberal Debating Club, c. February 1 to c. March 15, 1877, and the Editorial Note, "The Liberal Debating Club," *PWW*, Vol. 1, pp. 245-49.

conditions, and inter-collegiate athletics (which were beginning to play an important role in college life). Wilson, a strong partisan supporter of Princeton teams, emphasized organized practice, discipline, and good coaching. American football had just adopted the rules of English rugby; Wilson had a considerable knowledge of the game, probably from his reading of British periodicals. He was secretary of the Football Association[14] and also served as president of the Base-Ball Association.

Judged by grades alone, Wilson was not an outstanding student; he graduated at the bottom of the top third of his class. His best subject was history, followed by philosophy (including psychology, logic, and ethics). In Dr. McCosh's course for seniors, he received the spectacular grade of 99.8, which Dr. Wilson might have said was about one degree above normal. Professors Arnold Guyot in geology, Cyrus F. Brackett in physics, and Charles A. Young in astronomy were all good teachers, but Wilson's lack of interest in science was reflected in barely passing grades in these subjects. He received his worst marks in French, a course he cut frequently. Always poor at learning foreign languages, Wilson found his instructor, General Joseph Kargé, a flamboyant Polish ex-cavalryman and nationalist, somewhat ridiculous.[15] Wilson was particularly critical of his Greek professor, Henry Clay Cameron.[16] Professor Cameron liked to tell his students that he had never made a mistake in his life and had not changed his mind since he was eighteen. He would call on each man to translate two or three lines of Homer and parse each word. At the last meeting of the course, he would give a lecture during which the students took notes on toilet paper, while crossing and uncrossing their legs in unison. At the end of the lecture, they crowded about Cameron, presumably to ask questions, but actually to take his wide-brimmed felt hat, which would be cut into pieces and sold as souvenirs.[17] Cameron, a teacher at Princeton

[14] In this office, Wilson showed considerable business ability. The secretary had to raise money for equipment and travel expenses for a team of fifteen. Wilson raised the price of admission to games to fifty cents and defended his action in *The Princetonian*. At the end of the season, the Football Association had made a profit and contributed $100 to help pay off the baseball deficit. Princeton's undefeated football team of 1878 was scored upon only once and beat Yale and Harvard. Wilson noted that the team, overmatched in weight and strength, had won because of constant practice, teamwork, skill, and a more scientific game. See *The Princetonian*, December 5, 1878.

[15] Wilson diary, June 9, September 16, and November 18, 1876, *PWW*, Vol. 1, pp. 136, 194, 229.

[16] Wilson diary, June 13, 15, September 15, 18, and 29, 1876, *ibid.*, pp. 139, 141, 193, 195, 202.

[17] Bragdon, Memorandum of interview with Jacob N. Beam, December 19, 1939, Bragdon Collection.

for fifty years and an historian of Whig, kept not only the library keys but the other old traditions. His teaching was typical of the sterile pedagogy that McCosh strove so hard to eliminate.

Wilson felt at ease with a small group of close friends. They would meet at night in one of the rooms of the new Witherspoon dormitory for study and discussions, mainly about politics. Wilson had to strive to control his temper when questions about the Civil War arose, but the extent to which his horizons were widening is revealed in the fact that few of his friends came from the states of the former Confederacy. In Whig, Wilson was one of the few Southerners to vote for the admission of a "carpet bag" governor of South Carolina, Daniel H. Chamberlain. In addition, none of the members of the "Witherspoon Gang," the Liberal Debating Club, and Wilson's eating club, the Alligators, became a minister. The gatherings in Witherspoon Hall also provided scope for Wilson's talents as an entertainer. He had a great fund of anecdotes and loved to sing verses from Gilbert and Sullivan. Wilson was a member of the Glee Club and took the part of Marc Antony in a production of "The Sanguinary Tragedy of Julius Sneezer." Later he looked back on the comradeship of his college years with nostalgia.

Wilson, in maturity, recalled that he had been a shy and diffident youth at Princeton, and a number of fellow students saw him as cold and unfriendly. More than twenty years after graduation, he confided to a good friend, Edith Gittings Reid, "Plenty of people offer me their friendship; but, partly because I am reserved and shy, and partly because I am fastidious and have a narrow, uncatholic taste in friends, I reject the offer in almost every case; and then am dismayed to look about and see how few persons in the world stand near me and know me as I am,—in such wise that they can give me sympathy and close support of heart. Perhaps it is because when I give at all I want to give my whole heart, and I feel that so few want it all, or would return measure for measure."[18] Even with intimates, his pride might keep him from being completely open. When he was President, he told Cary Grayson that, once when money had not arrived from home, he went for days, literally without a penny, rather than ask a friend for a loan.[19]

Wilson kept a shorthand diary at Princeton regularly from June 3 to November 23, 1876, and sporadically afterward. It is highly revealing, and tells of his attitude toward his studies, relationships with his family, his keen interest in athletics and politics, fascination with

[18] WW to Edith Gittings Reid, February 16, 1902, *PWW*, Vol. 12, p. 272.
[19] Grayson, *An Intimate Memoir*, p. 37.

Lord Macaulay, and concern about his own health. The diary also gives an interesting picture of student life at Princeton in the 1870s.

Wilson began with the modest disclaimer that any resemblance between his diary and that of Samuel Pepys did not go beyond the circumstance that each was written in shorthand. Wilson then recorded his great satisfaction over the Harvard baseball team's victory over Yale. He had a "tiresome" Sunday, but in the evening he had a "right[20] pleasant time" walking with friends and discussing different forms of governments, especially "the relative merits of a limited monarchy and [a] republic." The boys agreed that a limited monarchy was "preferable."

The next few days were pleasant, and Wilson played baseball both at noon and after chapel. He was bitterly disappointed when Princeton lost again to Yale and took solace in reading Macaulay. He thought that Macaulay was the best of the English historians because of his "vivid imagination." The news of yet another Princeton defeat (this one to Amherst, eighteen to twelve) led Wilson to the consoling observation that failure in athletics did not, after all, "detract from the excellence of the college." On Saturday he was overjoyed when he received a letter from his mother. The following Saturday he began examinations and subsequently found the Greek test "very fair though rather hard." On several afternoons he read Macaulay, and he and his classmates attended a celebration with fireworks and cannon to mark the end of their freshman year. His spirits were dampened by a letter from his father taking him to task for his extravagance.[21]

The diary reveals that Wilson was a hard critic of sermons. On June 4 he heard one that was "spiritually uninteresting," but he admitted that it might have been less so had he paid closer attention. The following Sunday he listened to a "poor attempt" at the First Presbyterian Church in the morning and a "very dull" one at the Episcopal Church in the afternoon. In the evening, at the Presbyterian Church, he heard, not a profound discourse, but a good presentation of already grasped facts. The warm weather made it difficult to stay awake, but he felt that the effort could have been aided by the sight of some pretty girls. Two Sundays later, he got up late and went to the baccalaureate service, but, after hearing the opening anthem, he thought better of the idea and left. He lay outside in the shade with Bob McCarter and decided that the number of pretty girls coming out was not as great as he could see in the "sunny South."[22]

[20] "Right" was one of the few Southernisms in Wilson's speech. At least as an adult, he did not speak with a Southern accent.

[21] Wilson diary, June 3-23, 1876, *PWW* Vol. 1, pp. 132-45.

[22] Wilson diary, June 4, 11, and 25, 1876, *ibid.*, pp. 132, 137-38, 145.

Wilson was intensely interested in the presidential election of 1876. He wrote that he hoped that the nation would be sensible enough to elect the Democratic candidate, Samuel J. Tilden, over the Republican Rutherford B. Hayes. When the initial returns favored Tilden, Wilson and other campus Democrats lit a bonfire and made speeches, only to be jeered at by the Republicans when news came that Hayes was ahead. Two days after the election, Princeton was in an atmosphere of suspense. Woodrow spent that evening "loafing around unexcited and listless near unable to settle down to anything." He spent the following evening in the pleasant forgetfulness of Whig Hall.[23] Wilson must have engaged in some strenuous political arguments, as his mother implored him to disregard the "ignorance and fanaticism" of his infatuated "Radical companions" and, by all means, to stop talking "about knocking any body down."[24]

Wilson's diary and correspondence indicate his concern about health. He reminds himself repeatedly that his good health depends on regular exercise, and a typical day's entry closes with Pepys's ritual statement, "Thank God for health and strength." Despite the dreadful sanitary conditions in Princeton,[25] Wilson's health in his undergraduate years was good, with no more than the usual seasonal ills of student life. However, his mother worried about him constantly and became apprehensive when he did not send her detailed accounts of the state of his health and living conditions. In his senior year, for example, when he made some (unspecified) complaint about his eyes, probably from long hours of reading in inadequate light, she wrote: "I cannot tell you how I shrink from the idea of your putting yourself in the hands of a doctor. Your father was very much disturbed about it. It seems he has not known anything about it. You see, you and I talk over such matters here in the summer—and are apt to forget that he does not know all that we talk over. I wish you would write *to him* particularly about this matter—giving all possible particulars."[26]

Mrs. Wilson's obsessive concern with Woodrow's health—part of her general overprotectiveness—reflected her own fears of illness. His detailing of his symptoms was a filial duty, and the subject of his health was a special bond of intimacy with his mother. Even after Wilson was in law school, Mrs. Wilson expressed her amazement that

[23] Wilson diary, November 7-10, *ibid.*, pp. 221-24.

[24] JWW to WW, November 8 and 15, 1876, *ibid.*, pp. 223, 228.

[25] Poor sanitation and inadequate water supply were frequently mentioned in undergraduate periodicals and in the minutes of the board of trustees. Princeton had open cesspools and sewers, and a rectangle of brick latrines, known as the *cloaca maxima*, had been built to replace wooden outhouses. There was an epidemic of typhoid in 1880.

[26] JWW to WW, February 4, 1879, *PWW*, Vol. 1, p. 452.

he could ever conceal anything from his parents for "fear of being misunderstood." Her letter also illustrates her habit of expressing her feelings as if they were someone else's, in this instance, her husband's.[27]

As Woodrow was in good health at Princeton, his father did not worry about him unduly. One incident illustrates both Dr. Wilson's humor and his inordinate concern about the voice. A doctor had removed a fishbone from Woodrow's throat. Dr. Wilson wrote: "It is to be hoped that, however fishy you may be in some respects, you will hereafter make free to reject the bones of the literal finny fellows whose facility for being swallowed in toto is proverbial. Seriously do you think that bone which was surgically extracted from yr throat left no evil effects in the way of hindering your elocution? This is the principal bad consequence that I have feared. Your maw (not yr ma) is to be yr. chief dependence as a public speaker—and you ought to guard all its approaches with a care equal to its importance."[28]

Wilson returned home for summer vacation in 1876 to find that his father was away at Davidson College commencement and that his mother and brother Josie were "all alone." Several days later, Mrs. Wilson was in a "weak condition" and suffering from her old pains.[29] She continued indisposed over the summer. Wilson did a great deal of reading in Shakespeare, Macaulay's history and essays, and Gibbon, and annotated an anthology of literary works. He helped his parents with house and yard chores and, when his mother was not well, did the marketing. Woodrow played with his brother Josie; he drew ships and made toys for him, coached him in his school work, and appointed him an officer in the "Navy." He escorted his mother to church and found his father's sermons excellent. While Dr. Wilson was away on vacation in Saratoga, Wilson took over his duties as stated clerk. He also wrote some articles for *The North Carolina Presbyterian*, which his father was now editing. His activities outside the family were very limited. He went boating once with friends on the Cape Fear River, but despised the fishing.[30] Despite his mother's urging him to visit Wilmington girls, he found them uninteresting and preferred to remain home and read. Wilson was evidently so distressed by his mother's illness and depression and so identified with her suffering that, soon after his father left for Saratoga, he developed psychosomatic symptoms of his own. He awoke one morning with a "strange swimming" in his head. It lasted for several days and was followed by a headache.[31]

[27] JWW to WW, October 20, 1879, *ibid.*, p. 578.
[28] JRW to WW, October 23, 1877, *ibid.*, p. 304.
[29] Wilson diary, June 27, 29, 30, 1876, *ibid.*, pp. 146-47.
[30] Wilson diary, August 25, 1876, *ibid.*, p. 184.
[31] Wilson diary, July 28 and 29, and August 23, 1876, *ibid.*, pp. 161-62, 183-84.

An entry in Wilson's diary indicates the division of labor in the house. On the day before his father's departure for his vacation, Woodrow went out to order a carriage. He and his father played billiards before and after tea. Woodrow helped his mother pack his father's things and, as she was not feeling well, he brought down the trunk and dusted off his father's clothes.[32] The incidents suggest that, despite her ailments, Mrs. Wilson took her household duties conscientiously and that she and Woodrow felt that Dr. Wilson should not be bothered with menial tasks.

The Wilsons, especially Mrs. Wilson, were not happy in Wilmington. Years later, for Hale's biography, Wilson described Wilmington as "a city of gentlemen of good company and women who would have been esteemed brilliant the world over." Dr. and Mrs. Wilson, he said, immediately achieved great popularity, and the parsonage was a social center.[33] In a letter to his fiancée in 1883, however, Woodrow called the city "an exceedingly dingy, uninteresting town."[34] Jessie Wilson similarly found the city and its people "dull."[35] She felt that Dr. Wilson's talents were not appreciated and that her own status in the southern Presbyterian aristocracy was not acknowledged. She made few if any friends and complained of being ignored: "The way they treat us during your father's absenses has made it impossible for me to regard the people with the slightest affection. They never come near me even when they know that Josie & I are all alone."[36] She hoped to leave Wilmington when Woodrow's studies were completed and settle with him in Nebraska, where she had inherited property.[37]

While Dr. Wilson's sermons were well attended and highly praised, and he continued to be an important figure in the Presbyterian Church, he missed the intellectual stimulation of teaching. His preference for the homilectical aspects of the ministry and lack of enthusiasm for house calls left his parishioners discontented. "The fault they find with me is as to visiting. They want a gad-about gossip," he wrote to Woodrow.[38] One of the main reasons for leaving Columbia for Wilmington had been the unusually high salary of $4,000. Only one other southern Presbyterian church (one in Memphis) paid that much in 1874. But the Wilmington congregation was frequently in arrears. Dr. Wilson found editing *The North Carolina Presbyterian* onerous and

---

[32] Wilson diary, July 24, 1876, *ibid.*, p. 159.
[33] Hale, *Woodrow Wilson*, pp. 52-53.
[34] WW to ELA, December 8, 1883, *PWW*, Vol. 2, p. 571.
[35] JWW to WW, April 11, 1877, *ibid.*, Vol. 1, p. 257.
[36] JWW to WW, June 6, 1877, *ibid.*, p. 273.
[37] JWW to WW, February 23, 1878, *ibid.*, p. 361.
[38] JRW to WW, October 21, 1882, *ibid.*, Vol. 2, p. 147.

resigned less than a year after his appointment. His struggles with his fellow Presbyterians continued and, in October 1877, he survived an attempt to have him removed from his position as stated clerk—an effort, according to Mrs. Wilson, motivated by "private spite & jealousy."[39] Dr. Wilson reacted to such frustrations with "dark moods" in which he became morbidly self-conscious and introspective.[40] A suggestion of the sources of Dr. Wilson's difficulties is revealed in a letter to Woodrow from his mother: "[He] had a pleasant time at Synod. The members of Synod have gotten to understand him as much as they are capable of doing—and he rules them completely without making them conscious that he is doing so!"[41]

In the battles within the Presbyterian Church, Jessie Wilson could be as stern and unforgiving as any of her Scottish ancestors. She described her reactions in the highly emotional moments when northern and southern Presbyterians met in 1883 and agreed to bury the hatchet (but not to unite): "The Northern delegates were received yesterday morning. It was quite an impressive scene. Your father was *really* master of ceremonies—for nobody else knew what should be done. There were many tears shed. I fear I am hard hearted—for not a tear came to my eyes. Dr. Martin of Atlanta was seated just in front of me and had great difficulty in choking down his emotion. There was much less *gush* than I had feared, however."[42]

Woodrow was depressed and evidently felt a great deal of guilt or lack in himself over his mother's ill health and unhappiness. Shortly after his return to Princeton in September 1876, he wrote an article, "One Duty of a Son to His Parents," for *The North Carolina Presbyterian*. He admonished young men to be more polite to their parents. He urged his readers to remember how much they owed to the mother who had brought them forth, nourished them in their helplessness, loved them as only a mother could, trusted them when all others forsook them, and was ready to give her all to make them happy. "Are you to do nothing for her?"[43] Wilson's depression was evident when he began the article. As he wrote in his diary:

"My thoughts come hard this evening and I have no pleasure in *thinking* so I must not think any more. No one ought to try to write when it requires such an immense effort as it does from me this evening.

[39] JWW to WW, October 26, 1877, *ibid.*, Vol. 1, p. 305.
[40] JRW to WW, January 25, 1878; JWW to WW, June 5, 1880, *ibid.*, pp. 346, 659.
[41] JWW to WW, October 28, 1879, *ibid.*, p. 579.
[42] JWW to WW, May 20, 1883, *ibid.*, Vol. 2, p. 360.
[43] "One Duty of a Son to His Parents," October 8, 1876, *ibid.*, Vol. 1, p. 206.

My heart feels full and yet my thoughts will not clothe themselves in any suitable words and will not even put themselves into tangible form. Striving thus to express my thoughts which will not come and yet on the subject of which I am full is one of the most painful things I know of."[44]

Wilson remained in a depressed frame of mind for several weeks. He felt bad and had a recurrence of the "dull swimm[ing]" in his head. He prayed that God would give him more of the Holy Spirit and make him something more than the "cold Christian" he had been of late.[45] Under the pen name, Twiwood, he wrote a religious essay, in which he expressed the view that the good Christian should not be gloomy or depressed, and said that, under pain of punishment, one must obey God's command "*to the very letter*."[46] Some time later Twiwood, in a happier frame of mind, assured his readers that the darkness surrounding was "seldom so dense as to shut out the radiance of the Almighty's loving smiles."[47]

Mrs. Wilson's health did not improve over the autumn and winter. By December, she still did not feel well and expressed her disappointment that Woodrow had decided not to come home for the Christmas holidays. She wrote: "I must confess I am greatly disappointed and distressed by the news with reference to your vacation. I have allowed myself to think that you would almost certainly come home—and have been laying all my plans with reference to your coming. I dont see how I can wait till Spring to see you. But I must not be less brave than my precious son."[48]

This letter did not persuade Wilson to change his mind, but his mother had not given up the idea of his coming home. She told him how "very blue" his father had been and attributed this condition to his concern about her being "laid aside" and the prospect of not seeing Woodrow.[49] Mrs. Wilson's diagnosis of the causes of her husband's depression was not completely accurate. It is extremely unlikely that Wilson's father *was* depressed because he missed his son. He enjoyed talking with Woodrow, and the boy's presence undoubtedly lightened the dreariness of the household. However, he was generally not in favor of Woodrow's coming home for winter vacations while he was

[44] Wilson diary, September 23 and 24, 1876, *ibid.*, pp. 198, 199.
[45] Wilson diary, September 23 and October 5, 1876, *ibid.*, pp. 198, 204.
[46] "The Positive in Religion," October 15, 1876, *ibid.*, pp. 211-12.
[47] "Christian Progress," December 20, 1876, *ibid.*, p. 234.
[48] JWW to WW, December 1, 1876, *ibid.*, p. 232.
[49] JWW to WW, December 21, 1876, *ibid.*, p. 235.

at Princeton because of the expense, hazards, and length of the trip—
train to Baltimore, boat to Portsmouth, and train to Wilmington.[50]

The incident in 1876 is an example of Mrs. Wilson's way of ascribing
her own yearnings to others in order to appear selfless and unde-
manding. Woodrow got the emotional message and came to Wilmington after a visit in Baltimore with Hi Woods. He did not keep
a diary at home, but his visit evidently assuaged his mother's loneliness
only briefly. Shortly after his return to Princeton, she wrote to him:

"I have made a point of being *very busy* ever since you left—that
I might not be unhappy about you. It was such a relief to receive your
telegram, telling of your safe arrival in Princeton. I dare not tell you
how we missed you, darling, after you left. I want to tell you how
bravely dear little Josie behaved that morning. As soon as you had
gone, he burst into an uncontrollable fit of crying—but when I discovered a handkerchief I thought you had left, and I wanted him to
run after you with it—he made a desperate effort to control himself,
and ran after you. When he came back he said, 'Mama, I did not let
brother see that I was crying, for I smiled when I caught up with
him.' "[51]

It is likely that Josie Wilson's tears were as much a response to his
mother's distress over his brother's leaving as to the departure itself.
In either case, the account of his behavior dramatically represented
Mrs. Wilson's feelings and probably increased Wilson's burden of
guilt.

Dr. Wilson could also express self-gratifying motives on a devotional
and moral plane. In the summer of 1877, after a year of the depressed
atmosphere caused by his wife's ailments, he was particularly eager
to get the family off to visit relatives, while he stayed in Wilmington
prior to going to Saratoga. Dr. Wilson, to judge from his popularity
with the ladies, may have had some romantic interest in Wilmington
as well as concern for his wife's health. Woodrow dutifully escorted
his mother to Columbia, South Carolina, and Rome, Georgia. Dr.
Wilson began a letter to Woodrow, who was then in Rome, with some
criticism of an essay by Woodrow on Carlyle. Then, quite uncharacteristically, he exhorted Woodrow about the need for truthfulness:

"The Lie is always the bad and the detestable. It is of the Devil its
father. I am preparing to leave home for my summer vacation. I wish
it were not going further from you all that this preparation is making.
My heart longs for the dear ones upon whom its affections are set,

[50] JRW to WW, December 10, 1877; JWW to WW, November 20, 1878, *ibid.*, pp.
329, 435.
[51] JWW to WW, January 17, 1877, *ibid.*, p. 237.

with a longing that is sometimes almost intolerable. But, to do what is right is better than to follow mere inclination. Tell your dear mother that her letter of the 8th was received at the same time with yours. I will write to her once more before I leave. I am sure, dearest boy, that you show her all the love you feel, and that you feel as much as son ever felt for mother. She deserves the utmost of the affection and reverence and devotion of us all. There never was a truer wife or a better mother. I am so glad that she has in you a son of whom she feels that she has reason to be proud. Make her prouder still."[52]

Wilson's vacation was dull. He enjoyed the scenery, took long walks, and played croquet with his cousin, Jessie Bones.[53] He found little of interest in the Atlanta newspapers and spent most of his time writing. He amused himself by sending letters in shorthand to his friends and engaged in a long discussion with Bob McCarter on originality of thought.[54] After writing his essay on Carlyle, he attempted to compose a speech, "Independent Conviction," in which he analyzed the deficiencies of the American government and deplored the poor quality of its elected officials. Wilson completed it but discarded the manuscript in disgust, calling it "one of the most miserable productions of which I was ever guilty."[55]

Several months later, Wilson turned to the writing of "Prince Bismarck." In December, he delivered this biographical essay before the Whig Society. It was an exercise in hero worship and romantic idealization based on a sophomoric knowledge of German history and politics. It contained many florid figures of speech and many gross overgeneralizations. Wilson contrasted Bismarck's "noble purposes" with "Austrian intrigue" and found in Bismarck the "moral force of Cromwell," "the political shrewdness of Richelieu," "the comprehensive intellect of Burke, without his learning," the haughtiness of Chatham, and "the diplomatic ability of Talleyrand, without his coldness." Describing Bismarck's oratory, Wilson stated that "his eloquence partakes of the stern magnificence of the storm, rather than of the soft brilliancy of the cascade or the quiet beauty of deep, still waters." The young author was obviously carried away by his own love of oratory. If ever there was a statesman who was convinced that the great questions of the day would not be settled by speeches and parliamentary debate, it was Otto von Bismarck. Wilson dealt with this feature tactfully by admitting that the violence of Bismarck's pol-

[52] JRW to WW, c. August 10, 1877, *ibid.*, p. 288.
[53] Wilson diary, July 19 and 20, 1877, *ibid.*, pp. 285-86.
[54] WW to Robert Harris McCarter, c. July 18, 1877, *ibid.*, p. 284.
[55] Wilson diary, July 20, 1877, *ibid.*, p. 285.

icies had thrown a shadow on his otherwise fair name. However, he added, "this shadow only serves in his case to bring out into greater prominence many a shining virtue."[56]

The essay appeared in *The Nassau Literary Magazine* under the pseudonym Atticus.[57] As a reflection of his own development as a political scientist, Wilson, ten years later, had lost interest in Bismarck, the heroic leader, and was writing in scholarly fashion of Baron vom Stein's reforms of the Prussian administrative system. "Bismarck" not only represents a stage in Wilson's growth as a scholar; this essay is also an example of the florid style of writing as a source of pleasure to the boy and a way to relieve boredom and frustration.

Wilson's vacation in 1878 was more lively. He spent the summer in Wilmington and again visited relatives in Columbia with his mother. His correspondence with his Princeton friends was in a lighter vein. Sexual drives were beginning to develop. From Columbia he wrote that he was at "the scene of some of my old love adventures,"[58] and he joked with another classmate, Robert Bridges, about "a *walk* and a KISS."[59] He thought that religious camp meetings made flirting easy, and he was understanding: "Certainly one can hardly find courage enough to blame the young men and women for yielding to a temptation which everything conspires to make almost irresistable. I know well enough that I could pretty safely predict my own course under such circumstances."[60] Whatever Wilson might have done at a camp meeting, he avoided temptation in Wilmington. He kept away from the numerous pretty girls who attended amateur concerts, watched the regattas on the Sound, and went for moonlight excursions on the river. Instead, he read John Richard Green's *History of the English People*, which had supplanted the work of Macaulay in his estimation, and practiced oratory in his father's church.

His sexual awakening and some of the problems it created seem to be represented in another biographical essay, "William Earl Chatham." Wilson dwelt particularly on the elder Pitt's passionate, imperious, and energetic nature, his dramatic style, and his great popularity. He believed that the passionate intensity of Pitt's nature imparted a special quality to his oratory. Passion was the "pith" of his eloquence and "indeed the ground-work of his character."[61] "Chatham" is far su-

---

[56] "Bismarck," speech given before the American Whig Society of Princeton University, December 6, 1877, *ibid.*, pp. 325-28.

[57] "Prince Bismarck" (essay) November 1877, *ibid.*, pp. 307-13.

[58] WW to James Edwin Webster, July 23, 1878, *ibid.*, p. 384.

[59] WW to Robert Bridges, August 10, 1878, *ibid.*, p. 394.

[60] *Ibid.*, p. 395.

[61] "William Earl Chatham," October 1878, *ibid.*, pp. 407-12.

perior to "Bismarck," both in content and style. The essay has much colorful imagery, but the content corresponds closely to the facts of Chatham's life and contains fewer generalities and forced dichotomies and analogies. The editors of *The Nassau Literary Magazine* designated it as the magazine's prize essay. Interestingly, and perhaps significantly, it appeared under the authorship of Thomas W. Wilson, rather than a pen name.

Wilson's attitude toward work and accomplishment in his Princeton years are well documented. His "Index Rerum" included the maxim: "Keep busy; idleness is the strength of bad habits. Do not give up the struggle when you have broken your resolution once, twice, ten times, a thousand times. That only shows how much need there is for you to strive."[62] His diary contained many references to "loafing" and comments on how he might have used his time to better advantage. He was often self-critical and bent on improving himself. Despite the success of his essay on Chatham, Wilson was dissatisfied with it. "It is, I am afraid, rather a lame affair—some passages of it limp perceptibly and even painfully," he told Bobby Bridges.[63] He became wholly committed emotionally to any task or contest in which he was involved, either on the athletic field or in the debating hall. In his senior year he withdrew from the Lynde Debate rather than argue against his conviction that universal suffrage—meaning votes for Negroes and others without property—was wrong.[64] He tended to equate defeat with personal failure, and setbacks resulted in feelings of depression and a temporary doubting of his abilities.

Wilson's letters indicate his great affection and admiration for his father, whom he regarded as a model of clear thinking and verbal expression. While Dr. Wilson encouraged and praised Woodrow, he recognized his son's great ambition, competitiveness, and impatience for fame and sought to temper them. The following letter, written after Woodrow had failed to gain entry into the junior oratorical contest, illustrates Dr. Wilson's understanding of his son's temperament and his own theodicy. Dr. Wilson wrote: "We all sympathize with you in the matter of your contest disappointment. It must have been a sore grief—and the sorer because unexpected. But, let it go. It is not killing: only *stunning*. You will recover and be all the stronger for the blow. Indeed, to tell you the honest truth, I am not inconsolable

---

[62] Index Rerum, May 18, 1876, *ibid.*, p. 90.

[63] WW to Robert Bridges, August 10, 1878, *ibid.*, p. 395.

[64] Beam, *The American Whig Society*, pp. 191-92; Charles Andrew Talcott to WW, May 21, 1879, *PWW*, Vol. 1, p. 484; Editorial Note, "Wilson's Refusal to Enter the Lynde Competition," *ibid.*, pp. 480-81.

by reason of your failure. I rather like it. It will help to reveal your true worth, both as to quality and quantity; will show the stuff you are made of. If you shall continue to be disheartened—much more if you should become despairful—in view of what has happened—well, you can't be good for much. But, if, after the first days of depression shall have passed, you arise with new resolution and with at once an humbler and a mightier purpose to achieve success—trusting hereafter in God *and* yourself not so much in yourself alone—well, this will be prophetic of a noble and honorable manhood. I failed twice in pretty much the same way: but my competitors have never been heard of since—and I count myself as having only ordinary capacity.

"My darling, make *more* of your class studies. Dismiss *ambition*— and replace it with hard industry, which shall have little or no regard to *present* triumphs, but which will be all the time laying foundations for future work and wage. *I* know you. You are capable of much hard mental work, and of much endurance under disappointment. You are manly. You are true. You are aspiring. You are most lovable every way and deserving of confidence. But as yet you despise somewhat the beaten track which all scholars and orators (almost) have had to travel—the track of patient study in mathematics, in languages, in science, in philosophy. Dearest boy, can you hope to jump into eminency all at once? You say, though, that others who seem to be less worthy are succeeding where you fail. Pshaw, this is always the case, in all life. Brass is mightier even than gold—and favors are showered upon fools often until they are saturated, whilst the wise are forgotten. Buckle on the harness again."[65]

Fatherly advice, however, was overshadowed by fatherly example, and Woodrow had grown up in an atmosphere of striving and competition. The emphasis on success led him to structure situations in agonistic fashion and, at times, to regard the victory as more important than the substance. Each of Wilson's parents believed that he was destined for great things and that his capacities were unlimited: as Dr. Wilson's fortunes in the church waned, his expectations for his son grew. When Woodrow expressed gloom about the study of the law, his father replied that he could think of no other reason for the blues to come to him other than that Woodrow might fight and conquer them.[66] Throughout Wilson's career, failure and depression were followed by great undertakings.

Jessie Wilson's chronic depression and great longing for Woodrow

[65] JRW to WW, December 22, 1877, *ibid.*, pp. 331-32.
[66] JRW to WW, January 27, 1880, *ibid.*, p. 596.

suggest that she found only limited satisfaction in her marital life and that her happiness depended on his presence and achievement. She gave him the belief that he was not only intellectually, but also morally, superior to his associates. When, in his senior year, he expressed dissatisfaction with his grades, his mother told him that he had been treated in "miserably unjust" fashion.[67] Wilson idealized his mother: he saw her preoccupation with his health as devotion, her suffering as self-sacrifice, and her bitterness toward people as family loyalty. Observing her reactions to his father's successes and failures, Woodrow came to feel that he must return from battle either with his shield or upon it. Her clannishness contributed to his uneasiness with outsiders and to his reluctance to offer his friendship until he had received assurances of affection and admiration. The effects of Wilson's over-attachment[68] to his mother were reflected in the social immaturity which, in contrast to his intellectual development, characterized his behavior at the institution to which he was about to go—the University of Virginia.

[67] JWW to WW, January 20, 1879, *ibid.*, p. 448.
[68] See Chapter 4 for a discussion of attachment behavior.

CHAPTER III

The Law and Love

AS EARLY as his sophomore year at Princeton, Wilson had decided to study law in order to prepare himself for a career in politics.[1] He and Charley Talcott had made a pact to devote their legal careers to unselfish public service and the purification of American politics.[2] He chose the University of Virginia because of his pride in being born in the state—he had made calling cards with the inscription, THOMAS WOODROW WILSON SENATOR FROM VIRGINIA—and because it had the best law course in the South. Yet, by the time of the Princeton commencement, he had misgivings;[3] he looked forward to his summer vacation to provide a respite from "the dry dust of Law."[4]

Aside from this concern, Wilson spent a pleasant vacation with his family in the North Carolina mountains. His mother was feeling well and was pleased that Dr. Wilson, enjoying his stay at Saratoga, had been elected Moderator of the southern Presbyterian General Assembly. Woodrow's article, "Cabinet Government in the United States," had just appeared, and he wrote another long political essay, "Self-Government in France." This paper was turned down by *The International Review*, but Woodrow accepted the rejection in good spirit and admitted that he had not read extensively on the subject. Not all of his thoughts, however, were of the law and politics. He told Bobby Bridges that, although Horse Cove had every advantage of situation that a lover might desire, he had no one to love. He was, he said, reserving his powers of charm for the girls at the University, where he had heard they were numerous. He even asked Bobby if he thought that the law and love would mix well.[5]

The law and love did not mix for Wilson, not because of any intrinsic incompatibility, but because he was not interested in the practice of law and was not ready for love. The University of Virginia was very different from Princeton. Virginia's academic standards were higher,

[1] Wilson diary, September 15, 1876, *PWW*, Vol. 1, p. 193.
[2] Charles Andrew Talcott to WW, June 1, 1879, *ibid.*, pp. 485-86; WW to ELA, October 30, 1883, *ibid.*, Vol. 2, p. 500.
[3] WW to Talcott, July 7, 1879, *ibid.*, Vol. 1, pp. 487-88.
[4] WW to Robert Bridges, July 30, 1879, *ibid.*, p. 490.
[5] WW to Bridges, September 4, 1879, *ibid.*, p. 541.

undergraduate students were not separated from graduates, and all students had more freedom and responsibility. Attendance at religious services was not compulsory, as it had been at Princeton. There were few parietal rules, little faculty supervision, and classroom disorders were unknown. Wilson missed the college spirit and intense class loyalties of Princeton and thought nostalgically of the old gatherings in Witherspoon Hall. Charlottesville offered a far more sophisticated environment than Wilson had experienced either in provincial Wilmington or monastic Princeton. There were many social functions in Charlottesville, including Sunday night suppers at which faculty, students, and the ladies of the academic community mingled. Wilson was embarrassed at these gatherings because he had little small talk and, as he put it, could talk only if he had something to say.[6] While Wilson participated with the glee club in serenading young women, he was too shy to make more private associations. Since he did not dance, he was bored at cotillions; at one big party, he noted, "I was careful not to allow myself to be introduced to any [ladies] whom I was not sure of finding entertaining."[7]

On the positive side, Wilson made friendships among his fellow students, notably with Richard Heath Dabney and Charles William Kent. He recognized the high caliber of the student body and the professional faculty; he particularly admired the head of the small law faculty, John Barbee Minor. Minor, one of the great American legal scholars of the nineteenth century, was an authority on the common law and gave an outstanding course in English constitutional history. (Two of Minor's students were elected to the United States Senate from Virginia.) Wilson was also impressed by the way that faculty apartments and students' rooms faced on a court and thus assured contact outside of the classroom. Yet Wilson complained unhappily about the monotony of legal studies and the burden of work.[8]

Despite his protest that the law was a hard taskmaster, Wilson found time for many extracurricular activities. He continued his outside reading and wrote biographical essays on John Bright and William E. Gladstone. Shortly after the beginning of his first term he wrote "Congressional Government," a revision of "Cabinet Government in the United States," and tried unsuccessfully to get it published. He joined a debating club, the Jefferson Literary Society, and became first its secretary and then its president. He rewrote its constitution and

[6] WW to Harriet Woodrow, October 5, 1880, ibid., p. 681.
[7] WW to Harriet Woodrow, April [c.] 14, 1880, ibid., p. 648.
[8] WW to Talcott, December 31, 1879 and May 20, 1880, ibid., pp. 591, 656.

bylaws. He took elocution lessons and spoke frequently on campus occasions.

The annual debate of the Jefferson Society was perhaps the outstanding event at the University. Two prizes were offered: the Debater's Medal and a lesser one, the Orator's Medal. Wilson had come to Virginia with a reputation as an orator, and he and William Cabell Bruce[9] were favored participants for the contest of April 1880. The subject was "Is the Roman Catholic Element in the United States a Menace to American Institutions?" Wilson for the negative and Bruce for the affirmative expressed exactly the same views. They differed only in that Wilson thought that American democratic institutions were strong enough to withstand the influence of political Catholicism. The judges found it extremely difficult to choose the winner, and it took them several days to award the Debater's Medal to Bruce and the Orator's Medal to Wilson, with a special declaration of appreciation for the merit of his performance as a debater.

The events surrounding the debate illustrate Wilson's competitiveness, his tendency to underrate his opponents, his reluctance to accept defeat, and his determination to transform failure into ultimate victory. Wilson thought his award a sop and at first was inclined to refuse it. He was a debater, not an orator, he said. After he talked the situation over with one of his fraternity brothers, he decided to accept his medal and admitted that he had been fairly beaten. According to his friend's recollection, Wilson vowed in a tone of grim determination, "Bruce beat me on this, but I will beat him in life, for I'm a worker, he is not."[10] Nicknamed "Senator" by his friends, Bruce was an aggressive campus politician, and he and Wilson had clashed at one of the previous meetings of the Jefferson Society. Wilson made a cutting remark to Bruce at the time and reported it to his parents. His mother replied: "We were much amused at your downsetting of Mr. Bruce. I think he must be a puppy."[11] On the other hand, when Wilson sent his father a copy of Bruce's prize-winning article on John Randolph, along with some derogatory comments on the author and other students, Dr. Wilson wrote: "Above all, darling son, guard against the temptation of imagining yourself to be perfect, and that whatever does not measure well by T.W.W. is to that extent defective. I do not fear however, on your part, an egotism so gross—yet it is proper to plant a post here,

---

[9] Bruce was a member of a distinguished Virginia family. He later won a Pulitzer Prize for a biography of Benjamin Franklin and served for many years as United States Senator from Maryland. He was one of the early "Wilson-for-President" men.

[10] S. B. Woods to Bragdon, n.d., quoted in Bragdon, *Wilson*, p. 82.

[11] JWW to WW, October 28, 1879, *PWW*, Vol. 1, p. 579.

on which 'Dangerous' is labell[ed]. Your descriptions of yr companions are admirably touched—but are they not just a little bit acid?"[12] Lest Woodrow get the impression that he was not perfect, his mother hastened to assure him that his father had not meant to say that he, Woodrow, was "hard" in his judgment of others.[13]

The debate had interesting sequels. Despite Wilson's statement that Bruce was not a worker, he was, and he defeated Wilson again in the competition for the best article in the *Virginia Literary Magazine*. When, in the fall of 1880, Wilson revised the constitution of the Jefferson Society, he wrote in a provision for the award for only a single prize—for best debater. In similar fashion, as if to undo symbolically his withdrawal from the Lynde Debate at Princeton, he stipulated that no speaker should be made to argue against his convictions.

Wilson had been at Virginia barely a few weeks when he wrote to his family that he was not feeling well. When he complained of fits of the blues, his father advised him to be less introspective and self-conscious and more studious.[14] In the early spring of 1880, as at Davidson six years previously, he developed a persisting "cold," the manifestations of which seem to have been chiefly dyspeptic. Dr. Wilson attributed the condition to the climate of Charlottesville and bad food,[15] while Mrs. Wilson expressed alarm that his stomach would be "ruined for life" and urged him to change his boarding arrangement.[16] Wilson's father also suggested that he might return to Wilmington and continue his studies at home. To judge from the nature of these symptoms, and with knowledge of Wilson's subsequent medical history, his ailments were not due to bad climate or poor food, but were clearly a psychosomatic response to emotional tension.

One of Wilson's problems was his lack of commitment to his courses. It would be an oversimplification to say that he was uninterested in the law. His later career at Johns Hopkins and Princeton shows that he was deeply interested in the constitutional, historical, philosophical, and sociological aspects of the law. While at Virginia, he criticized Professor Minor's method of teaching; he later acknowledged that, next to his own father, Dr. Minor was the greatest teacher he had ever had. What Wilson objected to was the amount of work and study required. Here his problem may have been his slow reading, which made it difficult for him to amass detailed information.

---

[12] JRW to WW, November 19, 1879, *ibid.*, p. 585.
[13] JWW to WW, November 26, 1879, *ibid.*, p. 587.
[14] JRW to WW, January 27, 1880, *ibid.*, pp. 596-97.
[15] JRW to WW, April 2, 1880, *ibid.*, pp. 646-47.
[16] JWW to WW, June 18, 1880, *ibid.*, p. 661.

At the end of 1879 Wilson fell in love with his cousin, Harriet Woodrow. Hattie was the nineteen-year-old daughter of Jessie Wilson's eldest and favorite brother after whom Woodrow Wilson, as has been said, had been named. Hattie and Woodrow had known each other as children; they had written to each other when he was a senior at Princeton and she had visited him in Wilmington. But he had not previously been enamored of her. Hattie was a student at the Augusta Female Seminary at Staunton (now Mary Baldwin College), and they met there at the home of their Aunt Marion Bones. As Wilson put it later to his fiancée, Ellen Axson: "I was absolutely *hungry for a sweetheart*. I had always had a great capacity for loving the gentle sex, and had, of course, never been without a sweetheart until I went to Princeton. . . . I went to Virginia with a deep sense of the inconvenience and discreditableness of my condition and with a definite determination to find a lady-love if possible. Seriously, I *was* in need of a sweetheart."[17]

At the time, however, Hattie was not just the answer to Wilson's loneliness and biological needs: she was *the* girl. She was attractive, vivacious, popular, and a talented musician and singer. Woodrow was enchanted with her voice, which he thought the equal of Adelina Patti's, and he was especially ravished by her rendition of "The Last Rose of Summer."[18] He pursued her ardently in person and through the mails—too ardently, it turned out, because Hattie did not reciprocate and found the frequency and length of his visits embarrassing.[19] Also, he was reprimanded by the University of Virginia faculty for his many unexcused absences. Even after the faculty report in May 1880 had criticized Wilson's poor class attendance, he disregarded the warning and went, without permission, to Harriet's graduation exercises. There he embarrassed her further by his vociferous cheering of her musical performance.[20]

When the faculty, through Dean James F. Harrison, unofficially threatened to suspend or dismiss him, parental reactions were predictable. Dr. Wilson called the faculty action correct and reproached Woodrow for his "juvenile folly." Instead of his usual salutation of "my precious son" or "my dearest son," he addressed Woodrow as "my dear son" and in place of his customary "yr affectionate Father," he closed with "God bless and utterly reform you. Your own Father."[21] Wilson's mother, on the contrary, thought that Dean Harrison had

[17] WW to ELA, October 11, 1883, *ibid.,* Vol. 2, p. 466.
[18] Editorial Note, "Wilson's Proposal to Hattie Woodrow," *ibid.,* p. 84.
[19] WW to Harriet Woodrow, October 5, 1880, *ibid.,* Vol. 1, p. 679.
[20] Baker, *Wilson,* I, 130.
[21] JRW to WW, June 5 and 7, 1880, *PWW,* Vol. 1, pp. 658, 659-60.

been "wrong and cruel" in threatening him, even though the Dean had meant well. She asked Woodrow, for his father's sake, to go to Mr. Venable[22] and have him use his influence on his behalf. Lest Woodrow be upset by his father's reproach, she informed him that it had been written in one of Dr. Wilson's "dark moods."[23]

The Jefferson Society held a monthly oration and, in March, Wilson delivered an essay on the English statesman, John Bright. Like "Bismarck," it was an eulogy that expressed Wilson's aims and ideals and that contained many self-referential figures of speech. While he had written that Bismarck's eloquence did not partake of "the quiet beauty of deep, still waters," Bright's restrained style was suggestive of the "broad and *silent* river." Wilson found in both men a character "in whom the elements are so mixed, 'that Nature might stand up and say to all the world, This was a man.' "[24] Wilson had just received a letter from Charles Talcott, who had described the maneuvering for delegates at the New York State Republican Convention. He incorporated his reactions in his speech. John Bright's career, Wilson concluded, demonstrated "that duty lies wheresoever truth directs us; that statesmanship consists, not in the cultivation and practice of the arts of intrigue, nor in the pursuit of all the crooked intricacies of the paths of party management, but in the lifelong endeavor to lead first the attention and then the will of the people to the acceptance of truth in its applications to the problems of government; that not the adornments of rhetoric, but an absorbing love for justice and truth and a consuming, passionate devotion to principle are the body and soul of eloquence."[25]

Such rhetoric was the order of the day, and it served to lift the spirits of both speakers and audiences. For Wilson it was especially timely, and it restored his sense of direction. He expressed his exhilaration to Talcott: "Those indistinct plans of which we used to talk grow on me daily, until a sort of calm confidence of great things to be accomplished has come over me which I am puzzled to analyze the nature of. I can't tell whether it is a mere figment of my own inordinate vanity, or a deep-rooted determination which it will be within my power to act up to."[26]

---

[22] Charles S. Venable, Professor of Mathematics, who had served on General Lee's staff. The Wilsons had known him when he taught at South Carolina College in Columbia. Previous to the present incident, Mrs. Wilson had asked Woodrow if Venable was "as lazy as he used to be." JWW to WW, November 18, 1879, *ibid.*, p. 584.

[23] JWW to WW, June 5 and 18, 1880, *ibid.*, pp. 659, 661.

[24] "John Bright," March 6, 1880, *ibid.*, pp. 613, 620.

[25] *Ibid.*, p. 620.

[26] WW to Talcott, May 20, 1880, *ibid.*, p. 655.

Shortly after the Bright oration, Wilson completed an essay on Glad-stone, which similarly contains a number of highly self-referential passages. One reads:

"William Ewart Gladstone was born in Liverpool in the year 1809. He comes of sturdy Scotch stock; and his mind and body alike are cast out of strong Scotch stuff. We can easily imagine what sort of youth his was. He must have been a sober, thoughtful boy, full of spirits without being boisterous; eager and impetuous without being imperious; a leader in sport as in study; straightforward in everything, even in his hatreds; half-souled in nothing, not even in his faults."[27]

Despite his ailments and absences, Wilson completed his first year with satisfactory grades. He spent the summer at Fort Lewis in western Virginia, with relatives, since his mother had accompanied his father to Saratoga. He had expected Hattie to come there with her mother, but the girl, realizing the seriousness of his attachment to her and not wishing to encourage it, did not go. In a letter to Bobby Bridges, he reflected on his disappointments: "You are a little mistaken in your estimate of me, old fellow. Do not imagine that I am never discouraged. I hope that I'm never *conquered* by discouragement; but I'm absolutely ashamed of the weak fears and the unmanly dispair which have seldom failed to come after my numerous failures. I tell you one thing, Bobby, I'm absolutely dependent on sympathy—the sympathy we were able to feel in each others' work at Princeton was to me the most blessed part of the rare intercourse we enjoyed there; and the lack of any such sympathy has been just the hardest trial I've had to bear at the Uni-versity[.] There are no men like 79's to be found there."[28] Wilson exaggerated; Heath Dabney was a warm friend.

No sooner had Wilson returned to Charlottesville than he was writ-ing to Hattie (now at her home in Chillicothe, Ohio) of his loneliness. He dreaded intensely the possibility that they might drift apart, and only the hope of a letter from her brightened his disconsolate state. To forget his "lonliness," he told her, he was entering into fraternity affairs with "renewed vigor" and would try to improve on his "social accomplishments" by visiting girls, even though he was not interested in them.[29] He also remained active in the affairs of the Jefferson Society; throughout his stay at the University he missed only one meeting. To his father's satisfaction, he attended classes regularly. However, Dr. Wilson, reading between the lines of Woodrow's letters, discerned

---

[27] "Mr. Gladstone, A Character Sketch," *Virginia University Magazine*, XIX (April 1880), 401-26, printed in *ibid.*, p. 627.

[28] WW to Robert Bridges, September 18, 1880, *ibid.*, pp. 675-76.

[29] WW to Harriet Woodrow, October 5, 1880, *ibid.*, p. 681.

"a face of solicitude," and heard "sighs of anxiety."[30] Dr. Wilson's perception was accurate. By November 1880, Woodrow had developed another persistent "cold." With his failure to improve—there is no mention of his going to a doctor—his parents became frightened and told him that it was absolutely necessary for him to come home and attend to his health.[31] At first he refused, but on Christmas Day, without saying goodby to his friends or notifying the faculty, he left for Wilmington.

The state of Wilson's emotions was also shown in a dispute he had just had with Professor Minor. Wilson had proposed the holding of a moot court by the students, but Minor did not favor the idea. However, Wilson persisted with his proposal to the point where his mother urged him to abandon it rather than incur Minor's ill will. Wilson's comments on the matter are not recorded, but Mrs. Wilson thought that Minor's conduct was "simply contemptible" and his "want of candor in the matter . . . unpardonable."[32] As has been mentioned, Wilson regained his esteem for Minor, and the latter responded to Wilson's later letters and visits in friendly fashion.

After Wilson's return to Wilmington, both his estimate of the University of Virginia and the state of his health improved sharply. He told Bridges that, while Virginia lacked the charm and class spirit of Princeton, the fraternities provided close companionship and that he would miss the exercises of the literary societies. He explained that there was nothing seriously wrong with him, but he gave contradictory accounts to his friends. He explained to Bridges that he had contracted a "very severe cold" that made him "unfit for study."[33] He wrote to Richard Heath Dabney that his digestive organs had been found to be "seriously out of gear," and that he had been warned by a doctor not to neglect "systematic medical treatment."[34]

Wilson's return to his family in Wilmington marked the beginning of a dismal year. After a temporary improvement, his digestive troubles returned. He studied for his bar examinations, which he hoped to take at the end of the winter but did not in fact take until the following year. He taught his brother Latin, read, and practiced elocution. A major motive was the hope of establishing himself in a law practice so that he could marry Hattie, a match now being strongly supported by his mother.[35] From Wilmington, he wrote Hattie long and adoring

---

[30] JRW to WW, October 19, 1880, *ibid.*, pp. 685-86.

[31] JWW and JRW to WW, December 14, 1880, *ibid.*, p. 701.

[32] JWW to WW, December 9, 1880, *ibid.*, p. 700.

[33] WW to Robert Bridges, January 1, 1881, *ibid.*, Vol. 2, p. 9.

[34] WW to Richard Heath Dabney, February 1, 1881, *ibid.*, p. 17.

[35] JWW to WW, c. December 21, 1880, *ibid.*, Vol. 1, pp. 702-703.

letters, and he was thrilled when he was invited to stay at Hattie's home in Chillicothe during the summer of 1881, while he served as an apprentice clerk in the law office of their common uncle, Henry Wilson Woodrow. Wilson's initial effort at practice was as unrewarding as his courtship. According to Henry Woodrow's account, thirty years later, Wilson was an able lawyer and could put a contract in clear language; however, he was less successful in dealing with clients.[36] The romance came to an abrupt and unhappy end on September 4, 1881. Woodrow suddenly took Hattie from the dance floor at a party and proposed; she rejected him, and to spare his feelings, gave their blood relationship as the reason. He left the party abruptly and went to a hotel, where, after a sleepless night, he sent a note importuning her to reconsider and leave some faint hope to save him from the "terror of despair."[37] He was again refused.

In his discouraged state, Wilson put off his plans to open a law office. As he was to do on later occasions when he felt bereft of a woman's love, Wilson composed a poem for Hattie, "A River's Course." The verses indicate his feelings of solitude, lifelessness, and, probably, suppressed rage. (Later, he called Hattie "heartless.")[38] The flow of water was one of Wilson's favorite metaphors, and the poem relates how a deep river breaks in rage from the bondage of its rocky shores and finds a ruined castle, whose alarm bell in a crumbling turret has had its tongue rusted by silence. The river flows on, leaving scenes of death and decay, and, after passing through a bustling city, flows by a goodly mansion on a green lawn, in which dwells a lovely lady. At last, it peacefully pours its waters into the sea.[39] The poem is not only highly symbolic, but prophetic. In a second poem, "A Song," Wilson mourns and commemorates his lost song-bird as he bids feathered songsters raise their voices to win her love and make joy fill all his days.[40] These lyric expressions may have helped to raise Wilson's spirits and bring him out of his depressed state. He read and annotated a book of Professor Minor's and had an article, "New Southern Industries," published in the New York *Evening Post*.[41] In March 1882 he made the outline for a full-length book, "Government by Debate." He was able, in a letter to Bobby Bridges, to express his feelings about

[36] Louis D. Bannon, memorandum of conversation with Henry Wilson Woodrow, cited in Bragdon, *Wilson*, p. 91.

[37] WW to Harriet Woodrow, September 25, 1881, *PWW*, Vol. 2, p. 83; "Wilson's Proposal to Hattie Woodrow," *ibid.*, p. 84.

[38] WW to ELA, October 11, 1883, *ibid.*, p. 467.

[39] "A River's Course," December 1, 1881, *ibid.*, pp. 91-94.

[40] "A Song," December 8, 1881, *ibid.*, p. 94.

[41] Printed April 26, 1882. See *ibid.*, pp. 119-25.

the unhappy love affair with Hattie, who, he remained convinced, had rejected him only because of her "prejudice" against the marriage of first cousins. Wilson, evidently, also recovered his sense of humor, for he found an opportunity to indulge himself in satire and ridicule at the expense of the "conceited ignoramus who edits our chief daily, the *Wilmington Morning Star*."[42]

However, as Wilson approached leaving home for the practice of law, his digestive organs were again "out of gear." He also complained of constipation, which may have been brought on in part by his sedentary habits, and was treated by mail by his brother-in-law, Dr. George Howe, Jr. Dr. Howe advised Woodrow that the purges he was taking were unnecessary and recommended sulfur water to insure soft stools. Also, Dr. Howe prescribed the use of sulfur soap and a sitz bath of bicarbonate of soda, a regime which suggested that Wilson also had hemorrhoids. (He was operated on for them several years later.) His symptoms worsened soon afterward, and Dr. Howe decided that, rather than indigestion, he had "too much bile aboard" and ordered pills (perhaps calomel) to relieve the "liver torpor."[43] Eventually, it was Dr. Wilson who divined the source of his son's dysfunction when he told Woodrow he should conquer his "*mental liver*."[44]

Wilson opened a law office in Atlanta in partnership with Edward Ireland Renick, a former law student at the University of Virginia. Although Atlanta was a bustling city, neither he nor Renick had the connections or business enterprise to do more than try to collect "numberless desparate claims."[45] Despite his professed distaste for the practice of law, he gave a brilliant performance on his examination and was admitted to the Georgia bar in October. He found Atlanta unstimulating intellectually and read a great deal of political science, history, and literature.[46] He completed "Government by Debate," but it was rejected for publication several times. Wilson continued his advocacy of a governmental structure like that of the British cabinet system, but the book was poorly organized, repetitive, verbose, and highly rhetorical.[47] He visited the Georgia legislature and formed a low opinion of local politicians.[48] He also testified on the tariff before

---

[42] WW to Bridges, March 15, 1882, *ibid.*, pp. 107-108.
[43] George Howe, Jr. to WW, May 31, 1882, *ibid.*, p. 131.
[44] JRW to WW, February 13, 1883, *ibid.*, p. 304.
[45] WW to Bridges, January 4, 1883, *ibid.*, p. 281.
[46] WW to Bridges, May 13, 1883, *ibid.*, p. 355-56.
[47] Editorial Note, "Government by Debate," *ibid.*, pp. 152-57.
[48] WW to Bridges, February 27, 1886, *ibid.*, Vol. 5, pp. 126-27.

a Congressional committee. Characteristically, he organized and wrote the constitution for a debating club, the "Georgia House of Commons."

Wilson also improved his "social accomplishment" in a relationship which may not have been as casual as he later claimed. Katie Mayrant was the attractive niece of Mrs. J. Reid Boylston, at whose boarding house both she and Wilson lived. During the nine months that they were at Mrs. Boylston's, she and Wilson "romped" together; he entertained her and the other boarders with his comic speeches and antics. Woodrow and Katie read aloud to each other, and he taught her shorthand. After she returned to her home in South Carolina, they corresponded, and he visited her on his way from Atlanta to Wilmington. He wore a hat band she had given him until it was replaced by one from his future fiancée, Ellen Louise Axson. Ellen never quite believed that Wilson's affection for Katie was as completely platonic as he protested it had been.[49] Wilson hardly persuaded Ellen to the contrary when he described Katie as "jolly," "mischievous," "intelligent," and "affectionate," but "not deep" and capable of furnishing him with happiness only in his leisure hours.[50] In Atlanta, however, Woodrow did not seem to be concerned that Katie was "not deep" enough. Despite the drudgery of the law, he wrote Bobby Bridges that he was in fine spirits and had conquered the "catarrh" that had so persistently troubled him.[51]

A possibly serendipitous spinoff from Wilson's law practice was the occasion of his meeting Ellen Axson. He went to Rome, Georgia, to see James W. Bones about the estate of a deceased maternal uncle. Wilson was representing his mother in this matter. He attended services at the Presbyterian Church with the Boneses on April 8, where he saw an attractive girl. He soon discovered that she was the daughter of the minister, Samuel Edward Axson, an old friend of his father's. As he subsequently happily recalled: "I remember thinking 'what a bright, pretty face; what splendid, mischievous, laughing eyes! I'll lay a wager that this demure little lady has lots of life and fun in her!' " Wilson wasted no time in becoming acquainted.[52] The following evening he called on her father to inquire about his health. After introducing his

<hr />

[49] ELA to WW, October 15, 1883, *ibid.*, Vol. 2, p. 475.

[50] WW to ELA, July 4, 1883, *ibid.*, p. 381; WW to ELA, June 16, 1885, *ibid.*, Vol. 4, p. 720.

[51] WW to Bridges, January 10, 1883, *ibid.*, Vol. 2, p. 284.

[52] Actually, the Wilson and Axson families had known each other in Augusta. Ellen Axson had certainly known Wilson by reputation, and he may well have anticipated meeting her.

daughter, Mr. Axson opened the conversation by asking Wilson: "Why have night congregations grown so small?" Wilson must have given the correct answer, and the rest of the evening must have gone well, because Ellen was impressed.[53] She knew of Wilson's family background and his reputation as a scholar and thought that his appearance, now adorned with a mustache, was quite distinguished. The catalyst of the romance was Jessie Bones Brower, Wilson's cousin and a close friend of Ellen's. Jessie arranged a second meeting.[54]

Wilson had barely returned to Atlanta when he was certain that he was in love. By the end of June, he had visited Rome twice more and had made his intention unmistakably known. Wilson told Ellen about his earlier unhappy love affair, his need for a woman's love, and his poor prospects; he declared that he had no right to ask a girl to marry him. Ellen was noncommittal but not altogether unresponsive. As she sat in a hammock at a picnic several days later, they agreed to correspond.[55] The "poor prospects" to which Wilson alluded referred to the decision that he had made in late February 1883—to give up his law practice and seek an academic career. In April he had accordingly applied for a fellowship at the new Johns Hopkins University in Baltimore to study history and political science. He did not win the fellowship, but his father agreed to support him.

While Wilson had no reservations, Ellen did. Her mother had died in childbirth in November 1881, and she had taken over the management of the household and the care of her two younger brothers and baby sister. Actually, when Wilson first saw her, she was still in mourning and wore a black crepe veil. Also, she had taken over the duties usually carried out by a minister's wife, such as visiting sick parishioners. Her major worry was over her father's health; Samuel E. Axson had gone through a severe depression at his wife's death and had had several recurrences.

By an unusual coincidence, Woodrow and Ellen met again in September in Asheville, North Carolina. Wilson had gone to Flat Rock and then to Arden with his mother so that she could convalesce from a febrile illness. Ellen had traveled to Morganton to visit friends but was called back to Rome because her father was not well. Woodrow had hoped to see her in Morganton, but, as she had left by the time his letter to her had arrived, he went to Asheville to take the train to

---

[53] WW to ELA, October 11, 1883, *PWW,* Vol. 2, p. 468.

[54] Eleanor Wilson McAdoo, *The Priceless Gift: The Love Letters of Woodrow Wilson and Ellen Axson Wilson* (New York, 1962), pp. 5-6; Editorial Note, "Wilson's Introduction to Ellen Axson," *PWW,* Vol. 2, p. 335, n.5, qualifies Mrs. McAdoo's account.

[55] Editorial Note, "Wilson's Early Courtship of Ellen Axson," *ibid.,* pp. 362-63.

Baltimore. He had no knowledge that she was also in Asheville waiting for a train to Knoxville. To his delighted amazement, while he walked along the street, he saw her sitting at the window of her hotel. He persuaded her to delay her trip to Rome, and the next day, September 15, they drove out to visit his mother and Annie in Arden, a meeting at which Ellen was extremely nervous. The following day, shortly before his train was to leave, Wilson proposed and Ellen accepted.[56]

Ellen had good reason to be nervous because, ever since Woodrow had told his mother of his intentions, Mrs. Wilson had been opposed to the marriage. Although she had heard that Ellen was an attractive girl, she did not think that Woodrow should yet be involved in any way. Mrs. Wilson was "distressed" over the "weary waiting" that he would have to endure.[57] On another occasion, she wrote: "I need not assure you that we would not, either of us, wish you to sacrifice *anything* in the way of your own happiness. But *I do not believe that* your present plan is the best way to bring about that happiness. Miss Ellie has seen enough of you to know whether or not she likes you— enough at least to consent to *correspond* with you. And that is your true plan—the *only* plan you can adopt under the circumstances. I do not think it will do you any good to linger longer in Rome than is necessary to accomplish your business. If you were in a condition to marry, then it might be desirable for you to remain & push matters. I need not assure you, my precious boy, that you have our warmest sympathy in this matter. From all I have ever heard of Ellie Lou I feel assured that there does not live a sweeter or purer girl than she. So that if you succeed in winning her, some day, no one will be glader[58] than I. How is her health now? She used to be very frail."[59] (There is no evidence that anyone ever considered Ellen frail.) To reinforce her argument, perhaps, Mrs. Wilson mentioned several times in her letters that Dr. Wilson was not well and was suffering from dizzy spells. Her own illness, first thought to be malaria and then typhoid, had improved.[60]

Wilson disregarded this motherly advice. He may have been some-what perplexed by it, because two years earlier, when his financial prospects were no better, his mother had enthusiastically encouraged his courtship of Hattie Woodrow. She had wanted them to marry

[56] Editorial Note, "The Engagement," *ibid.*, pp. 426-27.

[57] JWW to WW, June 7 and 12, 1883, *ibid.*, pp. 365, 369.

[58] This slip of the pen might have been significant. Mrs. Wilson, unlike Woodrow, was an excellent speller.

[59] JWW to WW, June 21, 1883, *PWW*, Vol. 2, pp. 370-71.

[60] WW to ELA, July 16, 1883, *ibid.*, p. 387.

"without a moment's hesitation."[61] Possibly, Mrs. Wilson, who was fond of Hattie, felt that she would be closer to Woodrow if his wife was a blood relative rather than only an attractive and a highly eligible Presbyterian. On his arrival in Baltimore, Wilson promptly notified his parents of his engagement and wrote to Samuel E. Axson to ask for his formal permission. Ellen's father, just out of bed, gave his loving sanction, but the only surviving immediate response from the Wilson family was a letter of congratulation from Josie.[62] Woodrow received a letter from his father a week later. Dr. Wilson excused his tardiness by saying that he did not know Woodrow's Baltimore address; he cautioned him not to let his affections interfere with his studies. Dr. Wilson did not end the letter with his usual expression of affection but signed himself with the formal, "Believe me to be—Yours in every sense—Father."[63] However, Dr. Wilson soon became reconciled, and, a week later, in his customary warm fashion, expressed pleasure over his son's happiness, extended love to "Ella Lou," and signed himself "Your affc Father."[64] Also, he had almost recovered from his dizziness. Wilson's mother wrote to him and sent her love to Ellen, but she was apparently not well enough to write to her prospective daughter-in-law for another two months.[65] Wilson's elder sister, Marion Kennedy, wrote two warm messages of congratulations, but there is no record of a letter from Annie, who was much closer to their mother.[66] As events were to show, Woodrow Wilson had begun to cut the umbilical cord.

[61] WW to Harriet Woodrow, September 25, 1881, *ibid.*, p. 83.

[62] JRW, Jr., to WW, September 19, 1883, *ibid.*, pp. 431-32. ELA to WW, September 25, 1883, mentions a note of congratulation from Mrs. Wilson to WW, *ibid.*, p. 440.

[63] JRW to WW, September 25, 1883, *ibid.*, pp. 441-42.

[64] JRW to WW, October 4, 1883, *ibid.*, p. 455.

[65] JWW to ELA, December 1, 1883, *ibid.*, p. 559.

[66] Marion Wilson Kennedy to WW, October 15 and November 2, 1883, *ibid.*, pp. 474-75, 515.

CHAPTER IV

The Johns Hopkins and Marriage

THE JOHNS HOPKINS UNIVERSITY, opened in 1876 for graduate studies and research, was the first institution in the United States to attain German academic standards. Its Department of History, Politics, and Economics, which Wilson entered in 1883, was headed by Herbert Baxter Adams, a Ph.D. *summa cum laude* of Heidelberg University. Adams, the first great organizer of historical studies in America, introduced German research methods, with their emphasis on the use of original sources. Another of Wilson's teachers was Richard T. Ely, a political economist educated at Heidelberg, who acquainted Wilson with European administrative methods. This training, based largely on German scholarship, enabled Wilson to implement his main interest, which was the study of politics and government.

As at Princeton and the University of Virginia, Wilson had a self-generated project outside the regular curriculum. This was the writing of *Congressional Government*, a comparison of the American and British political systems modeled on Walter Bagehot's *The English Constitution*. Wilson had difficulty in combining this effort with his regular work and, following the completion of his first assignment—a paper on Adam Smith—he complained of eye strain.[1] This was probably the result of his compilation of an extensive bibliography under the handicap of his slow reading.[2] In order to avoid similar chores, he obtained permission from Professor Adams to drop some of his courses. Despite this dispensation, he continued to complain of the pressure of work, and, in December, developed a "cold" and digestive disturbances. Perhaps appropriately, he described his predicament to his fiancée in gastro-intestinal metaphors. He wrote: "I *can't* 'cram'; I must eat slowly and assimilate, during intervals of rest and diversion. My chief ground of indictment against my professors here is that they give a man infinitely more than he can digest. If I were not discreet enough to refuse many of the things set before me, my mental digestion would soon be utterly ruined."[3]

[1] WW to ELA, November 1, 1883, *PWW*, Vol. 2, p. 511.
[2] Editorial Note, "Wilson's Lecture on Adam Smith," *ibid.*, pp. 540-41.
[3] WW to ELA, December 22, 1883, *ibid.*, p. 596.

Wilson's problems may also have been expressed in his negative appraisals of his teachers. At the time when his "mental digestion" was about to be "ruined," Wilson made a comment reminiscent of his mother's reactions in similar situations. He characterized Adams as "superficial and insincere, no worker and a selfish schemer for self-advertisement and advancement."[4] Some of Wilson's criticism was apparently justified and was shared by fellow students. Adams had a "germ theory" of history—by which he tried to show that national institutions had evolved from village organizations—and he set his classes to work on the minutiae of colonial settlements. But much of Wilson's judgment was grossly unfair and seemed mainly to reflect his own dissatisfactions and unhappy state of health. Ten months later, when Wilson was feeling well and there were favorable indications that his book would be accepted for publication, Professor Adams' performance had somehow improved markedly. "Dr. Adams," Wilson magnanimously conceded, "is lecturing *much* better, and will be very serviceable to us, if he but keep up his present industry."[5] During Wilson's troubled first semester, he criticized Professor Ely's dribbling manner of speech and described him as "stuffed full of information but apparently much too full to have any movement."[6] Perhaps Wilson's constipation was bothering him. In any event, several months later, when he reported that he was completely cured of his ailments, he admitted that Ely wrote smoothly and clearly and was "quite full of encyclopaedic matter and Germanic doctrine."[7] Yet, while Wilson ridiculed "Germanic doctrine," he wrote to Heath Dabney (then studying in Munich), that he regretted that his ignorance of German kept him from a German university training.[8]

The weekly meeting of the Historical and Political Seminary, or seminar, was the most important academic exercise of the department. Outside speakers were invited, papers in the field were reviewed, and graduate students presented their work for discussion. Wilson read the first chapters of *Congressional Government* to the Seminary in the spring of 1884. The work was very favorably received: it prompted the offer from President Daniel Coit Gilman of a fellowship of $500 for the coming academic year and a request by Dr. Ely that Wilson collaborate with him and another student on a book on American political economists. G. Stanley Hall, the founder of American edu-

[4] WW to Bridges, December 15, 1883, *ibid.*, p. 586.
[5] WW to ELA, October 12, 1884, *ibid.*, Vol. 3, p. 350.
[6] WW to ELA, November 27, 1883, *ibid.*, Vol. 2, p. 552.
[7] WW to ELA, February 26, 1884, *ibid.*, Vol. 3, p. 49.
[8] WW to Richard Heath Dabney, February 17, 1884, *ibid.*, p. 26.

cational psychology, was also impressed. He asked Wilson to assist him in teaching an undergraduate course in logic and psychology, but Wilson declined, pleading ignorance of the subject.[9] Wilson's debating skill stood him in good stead in the Seminary; Professor Ely recalled him as a speaker of "unusual" effectiveness.[10] Despite Wilson's heavy schedule, he had a fairly active social life in Baltimore. His friends among the graduate students and younger faculty included Albert Shaw, Charles Howard Shinn, and J. Franklin Jameson.[11] He saw a good deal of Dr. Hiram Woods, his Princeton classmate, and consulted Woods casually about his health. Wilson described himself, jokingly, as looking so serious at social gatherings as to be taken for a minister, but he was more at ease than he had been at Charlottesville. He was in demand as a dinner speaker and entertainer and was one of the organizers of the Glee Club. One of the several ditties that he contributed is the following:

> We get our learning served in bits
> Of German literature
> With now and then an Eng[lish] word
> Our ears to reassure.[12]

Woodrow joined the Hopkins Literary Society, also known as the Hopkins Debating Club, rewrote the constitution, and renamed it, predictably, the Johns Hopkins House of Commons. The organization was a great success: when Wilson left Baltimore, the members expressed their appreciation of his efforts by presenting him with a pair of bronze figures of cavaliers.[13]

As at the University of Virginia, Wilson complained intermittently of digestive troubles during his stay in Baltimore. These were of psychosomatic origin. He had discomfort after eating, and, while he,

[9] WW to ELA, February 19, May 28, and June 3, 1884, *ibid.*, pp. 36, 197, 205.

[10] Richard T. Ely, *Ground Under My Feet: An Autobiography* (New York, 1938), p. 109.

[11] Shaw became editor of *The Review of Reviews*. He remained a close friend and edited the first collection of Wilson's public papers. At Hopkins he nicknamed Wilson "The Colonel" because of his southern political views. Shinn, who was deaf, had a varied career as managing editor of the *Overland Monthly* and then as forester with the University of California and the Department of Agriculture. Jameson received the Ph.D. degree from The Johns Hopkins University in 1882. He was Professor of History at Brown University while Wilson was at Wesleyan, and they retained an affectionate friendship.

[12] A fragment of a ditty, c. August 12, 1884, *PWW*, Vol. 3, p. 287.

[13] WW to ELA, December 15, 1884, *ibid.*, p. 543, n.3; WW to ELA, June 4, 1885, *ibid.*, Vol. 4, p. 682.

probably out of delicacy, was not specific about his bowel symptoms, the combination of constipation and urgency of stool[14] is highly suggestive of a "nervous" or irritable colon. Along with his gastro-intestinal symptoms, he had headaches, a sense of stuffiness in his head, and feelings of lethargy and depression. He was actually examined by a doctor on only one occasion, probably by his classmate, Dr. Charles W. Mitchell. Mitchell told his patient that he was suffering from the "natural after effects of a harmless disease" and gave him a "nauseous mixture" to be taken before each meal.[15] In his letter to his fiancée describing the encounter, Wilson, in an evident attempt to assure her of his good health, told her that it was only his first visit to a doctor in "six or eight years."[16] (Wilson was not accurate; he had seen a physician in Wilmington in January 1881.)[17]

Wilson's two years in Baltimore coincided with the period of his engagement to Ellen Axson. Their voluminous correspondence provides a record of his health and emotional state and gives a highly revealing and almost obsessional account of his thoughts and feelings. It discloses to a remarkable degree that Wilson was repeating the pattern of interaction that he had with his mother. He would usually begin his letters with a report of his ailments. After he had performed this ritual, he would assure Ellen that there was nothing wrong with him about which she should be concerned. After an episode which alarmed her greatly, he wrote: "You mus'nt take it so much to heart when I am sick, my little sweetheart. I've never been seriously ill in my life, and I certainly was not this time: and now I am perfectly well again. Whenever I write to you that I am unwell I am inclined to reproach myself afterwards for having told you anything about it: and yet I tell you such things *on principle*."[18] Wilson had a compulsion to tell Ellen everything about himself, and the *principle* was that neither he nor Ellen should ever conceal anything from each other. No matter how distressed he would be on hearing that she was unwell, he told her, he would be much more distressed by the thought that she was not letting him know everything. Woodrow worried so very much about anything that he suspected might be an indisposition that Ellen found it difficult to carry out the compact.

Wilson needed constant assurances that he was really loved, and, weighed down by his sense of responsibility for his unhappy mother,

---

[14] Axson Memoir.

[15] The "nauseous mixture" may have been an antacid or carminative (for gas).

[16] WW to ELA, February 2, 1884, *PWW*, Vol. 3, p. 4.

[17] WW to Dabney, February 1, 1881, *ibid.*, Vol. 2, p. 17.

[18] WW to ELA, July 8, 1884, *ibid.*, Vol. 3, p. 237.

he wondered if he could ever give another person happiness. When he was depressed, he wondered whether Ellen could love someone with his looks. He recalled how, after falling in love with Ellen, he was tormented by the fear that he would not win her.[19] When a letter from her would be late—they wrote almost daily—he was plunged into doubt, and, as Ellen soon learned, would get a headache. When he thought that Ellen was not confiding all her troubles to him, he felt that she was keeping him at arms' length. He was overjoyed when she revealed to him her apprehensions about the nervous condition of her brother, Stockton. Wilson recognized and was troubled by his compulsion to begin his letters with an account of his ailments and morbid thoughts, and he often told Ellen that he had destroyed the first few pages of a letter so that it would start on a brighter note.[20] Wilson realized that his fears about her were often without foundation, and he admitted that his anxieties were not wholly unhappy but "fraught with untold blessings." He once told her that, "aside from the unspeakable anguish of seeing you suffer [I would] esteem it a sweet privilege to nurse my darling through a *life-time* of ill health." This, for Wilson, was the supreme expression of devotion.[21]

In hundreds of letters, Wilson expressed his love eloquently and passionately. Writing to her liberated his heart from its loneliness. Her letters calmed his belligerence and soothed his impatience. He felt that she gave him a buoyancy of spirit that he had never had. He looked forward with indescribable happiness to the time when they would no longer be separated, and he recalled the anxieties and ecstacies of past meetings. Wilson urged Ellen to express her feelings as passionately as he poured forth his yearning for her. He wrote, not only of the purity and sacredness of their love, but also in explicit fashion of its physical joys. Several months after they had become engaged, he reported a delightful dream in which his excitement at finding her alone betrayed him into "one or two offences against decorum and 'principles.' " He assured her, however, that he was "not a youth to go an ell because once allowed an inch!"[22]

Wilson told Ellen of his hopes and his ambitions; his yearning to satisfy his instinct for leadership; and his aim to communicate the great thoughts and experiences of the past to the great mass of the

---

[19] WW to ELA, April 1, 1884, *ibid.*, p. 109. Wilson seems to have believed literally that he had a face only a mother could love.

[20] WW to ELA, March 11, April 25, and April 29, 1885, *ibid.*, Vol. 4, pp. 354, 527, 541.

[21] WW to ELA, January 15 and April 12, 1885, *ibid.*, Vol. 3, p. 611, 477.

[22] WW to ELA, January 8, 1884, *ibid.*, Vol. 2, p. 654.

people. He admitted candidly that he did not have the temperament for the tedium of scholarly research.[23] When he was feeling frustrated and depressed, he confessed his inadequacies—his temper, impatience, tendency to ruminate, and habits of self-scrutiny. When, in the spring of 1885, he was particularly unhappy, he wrote: "My bane, my worst enemy is self-consciousness, self-criticism—that communion with my anxieties, that impatience of my own weaknesses and faults, which fills my life when I am alone. I am too self-analytic; and it is only in the love-intercourse and love-services of home that I can forget, throw off this too morbid tendency."[24] In his depressed moods, he told Ellen: "[I come to] the conclusion that I am a shallow, thought-barren fraud, boundlessly ignorant, absurdly weak! I am filled with disgust for myself and with pity for all who love me."[25]

Wilson saw in Ellen the same qualities that he found in his mother—intelligence, integrity, womanly sweetness, purity, gentleness, and self-sacrifice. Yet Ellen differed in a number of respects. She was loyal and devoted to her family, as Jessie Wilson was, but, while reserved, she was more friendly with outsiders. Unlike Woodrow's mother, Ellen was not bitter toward people who might (she felt) not appreciate or offend her. Ellen was more self-sufficient and did not experience the intense loneliness that Mrs. Wilson suffered when Dr. Wilson and Woodrow were away. Although Ellen took Woodrow's side, she did not reinforce his resentments and competitiveness in the way that his mother did. When Woodrow complained that Dr. Adams was exploiting him, Jessie Wilson called Adams "a miserable humbug."[26] Ellen, however, thought that Adams had paid Wilson a compliment by asking him to collaborate with him. She could see his loneliness in proportion to larger problems. When Wilson complained of how miserable he would be at Christmas "alone" in Baltimore, she reminded him that her brother, Stockton, would be even lonelier in the "dismal village" where he was attending school.[27]

Ellen had a sense of humor that Wilson's mother lacked or had worn out over years of listening to her husband's puns. Woodrow could joke with Ellen in a way that he could not with his utterly serious mother. He wrote her that he had run into Hiram Woods, who told him that he (Wilson) looked about to break down and was working himself to death. Then he, Hiram, Hiram's sister, and another girl

[23] WW to ELA, February 24, 1885, *ibid.*, Vol. 4, p. 287.
[24] WW to ELA, April 4, 1885, *ibid.*, p. 451.
[25] WW to ELA, May 3, 1885, *ibid.*, p. 554.
[26] JWW to WW, April 2, 1884, *ibid.*, Vol. 3, p. 110.
[27] ELA to WW, January 7, 1884, *ibid.*, Vol. 2, p. 652.

went off to a baseball game and dinner and had a "jolly time."[28] In response, Ellen commented that she was very, very sorry to learn that he was trying to break himself down with overwork, and she hoped that Woods would "fairly *persecute*" him with ball games.[29] Ellen expressed surprise that the absence of a letter could have such a profound effect on him and told Woodrow that, if she were a man, she would not "condescend to get up a head-ache on any girl's account."[30] The couple had agreed not to make their engagement public, and Ellen wore her ring on her right hand. When he became jealous about the calls of a young minister, she could not resist some teasing. Once, when she had mentioned, half seriously, a planned visit to an art collection in Baltimore, and Woodrow was disappointed when she did not come, she joked about going to an exhibit in London for a day.[31] She learned, however, that Wilson was too serious about her affections and their enforced separation to appreciate such teasing.

In some respects, Ellen Axson underrated herself. She believed that she was not intellectual enough for Wilson, whom she considered the greatest and best man in the world. Actually, her knowledge of literature was wider than Wilson's, and she did much to broaden his narrow tastes in modern prose, poetry, and art. Regarding her painting, she was confident that, with proper training, she could become a successful professional artist. Ellen had more acquaintance than Woodrow with the world outside small southern towns and the campuses of universities. After she had lived in New York, she learned from observation the problems of poverty and economic insecurity that Wilson understood only academically. She, like Wilson, was the child and grandchild of Presbyterian ministers and was deeply religious. However, after the tragic death of her father in May 1884, she wondered, briefly but agonizingly, if her loss was truly a manifestation of God's love.[32] In her attitudes toward mental illness and her thoughts about the meaning of life and death, she had a far more inquiring mind than Wilson.

One reason for Ellen's difficulty in expressing herself as ardently as her lover wished was her concern about her father's illness. Samuel Edward Axson had been a nervous man, and, after the death of his wife in childbirth in 1881, he had periods of melancholy. Expression of suicidal ideas and episodes of physical violence caused him to be

[28] WW to ELA, April 20, 1884, *ibid.*, Vol. 3, pp. 138-39.
[29] ELA to WW, April 29, 1884, *ibid.*, pp. 149-50.
[30] ELA to WW, July 14, 1884, *ibid.*, p. 245.
[31] ELA to WW, March 13, 1884, *ibid.*, p. 85.
[32] ELA to WW, June 5, 1884, *ibid.*, p. 207.

admitted to the Central State Hospital at Milledgeville, Georgia, on January 10, 1884.[33] Ellen had not told Woodrow of the seriousness of her father's condition, and it was a great shock for him to learn that Axson had become acutely psychotic. Wilson, on hearing the news from a relative of Ellen's, consulted his friend, Shinn, and borrowed the money to go to Savannah, where Ellen had moved to be with her grandparents and other family after her father's hospitalization.[34] (Her grandfather, the Rev. Dr. Isaac Stockton Keith Axson, was pastor of the Independent Presbyterian Church of Savannah.) She offered to break the engagement because of the social stigma involved, but he dismissed the idea. Axson's course in the hospital was fluctuating. He became much worse in the middle of May and died suddenly, undoubtedly by suicide, on May 28.[35]

The death of Ellen's father came during a crisis in her relationship with Woodrow. The couple had been eager to see each other during the summer, and Ellen wanted Woodrow to visit her in Savannah. Wilson insisted that she come to Wilmington, citing his obligation not to leave his mother alone with Josie after Dr. Wilson went north. His mother, Woodrow said, had unselfishly offered to go to stay with her daughter, Annie, in Columbia so that he could go to Georgia, but he knew that this would be a great self-sacrifice because Mrs. Wilson could not really rest in Columbia since she found Annie "sensitive."[36] Jessie Wilson had only been "tolerably well,"[37] and, Woodrow, feeling it his duty to stay with her, pleaded with Ellen to change her mind.[38] Ellen, however, declined the invitation, because her grandmother and

[33] Samuel E. Axson's admission note to the Central State Hospital reads: "Lunatic from Chatham Co, Ga. Native of Liberty Co, Ga. Age about 47 years. Widower. Duration of insanity about four weeks. General health has been failing for some time. Cause supposed from bad health. Has been always a very nervous man, easily excited. Lost his wife about a year ago, which seemed to grieve him a great deal. Slight suicidal tendency. Is disposed to be violent occasionally. Patient is a Presbyterian preacher, and has been for quite a number of years, a devoted Christian. Eats well, sleeps but little. Has been in the habit of taking Chloral at night." Admission Records of the Central State Hospital, Milledgeville, Ga. (Georgia State Archives), Jan. 13, 1884.

[34] Charles Howard Shinn to WW, January 21, 1884, *ibid.*, Vol. 2, p. 662, n.3.

[35] *Ibid.*; WW to ELA, January 28, 1884, *ibid.*, p. 663. There can be little doubt that the cause of his death was suicide. Ellen's uncle wrote to her: "The place and manner of your father's death are inexpressibly sad: but you cannot doubt his 'acceptance in the Beloved.' It was a dark cloud which had settled upon his reason." Randolph Axson to ELA, June 12, 1884, the Papers of Woodrow Wilson, Library of Congress; hereinafter cited as the Wilson Papers.

[36] JWW to WW, November 23, 1883, *PWW*, Vol. 2, p. 547.

[37] JRW, Jr. to WW, February 5, 1884, *ibid.*, Vol. 3, p. 11.

[38] WW to ELA, April 6, 1884, *ibid.*, p. 113.

her Aunt Ella[39] did not consider the visit socially proper.[40] The refusal put Woodrow in low spirits; he assured Ellen that his mother's heart was set on her coming, and that Jessie Wilson, very old-fashioned and strict about such matters, regarded the visit as quite proper.[41] Again, Ellen refused, citing now her grandmother's opinion that the summer climate of Wilmington was not suitable.

Ellen obviously was being evasive. She admitted as much when she noted that her grandmother (Rebecca Randolph Axson) had made Ellen's mother (Margaret Jane Hoyt) spend the whole winter with her (Ellen's) father when they were engaged.[42] Ellen was not able to tell Woodrow her real reasons. One was that she did not want to leave her father, who was not doing well in the hospital; and she might have feared that Woodrow, who seemed to have little conception of the gravity of Axson's condition, might not have understood. The second was her concern that Woodrow, with the same fervor that he had shown the previous year in Asheville, might sweep her off her feet into an early marriage.

The question of marriage had come up in April, when Woodrow heard from his sister, Marion Kennedy, in Little Rock, that a professorship might be available at Arkansas Industrial University (now the University of Arkansas) in Fayetteville. He promptly asked Ellen what she would think of a home "amidst the pretty mountain lands of upper Arkansas."[43] Ellen was in no mood for marriage. She was torn by suspense about her father; worried about Stockton, who was experiencing the first symptoms of the mental illness which was to incapacitate him for long periods of his life; and upset over the severe stuttering that her eight-year-old brother, Edward, had developed. She wanted Woodrow to accept the fellowship he had been awarded and continue at the Hopkins. She, herself, was planning to take a position teaching art in Atlanta to improve her considerable talent and to ease the financial burden on her grandfather. Accordingly, she temporized by asking him for more information about the university and the position.[44] Wilson admitted that he knew very little about AIU except that it was a coeducational, land-grant institution; that he would be paid a salary of $1,700 a year; and that he would start teaching in

---

[39] Ella Law Axson, who was the wife of Randolph Axson.

[40] ELA to WW, April 7, 1884, *PWW*, Vol. 3, p. 118.

[41] WW to ELA, April 11, 1884, *ibid.*, p. 122.

[42] ELA to WW, April 15, 1884, *ibid.*, p. 129.

[43] Marion Wilson Kennedy to WW, April 15, 1884; WW to ELA, April 24, 1884, *ibid.*, pp. 131, 145.

[44] ELA to WW, April 29 and May 1, 1884, *ibid.*, pp. 150, 154.

September. He advised her that the opportunity was as favorable as he was likely to find at this stage of his training and made the completely implausible statement that, despite the absence of library facilities, he could study more effectively than at the Johns Hopkins because "a man learns best what he is under the immediate necessity of teaching."[45] He was so absorbed in the Arkansas business that he forgot to tell Ellen about his health and had to write another letter.[46] In her reply, Ellen reiterated her distress over her own family problems; however, if Woodrow insisted, she would agree to marriage and living in Arkansas.

Under the strain of trying to induce Ellen to come to Wilmington (as he waited for news of the Arkansas position), Wilson had an exacerbation of his psychosomatic ailments: headaches and a "terrible case of the 'blues.' " He was particularly upset over the prospect of Ellen's taking a job which would, he said, take her away from him and her friends, and he urged on her "the absolute necessity of letting me into all your counsels, if you would save me from infinite pain and anxiety."[47] He exacted from her the promise that she would make no decision about the teaching position for a week, at the end of which time he hoped to have more information about the Arkansas professorship. As he had done in his grief over his loss of Hattie Woodrow, he wrote her a poem, "To E.L.A. on Her Birthday."[48]

Woodrow's father had no faith in the Arkansas matter—it proved to be little more than a rumor—and both of his parents advised Wilson strongly against a precipitate marriage. Woodrow also seems to have had some idea of marrying and remaining at Johns Hopkins. Dr. Wilson warned him that, in such an event, his fellowship might be withdrawn. Despite their outspoken disapproval, his parents, characteristically, offered him continued financial support and a home for Ellen in Wilmington.[49] What finally brought Wilson to his senses was, not his parents' advice or a rational reconsideration of his plans, but the sudden worsening of Axson's condition which preceded his death. When Woodrow received the news of Axson's collapse, he abjectly

[45] WW to ELA, May 1, 1884, *ibid.*, p. 155-56.
[46] WW to ELA, May 1, 1884, *ibid.*, p. 156.
[47] WW to ELA, May 13, 1884, *ibid.*, pp. 176-77.
[48] "To E.L.A. on Her Birthday, May 15, 1884," enclosed with WW to ELA, May 13, 1884, *ibid.*, pp. 178-79. Although Ellen and Woodrow were fond of exchanging poetry, especially passages from Wordsworth, Tennyson, and Swinburne, it was only under conditions of great stress that Wilson himself composed poems.
[49] JWW to WW, May 15, 1884; JRW to WW, May 17, 1884, *ibid.*, pp. 181-82, 183-84.

apologized to Ellen for his "wild scheme"—and the "last manoeuvre of a wilful man bent upon having his own way."[50]

None the less, Wilson still disapproved of Ellen's working and expressed the fear that she might injure her health. This issue was resolved when, under the terms of her father's will, she received enough money to provide for a year's study at the Art Students' League in New York. But Woodrow continued to hope that he might find a position in some small college which would enable them to marry.[51] He took no active steps in this direction, however, and formally accepted the Hopkins fellowship. Soon afterward, to his delight and amazement, Ellen's grandmother changed her mind, and Ellen cordially accepted Mrs. Wilson's invitation. Mrs. Axson wrote that not only had she no objections to Ellen's trip to Wilmington, but she also strongly approved of the visit.[52] Needless to record, Woodrow's health improved markedly.

Wilson had a highly successful second year at the Hopkins. Despite the stresses of the summer, he had finished the last chapter of *Congressional Government*, and he sent the manuscript off to Houghton Mifflin in Boston on his return to Baltimore. The book, accepted in November and published in January, was an instant popular success. Its dedication to Dr. Wilson ran: "To His Father, the patient guide of his youth, the gracious companion of his manhood, his best instructor and most lenient critic, this book is affectionately dedicated by the Author."[53] Wilson was slowed in the work for his degree by the extra chore of his collaboration with Professor Ely on a history of American economic thought, but felt that he was making progress. In February he wrote to Heath Dabney: "I am considerably better contented with the University courses this year than I was last: whether because I am enjoying the acceptable emolument of the Fellowship stipend or because the courses—or rather the *coursers*[54]—have taken a brace is too recondite a problem for my present powers of solution."[55] He was in good health; at home, his mother was relatively well and pleased about leaving Wilmington for Clarksville, Tennessee, where Dr. Wilson had received an appointment to the faculty of the Southwestern Theological Seminary. In New York, Ellen was happy, enthusiastic about her art classes and the galleries, and was enjoying friends. Woodrow visited

[50] WW to ELA, May 17, 1884, *ibid.*, pp. 184-85.
[51] WW to ELA, June 29, 1884, *ibid.*, p. 221.
[52] WW to ELA, July 13, 1884, *ibid.*, p. 243.
[53] WW to ELA, December 1, 1884, *ibid.*, p. 503.
[54] Adams and Ely.
[55] WW to Dabney, February 14, 1885, *PWW*, Vol. 4, p. 249.

her over the Christmas holidays. On the same day that he received the first copies of *Congressional Government*—January 24, 1885—Wilson decided to accept an offer to teach history and political science at the newly established Bryn Mawr College, a woman's college.

It was a time for happiness, but, although Wilson's book established him as a scholar of note, and the Bryn Mawr appointment seemed to remove the last obstacle to marriage, success brought new problems. In a letter to Ellen, soon after he had heard that his book had been accepted, Wilson described one of the psychological aspects. He wrote: "I am quite well this morning and the 'blues' are altogether dispelled. It *was* unreasonable, I confess, to be low-spirited so soon after hearing of Houghton and Mifflin's decision about my *mss*; but then you must remember that I am constituted, as regards such things, on a very peculiar pattern. Success does not flush or elate me, except for the moment. I could almost wish it did. I *need* a large infusion of the devil-me-care element. The acceptance of my book has of course given me the deepest satisfaction and has cleared away a whole storm of anxieties: it is an immense gain every way. But it has sobered me a good deal too. The question is, What next? I must be prompt to follow up the advantage gained: and I must follow it up in the direction in which I have been preparing to do effectual political service. I feel as I suppose a general does who has gained a first foothold in the enemy's country. I must push on: to linger would be fatal. There is now a responsibility resting upon me where before there was none. My rejoicing, therefore, has in it a great deal that is stern and sober, like that of the strong man to run a race. The light-heartedness comes in when I think of the delight I have been able to give my darling. *You* are my *joy*, my pet. Your love is the effectual sunlight in my life."[56]

Wilson had accepted the Bryn Mawr position after a great deal of deliberation, and he had second thoughts after his decision. The college had the advantages of closeness to Philadelphia and its libraries and an intimate association with Johns Hopkins. The salary, though small, would still enable him to get married. On the other side, he and Ellen, knowing that the great majority of women's colleges of the day were little more than glorified boarding schools, were concerned that the post would be beneath his dignity. They were also concerned about his relationship to the Dean of the Faculty, the vigorous Martha Carey Thomas, who, on the recommendation of Professor Adams and President Daniel Coit Gilman of the Johns Hopkins, had been mainly instrumental in selecting Wilson. Having decided to forego the Ph.D.

[56] WW to ELY, December 2, 1884, *ibid.*, Vol. 3, pp. 506-507.

degree because of the amount of reading and his slowness in German, Wilson was deeply concerned that the lack of the degree would impair his standing with his German university-trained colleagues. Although the first edition of *Congressional Government* sold out in a few weeks and received, on the whole, favorable reviews, he expressed concern that his contribution had not been substantial enough. Also, he developed "a lurking sense of disappointment and *loss*" in the knowledge that an academic career would deprive him of the opportunity to participate more actively in politics.[57] Ellen, who addressed herself to the last point, sensibly suggested that no young man of twenty-eight, with his life before him, need be talking about disappointed ambitions.[58]

Wilson probably had no idea that *Congressional Government* would be such a great success and that it would immediately lead to offers of positions from important institutions. One attractive proposal came from the University of Michigan. Wilson, who debated whether he should ask President James E. Rhoads of Bryn Mawr to release him from his contract, sought his parents' advice. Their responses characteristically indicate the elder Wilsons' attitudes toward Woodrow's career and are examples of their styles of direct and indirect communication. Dr. Wilson wrote: "I hardly think I w'd break the engagement at *B.M.* A year or so there will be nothing lost; and, by keeping up a correspondence with yr. 'big-bugs' here and there, you will no doubt find a first-class opening. 'Festina lenti.' "[59] On the same day, Mrs. Wilson wrote: "Your sweet letter to papa was received this morning. I need not tell you, my darling, that we think of you constantly—and talk about you much every day. That we are inexpressibly proud of our beloved boy's success—unprecedented as it is. We are filled with joy & thankfulness. We took tea last night with Mr. & Mrs. Wm. Phillips. He has expressed his delight in reading your book, of which he bought a copy, before. He is very particular to claim you as an old classmate[60]—makes much of that—and last night he was asking us whether you were really bound to go to Bryn Mawr. It seems there is to be a chair in your department established at Chapel Hill— and *he* hopes to be elected Prof. of Chemistry—will apply for the place. He thinks it would be so delightful if you and he could work together there—and wants you to apply for the "English" chair—or

[57] WW to ELA, February 24, 1885, *ibid.*, Vol. 4, p. 287.
[58] ELA to WW, February 25, 1885, *ibid.*, p. 297.
[59] JRW to WW, March 17, 1885, *ibid.*, p. 377.
[60] William B. Phillips and Wilson were members of the Class of 1877 at Davidson College.

"History"—I am not sure as to the precise name of the new Chair. My darling boy—are you *bound* in honour to go to B.M.? Of course we cant tell what will be for the best. But your father says he will advise you to accept an invitation such as Prof Adams[61] of the Mich University proposes. But I will leave him to speak for himself as to that. Your father says he expects to be spoken of in the future as *your father!* "[62]

Dr. Wilson's advice was practical and straightforward; Woodrow carried it out with the eventual satisfactory result that his father had predicted. Dr. Wilson recognized that Woodrow had no teaching experience and knew that Woodrow's drive and the pressure of a large university would probably have adverse effects on his health. Mrs. Wilson, on the contrary, was devious. She obviously cited Phillips' remark that he wanted Woodrow as a colleague at North Carolina as the vehicle for the expression of her own wishes to have a prestigious post for Woodrow and to have him close to her. The use of this "third person" mode of communication also occurred in her quoting, or rather misquoting, her husband. The question of "honour" was hardly an issue, but she may have felt that its introduction might have given Woodrow justification for withdrawing from his contract. The whole incident illustrates how Wilson's mother could feed the flames of his ambition and influence him while maintaining her role as a non-dominating mother and a deferential wife.

No sooner had Woodrow accepted the Bryn Mawr job than he began to press Ellen to name the wedding day. He wanted early June; she suggested September. He pointed out that the college term began on September 15 and that he could hardly make the necessary preparations for his courses while he was, in effect, still in the heat of passion. Despite his pleading, Ellen was unwilling to commit herself; as she had done regarding the Wilmington visit of the previous year, she invoked the need to consult her Aunt Ella. To this evasion, Woodrow responded with a headache and a sudden trip to New York. The visit did not resolve the issue, and Wilson continued to have not only headaches, but also "colds" and "the blues."[63] One reason for Ellen's preference for a later date appears in a letter of February 12, in which she expressed the hope that, after the close of the term at the Art Students' League, she could spend at least a month taking lessons in landscape painting. She told Woodrow that she and several other

[61] Charles Kendall Adams, Professor of History, University of Michigan.

[62] JWW to WW, March 17, 1885, *PWW*, Vol. 4, p. 376.

[63] WW to ELA, January 29 and February 1, 1885; ELA to WW, January 30, 1885, *ibid.*, pp. 197, 205, 201-202.

students had an opportunity to rent a house at Hampton Beach, Long Island, where they would be chaperoned by the mother of one of the girls while their instructor lived nearby.[64] In an impassioned reply, Woodrow was "sorely puzzled" that she would prefer a "sketching class to my company."[65] A few days later he wrote that he missed her so much and was so worried about not getting his degree that if he did not break down in health this year, he surely would the next. Typically, to this dire prediction he added: "But I wont worry my darling about these things. It can't help me to distress her: it will only add to my disquietude to know that I have disturbed her peace of mind."[66] The news did indeed disturb her peace of mind. On the night that she received his letter, she had a blinding headache and a fainting spell. She struck her head in the fall and became momentarily stunned. Aside from a sizable contusion, there were fortunately no medical aftereffects.[67]

A more comic aspect of Wilson's problems was his jealousy over the attentions that his fiancée was receiving from a fellow boarder, Arthur Goodrich. This young man, to whom Ellen alluded as "that verrie parfait, gentil knight," had taken to bringing her home from class. She assured Woodrow that Goodrich was not a southern boy, with whom her experiments, she admitted, had not been brilliantly successful, but a cool-headed New Englander. She knew, she told Woodrow, in what direction his (Wilson's) thoughts would run, but it was all on a "*platonic* schedule."[68] Wilson informed her that she was quite right in her prediction about the direction of his thought, and, even though he had "*perfect* faith" in her discreetness, he knew from his knowledge of men that there was no such thing as a "platonic schedule."[69] He was particularly annoyed when Goodrich, who worked in Houghton Mifflin's New York office, promised Ellen a copy of *Congressional Government* fresh from the press. To Woodrow's satisfaction, she had earlier informed her admirer that she was engaged.[70] In his turn, Woodrow wrote to her that he had been told that a young lady in Baltimore had been most pleased to learn that he was

[64] ELA to WW, February 12, 1885, *ibid.*, p. 241.

[65] WW to ELA, February 14, 1885, *ibid.*, p. 51.

[66] WW to ELA, February 17, 1885, *ibid.*, p. 263.

[67] ELA to WW, February 19, 1885, *ibid.*, p. 270.

[68] ELA to WW, December 17, 1884, *ibid.*, Vol. 3, p. 551.

[69] WW to ELA, December 18, 1884, *ibid.*, p. 556.

[70] ELA to WW, January 11 and 12, 1885; WW to ELA, January 13, 1885, *ibid.*, pp. 600, 602, 603-04. Ellen was not wearing her engagement ring because it had become too small for her finger. ELA to WW, December 20, 1884, *ibid.*, pp. 562-63.

engaged "because she could be as nice to him as she chose."[71] He was not amused to learn that, after Ellen had supposedly dismissed Goodrich forever, he had escorted her to prayer meeting and the theater.[72] Ellen explained that she fulfilled these engagements because they had been made before her talk with Goodrich. After she refused to even speak with Goodrich, the young man, in her presence, burned some poems that he had written and persuaded a friend of Ellen's to take a note to her. When Woodrow heard of these activities he threatened to come to New York and take some means of delivering her.[73]

Any explanation of Ellen Axson's delaying tactics and flirtatious behavior involves some analysis of her character and her ambivalence about giving up her career in art for marriage. She had been regarded as a dreamy, impractical girl, always with a book in her hand, and her dream was of art and beauty.[74] After her graduation from the Rome (Georgia) Female Seminary, she went to New York to study at the Art Students' League. However, after her mother's death she had been obliged to return home to care for her father, infant sister, and two brothers. She had great self-discipline and was extremely conscientious and compulsive about work and duty. Like her father and her brother Stockton, she was introspective and had a tendency to depression, which she fought by keeping busy and maintaining total devotion to an ideal. She was an outstanding student at the Art Students' League; her friend, Antoinette Farnsworth (the bearer of the note from Arthur Goodrich), marveled at how anyone could work so hard at something that she was going to give up almost immediately.[75]

Wilson was proud of Ellen's ability but thought her painting only a pleasant pastime. When he was worried that his Bryn Mawr salary would be insufficient, she suggested that she work for a year. He rejected the idea. After she made her decision, Wilson felt "guiltily selfish" about her sacrifice. He was sure, he said, that she could find subjects to paint and could leave immortal portraits. His heart would be in any arrangements by which she could take time from her household duties for her studies. He pointed out that it was a subject that they had never discussed and asked her to tell him her feelings.[76]

[71] WW to ELA, January 13, 1885, *ibid.*, p. 605.

[72] WW to ELA, January 24, 1885, *ibid.*, Vol. 4, p. 4.

[73] ELA to WW, February 10, 1885, *ibid.*, p. 234; WW to ELA, May 15, 1885, *ibid.*, pp. 595-96.

[74] ELA to WW, April 3, 13, and 15, 1885, *ibid.*, pp. 443, 485, 491.

[75] ELA to WW, April 11, 1885, *ibid.*, p. 475.

[76] WW to ELA, January 17, 1885; ELA to WW, January 21, 1885, *ibid.*, Vol. 3, pp. 617, 625-26; WW to ELA, March 1 and 27, 1885, *ibid.*, Vol. 4, pp. 316, 420.

She expressed some of her feelings and concealed others in a way which showed movingly the crisis of commitment through which she had passed. She wrote: "It never occurred to me that there might be any question in your mind as to my course with regard to my work hereafter, yet now that such a thought is suggested I can easily understand your uncertainty. . . . Sweetheart, I would never give you a divided allegiance; I owe you my little *all* of love, of life and service, and it is all my joy to give it. Believe me, dear, it is an absolutely pure joy—there is in it *no* alloy, I have *never* felt the *slightest* pang of regret for what I must 'give up.' *Don't* think there is any sacrifice involved, my darling, I assure you again there is *none whatever*. . . .

"But to answer your questions more in detail,—I must remind you that I never had any ambition, and that I can't give up what I never had! Nor had I ever any faith in myself; I never even dreamed of painting 'immortal portraits.' My experience and observation since I have been here have driven me to the conclusion that I *have* talent, above the average among the art-students. It is *barely* possible that my talent for art combined with my talent for work *might*, after many years, win me a place in the first rank among American artists. . . . I wish if possible to take some lessons in landscape painting, partly because some knowledge of it is necessary to that practical equipment . . . and partly because I think it must be one of the most delightful and healthful of recreations. . . . But the chief reason . . . to give up, once for all, every thought of art as a serious study lies in my disposition. You don't know *yet* what a curious disposition that is, though I have tried to tell you several times! I am not at all well-balanced, I have entirely too much badly regulated energy and concentration; it is well-nigh impossible for me to divide up a day into bits as other women do;—I must do one thing all day long. It makes no difference whether it be something I *like* to do or not,—for that matter I like,—I grow interested in any work when I have once begun it,—but I may not have wished to begin it and I may be dreadfully tired, physically and mentally, yet all the same I want to *go on* to the end. . . . And if I did not forget then that I had ever thought to be an artist, I should be a *caution* as a house-keeper!—that is I should be all house keeper one day all artist the next!—and you would be the most uncomfortable of men!"[77]

Despite his joy over Ellen's surrender and the ardent expression of her love, Wilson continued to complain of feelings of loneliness and depression, and his psychosomatic symptoms persisted. He also be-

[77] ELA to WW, March 28, 1885, *ibid.*, pp. 428-30.

came extremely concerned about Ellen's health, although she was quite well. She wrote to him almost every night; but, because of her classes, visits to galleries, lectures, and shopping, and with the convivial atmosphere of her boarding house, she was sometimes too tired to make each letter a long one. Woodrow scolded her for overtaxing her strength in "the debilitating spring weather." He was haunted, he said, by the thought that she was sitting all day at her easel, "doing all that it is possible to do to drive the bloom out of your cheeks and to bring dark lines under your eyes." He warned her that no one could "break the laws of health with impunity" and advised her to give up some of her work and take regular exercise. He wondered why she did not have headaches from fatigue oftener than she did.[78] In reply, Ellen assured him that she was getting plenty of exercise and was feeling very well; she was tired at night only when she had been standing on her feet a great deal.[79]

Such overwrought fancies were probably morbid projections of Wilson's concern about his own malaise. He was working extremely hard and was taking no exercise. Actually, as he wrote the letter, he was having a nervous headache.[80] After he received her report of her health, he conceded that he, not she, should visit a doctor.[81] The entire sequence reveals how important a symbol illness was to Wilson in communicating his emotional identifications with Ellen. He had no wish for her to be actually ill, but the fantasy of the bloom fading from her cheeks made him feel more closely attached to her and eased his loneliness. His threat that he might become ill elicited the desired reaction. Ellen wrote: "You *must* know how much more eagerly I have longed to be your wife since I have seen that you had in your 'precarious' health a special need for a wife's loving care." For that, she said that she needed her own health. She recalled that, while still in Georgia, she had looked around her and seen that, to a greater or lesser degree, two-thirds of the women she knew were invalids. She had then decided that when she came to New York she would be examined by the best woman doctor she could find, and, if she was not judged completely fit, she would break the engagement. However, she had felt so well that she had forgotten about her plan.[82]

As the wedding day approached, Woodrow's feelings of rapturous anticipation were mingled with fears and doubts. He was tortured by

[78] WW to ELA, April 12 and May 23, 1885, *ibid.,* pp. 477, 618.
[79] ELA to WW, April 13, 1885, *ibid.,* p. 484.
[80] WW to ELA, April 12, 1885, *ibid.,* p. 476.
[81] WW to ELA, April 15, 1885, *ibid.,* pp. 488-89.
[82] ELA to WW, April 13 and 16, 1885, *ibid.,* pp. 485, 493-94.

such thoughts as "What if I should lose her?" and "What if God says no to our plans." He was "a little heart-sick" on a day when he did not receive a letter[83] and, he told Ellen, his loneliness increased even as his love grew. He was ashamed of himself that he had "the blues" when he should have been happy, but he could not control his feelings.[84] His state of tension is revealed by his answer to a letter from Ellen which he received as he was about to leave Baltimore to stay with his family in Columbia until the wedding. Ellen said that she could feel no grief about his departure; she felt that "the best and most restful" change for him would be to join the home circle. She added—playfully, she thought—"No, I won't say that either! why shouldn't I humour your fancy that there will be *one* change still better for you?"[85] She must have been staggered by his reply. Wilson scolded her for doubting his love by suggesting that he would be happier with his family than with her, which of course, Ellen had not done. If Ellen was humoring a fancy of his, he went on, then it followed, as night did the day, that there was no truth in his love for her. He begged her never to say such things again, even in fun.[86]

Wilson's uncertainty about Ellen's love for him persisted almost to the time of the wedding. Two weeks before they were married, he wrote: "One whit's abatement in that love, one moment's pause in its growth, would kill me. I am nothing, if my heart be broken: and it would break if I could not have your love as absolutely as you have that of Your own Woodrow."[87] Happily, there was no pause or abatement, and the couple were married on June 24, 1885, in the parlor of the residence of Ellen's grandfather. Dr. Axson and Dr. Wilson performed the ceremony.

For Wilson, the validity of the experience of love depended upon physical proximity. Without such closeness, he could not be certain that Ellen really loved him. He was desperately lonely when he was away from her, and her repeated verbal assurances gave him only temporary relief. Wilson was most lonely just after they had separated; he felt that she was a part of him, and that that part had been torn away or left behind. This sense of bereavement, which defied all of Wilson's efforts to deal with it rationally, led to his compelling need for an early marriage and a lack of appreciation for Ellen's reasons for postponement. He perceived any assertion of her own identity,

[83] WW to ELA, June 8, 1885, *ibid.*, p. 691.
[84] WW to ELA, March 11 and May 24, 1885, *ibid.*, pp. 353, 621.
[85] ELA to WW, May 26, 1885, *ibid.*, p. 666.
[86] WW to ELA, May 28, 1885, *ibid.*, pp. 667-68.
[87] WW to ELA, June 12, 1885, *ibid.*, p. 707.

apart from his own, as loss of love. When they were separated, Woodrow's passionate feelings substituted for her presence. Even such emotions as sadness, grief, and frustration were mingled with ecstasy because they brought Ellen close. Several years after their marriage, he wrote:

"The trouble is with my heart. It is not rested. It is weighted down with an unspeakable sadness from which it seems impossible to escape. I am not *unhappy*—that is not it. I am calm and as full of quiet, untroubled purpose as ever; but there's no heart in the purpose— nothing seems worth while without you—nothing seems to promise anything in the midst of this drear loneliness. I shall do better presently; but for the time I do not *care*, somehow, to feel differently."[88]

With considerable insight, Woodrow told Ellen: "My only disease is loneliness."[89] Yet loneliness is not a disease. It is a condition of modern man. In one of the few discussions of loneliness in psychiatric literature, Frieda Fromm-Reichmann writes: "The longing for interpersonal intimacy stays with every human being from infancy throughout life; and there is no human being who is not threatened by its loss. ... Anyone who has encountered persons who were under the influence of real loneliness understands why people are more frightened of being lonely than of being hungry, or being deprived of sleep, or of having their sexual needs unfulfilled."[90] It is difficult to separate sexual feelings from the need for closeness, but Wilson's behavior cannot be attributed simply to the strength of his "sexual drive" or even to his dependence on Ellen. Loneliness is different from dependence. Loneliness has a quality of exclusiveness in that it relates to a specific individual, while dependence has a more generalized range. In contrast to loneliness, dependence does not necessarily involve a strong emotional tie, nor does it imply an enduring bond. In addition, loneliness involves the absence of physical proximity, while one can be dependent on people who are, in spatial terms, far away.

In the psychiatric literature, the most attractive formulation of the genesis of loneliness is the attachment theory of the psychoanalyst John Bowlby,[91] who was influenced by Konrad Lorenz' work on im-

[88] WW to EAW, March 6, 1892, *ibid.*, Vol. 7, p. 447.

[89] WW to ELA, March 11, 1885, *ibid.*, Vol. 4, p. 352.

[90] Frieda Fromm-Reichmann, "Loneliness," *Psychiatry*, XXII (1959), 3, 7; Ben Mijuskovic, "Loneliness: An Interdisciplinary Approach," *ibid.*, XL (1977), 113-32.

[91] A British psychoanalyst who did pioneer observations of mother-infant relationships. Bowlby's studies have been expanded and further systematized by Mary D. S. Ainsworth and S. M. Bell, "Mother-Infant Interaction and the Development of Competence," in K. J. Connolly and Jerome Bruner, eds., *The Growth of Competence*

printing. Bowlby developed a hypothesis of attachment which, unlike the hunger and sex drive explanations of orthodox psychoanalysis, was based on methodical observations of the behavior of mothers and infants. Attachment behavior includes sucking, clinging, crying, smiling, and laughing; it is activated by strangeness, hunger, fatigue, and anything frightening, and is terminated by the sight, sound, or touch of the mother. The infant internalizes the interaction with the mother in pictorial image formation, and feelings of pleasure and contentment are inseparable from the child's image of himself (I refer to the infant as "he") and his mother. The alternate image, separation, is distressing and may be the precursor of the fear of death. In normal development, attachment behavior wanes by the third year of life and is replaced by the child's exploration of the environment. When he becomes mobile, he can, by sharing play with the care-giver at a distance, maintain contact while operating independently. The emotionally healthy mother provides a secure base from which the child can venture out and to which he can return. An anxious, lonely, unhappy mother prolongs attachment behavior.

Jessie Wilson was such a lonely, fearful, discontented mother. The early death of her own mother and the dilution of her father's affection probably contributed to her overprotective attitude toward Woodrow and her definition of being "all alone." Her loneliness, as we have seen, was associated with ill-health, depression, and premonitions of disaster. When Woodrow first left home—to go to Davidson College— the separation made mother and son so lonely and depressed that he was obliged to return home. The memory was apparently painful enough for Wilson in later life to invent such fictions as measles and scarlet fever to explain his leaving Davidson.[92] Wilson's notable lack of curiosity and reluctance to engage in new experiences[93] may also have been related to events of early life.

(London and New York, 1974). See also L. Alan Stroufe, "Attachment and the Roots of Competence," *Human Nature*, I (1978), 50-57.

[92] The pattern of a mother who urges her son on to great achievement in the outside world, but who maintains him in a state of infantile dependence at home, is a common one in school phobias.

[93] Ray Stannard Baker and Cary Grayson emphasized that Wilson enjoyed reading the same books over and over and going to the same places. He did not visit the Capitol before writing *Congressional Government*, and he did not go with Dr. Adams and most of his Hopkins students to attend Grover Cleveland's inaugural. See WW to Albert Shaw, March 7, 1885, *PWW*, Vol. 4, p. 341; Baker, *Wilson*, I, 232-33; Grayson, *An Intimate Memoir*, p. 12. When Ellen Axson suggested that he inspect Bryn Mawr before he accepted an appointment there, he answered that it would interfere with his "uppermost wish to have my darling all to myself for a few days." WW to ELA, December 11, 1884, *PWW*, Vol. 3, p. 532.

Throughout his life, Wilson needed the close companionship of women, particularly in stressful situations. However, Ellen Axson did far more for him than to relieve his loneliness and depressions. She made a reality out of the rhetoric by which he idealized women. She gave him a better self, free of much of his mother's gloom, apprehensions, and bitterness. As he was so often to write, she liberated his heart from bondage. She provided the secure base from which he could venture out into the world.

CHAPTER V

Bryn Mawr
and the Opposite Sex

WOODROW WILSON'S BELIEFS and feelings about the relationship of men and women were in accord with the biologically based, sex-dichotomist views of his time. Science and religion alike taught that the sexes differed in their mental as well as in their physical qualities, and that gender determined not only social role but also personal character. The classification provided a guide to living and a way of structuring situations, even some not basically related to sex. Its validity was affirmed in custom and everyday language. Wilson, like his father, used the word "manly" to indicate courage and forthrightness, and the term "womanly" to denote gentleness, modesty, and the possession of finer sensibilities. His concept of the role of the male as protector was expressed in his usual habit of addressing Ellen in his letters as "my little wife," and in her so signing herself. On one occasion, he made a slip of the pen and called her "my own sweet, precious, *precious* little little wife." He thought that the extra "precious" represented deep "unconscious striving" but did not think that the second "little" had any meaning.[1]

Wilson's pronouncements about the social order of the sexes could be sweeping. When Ellen was living in New York during their engagement, she became acquainted with women who lived outside the conventional family pattern and worked for a living outside the home. When Ellen expressed some interest in the new subject of women's rights, Wilson, in his impatience for her to set the wedding date, denounced the issue as "false talk." He went on to assure her that for men and women to live apart was "untrue to the teachings of history, to the manifestations of Providence, and to the deepest instincts of the heart."[2] Such basic assumptions, on one occasion at least, influenced his academic thinking. For a course at Johns Hopkins, he reviewed a book on the early history of the family in which the author discussed Johann Jakob Bachofen's theory that matriarchal social systems could have been a normal practice. Wilson rejected the idea that anything

[1] WW to EAW, April 30, 1886, *PWW*, Vol. 5, pp. 185-86.
[2] WW to ELA, March 1, 1885, *ibid.*, Vol. 4, p. 316.

but a patriarchal organization could have existed, except under very unusual circumstances. He regarded matriarchy as highly abnormal and equated it with promiscuity.[3]

Wilson was drawn to attractive, feminine women and was repelled by those whom he felt reversed the natural social order. His feelings in this respect, as well as his prejudice against New Englanders, were expressed in his comments on attending a congress of the American Association for the Advancement of Women in Baltimore. He went to the meeting despite "the chilled, scandalized feeling" that always came over him when he saw and heard women speak in public. The only "noticeable 'orator,' " he wrote, was a "severely dressed person from Boston, an old maid of the straitest sect of old maids." "Not trousers and a Prince Albert coat," he continued, "could have made her more manly in her bearing. She was a living example—and lively commentary—of what might be done by giving men's places and duties to women—a very dialectic Amazon!" On the other hand, he was favorably impressed by the chairwoman, Julia Ward Howe—"a most attractive, motherly old lady."[4]

Wilson approved of higher education for women but objected to coeducation because he felt that it would lead to undesirable sexual relationships and hamper studious work. He did not believe that women were less intelligent than men. However, he thought that their minds were different, and that their intelligence was largely "sympathetic." Women were, in his view, endowed with a particular quality of understanding which, by divine plan, provided men with intellectual stimulation and satisfaction. A less than convincing, but amusing, demonstration of this thesis occurred after Ellen had read Charles Egbert Craddock's *The Prophet of the Great Smoky Mountains* and was impressed by his powerful and beautiful style.[5] Wilson agreed with her evaluation, and both were then amazed to learn that "Craddock" was the pseudonym of Mary Noailles Murfree. Wilson, on second thought, decided that this discovery did, after all, bear out his belief that women's mental powers were almost entirely of the "sympathetic sort."[6] After Wilson had had some experience at Bryn Mawr, he admitted that women students could do extremely well in English, Greek, and Latin.[7]

[3] A class report, "Some Words upon An Essay on the Early History of the Family, by A. Lang," c. November 19, 1884, printed as an addendum in *ibid.,* Vol. 12, pp. 480-85.

[4] WW to ELA, October 31, 1884, *ibid.,* Vol. 3, p. 389.

[5] ELA to WW, February 27, 1885, *ibid.,* Vol. 4, p. 307.

[6] WW to ELA, March 19, 1885, *ibid.,* p. 385.

[7] Baker, *Wilson,* I, 290.

Wilson's views of the proper role of women and the function of their brains ran directly counter to those of Martha Carey Thomas, Dean of the Faculty at Bryn Mawr. Miss Thomas, who was exactly Wilson's age, had gained her education in the face of male skepticism and opposition. After she had been refused regular admission for graduate study at the Johns Hopkins and at German universities, she had earned the Ph.D., *summa cum laude*, in Germanic philology from the University of Zurich. She believed that women were in every way the intellectual equals of men and were fitted for the best education that any male college could provide. Like Wilson, she was devoted to the life of the mind and was determined that Bryn Mawr should prove her beliefs. Miss Thomas derided the finding that men's brains were slightly heavier than those of women; all it showed, she said, was that, for thousands of years, women had had an inferior education. She vowed that she would, if study and learning could do it, make her brain weigh as much as that of any man, so that no "miserable man" could stand up and tell any "miserable audience" that her brain weighed a few ounces less than a man's![8]

Wilson, of course, was painfully aware of Dean Martha's—as he jokingly called her in private—academic accomplishments and his own lack of the Ph.D. Miss Thomas was also strikingly handsome and well-dressed and never married or showed the slightest interest in men. Although she represented all that Wilson resented and feared in women, there were marked similarities in their backgrounds and personalities. Miss Thomas was of the Quaker aristocracy, as Wilson was of the Presbyterian elite. Each had a dominating father and an outwardly submissive mother who exercised subtle control. Each was ambitious and achieving and conscious of a strong sense of intellectual superiority and leadership. Each tended to be also shy in unstructured social situations. After they assumed the presidencies of their respective institutions, their policies were similar—insistence on high academic standards, introduction of a tutorial system, and placement of scholarship ahead of religious beliefs. At Bryn Mawr, their relationship was formal and guarded. Her attitude toward Wilson is summed up in a quotation from Tennyson that she placed under his name in a projected memoir. It was, "Put thy sweet hand in mine and trust me."[9]

Wilson's three years at Bryn Mawr were a period of high academic success. He had envisioned his stay at the college as preliminary to a chair of political science at a larger institution, preferably Princeton or the Johns Hopkins, and he worked diligently to attain the necessary

[8] Edith Finch, *Carey Thomas of Bryn Mawr* (New York, 1947), p. 31.
[9] *Ibid.*, p. 175.

competence and recognition. In his first year, at the urging of his wife and Dean Thomas, and through the kindness of Dr. Adams, who permitted him to use *Congressional Government* as his thesis, he obtained the Ph.D. from the Johns Hopkins. His paper, "The Study of Administration" (completed in the autumn of 1886), set forth the need to adapt European bureaucratic methods to democratic government and is regarded as the pioneer article on the subject in English.[10] Wilson was still unable to read German at sight, but he painstakingly translated the multivolume *Handbuch des Oeffentlichen Rechts des Gegenwart* (the major source of his most widely read work, *The State*). He was the only member of his department and thus covered a wide range of historical subjects in the classroom: ancient Greece and Rome, modern European history, American history, and constitutional history. He also wrote numerous articles and reviews, accepted invitations for outside lectures, and, in the winter of his last year, gave the first of his annual series of lectures on administration at Johns Hopkins.

One of his first outside appearances was a tragicomic fiasco, which stands in contrast to his later brilliant career as an after-dinner speaker. Wilson's classmate, Robert Bridges, had secured for him an invitation to address the banquet of the Princeton alumni in New York; Wilson, conscious of the opportunity to advance his fortunes, grasped it eagerly. In his haste, zeal, and nervousness, however, he failed to sense what sort of talk would be appropriate for an evening of fun and song. Instead of applying a light and humorous touch, he spoke seriously and at length on the theme of the scholar in politics. His main thrust was that Princeton should establish a chair of politics, with the not so subtle implication that Wilson was the man for it. Despite rude interruptions and a dwindling audience, Wilson pressed on, and he closed with the toast, "I ask you to drink to the future professor of politics: may he be no less a scholar for being studiously a man of the world!"[11] Wilson was so discouraged by his setback that, two weeks later, he looked unsuccessfully for a governmental position in Washington. He probably did this on the spur of the moment; he was in Washington since he had escorted his wife on her way south for her first confinement.[12]

The Wilsons' expectations of a happy marriage were fulfilled in

[10] Arthur S. Link, "Woodrow Wilson and the Study of Administration," in Link, *The Higher Realism of Woodrow Wilson and Other Essays* (Nashville, Tenn., 1971), pp. 38-44.

[11] Editorial Note, "Wilson's 'First Failure' at Public Speaking," *PWW*, Vol. 5, pp. 134-37. Wilson's address is printed in *ibid.*, pp. 137-41. See also Baker, *Wilson*, I, 264-66.

[12] *Ibid.*, p. 266.

Bryn Mawr. Wilson delighted in their physical proximity and Ellen's domesticity. She sewed while he worked, and he read aloud to her everything that he wrote. She learned enough German to assist him in translation and filing. Before her marriage, Ellen had not known how to cook, so she went to Philadelphia for a course in domestic science.[13] The Wilsons' social life was very restricted because of her two difficult pregnancies and the illnesses of the babies. Her poor health forced Wilson to give up a plan to go to Germany with his family so that he could learn enough of the language to emancipate himself from the dictionary.[14] Ellen went to her aunt in Gainesville, Georgia, for the birth of the children because she feared that Woodrow would become upset by her condition and she did not want to interrupt his work. He tried to persuade her to stay, but, according to family legend, he yielded to her argument that she did not want any child of theirs to be born north of the Mason-Dixon line. When he accepted his wife's decision, Wilson disregarded the advice of his mother, who warned him that he would not be able to bear the loneliness of the separation.[15]

Contrary to his mother's prediction, he bore the separation well. He worried a great deal about passing his Ph.D. examinations and, on the eve of taking them, developed headaches and a "mutiny on the part of my bowels."[16] However, on the whole, his health at Bryn Mawr was good. He worried much more about Ellen than himself. When she developed postpartum complications after the birth of their first daughter, Margaret, he wrote: "My little wife has taken all real pain out of my life: her wonderful loving sympathy exalts even my occasional moods of despondency into a sort of *hallowed* sadness out of which I come stronger and better. She has given to my ambitions a meaning, an assurance, and a purity which they never had before: with her by my side, ardently devoted to me and to my cause, understanding all my thoughts and all my aims, I feel that I can make the utmost of every power I possess. She has brought into my life the sunshine which was needed to keep it from growing stale and and [*sic*] morbid; that has steadily been bringing back into my spirits their

[13] *Ibid.*, pp. 275-76; Eliott, *My Aunt Louisa*, p. 114. The newly developed domestic science, or home economics, movement had grown largely out of studies of food chemistry, nutrition, and home management carried out by Ellen Swallow Richards, instructor in chemistry at the Massachusetts Institute of Technology. Samuel C. Prescott, *When M.I.T. was "Boston Tech," 1861-1916* (Cambridge, Mass., 1954), pp. 122-23.

[14] WW to Robert Bridges, November 28, 1886 and January 23, 1887, *PWW*, Vol. 5, pp. 410, 433.

[15] JWW to WW, January 4, 1886, *ibid.*, p. 98.

[16] WW to EAW, April 23, 1886, *ibid.*, p. 168.

old gladness and boyhood, their old delight in play and joyous laughter:—that sweetest sunshine of deep womanly love, unfailing, gentle patience, even, happy spirits, and spontaneous, girlish mirth, that is purest, swiftest tonic to a spirit prone to fret and apt to flag. She has given me that perfect *rest* of heart and mind, of whose existence I had never so much as dreamed."[17]

Margaret Woodrow Wilson was born on April 16, 1886. Wilson spent several weeks in the summer visiting his parents and brother in Clarkesville and his elder sister, Marion, in Little Rock. The summer of 1887 was more eventful and proved to be thoroughly miserable. Ellen went to Gainesville for the delivery of their second child, Jessie WoodrowWilson, and suffered there from the intense heat, the insects, and from back trouble, which made it impossible for her to sleep comfortably. Wilson worried about the birth and feared that nursing would be as difficult for her as it had been with the first baby. He may also have been disturbed by the knowledge that Ellen's mother had died in childbirth. Little Margaret had a series of ailments, including bloody, mucoid stools and a skin eruption. Awaiting Ellen's delivery, Woodrow spent several weeks at his sister's home in Columbia, where his mother had gone to consult Dr. George Howe about her health. In Columbia, he had a recurrence of his digestive disturbances, along with constipation and diarrhea. He was also bothered with piles and underwent a hemorrhoidectomy, which was followed by intense postoperative pain.[18] To add insult to injury, he learned that his manuscript, "The Eclipse of Individuality," which he had sent off to a publisher in April, had been rejected. A further disappointment was word from President Rhoads that Bryn Mawr had postponed until the following year the appointment of an assistant for him.[19]

In the midst of his suffering, Wilson (as in previous periods of intense stress) engaged in a literary effort. This time it was not a catalogue of the Royal Navy, a romantic biography, or a love poem, but a highly autobiographical short story, "The World and John Hart," written under the pen name of Edward Coppleston.[20] "The World and John Hart" is the story of a man's liberation from the depressing effects of a stern mother figure through his writing and the love of a vivacious

[17] WW to EAW, May 9, 1886, *ibid.*, pp. 207-08.

[18] EAW to WW, July 13-20, 22-29, 1887; WW to EAW, July 15, 1887, *ibid.*, pp. 522, 523, 525, 526, 527, 528-29, 530, 532, 535, 536, 537, 538, 539, 540, 541-42, 543, 544-45, 524-25.

[19] EAW to WW, July 20, 1887; James E. Rhoads to WW, August 25, 1887, *ibid.*, pp. 533, n.2, 563-64.

[20] "The World and John Hart: A Sketch in Outline," c. September 1, 1887, *ibid.*, pp. 567-84.

girl. In it, Wilson fictionalized his own problems in thinly disguised
fashion and took the opportunity to satirize his literary critics and
indulge in several puns. The following synopsis is a paraphrase of
Wilson's own words.

John Hart was a young lawyer, unhappy with his practice, who
yearned for a literary career. He lived a dismal existence with his elder
sister, Sarah, a stern humorless spinster, who kept the family under
the shadow of her sober and vigilant conscience. She believed that
John should follow the law, his father's profession, rather than write
stories. Sarah was not really disagreeable, but made herself that way
out of a sense of duty. Like Sarah, John had a grave, serious demeanor,
but within he was all poetry and laughter. He expressed his inner
gaiety in his stories, which, in reaction to the austere sister, were
humorous, cheery, and racy. John was manly and handsome and
blessed with an especially strong digestive system. His digestion was
so good that he could write after a hearty dinner, when he would
retreat to his study and preserve his privacy with the fumes of his pipe.
He wrote from a heart which found cheer amid hardships because of
his faith in the balanced rightness of the world, which was like his
own good stomach. It digested good and bad alike and produced
abounding health as a result.

There were no women in John's life until he met a medium-sized,[21]
lovely, blue-eyed sunbeam of a girl named Edith Albright. They married and had a son; no husband was ever happier, and Edith realized
her ideals by devoting her life to John and his career. Under her
inspiration, John wrote a story, "The Minister's Experience," that
embodied a more satisfactory expression of his ideals than he had ever
been able to frame before. However, to his great disappointment, the
story was rejected by *Piper's* [Piper = *Harper's*] *Magazine*. When he
read the story to Edith, she recognized that it had been rejected because
it was too sober and intense and lacked humor. She got his consent
to send it to the editor of the *Old Dauphinville* [*New Princeton*]
Review, who eagerly accepted it. John's writings, however, had lost
their old breezy gladness and blithe freedom. At first Edith blamed
herself, but she then discovered that the cause of the problem was the
trouble that John was having with his family.

After Sarah had been replaced by Edith, Sarah fulfilled her long held
ambition to be the matron of an orphan asylum. Ill health, however,
forced her retirement and she then led a life of invalidism and spent

---

[21] Later in the story, Edith was John's "little wife," reflecting, no doubt, not a decrease
in her stature, but a growth in his affection.

half of her time with John and Edith and the other half with her younger sister, Mary. The sisters quarreled mainly about Mary's children, whom Sarah criticized for their bad manners. At the opening of the story, one child had the measles and the other a dreadful skin eruption.[22] Mary was expecting another baby, an event which Sarah looked upon with disfavor. She likened the experience to Socrates drinking the hemlock. John had previously no more been aware of the effect of these tensions on his thinking and writing than he was of his own digestion.

After John's little manager had revealed his problem to him, she took him off to beautiful Lake George, where, over a long summer, he wrote a tale of sustained passion, swift plot, and elevated morals such as made the critics rub their eyes, doff their caps, and pour the milk of human kindness into their inkwells wherewith to write their notices of the story now called "John Marsden's Faith." After this success, Edith took her author to London for the winter and made him devote all his leisure to taking her among the poor of the great metropolis so that she might indulge her love of serving the homeless and destitute. Unfortunately for Wilson, the editor to whom he sent "The World and John Hart" did not have the milk of human kindness in his inkwell and sent back a rejection.

There is much striking autobiographical material in Wilson's story. Wilson's equating of Edith Albright with his wife, his ambitions to become a writer, his yearning for a son, and his envy of people with good digestion are obvious. The relationship between Sarah and Mary strongly resembles that between Wilson's mother and Sister Annie. Jessie Wilson and Annie Howe were a devoted mother and daughter, but they got on each other's nerves when they were together.[23] Mary's son, called George in the story, was a "rampant boy" ("obstreperous" in the original draft) who resembled Wilson's nephew, Wilson Howe, who had fought with Edward Axson at Woodrow and Ellen's wedding, and who was a behavior problem growing up.

It seems that Wilson was both aware and conscious[24] of the tensions in his own family. However, one wonders how conscious he was of the way in which he endowed Sarah Hart with so many of his mother's

[22] In Wilson's original draft, he had designated a baby as the victim of the skin eruption but crossed it out and substituted "child," as the identity of "baby" might have been too obvious.

[23] JRW, Jr. to WW, January 25, 1885; Marion Wilson Kennedy to WW, February 9, 1885, PWW, Vol. 4, pp. 185, 231.

[24] We may be aware of happenings without being conscious of them. Consciousness involves a recognition of meaning.

qualities—her sense of duty, proper behavior, stern moral code, cheer-lessness, lack of humor, and invalidism. It is unlikely that he was completely conscious since this knowledge would probably have caused him great anxiety. In none of his other writings did Wilson openly criticize his mother; yet one's otherwise unarticulated feelings can be expressed eloquently in fiction and fantasy. For Wilson to have come this close may be a tribute to the liberating influences of his marriage. It is interesting that Wilson made no mention of Dr. Howe, and the only obvious reference to his own father was the pipe-tobacco smoke for which Dr. Wilson was famous in the family. The reasons for these omissions may be that Wilson's relationship with his brother-in-law and with his father at the time were relatively tension- and worry-free. One also notes the homonyms "Hart" and "heart." The latter was Wilson's favorite word when he described his emotional state.

Much has been written about Woodrow Wilson's distaste for teach-ing women, but his first two years at Bryn Mawr were pleasant ones. By teaching "demure Friendly damsels," he wrote to Charley Talcott on March 25, 1885, he could ground himself in history. After the beginning of the fall term, he observed to Heath Dabney: "I haven't left myself time to speak of my work here. I can say, however, that I am enjoying it, improving under it, and find the girls interested and intelligent."[25] In January 1887, when he was trying to induce Dabney to come to Bryn Mawr, he wrote: "Since one must struggle with classes, he ought to be thankful for so comfortable a berth—where the classes are docile, intelligent, and willing,—where the administra-tion is honest, straightforward, and liberal."[26] In May 1887 he signed a contract for an additional two years at Bryn Mawr, and, at the end of the month, evaluated his situation in a letter to his old Johns Hop-kins friend, Albert Shaw. He was better suited to a "professorship," he thought, than to the "practical" professions of law, medicine, or journalism. Though he "chafed bitterly" at the grind and drudgery of teaching, he was conscious that he needed time to mature his thought, and he believed that a professor's chair gave him the opportunity to take a detached view of practical affairs. He told Shaw of his plans for a textbook on government and for an extended study and analysis of democracy.[27]

Wilson's teaching schedule was light—five undergraduate lectures

[25] WW to Talcott, March 25, 1885, PWW, Vol. 4, p. 414; WW to Dabney, October 28, 1885, ibid., Vol. 5, p. 38.

[26] WW to Dabney, January 25, 1887, ibid., p. 437.

[27] WW to Albert Shaw, May 29, 1887, ibid., pp. 511-12.

a week during his first two years—and allowed him time for writing and travel. He organized a Bryn Mawr House of Commons and held fortnightly discussions on current topics. His students, as did all those whom Wilson taught, found him witty and pleasant and his lectures absorbing. Lucy Maynard Salmon, a graduate fellow in 1886-1887, and later Professor of History at Vassar for many years, agreed that his lectures, with their vivid descriptions of characters and events and explicit, dictated statements of the main ideas, were inspiring. In individual sessions, Wilson was evidently relaxed and expansive. Miss Salmon recalled that he liked to talk about his ambitions and that he told her that, if the American political system was like the English, he could have entered Parliament and risen to the top. She also remembered Wilson's great interest in literary style (often, she thought, at the expense of content), and she commented on his lack of curiosity about anything that did not fit into what he was doing at the time.[28] Miss Salmon and Jane Bancroft, another graduate student, thought that Wilson was patronizing, and the feminist Miss Salmon was particularly annoyed when Wilson once said that a woman who had married an intellectual man was often better educated than a woman who had had college training.[29]

Wilson's derogatory remarks on the hardships of teaching women have been widely quoted, but the fact that Bryn Mawr was a woman's college was not the primary source of the dissatisfactions that he experienced there in his last year. The problems were multiple. They arose from Wilson's low salary and his need to provide for a growing family; the separations necessitated by his wife's second pregnancy and continued illness; the frustrations of his literary efforts; the failure of President Rhoads to carry out what Wilson felt was an unqualified promise to provide him with a teaching assistant; and, perhaps above all, Wilson's impatience and desire to go on to higher things. All of these problems could easily have occurred at an all-male or coeducational institution,[30] but, given Wilson's social background and "world view," it is not surprising that he should have attributed his

[28] Lucy Maynard Salmon to RSB, January 6 and 15, 1926, Baker Papers.

[29] *Ibid.*

[30] Wilson's discontents were hardly more exasperating than those that his friend Heath Dabney was experiencing at Indiana University. Aided by Wilson's recommendation, Dabney had obtained a post teaching English. Feeling that he had been shabbily treated by the president of the university, David Starr Jordan, Dabney called Jordan "a snake-in-the-grass & a hypocrite of the rankest kind." Dabney to WW, January 25, 1887, *PWW*, Vol. 5, p. 435. For examples of Wilson's complaints about Bryn Mawr, see WW to EAW, October 8, 1887; WW to Bridges, November 30, 1887; WW to Dabney, March 26, 1888, *ibid.*, pp. 612-13, 632-33, 715-16.

difficulties to the differences between the sexes, and that the sexual metaphor should have affirmed the validity of his feelings.

Wilson became outspoken in his disparagement of women students on his return to Bryn Mawr following the disastrous summer of 1887. He left his wife and the two babies in Gainesville, and arrived at the college after a twenty-six-hour railroad journey. During three days of pouring rain, he searched fruitlessly for quarters where he could stay until the house he had rented was available.[31]

His household now included the two infants, Ellen's younger brother, Edward, and a cousin, Mary Eloise Hoyt, who lived with the Wilsons while attending Bryn Mawr. The situation was particularly difficult because Wilson was in straitened financial circumstances and had been forced to borrow money from his father.[32] He was also annoyed because President Rhoads was not interested in finding a way for him to buy coal at college prices.[33] Wilson's mind was not on academic matters, but he immediately faced the reading of entrance examinations (always a slow process for him), and the initial interview with his graduate student. Of this meeting he wrote to Ellen: "I have just come from a long and exhausting interview with Miss Benneson, the new Fellow in History. I dread these first interviews, and am very glad that this one is over with. Miss B. turns out to be a pleasant small person of a mind which it will be very hard, but I trust not impossible, to impress—a mind which has been pressed so often by other things at every point at which you press it that it yields in a *habitual*, acquired way rather than in the way you wish. She seems to herself, evidently, to have heard something of that sort before at the very opening of your remark and so takes it to be what she has heard before to the end, or is only a little confused by something in its course which does not quite exactly tally with what she expected. She seems to talk largely out of her memory; her travels overshadow her reasoning powers; her knowledge of the world makes her ignorant of conclusions which interpret the world. . . . But she is amiable—'not wilful,' she says— has some wholesome awe (quite diverting of course to me) of what is expected of her at Bryn Mawr, and can, I confidently expect, be dominated. . . . Dominating Miss Bancroft cost me sore, as you know. Miss Salmon needed only constant encouragement—but that amounted to carrying her on my shoulders. I'm *tired* carrying female Fellows on my shoulders! But you are coming to me, sweetheart,—that's the balm of hope that cures all my ills. What can I not stand or be or accomplish

---

[31] WW to EAW, September 30, 1887, *ibid.*, p. 594.

[32] JRW to WW, September 22, 1887, *ibid.*, pp. 592-93.

[33] WW to EAW, October 8, 1887, *ibid.*, p. 612.

with my Eileen by my side! When I think of you, my little wife, I love this 'College for Women,' because *you* are a woman: but when I think only of myself, I hate the place very cordially."[34]

Wilson was indeed tired physically, as well as figuratively. But he could not in fairness blame his fatigue on Cora Benneson, who had come to Bryn Mawr with an impressive academic record, including a law degree from the University of Michigan. Later, in a contrite mood, Wilson commented that he thoroughly liked "Miss Bennison [*sic*]."[35] If he had had indeed to carry Lucy Salmon on his shoulders, then her performance must have deteriorated under Wilson's tutelage, because two years earlier at the Johns Hopkins Seminary he had reviewed and praised her paper, "The History of the Appointing Power of the President."[36] He was not more charitable toward his undergraduate students, for, two weeks later, he noted that "lecturing to young women of the present generation on the history and principles of politics" was "about as appropriate" as "lecturing to stone-masons on the evolution of fashion and dress." He had by then evidently recovered some of his equanimity because he added, "perhaps it is some of it due to undergraduateism, not all to femininity."[37] A month later he expressed his dissatisfaction in a letter to Bobby Bridges about the six or eight additional lectures he had been assigned and the faint prospect of obtaining an assistant, as well as his fears that he would break down in health if he remained at Bryn Mawr.[38] The "damsels" who two years previously had been "demure" and "interested and intelligent" were now so docile and unchallenging that they relaxed Wilson's "mental muscle."[39] As he had done after his unfortunate appearance before the Princeton alumni, he inquired about a governmental position—this time as an Assistant Secretary of State—again with no success.[40]

By the end of the year, Wilson wanted to leave Bryn Mawr,[41] and he so notified President Rhoads in June. Bryn Mawr had hired an assistant by this time, but Wilson no longer believed that he was bound by his contract. Dr. Rhoads refused to release him, but, after each side had sought legal advice, Wilson's resignation was accepted. In June

[34] WW to EAW, October 4, 1887, *ibid.*, p. 605.

[35] *Ibid.*, n.1; WW to Lucy Maynard Salmon, November 23, 1887, *ibid.*, p. 631.

[36] Minutes of the Seminary of Historical and Political Science, March 6, 1885, *ibid.*, Vol. 4, pp. 336-37.

[37] Wilson's confidential journal, October 20, 1887, *ibid.*, Vol. 5, p. 619.

[38] WW to Bridges, November 30, 1887, *ibid.*, p. 632.   [39] *Ibid.*, p. 633.

[40] WW to James Burrill Angell, November 7, 1887; Angell to WW, November 12, 1887, *ibid.*, pp. 625-27, 628-29.

[41] WW to Bridges, November 30, 1887, *ibid.*, pp. 632-33.

1888 Wilson accepted the Hedding Professorship of History and Political Economy at Wesleyan University in Middletown, Connecticut.[42]

Wilson's mother died suddenly on April 15, 1888. What fatal disease supervened to cause her death cannot be determined from the scanty information available. Dr. Wilson had written to Woodrow that she was "quite feeble"[43] and she, herself, had told Woodrow that she was "far from well."[44] This was unusual for her, since she did not want him to worry about her. Her weakness may have contributed to a fall downstairs in which she suffered a severe blow to her head.[45] She was unwilling to see a doctor other than George Howe, and her condition went undiagnosed. Three days before her death, she had what appeared to be one of her "too common attacks." Dr. Wilson was away, and, when Mrs. Wilson did not improve, Joseph, Jr., called a local physician, who found her in no immediate danger. That afternoon, Josie went to summon his sister Annie and, in his absence, Mrs. Wilson died, attended only by her servant. When Woodrow arrived, he was told that she had probably died of congestion of the liver.[46] This is an unspecific diagnosis and does not explain the course of events.

In an oft-quoted letter to Ellen, Wilson expressed his sense of desolation. "As the first shock and acute pain of the great, the irreparable blow passes off my heart is filling up with tenderest memories of my sweet mother, memories that seem to hallow my whole life—which seem to explain to me how it came about that I was given the sweetest, most satisfying of wives for my daily companion. My mother, with her sweet womanliness, her purity, her intelligence, her strength, prepared me for my wife. I remember how I clung to her (a laughed-at 'mamma's boy') till I was a great big fellow: but love of the best womanhood came to me and entered my heart through those apron-strings."[47] To Heath Dabney he expressed the feeling that his mother's death had left him with an "oppressive sense of having" lost his youth.[48] Wilson grieved for his mother, but he was now free of her depressing presence.

---

[42] WW to James E. Rhoads, June 7, 1888; Rhoads to WW, June 27, 1888; WW to the President and Trustees of Bryn Mawr College, June 29, 1888; Minutes of the Executive Committee of the Bryn Mawr Board of Trustees, June 27, 1888; Edson Wyllys Burr to WW, June 30, 1888, *ibid.*, pp. 736, 741, 743-46, 739-40, 748.

[43] JRW to WW, June 11, 1887, *ibid.*, p. 516.

[44] JWW to WW, Oct. 17, 1886, *ibid.*, p. 352. JWW to WW, May 3, 1887, *ibid.*, p. 501.

[45] JRW, Jr., to WW, Nov. 21, 1886, *ibid.*, p. 393.

[46] WW to EAW, April 18, 1888, *ibid.*, pp. 718-19.

[47] WW to EAW, April 19, 1888, *ibid.*, p. 719.

[48] WW to R. H. Dabney, May 16, 1888, *ibid.*, p. 726.

CHAPTER VI

From Wesleyan to Princeton

WOODROW WILSON'S STAY at Wesleyan and the period of the early 1890s after his return to Princeton were the happiest years of his life. He suppressed his ambitions for a political career, accepted the role of a political scientist, and became an outstanding teacher, lecturer, and writer. He completed his most important work in political science, *The State*, in 1889 and began his first important historical study, *Division and Reunion*. He continued his annual lectures at Johns Hopkins and, in 1890, realized his dream of a professorship at Princeton. He showed a greater maturity in his relationships with his family and colleagues, and the satisfactions of his professional and personal lives were reflected in excellent health.

Contrary to Wilson's stereotyped ideas about cold New Englanders, he and his wife received a warm welcome in Middletown. They found a comfortable Greek-revival house adjacent to the campus, where Ellen's two brothers lived with them. Edward, eleven, accompanied them from Bryn Mawr, while Stockton transferred from the University of Georgia in 1889 to take his senior year at Wesleyan. Stockton had intended to leave school (because of financial difficulties) and to enter business; but Wilson, who well knew his brother-in-law's devotion to English literature, invited him to Middletown so that he could study under Professor Caleb T. Winchester. Although Wesleyan was a small institution of 215 students, fifteen of them girls, its faculty was of high caliber. Years later, Wilson remarked that there was less dead wood among the professors at Wesleyan than at any place he had ever been. He particularly admired Winchester, whom he rated, along with Professor Minor, as one of the best teachers he had known. Wilson developed warm friendships with Winchester and with the Rev. Dr. Azel W. Hazen, the minister of the Congregational Church that the Wilsons attended. Another good friend was J. Franklin Jameson, now a professor of history at Brown. Jameson, a bachelor, spent several weekends with the Wilsons at Wesleyan and later at Princeton. He had an excellent sense of humor and would tease Woodrow and Ellen about living in the lands of the Yankee.[1] Wilson also enjoyed cordial rela-

---

[1] WW to EAW, March 8, 1889, enclosed in WW to EAW, March 9, 1889, *PWW*, Vol. 6, p. 141.

tionships with Frederick Jackson Turner (later the great historian of the American frontier), then a student of Wilson's at the Hopkins, and with Albert Bushnell Hart of Harvard, editor of "Epochs of American History," the series in which *Division and Reunion* appeared.

At the Hopkins, Wilson had been very sensitive to criticism of his work. At Wesleyan, he was secure enough to be receptive. Jameson was candid with him about deficiencies in *The State*,[2] and, when the book received a negative review in *The Nation*, Wilson was able to joke about it. He felt that the reviewer had been unfair, but he was mainly worried that his chances for an appointment at Princeton would be affected.[3] When Munroe Smith, editor of the *Political Science Quarterly*, severely criticized *The State* in manuscript, Wilson remarked that he regarded criticism "as a means of grace." At Princeton, later, he received a great deal of editorial criticism from Hart. Wilson accepted Hart's comments on content and emphasis but firmly rejected those that involved his literary style.[4]

Wilson's teaching load at Wesleyan was light, and he prepared his lectures meticulously. He talked with a controlled intensity and seemed to put his whole energy into maintaining rapport with his class. According to Stockton Axson, he was so emotionally spent after each lecture that he would go home and lie down for a half hour. Wilson's wit and anecdotes made him highly popular. The college yearbook, *Olla Podrida*, characterized him as

Prof W-l-n:
A merrier man
Within the limits of becoming mirth
I never spent an hour's talk withal

When he returned to Wesleyan for a talk in 1891, the students gave him the college cheer as he stepped on the platform.[5] Disorders and pranks were as common at Wesleyan in the 1880s as they had been at Princeton in the 1870s. Some members of the Class of 1892 celebrated Washington's birthday in 1889 by exploding bombs which seriously injured a student.[6] According to alumni whom Henry W. Bragdon interviewed many years later, Wilson kept order in the class-

[2] J. Franklin Jameson to WW, March 9, 1890, *ibid.*, p. 547.

[3] WW to Jameson, January 6, 1890; WW to Bridges, January 6, 1890, *ibid.*, pp. 472-73.

[4] WW to Munroe Smith, November 12, 1888, *ibid.*, p. 22; WW to Albert Bushnell Hart, November 15, 1892, *ibid.*, Vol. 8, p. 44.

[5] Axson Memoir; *Olla Podrida* '91 (Middletown, Conn., 1890), p. 136.

[6] *Wesleyan Argus*, XXII (March 1, 1889), 109, printed in *PWW*, Vol. 6, pp. 118-20.

room by a tap of his pencil and a sharp look.[7] In the hope of providing an area of competition which would transcend the narrow partisan spirit bred by the fraternities, Wilson established a Wesleyan House of Commons. There was initial interest, but the students made a farce of the proceedings and they were discontinued.[8] A major reason for the failure was that, with the growth of intercollegiate athletics, the popularity of debating and oratory among undergraduates declined.

Wilson took an active part in Wesleyan athletics. He arrived in Middletown with a considerable football reputation indicated by the following news item in the *Wesleyan Argus*: "Professor Wilson, who graduated from Princeton in '79, was for some years editor in chief of the *Princetonian* and referee and one of the directors of the Princeton Foot-ball team at the time of its greatest success, and when the championship of the game resided with Princeton College. At one time he was hindered from playing in the victorious team only by a prolonged sickness. He is an admirer of the game and will be an enthusiastic supporter of the Wesleyan team."[9] It is likely that, in view of Wilson's passionate identification with Princeton teams and his tendency to give fictitious illnesses as an excuse for inadequacies, he may have misinformed the writer. According to Bragdon, who interviewed a number of people associated with Wesleyan football during Wilson's time there, the often-repeated story of Wilson rushing on to a muddy field in raincoat and rubber boots to drive the team to a come-from-behind tie with Lehigh may be apocryphal. In any case, it indicates Wilson's intense interest: he did plan strategy, attend practices, and sometimes accompanied the squad to out-of-town games. He and a graduate student at Wesleyan, Seward V. Coffin, coined a slogan: "The College First the Fraternity afterward." At the close of the season of 1889, the Wesleyan undergraduates formed a victory parade during which they serenaded Wilson at his home.[10]

At Wesleyan, Wilson made none of the derogatory comments about the work of women students that he made at Bryn Mawr. When the only girl in his political science class wrote the prize-winning examination on *The State*, Wilson praised her highly. He said that not only was he certain that she deserved her rank but also that he was glad

[7] Bragdon, *Wilson*, p. 167.

[8] Constitution of the Wesleyan House of Commons, c. January 5, 1889; *Wesleyan Argus*, XXIII (October 9, 1889), 2; WW to Jameson, March 20, 1890, *PWW*, Vol. 6, pp. 39-44, 401-402, 556 ns. 3, 4.

[9] *Wesleyan Argus*, XXII (October 12, 1888), 17, printed in *ibid.*, pp. 14-15.

[10] Bragdon, *Wilson*, pp. 172-73; Carl F. Price, "Woodrow Wilson at Wesleyan," *Wesleyan University Alumnus*, VIII (March 1924), 3-7.

that she had won the award.[11] Because he felt that he might be prejudiced by knowing the participants, Wilson asked Jameson to be the judge of the contest. This led to an amusing correspondence. In casting his vote, Jameson addressed Wilson as "Herr Geheimoberregierungsrath,"[12] a comment on the severity of the examination and possibly a joking tribute to the huge German bibliography that Wilson had laboriously compiled for *The State*.[13]

Wilson enjoyed very good health at Wesleyan. His only illness was an attack of grippe in Baltimore in February 1890. The acute attack was followed (as is usual in such cases) by a period of fatigue, but Wilson did not interrupt his teaching schedule. Characteristically, he referred to the disease in humorous fashion: "Have you had 'la grippe'? The worse thing about the vile thing, it seems to me, is its name: it sounds for all the world like the name of some venereal disease: it is short and significant of hidden things like 'clap.' "[14] Wilson had no digestive disturbances and boasted that marriage had cured them. He told Turner in Baltimore: "I used to have dyspepsia when I boarded—but now that I have a home and have what I prefer to eat and can talk with those I like at my table I am *happy* and have an excellent *digestion*."[15] In Middletown, he was relaxed enough to go bicycling and play tennis, usually with Stockton Axson and Winchester.[16]

Ellen Wilson, on the other hand, had a miserable time on account of her health. After she became pregnant again in January 1889 (shortly before Wilson's departure for Baltimore) she had an episode of vaginal bleeding and developed nausea, dizziness, headaches, and severe constipation. The constipation cleared up, but the other symptoms persisted until the latter part of the pregnancy. Medical advice to stay off her feet was as futile as it would be if given today to a conscientious mother of two small children. To add to her troubles, little Margaret and Eddie Axson fell ill, and the maid left when she, too, became sick. Ellen became very depressed and fearful that she, like her father, would have a nervous breakdown which would leave her mentally incapacitated.[17] She was self-deprecatory: she reproached

---

[11] WW to Jameson, June 27, 1890, *PWW*, Vol. 6, p. 679.

[12] "Mr. Secret Senior Government Official."

[13] Jameson to WW, June 15, 1890, *PWW*, Vol. 6, p. 643.

[14] WW to Bridges, January 6, 1890, *ibid.*, p. 474.

[15] Frederick Jackson Turner to Caroline Mae Sherwood, c. March 6, 1889, *ibid.*, p. 133.

[16] Axson Memoir.

[17] EAW to WW, February 15 and 19, 1889, *PWW*, Vol. 6, pp. 97, 107.

herself for her lack of self-control and thought her marriage a failure because she was tormenting rather than helping her husband.[18] Wilson was alarmed and returned home for several days at the end of February. Ellen got over her depression, but the physical symptoms remained for a time. Consultation with a New York specialist revealed albumin in the urine so she may have had an upper urinary tract infection or a toxemia of pregnancy with kidney damage. Either could have led to the chronic nephritis from which she died in 1914.[19] By summer, however, she was well enough for Woodrow to invite his father, sisters, and brother to visit Middletown. Ellen was being cared for by a woman physician, Dr. Florence Taft, and Wilson asked the advice of his brother-in-law, George Howe, about switching to a male doctor. Dr. Howe, in line with the standard medical opinion of the time, replied that women could be as efficient as men, but that the "nervousness" from which most women suffered during their menstrual periods made them unfit for emergencies.[20] The Wilsons decided to retain Dr. Taft. Either no emergency arose or Dr. Taft was not menstruating, since on October 22 the delivery of Eleanor Randolph Wilson was performed to the great appreciation and gratitude of her parents.[21]

Ellen wept when Dr. Taft told her that she had had another girl.[22] During her pregnancy she had fantasized about the arrival of the baby. The doctor announced that it was "a fine boy" and she told Woodrow the glad news.[23] Wilson had assured her that a girl would be as welcome as a son, but even he referred to "him" in writing of the baby.[24] Emotional factors, in addition to organic ones, may have contributed to the stormy early course of Ellen's pregnancy. She may not have wanted another child at the time because Margaret and Jessie were so young. She had had two previous difficult pregnancies and post-partum periods, and there was always the memory that her mother had died in childbirth. Whatever the situation, the events reveal Ellen's character: her shame over giving in to illness, her tendency to blame

210078

[18] EAW to WW, February 17, 1889, *ibid.*, p. 102.

[19] WW to EAW, February 19, 1889; Turner to Sherwood, February 22, 1889, *ibid.*, pp. 106, 109. See WW to EAW, September 2, 1889, *ibid.*, p. 387.

[20] JRW to WW, June 17, 1889; Marion Wilson Kennedy to WW, June 18, 1889; JRW, Jr. to WW, July 7, 1889; George Howe, Jr. to WW, August 23, 1889, *ibid.*, pp. 323, 324, 329, 371.

[21] M. Florence Taft to WW, January 4, 1890, *ibid.*, p. 471.

[22] McAdoo, *The Priceless Gift*, p. 171.

[23] EAW to WW, February 19, 1889, *PWW*, Vol. 6, p. 106.

[24] WW to EAW, March 1, 1889, *ibid.*, p. 122.

herself, and the feeling that she must be the perfect wife. She had the additional misfortune, at the end of the year, to suffer a painful scalding of her foot. It took several months to heal.[25]

Wilson's letters from the Johns Hopkins in 1889 and 1890 show a change from those he had written in the past. Much of the content of those in 1889 dealt with Ellen's illness, about which he was wholly supportive and sympathetic. Despite her suffering, or because of it, he expressed none of the irrational fears and morbid preoccupations in which he had previously indulged.[26] He talked about his everyday activities and other people rather than concentrating on his ambitions and self-doubts. He was lonely for Ellen, and days without a letter from her were dreary, he said; but he admitted that life could be pleasant at times when he was not writing to her or reading her letters. Nor did he complain that her letters were not sufficiently frequent, long, or passionate. His letters had also lost much of their portentous seriousness, and he spared Ellen the ritual recitation of the state of his health. He seemed to have outgrown his jealousies, or at least he ceased writing about them, and made no bitter comments about his colleagues. He even had a kind word for Bryn Mawr, warning Turner, who was considering a position there, that it was "a very dangerous place for a young unmarried man."[27]

Frederick Jackson Turner's letters to his fiancée give a picture of Wilson at the Hopkins in 1889. Turner was a graduate student and boarded at Miss Mary Jane Ashton's with Wilson. After their first meetings outside the classroom, he wrote: "Dr Wilson is here. Homely, solemn, young, glum, but with that fire in his face and eye that means that its possessor is not of the common crowd. He talks but little, Miss Lovell's [a fellow boarder] chatter bores him—but I had a little time with him the other evening. Miss Ashton has some cider and she made up a little company consisting of her niece, Dr Wilson and myself, and we had a pleasant conversation on all sorts of subjects . . . and we kept it up until Miss Ashton said 'Well, gentlemen, you have drunk all the cider, eaten all the cake, and it is after eleven o'clock—I confess to being very sleepy.' "[28] Again, "Dr Wilson is back. He is a happy father. If you had seen him seated on the footboard of my bed this afternoon talking the most delightful stream of annecdote and epigram to Haskins, Broughall, and myself, while we fairly shook the room

---

[25] WW to Bridges, January 6, 1890; George Howe, Jr. to WW, April 2, 1890; WW to Jameson, May 2, 1890, *ibid.*, pp. 472-73, 611-12, 621.

[26] When real life problems occur, people may lose their irrational anxieties.

[27] Turner to Sherwood, March 30, 1889, *PWW*, Vol. 6, p. 165.

[28] Turner to Sherwood, February 13, 1889, *ibid.*, p. 88.

with laughter, you would never have recognized him as the grave author of a book that has called out the admiration of the ablest statesmen and historians of the world."[29] Turner liked Wilson and provided the atmosphere that stimulated him. On another occasion: "Dr W. was in excellent talking trim and I kept him stirred up. I like to talk with him. One is always sure that he must keep his wits about himself or be voted commonplace, and besides he knows that if he does find an idea it will be readily seized by Wilson." Turner observed that Wilson was "perfectly familiar and companionable with the graduate students."[30] As Wilson was to write ten years later, one comes to one's self through relationships with others.[31]

In a letter in 1889 to his wife, Wilson again expressed the sense of maturity that he felt after the death of his mother: "Since I have been here," he wrote, "a distinct *feeling* of maturity—or rather of maturing—has come over me[.] The *boyish* feeling that I have so long had and cherished is giving place, consciously, to another feeling—the feeling that I am no longer young (though not old quite!) and that I need no longer hesitate (as I have so long and sensitively done) to assert myself and my opinions in the presence of and against the selves and opinions of old men, 'my elders.' It may be all imagination, but these are the facts of consciousness at the present moment in one Woodrow Wilson—always a slow fellow in mental development—long a child, longer a diffident youth, now at last, perhaps, becoming a self-confident (mayhap a self-assertive) man. I find I look older, my former (Princeton) college friends here being the witnesses."[32]

This self-realization also came out in a note in Wilson's journal on his thirty-third birthday: "If slow development is an intimation and promise of long life, I may certainly expect length of days sufficient for the accomplishment of all I have planned to do. I have come slowly into possession of such powers as I have, not only, but also into consciousness of them, into the ability to estimate them with just insight. Now that I am getting well into the thirties I begin to see my place in the general order of things."[33]

Wilson's appointment to the Princeton faculty came about not only

[29] Turner to Sherwood, February 28, 1889, *ibid.,* p. 118. James Samuel Broughall and Charles Homer Haskins were then graduate students at the Hopkins. Haskins became one of the leading medievalists of his time and later taught at Wisconsin and Harvard.

[30] Turner to Sherwood, c. March 6 and February 22, 1889, *ibid.,* pp. 133, 109.

[31] "When a Man Comes to Himself," c. November 1, 1899, *Century Magazine,* LXII (June 1901), 268-73, printed in *ibid.,* Vol. 11, pp. 263-73.

[32] WW to EAW, March 9, 1889, *ibid.,* Vol. 6, p. 139.

[33] Wilson's confidential journal, December 28, 1889, *ibid.,* p. 462.

in recognition of his writings but also by his own efforts and through the help of Robert Bridges and four other members of the Class of 1879—Cyrus H. McCormick, Cornelius C. Cuyler, Cleveland H. Dodge, and Edward W. Sheldon. They were men of wealth and influence, and all became Princeton trustees. President McCosh resigned in 1888. Wilson, upon hearing that Professor William Milligan Sloane might succeed President McCosh, asked Bridges to ascertain his chances of election to Sloane's chair in history. This probe came to naught as Sloane retained his professorship when the Rev. Dr. Francis Landey Patton was selected as the new president. Another step in Wilson's campaign was the publication of an article on Adam Smith, "An Old Master," in *The New Princeton Review*. Ostensibly a biography, the paper (based on one that Wilson had written for the Johns Hopkins Seminary) was an essay on the art of academic lecturing in which Adam Smith's importance as an economist was subordinated to the excellence of his literary style. When Frederick Jackson Turner read the article, he called it Woodrow Wilson's plea for a professorial chair.[34] The death in the summer of 1889 of Alexander Johnston, Professor of History and Political Economy at Princeton, created a vacancy, and Bridges set the Wilson candidacy in motion. A meeting with President Patton was arranged, and Wilson was offered Johnston's chair; his duties would begin in the fall of 1889. Wilson temporized for several reasons. He did not want to leave Wesleyan in the lurch on short notice; he wanted to continue his affiliation with the Johns Hopkins; and he did not want to teach economics along with history. Patton had also indicated to him that there were plans afoot for a professorship of public law, to include the history and philosophy of politics, the subjects nearest Wilson's heart.[35]

While Wilson anxiously waited for a decision, opposition developed among the trustees. Wilson had supported the theory of evolution in *The State*. He was now being criticized on grounds of religious orthodoxy. He was also charged with giving too much credit to Roman law and too little to the influences of Christianity in the genesis of the modern state.[36] His southern origin and fondness for English institutions were held against him, and it was said that he was too deep and learned to hold the attention of students.[37] Upset, Wilson wondered if the charge about the depth of his learning could have grown out of his "unfortunate after-dinner prose" at the alumni dinner in

[34] Turner to WW, December 20, 1893, *ibid.*, Vol. 8, p. 417.
[35] WW to Bridges, July 23, 1889, *ibid.*, Vol. 6, p. 356.
[36] Francis Landey Patton to WW, February 18, 1890, *ibid.*, p. 527.
[37] Bridges to WW, November 5, 1889, *ibid.*, p. 411.

New York in 1886.[38] Wilson offered a compromise to Patton: he would take Johnston's chair and teach both economics and history for two years if he had the assurance that, by the end of that time, he would be transferred to a post of public law.[39] An agreement was reached. Wilson had asked for a salary of $3,500 but took $3,000, with permission to continue his lectures at the Johns Hopkins.[40] He was fortified in the negotiations by an offer from Williams College of a new chair of American History, Literature, and Eloquence—and a very attractive counterproposal from Wesleyan. In contrast to the unpleasantness of his departure from Bryn Mawr, his farewell to Wesleyan took place amid expressions of mutual esteem.[41]

The only negative comment about Wesleyan that Woodrow Wilson ever made was during the period of suspense when he was urging Bridges to impress on the Princeton trustees his desire to return to his alma mater. Although Wesleyan was "a delightful place to work," Wilson said, it was not "sufficiently *stimulating*" because of the narrowness of New England thought.[42] The remark illustrates Wilson's tendency, especially in situations of stress, to use traditionally derived concepts and classifications as metaphors possessing little literal truth. Similarly, later in Princeton, on the arrival of a shy, tense, young southern relative, he wrote to his wife: "Willie Hoyt arrived yesterday. . . . I expected a delicate chap, not a prim one, a southern, not a New England, boy."[43] As we have seen, the Wesleyan undergraduates, the great majority of whom were from New England, were far from prim. Regarding the "narrowness" of New England thought, Wesleyan did not have the religious and political tests for office that Princeton had— and Wilson deplored. In any other situation, Wilson would have been the first to defend the liberal attitudes of the members of the Wesleyan faculty, even those born in New England.

The death of Wilson's mother was followed by significant changes in his family relationships. Wilson, absorbed with his new duties at Wesleyan, became remiss in his correspondence. Marion Kennedy complained of the "fearful silence" and begged him to write.[44] Annie

[38] WW to Bridges, November 6, 1889, *ibid.*, p. 413.
[39] Wilson pocket diary, February 13, 1890, *ibid.*, p. 523.
[40] *Ibid.*, WW to Bridges, February 13 and 18, March 8, 1890; Bridges to WW, February 20, 1890; Patton to WW, March 5, 1890; WW to Azel Washburn Hazen, March 8, 1890, *ibid.*, pp. 523, 524, 528-29, 546, 529-30, 542-43, 545.
[41] Horace Elisha Scudder to WW, December 20, 1889; Azel Washburn Hazen to WW, March 4, 1890, *ibid.*, pp. 454-55, 540.
[42] WW to Bridges, January 27, 1890, *ibid.*, p. 481.
[43] WW to EAW, September 9, 1893, *ibid.*, Vol. 8, p. 363.
[44] Marion Wilson Kennedy to WW, November 6, 1888, *ibid.*, Vol. 6, p. 18.

wrote of Dr. Wilson's loneliness and told Woodrow that she felt cut off from him.[45] Joseph, Jr., wrote: "Please brother write to father as often as you possibly can. When he don't hear from you and sisters frequently, he feels hurt. He sometimes intimates that *mother* was the one we cared most for, and since she is gone, we don't care as much for him. Of course it is only when he is blue that he says this."[46]

In this setting, Woodrow Wilson wrote his famous, often quoted "incomparable father" letter:

> My precious father,
> My thoughts are full of you and dear "Dode" all the time. Tennessee seems *so* far away for a chap as hungry as I am for a sight of the two men whom I love. As the Christmas recess approaches I realize, as I have so often before, the *pain* there is in a season of holiday and rejoicing away from you. As you know, one of the chief things about which I feel most warranted in rejoicing is that I am your son. I realize the benefit of being your son more and more as my talents and experience grow: I recognize the strength growing in me as of the nature of your strength: I become more and more conscious of the hereditary wealth I possess, the capital of principle, of literary force and skill, of capacity for first-hand thought; and I feel daily more and more bent toward creating in my own children that combined respect and tender devotion for their father that you gave your children for you. Oh, how happy I should be, if I could make them think of me as I think of you! You have given me a love that grows, that is stronger in me now that I am a man than it was when I was a boy, and which will be stronger in me when I am an old man than it is now—a love, in brief, that is rooted and grounded in *reason*, and not in filial instinct merely—a love resting upon abiding foundations of *service*, recognizing you as in a certain very real sense the author of all I have to be grateful for. I bless God for my noble, strong, and saintly mother and for my incomparable father. Ask "Dode" if he does not subscribe? And tell him that I love my brother passionately.[47]

The tone of this eulogy suggests that Wilson not only was expressing his great affection for his father but also was making amends for his neglect. He was trying to bolster the old man's spirits. Yet the letter

[45] Annie Wilson Howe to WW, November 26, 1888, *ibid.*, pp. 24-25.
[46] JRW, Jr. to WW, December 16, 1888, the Wilson Papers.
[47] WW to JRW, December 16, 1888, *PWW*, Vol. 6, p. 30.

has been interpreted by some biographers as evidence that Wilson's dependence on his father extended far into adult life. Alexander and Juliette George regard it as typical of Wilson's excessive devotion and subservience to his father, as well as unconscious hatred of him.[48] Even Ray Stannard Baker makes the erroneous statement that, until he was forty years old, Woodrow Wilson never made an important decision without consulting his father.[49] There is no evidence that Dr. Wilson directly influenced his son's decision to go to Wesleyan, and there is no indication that he guided Woodrow's strategy in obtaining the Princeton appointment. Intellectually, Woodrow Wilson had long been independent; in fact, in 1884 his father had asked his son's assistance in preparing an inaugural address to the Southwestern Theological Seminary.[50] From 1888 onward, Dr. Wilson approved of Woodrow's actions after the fact, but the only advice that he offered (other than discussions about money) was an occasional comment on literary style and an admonition to Woodrow that he not work too hard.

Woodrow Wilson, following his mother's death, became the dominant member of his family and the focus of its activities. His brother and sisters sought his advice and help rather than that of Dr. Wilson, who had sold his house in Clarksville and taken up an itinerant existence. Joseph, Jr., in particular, missed his mother and the loss of his home. In the summer of 1889 he was very upset by the rumor that his father would remarry.[51] Josie turned to his brother for reassurance about his father's intentions and for advice about his personal business affairs.

As Wilson's fortunes had been rising, his father's had been declining. He had never been happy in Clarksville. In 1887 he described himself as "ding-donging theology and Greek exegesis into dull brains—and sighing over the poor prospects of the church's oncoming ministry."[52] His dizzy spells had cleared up prior to his wife's death, but, after his bereavement, he complained for a time about arthritis and neuralgia. Even before Jessie Wilson died, Dr. Wilson had expressed gloom about the future and pathetically envied his son's youth, talent, and reputation.[53] He was particularly hurt when, after being the favored candidate for the position of chancellor of the University of Georgia, he

---

[48] *Woodrow Wilson and Colonel House*, p. 10.

[49] Baker, *Wilson*, I, 30.

[50] JRW to WW, December 17, 1884, *PWW*, Vol. 3, p. 549.

[51] JRW, Jr. to WW, August 25, 1889, *ibid.*, Vol. 6, p. 372.

[52] JRW to WW, January 12, 1887, *ibid.*, Vol. 5, p. 431.

[53] JRW to WW, March 5, 1888, *ibid.*, p. 707; JRW to WW, January 10, 1889, *ibid.*, Vol. 6, pp. 47-48.

was defeated in the election by an old opponent from his days at Columbia Theological Seminary.[54]

Dr. Wilson did not visit Middletown until the summer of 1890, despite repeated invitations from his son and daughter-in-law. He was striving to maintain his independence and did not wish to become a burden. Gradually, he adjusted to his reduced status and became more of his old self. He had earlier complained that the students in the seminary were a tax on his nerves, but in the fall of 1891 he found them both more numerous and more promising.[55] He recovered some of his pristine vigor and gained a victory in a struggle in the General Assembly. He routed his opponents "horse, foot & dragoon."[56] He was still bothered by rheumatism and had an uncomfortable episode of urinary retention necessitating catheterization; however, after the acute stage, he continued his classes and rode to them in a closed carriage.[57] Dr. Wilson resigned from the Southwestern Theological Seminary in June 1892 but remained as Stated Clerk of the General Assembly until 1898. He filled in as stated supply at various churches and was very gratified by a cordial welcome at his old church in Wilmington, where he preached the seventy-fifth anniversary sermon.

Dr. Wilson formed a close friendship with a widow in New York, Elizabeth Bartlett Grannis. She restored his spirits, and he spent considerable time in her house and enjoyed her "loving ministries."[58] Mrs. Grannis was an active person[59]—editor of the New York *Church Union* and of the *Children's Friend and Kindergarten Magazine*. She lectured on the sanctity of the home and was active in the movement for the sterilization of criminals and mental defectives.[60] Woodrow and Ellen disapproved of the relationship, but it is not clear whether they did so because of the irregularity of the liaison, or because of Mrs. Grannis' particular interests. Actually, her activities were not as radical as they might sound today. They were consistent with the eugenics movement of the late nineteenth century, which held that healthy living habits, social reform, and the modification of heredity would eradicate mental and moral defects. Dr. Wilson broke his relationship with Mrs. Grannis in 1894, and he and Woodrow stayed

[54] JRW to WW, October 10, 1888, *ibid.*, p. 14.

[55] JRW to WW, September 13, 1891, *ibid.*, Vol. 7, p. 288.

[56] JRW to WW, November 7, 1891, *ibid.*, p. 323.

[57] JRW to WW, March 16, 1892, *ibid.*, p. 489.

[58] JRW to WW, September 2, 1891, *ibid.*, p. 285.

[59] She lived until 1926. Her correspondence with Dr. Wilson was of such an "intimate" nature that her executor did not consider it suitable to be shown. J. Aspinwall McCuaig to RSB, May 15, 1926, Baker Papers.

[60] JRW to WW, July 25, 1889, *ibid.*, Vol. 6, p. 358 n.1.

together in Miss Ashton's boarding house in Baltimore.[61] Afterward
he spent most of his time in Princeton, Columbia, Wilmington (where
he fell in love again, twice), and Richmond.

When Woodrow Wilson returned to Princeton in 1890 he had—to
use one of his favorite expressions—come to himself. He was in the
midst of the most productive years of his academic career and had
matured as a person. After his mother's death, he retained a tender
devotion to her memory, but his guilt about her chronic unhappiness
faded. With his father's decline, he accepted the leadership of his family
and responsibility for it. His wife's devotion made his home life idyllic.
Although he still referred to his "nervous disposition" when it suited
his purpose[62] (and he was hardly easygoing), he was in good health,
was less tense, and showed more capacity to enjoy himself. He had
been able to work with colleagues and accept criticism and compromise. At Wesleyan, he had found the world less threatening and de-
manding. According to John M. Mulder, there was a corresponding
change in his religious attitudes; he was not as stern in the struggle
to carry out his duty to God and was more accepting of God's love
and grace.[63]

[61] WW to EAW, February 4 and 7, 1894, *ibid.*, Vol. 8, pp. 453, 462.
[62] WW to Albert Bushnell Hart, May 13, 1889, *ibid.*, Vol. 6, p. 240.
[63] Mudler, *Wilson*, pp. 107-10.

CHAPTER VII

Princeton, 1890-1896

IN 1890, Princeton was a small college of six hundred students with an informal atmosphere. The bowler hats and stiff collars of Wilson's undergraduate years had given way to black turtleneck sweaters and corduroy trousers. There were a number of new buildings. Otherwise, there had been little change. Class spirit was still intense, and the hazing of freshmen and the ritual stealing of the chapel bell clapper by each class still went on. Football was played with religious fervor, and the final game with Yale was figuratively a matter of life and death.[1] Theatrical performances were still held in the secrecy of Whig Hall; it was not until 1893 that the Triangle Club, begun by Booth Tarkington, performed openly. Nor had Princeton greatly improved its academic standing. It was still not a university, in spite of McCosh's efforts. Because of its reputation as a sectarian, inbred institution, it had not attracted many trained scholars and scientists. One of Wilson's actions as president was to have Princeton declared a non-sectarian institution.

Francis Landey Patton, the new president, inaugurated in 1889, was a strong defender of theological orthodoxy. He had come into prominence when he brought charges of heresy against the Rev. Mr. David Swing, a leading representative of Presbyterian liberalism.[2] The charges were voted down in the General Assembly, but Patton's eminence as a theologian and logician led to his election as Moderator of the General Assembly of the Presbyterian Church in the United States of America (northern). Patton, who was against change, was dilatory rather than actively obstructionist at Princeton. As Wilson told his friend Turner in 1896: "We are under the reign of 'King Log' rather than 'King Stork.' "[3] Although Patton was witty and a brilliant speaker,

---

[1] After Princeton beat Yale in the championship game of 1893, a coach asked the players to sing the doxology. Standing naked in the dressing room covered with mud, blood, and perspiration, they sang it from beginning to end. See Frank B. Presbrey and James Hugh Moffatt, eds., *Athletics at Princeton* (New York, 1901), p. 361.

[2] About this celebrated affair, see William R. Hutchison, "Disapproval of Chicago: The Symbolic Trial of David Swing," *Journal of American History,* LIX (June 1972), 30-47. For a general study of the issues involved, see Lefferts A. Leotscher, *The Broadening Church* . . . (Philadelphia, 1954), pp. 12-15.

[3] WW to Frederick Jackson Turner, November 15, 1896, *PWW*, Vol. 10, p. 52.

he was a poor administrator. He hated to discipline students or to get rid of incompetent teachers. Thus discipline was lax and academic standards were low. It was reputed that Dr. Patton said that it was better to have gone to college and loafed than never to have gone at all.[4]

Princeton students greatly enjoyed Wilson's courses; and, unlike some other professors, he had no problems of discipline. He worked hard to make his lectures interesting, and his classes, though electives, were always crowded. He opened his lectures with a fifteen-minute reading of his main points, which the students were required to take down. Then he would talk less formally for the remainder of the hour; he would give illustrations and anecdotes and refer to current events. Long after other memories of college courses had faded, Princeton alumni remembered his thrilling descriptions of such events as the signing of the Covenant. Booth Tarkington wrote that the class of 1892 worshiped him. He was very accessible, and students would call informally at his home to discuss their various problems.[5] After some southern students complained of the frequent cheating on examinations and the proctoring system, Wilson, at the urging of his wife, supported their plea for an honor system.[6] Despite his high academic standards, the students, year after year, voted Wilson the most popular professor. Two of his few graduate students were less appreciative. While they found Wilson pleasant and hospitable, they felt that he was a better lecturer than a teacher and that he was not interested in scholarly historical research.[7]

Wilson served on the Discipline Committee and became chairman of the Committee on Special and Delinquent Students. Grover Cleve-

[4] What he actually said was: "I am not prepared to say that it is better to have gone and loafed than never to have gone at all, but I do believe in the *genius loci*; and I sympathize with Sir Joshua Reynolds when he says, that there is around every seminary of learning, an atmosphere of floating knowledge where every one can imbibe something peculiar to his own original conceptions." Quoted by David W. Hirst, "Francis Landey Patton," in Alexander Leitch, ed., *A Princeton Companion* (Princeton, N.J., 1978), p. 355.

[5] McAdoo, *The Woodrow Wilsons*, p. 20.

[6] The Wilsons believed that students should be on their honor as gentlemen, and Wilson had seen the honor system work quite successfully at the University of Virginia. In a dramatic debate with Wilson, President Patton expressed skepticism about a code which permitted the killing of a friend in a duel or the seduction of a woman, but not cheating at cards. Patton was also concerned about giving undergraduates the virtual power of expelling a student. Wilson resented Patton's ridicule of Southern chivalry and made an impassioned speech that carried the faculty. Bliss Perry, *And Gladly Teach* (New York, 1935), pp. 130-31.

[7] Interview with Robert McElroy, November 22, 1942, and Max Farrand, November 1, 1942, Bragdon Collection.

land recognized his labors in 1900 by giving him a copy of his privately printed *Defense of Fishermen* with the inscription: "*Woodrow Wilson, the kindliest and best beloved of those who correct the mendacity of others.*"[8] Wilson was class officer to the seniors and frequently served as the liaison between the faculty and the board of trustees. Bliss Perry, a professor of English at Princeton during the 1890s, recalls that Wilson in committee presented his ideas clearly, but not insistently, and took defeat well. He was efficient as a presiding officer, allowed free discussion, commented only at the end, and closed the meeting promptly on the hour. Perry also noted that Wilson was impatient with slower minds and lacked respect for the older faculty members, whom he treated with scant courtesy in debate at faculty meetings.[9] Wilson was not inclined to defer to ministers by reason of their cloth, because he had witnessed both his father's experience in the controversy at Columbia Theological Seminary and James Woodrow's trial for heresy in the General Assembly. Perry was impressed by Wilson's high spirits, energy, and self-confidence. It was obvious that he had a temper, but he kept it under control. Perry also commented on Wilson's nationalistic, militaristic fervor. Perry had left Princeton by the time of the controversies over the quadrangle plan and graduate college battles from 1907 to 1910, so his recollections of Wilson, unlike those of participants in these struggles, are relatively uncolored by later events.

Wilson was also active on athletic committees and was as involved in the fortunes of Princeton teams as he had been as an undergraduate. When Princeton lost to Harvard in baseball, he was "the most profoundly 'blue' man on the continent."[10] When Ellen Wilson expressed to a friend her pleasure over Cleveland's election in 1892, she commented that Woodrow would have had "some sort of collapse" if both the Democrats and the football team had lost.[11] Overemphasis on football was a problem, and Princeton and Harvard had broken off athletic relations in 1889 in a squabble over certificates of amateurism. Wilson debated with Professor Burt G. Wilder of Cornell the question, "Foot Ball: Ought The Game To Be Encouraged?" Wilson took the affirmative position: he expressed the belief that the game made students more "manly" and developed their moral qualities. He favored playing big games in large cities because of the gate receipts. Wilder, a physiologist and neurologist, and a former football player himself, was considerably less impressed with the character-building features

[8] Perry, *And Gladly Teach*, p. 146.   [9] *Ibid.*, pp. 155-56.
[10] WW to EAW, May 8, 1892, *PWW*, Vol. 7, p. 624.
[11] EAW to Anna Harris, November 22, 1892, *ibid.*, Vol. 8, pp. 47-48.

of the game. He wanted the schools to make certain that players were bona fide students, deplored the betting and extravagance, and suggested that these undesirable features could be avoided by limiting football to intramural contests.[12] After Wilson became president of Princeton, he worked out, in 1906, agreement with the heads of Harvard and Yale to eliminate the abuses.

Wilson demonstrated the competitive aspect of his personality as a coach of the Princeton debating team. Here he enjoyed matching minds with men like Professors Arthur T. Hadley of Yale and George P. Baker of Harvard. Winthrop More Daniels, another debating coach, told Ray Stannard Baker: "I have seen him pacing back and forth through the ambulatory of the Commencement hall when a debate was in progress, unable to keep away, and still less able to sustain the verbal affront which the crudeness and immaturity of his protégés were almost certain to inflict."[13]

Social life for the Wilsons in Princeton was as delightful as it had been at Wesleyan. They made many friends and enjoyed company, small dinners, and evenings of conversation. Wilson was sometimes reluctant to meet new people, but, after his wife coaxed him, he would go and enjoy himself. No one in Princeton in the early nineties thought of Wilson as cold, arrogant, autocratic or selfish—adjectives applied to him at a later time. When there was family illness, the community showed a warm and cooperative spirit. When his wife was away, Wilson received many dinner invitations; on one occasion he was asked by Dean Andrew F. West to be his house guest. According to Bliss Perry, Wilson was easily the most popular member of the faculty. When he stopped at the Nassau Club for a chat or a game of billiards, the members would flock about him. He rode a bicycle both for utility and recreation and also played tennis.[14] Except for an occasional digestive upset, Wilson's health was excellent until 1895. In describing the benefits of marriage to his friend Albert Shaw, he included its salutary effects on the digestion.[15]

An intimate picture of the Wilsons' family life comes from their correspondence, the memoirs of their youngest daughter, Nellie, and the recollections of Margaret Randolph Axson, Ellen's young sister, who lived with them. The house was often filled with relatives; in 1896 it held an average of ten family members, including the two servants. The Wilsons especially enjoyed the young relatives who

[12] Philadelphia *Public Ledger*, February 14, 1894, printed in *ibid.*, pp. 482-84.
[13] Winthrop More Daniels to RSB, quoted in Baker, *Wilson*, II, 14.
[14] Axson Memoir.
[15] WW to Albert Shaw, July 18, 1893, *PWW*, Vol. 8, p. 281.

stayed with them while they attended school. Wilson was particularly fond of Ellen's younger brother, Edward, who in many respects was the son that he never had. Although he was not mechanically curious himself, Wilson liked to talk with Eddie about the boy's inventions and gadgets. The only regular house chore that Margaret Axson recalled that her brother-in-law performed was the Saturday-night winding of the grandfather clock. She thought that Wilson did this because he enjoyed the opportunity of relating the story of the Irishman who, when told that a clock would run for eight days without winding, asked how long it would run with winding.[16] Actually, Wilson did some of the household chores; he stoked the furnace when Eddie was away and liked working in the garden under his wife's direction.[17]

There were daily prayers and readings from the Bible, yet the family atmosphere was gay. Wilson especially charmed his children. He amused them by playing games, telling stories, and doing imitations. He would be the drunken man, the stuffy monocled Englishman, and, in a lady's hat and feathered boa, would gush in the high falsetto of a grande dame.[18] When his daughters were young, he sang them to sleep with lullabies, and when they were ill in bed, he entertained them. For Nellie, he built replicas of buildings at Oxford out of bits of colored tile. When Margaret Axson had chills and a fever, he told her a story of a man with the same condition who drank a glass of milk and shivered so that the milk turned to butter.[19] Wilson did not work in the evenings during his early years at Princeton; and, when the girls were old enough to stay up, he and Mrs. Wilson would read aloud to them. When the girls had their own social lives, he would ask the Ouija board the name of the latest beau of one of them and have it spell out the name of some campus character.

Like their father as a child, the Wilson girls engaged in much imaginary play. They acted out scenes from Shakespeare and incidents from Greek and Roman history.[20] One day they marched about the house for a half hour, chanting the oath of the ancient Persians, "to ride to shoot and to speak the truth."[21] Jessie, the middle child, had an imaginary companion. Jessie said that she herself was Homer, "the other man of the same name," who lived when Homer did and who made up poems together with him.[22]

[16] Elliott, *My Aunt Louisa*, p. 119.   [17] Axson Memoir.
[18] Arthur Walworth, *Woodrow Wilson*, 2nd edn. (Cambridge, Mass., 1965), p. 77.
[19] Elliott, *My Aunt Louisa*, p. 102.
[20] Walworth, *Wilson*, p. 77.
[21] EAW to WW, February 15, 1894, *PWW*, Vol. 8, p. 489.
[22] EAW to WW, February 16, 1895, *ibid.*, Vol. 9, p. 202.

The primary school in Princeton was very poor, and Ellen taught the children at home. Wilson considered the learning of German important, and he engaged a governess, Clara Böhm,[23] in 1897. The children were extraordinarily well-behaved; at mealtimes they were quiet while their parents talked. Like his own father, Wilson was strict mainly about lying, punctuality,[24] and proper diction. He could turn chores into a game as when, at the end of a meal, in a sing-song way, he would chant: "Now chickens, run upstairs wash your face and hands brush your teeth and put your bibs away before I count three— or I'll tickle, pinch and spankdoodle you."[25] When necessary, discipline was enforced with only a glance. Madge Axson never remembered the Wilsons' raising their voices to the children or, for that matter, to each other.[26]

Ellen Wilson (like Edith Hart in Wilson's short story) was the complete helpmate. She managed the household, estimated the budget, and, despite strict economy, set a bountiful table. She made her own clothes and did over the children's things long after the family was financially comfortable and good ready-made clothing was available in the stores. As Wilson's mother had said of him, Woodrow was not good at bargaining, and Ellen attended to most of the family business transactions. She persuaded the owner of the house that they had rented to let her decorate it at his expense, and she sublet the stable in the backyard to students. Before he gave a lecture, Wilson would read it or go over his outline with her. On his return from a lecture trip, he would immediately, unless it was mealtime, sit down and tell her about it. Wilson invariably consulted his wife before making any important decision, and generally took her advice. When he exaggerated or made some rash statement, she would exclaim, "Oh Woodrow," to which he would regularly reply, "Madam, I was venturing to think that I meant that until I was corrected."[27] Although Ellen rarely articulated open opposition and never expressed resentment,

---

[23] Although the children prattled in German, Wilson never spoke it with them. He would occasionally use brief German phrases, usually in jest. He was especially fond of quoting Mark Twain's comments on "that absurd language." See Stockton Axson to RSB, July 6, 1929, Baker Papers. Ellen tried to learn to speak the language and attended German classes. EAW to WW, February 4, 1898, *PWW*, Vol. 10, p. 375. Wilson never did learn the proper place of the umlaut in "Fräulein." He persisted in placing it over the "u."

[24] Both Woodrow and Dr. Wilson were extremely punctual. Dr. Wilson invariably arrived ahead of time. See Axson Memoir.

[25] McAdoo, *The Woodrow Wilsons*, p. 21.

[26] R. S. Baker, interview with Stockton Axson, March 17, 1925, Baker Papers.

[27] McAdoo, *The Woodrow Wilsons*, p. 22.

she could hold her ground. Then she would stand with her arms folded, a gesture that disturbed Wilson. "Don't do that, Nell; it pushes out your upper arm," he would say, only to have her resume the position.[28]

Wilson was a man of remarkably orderly habits; he felt that a clean desk was a sign of an orderly mind. No letters or papers lay about unsorted or in temporary confusion. Books which had been used were promptly replaced in their assigned locations on the shelves. He never seemed to be hurried or worried about his work and seemed always to be in perfect control. He told Bliss Perry that, when he could not think of a word, he would not light up his pipe and walk around, but would sit with his fingers on the typewriter keys and *make* the word come to him.[29] Stockton Axson described Wilson's routine when he finished his morning's writing. He would fold away his manuscript, open the drawer, take out his wiper and wipe his pen, close the drawer, place the cap on the inkstand, arrange his pencils in a straight line, go to the bathroom to wash his hands and brush his hair, and appear on the threshold of the dining room precisely at one.[30]

Wilson's all-encompassing interest after his return to Princeton was the establishment of a law school. He had come with the understanding that a school of law was one of President Patton's first orders of business with the board of trustees. Wilson had worked out a plan for a school of public affairs to be affiliated with The Johns Hopkins University, and he set up his undergraduate courses with the specific objective of developing a core program to prepare undergraduates for the new Princeton school of law.[31] The school was meant not only to prepare graduates for the practice of the law but also to be part of the general education of undergraduates and training for citizenship. Wilson had never lost interest in the application of the law to politics and government, but he also had an emotional commitment. He saw the law as the codification of the habits of a society and as the expression of a national spirit. Law assures liberty because it insures order, Wilson stated, and he likened the suspensions of laws to a disease.[32]

As usual, Dr. Patton was dilatory and ineffective. He asked Wilson to go ahead with his plans and to join him in eliciting interest among the alumni. Wilson campaigned vigorously and made many speeches to alumni groups in 1891, 1892, and 1893, while Patton did nothing. Not only did Patton not obtain an endowment, but also he never even

[28] *Ibid.*, p. 52.   [29] Perry, *And Gladly Teach*, p. 157.
[30] R. S. Baker, Axson interview, March 17, 1925.
[31] Editorial Note, "Wilson's Plans for a School of Law at Princeton," *PWW*, Vol. 7, pp. 63-68.
[32] *Ibid.*; notes for a lecture, July 2, 1894, *ibid.*, Vol. 8, p. 605.

proposed the project of a law school to the board of trustees.[33] Dr. Patton was probably afraid that new economic theories might be heretical. He disapproved of Wilson's proposal to have his new colleague, Winthrop More Daniels, give a course on socialism, which Wilson had covered (Patton probably did not know the fact) in his course in advanced economic theory. Disappointment over the lack of progress toward establishment of a law school was probably the major factor in precipitating the emotional crisis that Wilson experienced in the winter and spring of 1892.

While at the Johns Hopkins with his family in 1892, Wilson expressed doubts about his future at Princeton. Along with his unhappiness over the law school, he complained to his wife that his many duties, including the performance of some of Dr. Patton's speaking chores, did not allow him time for writing. He was annoyed that Professor Sloane was teaching courses that he wanted to give.[34] Wilson also complained that his salary of $3,000 was insufficient to support his present family and the son that he and his wife so desired and expected.[35] After the completion of his lectures, Ellen and the children went south to visit relatives while he went back to Princeton.

Soon after his return, Wilson became depressed and anxious and had a recurrence of his gastrointestinal symptoms. These included a pain in the region of his appendix for which he consulted a local physician and was told that he had a "partial obstruction of the *bile duct*."[36] Wilson was skeptical of the diagnosis since his pain was not near his liver, but he accepted the prescribed medication and felt better temporarily.[37] Wilson rarely consulted doctors formally but rather relied on the advice of his medical friends and his brother-in-law, George Howe. Thus his visit to Princeton's Dr. James H. Wikoff suggests that he was very worried. While Wilson's gastrointestinal symptoms improved, he developed another, probably psychosomatic, manifestation—a "raging headache," which he attributed to some California claret that Dean West had "made" him drink.[38] Along with these indicators of stress, he became extremely lonely and restless. Another week of separation, he wrote to his wife, would be like killing him.[39] His letters to her were gloomy and unhappily introspective. He told

[33] Editorial Note, "Wilson's Plans for a School of Law," *ibid.*, Vol. 7, p. 67.
[34] WW to EAW, May 6, 1892, *ibid.*, p. 621.
[35] WW to EAW, March 17, 1892, *ibid.*, p. 492.
[36] A diagnosis on a par with "sluggish liver."
[37] WW to EAW, March 21, 1892, *PWW*, Vol. 7, pp. 502-503.
[38] WW to EAW, March 25, 1892, *ibid.*, p. 519.
[39] WW to EAW, March 28, 1892, *ibid.*, p. 527.

her that he felt guilty that his selfish self-indulgence in his miseries was spoiling her trip. In his depression, he became self-deprecatory and described "that skeptical feeling that always haunts me about the possibility of *my* giving one any unhapppiness."[40]

Wilson also felt guilty about his state of sexual turmoil. He was tormented, he wrote, by the force of his sexual passions and feared for his self-control.[41] On a day that he lectured in New York (he was then giving a course of lectures at the New York Law School), he took the precaution to return to Princeton for the night to avoid temptation. One evening at home he translated, from the French, a highly erotic boudoir scene from Théophile Gautier's *Mademoiselle de Maupin*.[42] He also developed what seem to be overimaginative sexual fears. His wife had written that Margaret Axson, then age eleven, might be going to live with relatives in Athens, Georgia. Wilson became alarmed that she would be in a college town where "the restraints upon the intercourse of the two sexes are at a minimum." "It must be the riotous elements in my own blood," he admitted, "that make me fear so keenly what even the most honorable young fellows might be tempted by mere beauty to do."[43]

It is impossible to separate causes from effects in the sequence of Wilson's emotional disturbances, since the elements are so mutually interactive and reinforcing. Separation from his wife always made him more sensitive to frustrations in his work, and this in turn enhanced his loneliness. When he felt isolated, his sexual passions were stirred, and his guilt over these passions made him even more depressed. In this unhappy state, despite his loneliness and love for his wife, he became insensitive to her actual feelings.

While Ellen was in Georgia with the children, Woodrow suggested that she take them to see his sister, Annie, in Columbia. Annie, as usual, was unwell, and Woodrow thought that a family visit would cheer her. In his lonely and depressed state, he probably had a special need to feel a sense of family solidarity. By this time, Ellen had been away from home for over two months, and she was weary of traveling with three small children—now ages six, four, and two. She gave as excuses of why not to go to Columbia the fact that the Howes had guests and that an additional trip would be expensive. Despite his own

[40] WW to EAW, March 16, 1892, *ibid.*, p. 490.

[41] WW to EAW, March 9, 1892, *ibid.*, p. 461.

[42] WW to EAW, March 17, 1892, *ibid.*, p. 492; translation of a boudoir scene from Théophile Gautier, *Mademoiselle de Maupin*, 2 vols. (Paris, 1835-36 *et seq.*), Chapter XVI, printed in *ibid.*, pp. 462-66.

[43] WW to EAW, March 10, 1892, *ibid.*, pp. 466-67.

loneliness for her, Wilson insisted that she go to visit Annie. Ellen objected that it would be a "terrible day's journey for babies," involving a start at 4 a.m., changing trains on a close schedule, and arriving in Columbia at 10 p.m. Wilson did not get the real sense of her message, but urged her not to "grieve" Sister Annie by making her stay too brief. He reminded Ellen of how much Annie loved her and told her how gratified he was at the thought of the family's being together.[44] Ellen agreed to go, and, with a degree of understatement equaling her assurance that giving up her art career was not a sacrifice, said that she did not "dread this journey at all."[45] Shortly after her arrival in Columbia, Jessie broke her collar bone and Ellen strained her side and hip carrying the child upstairs. She was quite lame, she wrote to Woodrow, and needed him to massage her. If other Princeton faculty members could go to Europe, she thought, he could certainly come south to her.[46] Wilson, occupied with his own affairs, felt that he was unable to come short of "an absolute necessity."[47] He suggested, most imperceptively, that she get professional massage and told her that, even though staying away violated his "almost every wish and instinct," his judgment told him that he would be of more service to her by staying in Princeton and getting the house ready for her return.[48]

Ellen as usual, did not express her feelings and resentments openly. Rather, they may have been manifested psychosomatically, for example, in the way in which she hurt her back. Shortly after Ellen's return to Princeton, Woodrow left for Columbia to attend Josie's wedding. By then, Ellen was severely depressed, and her emotional state came out in the following letter: "I still have an uneasy conviction that it would not be good for me to 'invite my soul' *too* much just now. I am in danger of taking this separation all too tragically. There is something *terrible* in having so much at stake in life; it involves sometimes an acute agony. May God help me,—make me a better Christian,—more spiritual-minded! There is no other help *possible* for one who loves so intensely. How else may she hope to win *peace*? *Joy* indeed she has in fullest human measure, but *peace*,—*security*—who save the infinitely Great,—the infinitely Merciful can ensure her that?"[49] Such language was unusual for her and strongly suggests that

---

[44] EAW to WW, April 20, 1892; WW to EAW, April 22 and 24, 1892, *ibid.,* pp. 583, 587, 590.

[45] EAW to WW, April 21, 1892, *ibid.,* p. 585.

[46] EAW to WW, April 26, 1892, *ibid.,* pp. 592-94.

[47] WW to EAW, April 27, 1892, *ibid.,* p. 597.

[48] WW to EAW, April 28 and May 2, 1892, *ibid.,* pp. 600, 609.

[49] EAW to WW, June 18, 1892, *ibid.,* Vol. 8, p. 7.

her resentment had been turned inward. For Wilson, the episode shows how, in an emotional state, one can feel another person to be part of one's self and remain unaware of the other's actual feelings as an independent person in his or her own right.

The affair which occupied Wilson and kept him from going to his wife was the offer of the presidency of the University of Illinois at the large salary of $6,000. He was favorably impressed by the Illinois emissaries, and immediately sought Ellen's opinion.[50] She was practical and asked him to find out more of the substance of the proposal, such as the perquisites, the size of the student body and faculty, the endowment, and the relationship of the university to the state legislature.[51] She also suggested that the Illinois offer would be useful in bargaining with Princeton. Perhaps the college might buy a lot owned by the Wilsons and build a house for them on it. When she was in Columbia, after consulting with Uncle James Woodrow, she urged her husband to go to Urbana and see the university at firsthand (a suggestion which he did not follow).[52] Ellen Wilson viewed the situation as possibly a turning point, both in their lives and in the affairs of Princeton. She did not want her husband to miss what might be a great opportunity to lead a scholarly life, with freedom from classes and time to write and travel abroad. She believed that the time had come for Princeton to decide between remaining a small college or raising its salary scale to attract the men who could make it into a great university.[53]

After much consideration, Wilson decided to turn down the Illinois offer. He had asked the advice of his classmate, Cyrus H. McCormick, who told him that the university was little more than an agricultural college and had a standing far below that of the universities of Wisconsin and Michigan. Moreover, McCormick told him that the state legislature was not contemplating any substantial increase in endowment. The large salary, in McCormick's opinion, meant that the burden of establishing the institution would be placed almost entirely on Wilson. McCormick, along with other prominent Chicago businessmen and Princeton alumni, strongly advised him to remain at Princeton.[54]

Wilson's decision to turn down the Illinois offer was based on the sound grounds that assuming the presidency of an agricultural college

[50] WW to EAW, April 28, 1892, *ibid.,* Vol. 7, p. 600.
[51] EAW to WW, April 30, 1892, *ibid.,* p. 604.
[52] EAW to WW, May 1 and 3, 1892, *ibid.,* pp. 607, 609.
[53] EAW to WW, May 1 and 6, 1892, *ibid.,* pp. 607, 620.
[54] Cyrus H. McCormick to WW, May 4, 1892, *ibid.,* pp. 613-14.

was far different from taking charge of an institution with scholarly and literary traditions, and that his literary plans would be utterly frustrated. Characteristically, however, he then went on to justify and validate his action to himself in terms of his symbolic values. He cited his lack of sympathy with coeducation, although he seems not to have mentioned this matter at the outset. He also gave his decision an ethical sanction. It would not be fair to the university, he wrote his wife, to have as its head someone who would not for many years give his best thoughts and energies to the task of its development. It was wrong, he concluded, to sacrifice his highest aims to material comfort.[55]

Once the decision was made, Wilson went to Columbia. He had a refreshing sea voyage back from South Carolina and, on his return to Princeton, he and Ellen vowed never to leave each other again.[56] For the next year, they were separated only briefly. The family went with him to Baltimore that winter, and they vacationed during the following summer together on Long Island. Wilson lectured at the Chicago World's Fair; on his return, he persuaded Ellen to visit the exposition while he took care of the children. The situation at Princeton improved somewhat; he was given an assistant to teach economics and received a modest raise in salary. He compensated productively for the fading of his dream of a law school by giving undergraduate courses in administration, public law, constitutional law, the history of the English common law, and so on, and completed an extensive bibliography of public law, jurisprudence, and the history of the law, which drew heavily on German writers. Wilson was probably responsible for the decision of the Princeton Class of 1883 to give a library in political science as the class decennial gift to the college.[57] On completing *Division and Reunion* in the summer of 1892, he made an outline of what was to be his magnum opus, "The Philosophy of Politics." A year later, he began work on "A Short History of the United States," a text modeled on Green's *History of the English People.*[58]

The frustration of Wilson's plan for a law school created, or accentuated, a conflict between a career as a historian and writer and a more active political role. From 1893 onward, Wilson became increasingly prominent as an educator and lecturer on political, bio-

[55] WW to EAW, May 4, 1892, *ibid.*, p. 616.

[56] McAdoo, *The Priceless Gift*, p. 181.

[57] Editorial Note, "Wilson and the Class of 1883 Library of Political Science and Jurisprudence," *PWW*, Vol. 8, pp. 228-30.

[58] Editorial Note, "Wilson's *Division and Reunion*"; outline of "The Philosophy of Politics," August 28, 1892; Editorial Note, "Wilson's 'Short History of the United States,' " *ibid.*, pp. 27-28, 141-48, 279.

graphical, and patriotic topics. Among his subjects were "Democracy," "Political Liberty," "Municipal Government," "Religion and Patriotism," "Leaders of Men," and "University Training and Citizenship." He also talked on Bagehot, Burke, Tocqueville, Montesquieu, and Machiavelli. Some of the diffusion can be attributed to financial necessity, since only professors who were independently wealthy could subsist without outside lecturing and writing. Wilson, as he often said, was not primarily a historian but a political scientist, and his lasting contributions in that field were in administration.

Wilson's career as a historian was hampered by his action-oriented, impatient disposition, and unwillingness, perhaps because of his slow reading, to amass the amount of data necessary for the documentation of his ideas. However, for *Division and Reunion* he had to do much new reading. Wilson introduced the thesis that the fundamental cause of the Civil War was not slavery, but a sectional difference in the interpretation of the Constitution. He said that, while the South's ideas of state rights had not changed because its economy had remained stationary, the outlook of the North had shifted because of its industrial development and the growth of the West. The book, generally regarded as Wilson's best work, was received favorably by a public eager to forget the hatreds of the Civil War. Some historians were critical; even Wilson's good friend Frederick Jackson Turner could not believe that the South had remained "*preserved* by the ice of slavery like a Siberian mammoth."[59] *Division and Reunion* was also criticized for its generalities; Frederic Bancroft, a noted historian, thought that Wilson was more occupied with brilliance of style than with the presentation of facts.[60] Even so, *Division and Reunion* was the first book to cover the period 1829-1889, contained many brilliant insights, and was long regarded as the standard short work. Writing it also led Wilson to do some serious thinking about methodology and historical writing.

In part, at least, to adapt to his circumstances and literary style, Wilson developed the thesis that history was not a record of the facts, but of some of the facts selected for their significance and set forth in such order and combination, with a touch of the writer's imagination (Wilson called it divination), as to give the spirit of the age. This formulation led Wilson to some brilliant and heuristic ideas, as well as to some vague thinking. In a remarkable essay, "Mere Literature,"

[59] "Wilson's *Division and Reunion*"; Turner to WW, July 16, 1893, *ibid.*, pp. 148, 279.

[60] Review of *Division and Reunion*, in the *Political Science Quarterly* VIII (September 1893), 533-35, printed in *ibid.*, pp. 344-46.

he stated that one could not understand the laws and politics of a people without knowledge of their ideals, literature, traditions, social relationships, songs and conversations, attitudes toward authority, property, and privilege, and feelings about life and death.[61] By literature, Wilson meant the whole network of communications in a society. He stated that the historian needed "nothing less than the insight of the best novelists into character and the grounds of action."[62] He criticized a biography of Abraham Lincoln because the author had not dealt sufficiently with Lincoln's personality.[63] Unfortunately for his career as a scholar, Wilson, to implement his views, would have had to draw upon the yet undeveloped disciplines of psychology, sociology, anthropology, and demography.

On the negative side, Wilson was sometimes careless with the facts and gave the impression that he regarded digging for them as a routine task for lesser minds. After *Division and Reunion*, he rarely consulted primary sources. Too much knowledge, he warned, would break the spell of the imagination. In "Mere Literature," he seemed to deprecate scholarship when he claimed that it could not attain the essence of immortal truth found in poetry and prose. Wilson was stung by a criticism by Franklin W. Hooper, director of the Brooklyn Institute of Arts and Sciences, that his lectures were not sufficiently scholarly and instructive, but too much given to popular entertainment.[64] Wilson defended the privilege of a writer to write in the style of any period he chose, provided he had really absorbed the spirit of the age. He cited Charles Lamb, a favorite of his youth, who wrote as if he lived in Shakespeare's day and whose quaintness, according to Wilson, reflected the Elizabethan age.[65]

Wilson's conflicts over a career were associated with a resurgence of his political ambitions. These interests were quickened by the labor disturbances, agrarian discontent, and political unrest that followed the Panic of 1893. In his speeches he warned against revolution and populist excesses, and pleaded for a discipline of the intellect. In an historical essay, "A Calendar of Great Americans," Wilson praised the conservative Alexander Hamilton and criticized Thomas Jefferson as

[61] "Mere Literature," c. June 17, 1893, *ibid.*, p. 245.

[62] Wilson was commenting on James Ford Rhodes' *History of the United States from the Compromise of 1850* (New York, 1893) in "Anti-Slavery History and Biography," *Atlantic Monthly*, LXXII (August 1893), 268-77, printed in *ibid.*, p. 301.

[63] In this context, Wilson criticized John T. Morse, *Abraham Lincoln*, 2 vols. (Boston and New York, 1893), in *ibid.*, p. 297.

[64] Franklin William Hooper to WW, November 4, 1895, *ibid.*, Vol. 9, p. 334.

[65] "On an Author's Choice of Company," *Century Magazine*, LI (March 1896), 775-79, printed in *ibid.*, pp. 338-47.

a radical. According to Wilson, Jefferson was "not a thorough American because of the strain of French philosophy that permeated and weakened all his thought."[66] In a lecture which he gave many times, Wilson defined liberty as obedience to popular authority and participation in an orderly social system.[67] The shift to a more active orientation toward political life was most significantly signaled in Wilson's adoption of Edmund Burke as his "master" in place of Walter Bagehot. Wilson had long admired Burke, the eighteenth-century English statesman who advocated conciliation with the American colonies and condemned the excesses of the French Revolution. As a student at Princeton, Wilson had included in his Index Rerum an excerpt from Burke's famous speech on conciliation and a biographical sketch. He gave his first lecture on Burke to the Johns Hopkins Seminary in 1894. Wilson believed not only that Burke's writing and speeches reflected his own political views, but that Burke's style provided a model for their expression.[68]

The facts of Burke's life as given in the eleventh edition of the *Encyclopædia Britannica* and Wilson's biography suggest that Wilson felt a strong personal identification with him. Burke, who was born in Ireland (a conquered province like Virginia), studied law but disliked legal practice. So he turned to the application of the law to political problems. Burke had a nervous, excitable temperament but married a wife whose gracious charm soothed his mind and whose affection satisfied his ardent nature. The most serious part of his intellectual life began after his marriage. Burke, a man of sensitive imagination and elevated moral sense, had a passion for the sacredness of the law and thought that good government, like virtue, was a practical habit of conduct rather than a matter of constitutional structure. A brilliant debater, Burke formed his political judgments on the basis of prudence and expediency, and he made his appeal to the public on grounds of the highest sympathies of human character. His flair for dramatic description was shown in his account of the atrocities of the wars in India and his sentimental picture of the beautiful Marie Antoinette. He got at the heart of books through their spirit rather than through their grammar. He avoided direct references to what he read but smelted and recoined the material that he had received. Burke's career

[66] "A Calendar of Great Americans," New York *Forum*, XVI (February 1894), 715-27, printed in *ibid.*, Vol. 8, pp. 368-80.

[67] "Democracy," December 5, 1891, *ibid.*, Vol. 7, pp. 363-65.

[68] Editorial Note, "Wilson's First Lecture on Burke," and Wilson's lecture at the Hopkins, "Edmund Burke: The Man and His Times," c. August 31, 1893, *ibid.*, Vol. 8, pp. 313-18, 318-43.

demonstrated that the world of books was a better preparation for statesmanship than training in subordinate posts. It was an idea especially congenial to Wilson.

Wilson's discontents in the winter of 1894 at the Johns Hopkins came out in the form of an episode of depression characterized by loneliness, over-concern about his wife's health, and sexual preoccupation. He spent the first two weeks in Baltimore pleasantly enough; he went to the theater frequently and accepted a number of invitations to dinner. At a reception he found the Dean-President of Bryn Mawr (as he called Carey Thomas) "astonishingly cordial." He was also pleased to hear that his father had left Mrs. Grannis.[69] Ellen, at the same time, was enjoying herself in Princeton, going to a concert and several dinners. After several busy days, she was too sleepy and tired to write, and Wilson reacted with extreme alarm that she was overworking herself.[70] Wilson expressed not only loneliness but perhaps jealousy also. After Ellen wrote that she had stayed up late to finish a black silk evening gown, for the price of thirty cents, he replied that he could not approve of a gown which made her sit up so late and neglect him even though the price was a triumph.[71] He was envious, he wrote, of the man who sat next to her, in all her beauty, at a dinner. In the same letter, Wilson described how, in his loneliness, he had walked up and down Charles Street looking into each pretty face that passed, comparing them to Ellen's. He told Ellen that he was not worthy of her and asked her to pray with him that he might get the devil out of him and be less subject to temptation.[72] Ellen was in turn depressed by the thought that a "poor little creature" like herself might have said something to turn him to self-reproach.[73] Wilson may also have had some gastrointestinal symptoms. This is suggested by his reference to his wife as "a dear normal, light-hearted little woman, with a good conscience and an equable digestion."[74]

After a week, Wilson had recovered and was again writing enthusiastically about his social activities. He expressed particular pleasure at meeting Edith Gittings Reid, the wife of a Hopkins professor, Harry Fielding Reid, and a member of a prominent Baltimore family. Wilson

[69] WW to EAW, February 4, 1894, *ibid.*, pp. 453-54.

[70] EAW to WW, January 31 and February 4, 1894; WW to EAW, February 9, 1894, *ibid.*, pp. 444, 456, 467-68.

[71] EAW to WW, January 26, 1894; WW to EAW, January 31, 1894, *ibid.*, pp. 434, 445.

[72] WW to EAW, February 10-11, 1894, *ibid.*, pp. 470-71.

[73] EAW to WW, February 12, 1894, *ibid.*, p. 479.

[74] WW to EAW, February 15, 1894, *ibid.*, p. 487.

wrote: "The feature of the evening, for me, was meeting Mrs. Harry Reid,—by far the most charming woman I've met here. . . , so bright, so whimsical, so sweet, so pretty! How I should like to see you two together,—as Mrs. Bird[75] said! She is not at all *intense*, neither is she a bit 'advanced,' except in the power to think and to see. She engages one's affections at the same time that she captivates his mind. She seemed (I must say, even at the risk of alarming you) to take as much of a fancy to me as I took to her." He assured Ellen that, while Mrs. Reid delighted him, she, Ellen, enslaved him.[76] In reply Ellen said that she was glad that Woodrow had become such a "social lion" and wondered if home might not seem dull after such good times.[77] Wilson continued to correspond with Mrs. Reid and tell her about his work and ask her opinions about his literary style. Ellen encouraged the friendship and urged him to see interesting and bright people so that he would not be lonely.[78]

Wilson did not take a vacation with his family in the summer of 1894, but gave a series of lectures in Plymouth, Massachusetts, and Colorado Springs. At Plymouth, he at first found it hard to feel at home in a New England crowd; then he became acquainted with the wife of a Harvard professor, Nancy Saunders Toy,[79] whom he found "delightful."[80] The Toys were both Southerners. Soon after his return to Princeton, Wilson went to Saratoga Springs to address the annual meeting of the American Bar Association on legal education. He also discussed the national scene, particularly the recent strikes that had shaken the nation and the repressive measures taken by the courts. He blamed reactionary judges and lawyers as much as agitators and strikers and called for reforms.[81]

When he arrived in Baltimore for his annual lectures in 1895, Wilson wrote to his wife: "[I am] enjoying in a certain degree a sense of power,—as if I had gotten some way upon the road I used so to burn to travel, and yet fairly restless and impatient with ambition, as of old—a boy and yet a man—carrying about with me the marks and records of all the turns and experiences in my life of which this room

[75] Sarah, or Sallie, Baxter Bird (Mrs. William Edgeworth Bird), who lived in Baltimore and was an old friend of the Wilson family.

[76] WW to EAW, February 24 & 25, 1894, *PWW*, Vol. 8, pp. 507-08.

[77] EAW to WW, February 26, 1894, *ibid.*, p. 512.

[78] EAW to WW, February 5, 1897, *ibid.*, Vol. 10, p. 150.

[79] Crawford Howell Toy, Hancock Professor of Hebrew at Harvard.

[80] WW to EAW, July 16, 1894, *PWW*, Vol. 8, p. 615.

[81] Editorial Note, "Wilson's Address on Legal Education"; "Legal Education of Undergraduates," address before the American Bar Association, August 23, 1894, *ibid.*, pp. 646-47, 647-57.

reminds me! I talk as if I have seen the world, boxed the compass in the vicissitudes of my life, don't I! Well, I *have*,—*inside* of me; quiet and even and uneventful as the outside *fortunes* of my life have been. Oh, love, love, what a passion it has all bred in my heart for you, my delightful lover, my perfect wife. I love you and long for you more than I dare say! . . . I am quite well and *tame*."[82]

Wilson's state of serenity and "tameness" was short-lived. During the preceding months in Princeton, the Wilsons had begun planning their own home. They had bought a wooded lot adjoining the property that they were renting, and an architect had submitted plans for the house. He made these from plans that Mrs. Wilson had drawn and a clay model that she had constructed. Three days after he had assured Ellen of his well-being, Wilson was crushed to learn that he had miscalculated the amount of interest on the mortgage. Never, he told his wife, had he been so driven and beaten by a passion of grief as he was at the prospect of postponing their plans. If they had to pay 5½ rather than 5 percent, he would have to devote all his energies to making money, and the worry would perhaps kill him and wound her irreparably.[83] To tell her of his mistake, he wrote, was like "thrusting a knife" into her.[84]

Ellen took the disappointment calmly. She assured him that the mistake was not his fault, and that she would be perfectly happy to live with him "in *any* house."[85] She urged him not to grieve about the matter; it was she who was responsible for his distress, she claimed, as the house-building scheme was hers from the first. The only suffering she had ever endured in her marriage, she maintained, was from the consciousness that he was torturing himself.[86] Fortunately, Ellen suggested some alterations that brought the expense down, and the house was built. In retrospect, the mistake was a relatively trivial one, related to Wilson's deficiency as a calculator. However, the disturbance that it caused suggests that he was in a greater state of emotional tension than he realized.

The winter of 1894-1895 was unusually severe, and Wilson felt guilty over the fact that he was warm and comfortable in Baltimore while his loved ones were suffering in Princeton. When Ellen complained of some aches and pains, he wanted to know all the details and asked her to promise to see a doctor.[87] Wilson was also troubled

---

[82] WW to EAW, January 24, 1895, *ibid.*, Vol. 9, p. 124.
[83] WW to EAW, January 28, 1895, *ibid.*, p. 137.
[84] WW to EAW, January 27, 1895, *ibid.*, p. 133.
[85] EAW to WW, January 28, 1895, *ibid.*, p. 139.
[86] EAW to WW, February 4, 1895, *ibid.*, pp. 170-71.
[87] WW to EAW, February 10, 1895, *ibid.*, p. 184.

by a resurgence of his erotic impulses. He was having, he told his wife, "all the roving, Bohemian impulses the wildest young colt could have," and it was just as well that he had to sit in his room and correct the last semester's examination papers.[88] Jokingly, he assured her that he was safe because his father was watching over his morals.[89] As Wilson had done previously in states of stress, he composed another poem to Ellen:

And so by you my heart was loosed,
Was freed from bondage, and the fear
Of what is coarse and dull and dread.
You brought me life, you gave me speech.[90]

Despite her previous suggestion that he give up writing poetry, Ellen was deeply touched by the sentiment.[91]

Wilson also had a recurrence of his gastrointestinal symptoms, and, toward the end of his stay in Baltimore, he had an attack of the grippe. He received a "sovereign remedy" from his friend Charlie Mitchell which enabled him to "master it very promptly."[92] However, his digestive disturbances persisted, and in the following autumn he came under the care of the distinguished physician. Dr. Francis Delafield of New York. Dr. Delafield concluded that his patient's troubles were caused by excess stomach acid or mucus and instructed him in washing out his stomach with a siphon attached to a large rubber tube. Wilson was fond of describing his first meeting with Dr. Delafield. The Doctor approached him, tube in hand, saying as if in benediction, "You will find this extremely disagreeable but not intolerable." (Actually, the treatment, now happily extinct, was not only scientifically useless but potentially dangerous because the depletion of stomach acid may cause alkalosis and tetany. Fortunately, the complications for Wilson were less serious.) One day, after Wilson had filled his stomach with water, the siphon failed to work. He hastened to Dr. Delafield's office but was told by the nurse that the Doctor's office hours were over. Wilson then inquired if the Doctor had left the building. He had not, the nurse responded, but he would not see any more patients. Wilson then spied the Doctor and said, "I will have to hold you up, Doctor, I am waterlogged."[93]

Wilson was intent on making enough money to pay for the house and also was goaded by his literary and political aspirations. Due to

[88] WW to EAW, February 1, 1895, *ibid.*, p. 148.
[89] WW to EAW, February 3, 1895, *ibid.*, p. 166.
[90] WW to EAW, February 16, 1895, *ibid.*, p. 201.
[91] EAW to WW, February 17, 1895, *ibid.*, p. 204.
[92] WW to EAW, February 22, 1895, *ibid.*, p. 219.   [93] Axson Memoir.

the conflicts between these aspirations, he carried on a punishing schedule through 1895 and into 1896. It is only a slight exaggeration to say that, over this period, he spent as many working days away from Princeton as at the college. In the spring of 1895, he talked at meetings of Princeton and University of Virginia alumni and gave commencement addresses at Wellesley and Oberlin. He was too busy to work on his projected history of the United States (a school text, not the later *History of the American People*), and too overwhelmed with work to go to his family in Columbia after the death of George Howe.[94] However, he accepted with alacrity an offer from *Harper's Magazine* to write a serialized popular biography of George Washington, at $300 for each of six articles, and began work in the autumn of 1895. Between October 10, 1895, and the beginning of his Johns Hopkins lectures in mid-January 1896, he took eighteen out-of-town trips to deliver popular lectures under the auspices of the Brooklyn Institute of Arts and Sciences and the American Society for the Extension of University Teaching.[95] In 1895 he received more money in lecture fees than he did from his professorship.

Wilson's health suffered, and his ailments, unlike previous ones, interfered with his work. In late September 1895 some unspecified illness held up the writing of *George Washington* and obliged him to delay the start of his lectures at the Brooklyn Institute.[96] A "sharp attack of indigestion" sent him to bed for several days in November.[97] At the Johns Hopkins, in January 1896, episodes of colic caused him to miss several lectures. Dr. Mitchell thought that the stomach tube had caused a kink in the small intestine and had produced pain by dilating the stomach. Mitchell advised him to discontinue it. He recognized how tense his old classmate had become and urged him to take a summer vacation abroad. Wilson's condition was obvious to others as well; Professor Theodore Whitefield Hunt, an old friend and teacher, urged him to cut short his Hopkins classes.[98] Wilson also developed a nervous tic of his left upper facial muscles. It so alarmed his father that Dr. Wilson exclaimed, "I am afraid Woodrow is going to die."[99] Woodrow did not die, but in May, as he was about to sail for England, he suffered the first of a series of incapacitating strokes.

[94] WW to Annie Wilson Howe, April 21, 1895, *PWW*, Vol. 9, pp. 247-48.

[95] WW to Harper & Brothers, May 16, 1896; Editorial Note, "Wilson's Lectures on Great Leaders of Political Thought," *ibid.*, pp. 504-05, 326-27.

[96] WW to Howard Pyle, October 7, 1895, *ibid.*, p. 324.

[97] WW to Henry Mills Alden, November 30, 1895, *ibid.*, p. 353.

[98] WW to EAW, January 29, 1896; WW to William Rainey Harper, February 5, 1896; Theodore Whitefield Hunt to WW, February 6, 1896, enclosed in WW to EAW, February 11, 1896, *ibid.*, pp. 395, 406 n.1, 417.

[99] Axson Memoir.

CHAPTER VIII

Wilson's Imagery:
Language and Stress

SOMEONE HAS SAID that Woodrow Wilson was born between the Bible and the dictionary. He used language to express his thoughts and feelings, and, to an unusual degree, his language influenced his cognitive and emotional behavior and his perception of reality. Wilson's linguistic style and his emphasis on proper English were outstanding elements of his personality, and language provided him an important mode of adaptation to stress.

Wilson had a gift for word description and a remarkable facility for retaining impressions of scenes which he had witnessed, read about, or only imagined. This was the quality which he had so admired in Macaulay. He could remember the roar of the furnaces and the sheets of flame in the factories, which, as a child, he had visited with his father. He could recall the taste of cow-pea soup, the sound of his father's laughter, and the smell of Dr. Wilson's books.[1] His evocations of such events as the signing of the Covenant and the Battle of Princeton were colorful and dramatic. At the time that he wrote *Congressional Government* he had not visited the Capitol, and he described the House of Commons long before he saw it.

Wilson had difficulty in separating words from the images they evoked. Among his favorite passages of poetry were the lines from Swinburne's *Tristram of Lyonesse* which describe Iseult's voyage across the stormy sea to Cornwall to marry King Mark. He told Ellen that nothing could surpass Swinburne's description of the brewing and breaking of the storm, followed by the appearance of the sun, and the fearlessness of Iseult throughout these events. He would read these lines to prepare himself for lectures at the Johns Hopkins Seminary. "From Shakspere, or from any finely figurative writing," he said, "I get a stimulus for extemporaneous expression, with either my tongue or my pen, such as I can get in no other way and from no other source. It sets my mind aglow, seeming to make it nimble and strong."[2] Words-

[1] Axson Memoir.
[2] WW to ELA, April 22, 1884, *PWW*, Vol. 3, pp. 143-44.

worth's poems brought tears to his eyes, and he was emotionally affected by sad stories. Mary Hoyt, Ellen's cousin who lived with the family in Bryn Mawr, recalled that his voice would break when he read aloud and came to a tender part.[3]

Wilson's historical writings abound in imagery. He wanted his readers to feel things as he believed they had actually happened—to hear the clang of battle and the bustle of the cities, and to sense the calm of the countryside. The spirit of an age, he told the graduating class of a girls' school, was part of a universal human spirit which "touches the springs of fancy or of action within us, and makes our own life seem more quick and vital." The historian, he said, must not only give the facts; he must also learn to write with such color and imagination that he can make dead generations breathe again. Like his model, Bagehot, Wilson believed that he could revive the spirit of the Roman Empire through the use of adjectives and generalizations such as "stately Roman," "keen-eyed Greek," "watching Jew," and "horrid Hun."[4]

The type of cerebral hemisphere organization associated with Wilson's childhood dyslexia, and his father's insistence that he reproduce his sensory impressions verbally, may have influenced his linguistic style. The hemispheres of the brain process information differently. The left hemisphere uses a strategy based on combinatorial individual feature analysis, while the right has a holistic, global approach. The right hemisphere retrieves the meaning of a word by its auditory gestalt, while the left hemisphere analyzes the utterance into its phonetic components. Thus, the left hemisphere may be said to be dominant for the phonetic, syntactic, and sequential aspects of language, while the right is more specialized for the sensory aspects and perceives words as visual and auditory gestalts. Normally, however, the hemispheres do not work in isolation, and the performance of the whole person exceeds the sum of the individual hemispheric competencies. The nature of the task determines which hemisphere assumes control of the totally behaving organism, and a preference for one linguistic-cognitive style does not mean a deficiency in the other.[5] Wilson distinguished in himself two styles, one political and concrete, the other imaginative; and he praised Thomas Jefferson for his ability to think simultaneously in visual and concrete terms.[6] In his speeches Wilson

[3] Mary E. Hoyt, memorandum on Wilson, October 1926, Baker Papers.

[4] "On Being Human," commencement address at Miss Hersey's School in Boston, June 2, 1897, printed in *PWW*, Vol. 10, p. 246.

[5] Zaidel, "Lexical Organization in the Right Hemisphere."

[6] WW to ELA, October 30, 1883, *ibid.*, Vol. 2, p. 502; address on Thomas Jefferson,

seems to have been able to visualize scenes and ideas, which he translated into images and figures of speech and delivered in perfect syntax. At his best, he combined superbly factual narrative, conceptual clarity, and vivid metaphor.[7]

Cognitive style also involves memory. Wilson had excellent recall for material which fitted into perceptual and ideational patterns. It is said that he knew the speeches of Burke almost by heart, and on several occasions he demonstrated his ability to remember the exact wording of political speeches. His addresses were usually extemporaneous in the sense that he did not read from a prepared copy, but from a brief outline of his main points. These he fleshed out with illustrations, analogies, and figures of speech. On the rare occasions when he later read transcripts of his speeches, his memory for what he had said—or his familiarity with his habitual style—was such that he could detect any error; his accuracy was evidenced by the correspondence of his corrections with the original shorthand recording.[8] He demonstrated his capacity for auditory and visual recall on other occasions. Colonel House noted in his diary: "Page also sent me a remarkable letter from a lady of the nobility which he asked me to burn after reading to the President. I started to burn it when the President remarked, 'let me see if I have the facts in the letter right.' He then repeated it almost verbatim."[9]

On the other hand, Wilson had a poor memory for individual items which did not form a thematic pattern. Herbert Baxter Adams said that he had never had a student with as poor a memory for facts and a better memory for ideas. Wilson told a friend that he had trouble remembering engagements unless he connected them with the date of some historical event.[10] His inability to retain German and French despite a great expenditure of effort has been cited, and he confessed to a Princeton class that he was unable to remember anything word for word.[11] Wilson's verbal memory was very sensitive to emotional

---

delivered at the annual Jefferson Day Dinner of the National Democratic Club in New York, April 16, 1906, printed in *PWW*, Vol. 16, p. 364.

[7] According to Arthur S. Link, Wilson's address, "Leaders of Men," first delivered on June 17, 1890, at the University of Tennessee's commencement exercises, is one of the best illustrations of these qualities. See Editorial Note, "Leaders of Men" and address, *ibid.*, Vol. 6, pp. 645-46, 646-71.

[8] *Ibid.*, Vol. 25, ix; see Wilson address in Mobile, Ala., October 27, 1913, *ibid.*, Vol. 28, p. 452 n.4.

[9] The diary of Colonel Edward M. House, December 12, 1913, Yale University Library; hereinafter cited as the House diary.

[10] Undated interview with Jacob N. Beam, Bragdon Collection.

[11] Undated interview with Gordon Pierce, Bragdon Collection.

factors. He told Mary Hoyt that he could not remember a single rhyme from *Childe Harold's Pilgrimage* by Byron—whom he detested.[12]

When one considers Wilson's love of language and his frequent quotations of poetry, it is surprising to learn that he read so narrowly. He took little interest in the scientific and technological developments of his time, and showed no intellectual curiosity about philosophy or the metaphysical aspects of religion. His tastes in prose and poetry were selective and limited. He passionately admired and cited passages from Keats, Wordsworth, Shelley, Browning, and Matthew Arnold, but he did not read their works extensively. Aside from *Tristram*, he did not care for Swinburne. He had little knowledge of the world's great literature.[13] He was not interested in travel beyond his orbit of England and Scotland; he once told Lucy Salmon that the best traveled man he ever knew had never been outside of Georgia.[14] Wilson enjoyed the Biblical language of sermons and the wit of a preacher, but he did not care for ministers who engaged in discussion of political or social topics.[15] He was fond of all forms of theater, including vaudeville and the movies. His daughter Eleanor recalled him as an enthusiastic and uncritical viewer.[16]

In no area did Wilson take more pride than in speaking and writing perfect English. He regarded his father as his best teacher, and, like Dr. Wilson, tended to judge a man's mental capability by the conciseness and clarity of his language. Slang, he believed, was a device for avoiding the intricacies of English grammar. As has been mentioned, he accepted criticism of his ideas from editors, but he rejected any suggestions that he change his writing style. At times, he was pedantic: he insisted, for example, that the only correct spelling of the term "OK" was "okeh," since, he said, it was derived from the Choctaw. When Wilson was President he often used over-literal interpretations to evade direct answers to reporters' questions. Language was a lively topic in personal relationships. He liked to imitate his wife's southern accent and delighted in catching friends up on their forms of speech.[17] The importance of proper English as a symbol was shown in the early months of the Great War, when, distressed by the conflict

[12] Hoyt, Memorandum on Wilson, October 1926, Baker Papers.

[13] Baker, *Wilson*, I, 202-203; Link, *Wilson*, II, 62.

[14] A Neutral, "Woodrow Wilson: The President's Policies Analyzed in the Light of His Natural Inhibitions and His Past Record," *The Nation*, CIII (September 14, 1916), 258.

[15] Axson Memoir.

[16] McAdoo, *The Woodrow Wilsons*, p. 233.

[17] Grayson, *An Intimate Memoir*, p. 47.

and deeply depressed over the death of his wife, he seemed to sum up his unhappiness by criticizing the English used in State Department dispatches.[18]

The purposes of oratory, in Wilson's view, were "to please the ear," "govern the emotions," "give a sense of definiteness," and impart "a sense of *reality*."[19] He spoke in cadence with clear diction; he did not hesitate or fumble for words. His father had taught him not to use stereotyped gestures and vocal effects, and their absence seemed to enhance the power of his words. He told his fiancée that speaking in public was an exhilarating experience: "I enjoy it (speaking) because it sets my mind—all my faculties—aglow: and I suppose that this very excitement gives my manner an appearance of confidence and self-command which arrests the attention. However that may be, I *feel* a sort of transformation—and it's hard to go to sleep afterwards."[20] He found "absolute joy in facing and conquering a hostile audience . . . or thawing out a cold one."[21] Wilson also had the power to make his audiences laugh, as is evidenced by the frequent notations of "laughter and applause" in transcripts of his speeches.

Long before he entered politics, Wilson had worked out a philosophy of political leadership based on language. He believed that his hold on a political audience was due to his literary training, because he could put into words what people were thinking but were unable to articulate. He stated that the successful leader did not bring new ideas to his audience but that he embodied the projected consciousness of his time and people. Political parties, he said, wanted to be led by absolute opinions without consideration for the views of the opposing side. He differentiated the qualities of the literary man from those of the politician. Speakers who could move masses of men lacked the finer sensibilities that appealed to individuals. Thus, in Wilson's opinion, no poet could become a politician and no political leader, with the exception of Benjamin Disraeli, could write fiction. Politicians, at times, had to shock people, and methods which would infallibly alienate individuals would master multitudes.[22]

Wilson could also be inspiring and persuasive in private conversation. One of the men who had been recruited for the preceptorial system at Princeton told how he had been carried away: "My interview

[18] House diary, December 18, 1914.
[19] Notes for a talk at Whig Hall Graduation, "The Power of Literary and Oratorial Form," April 4, 1910, *PWW*, Vol. 20, p. 315.
[20] WW to ELA, November 25, 1884, *ibid.*, Vol. 3, p. 484.
[21] WW to ELA, March 18, 1884, *ibid.*, p. 89.
[22] "Leaders of Men," *ibid.*, Vol. 6, pp. 646-71.

lasted some forty minutes. Mr. Wilson asked me no questions about myself, but spoke with winning eloquence about his plans for Princeton. Before five minutes had passed I knew that I was in the presence of a very great man. Of course I was not sufficiently a prophet to foresee the scope of his subsequent achievement . . . . But I did recognize that I had never before talked face to face with so compelling a person. Before the talk was over my loyalties were entirely committed to him. Had Woodrow Wilson asked me to go with him and work under him while he inaugurated a new university in Kamchatka or Senegambia I would have said 'yes' without further question."[23]

Wilson lost his self-consciousness in his public speeches and his writings. He could put affectionate sentiments in letters to friends and acquaintances which he would have been embarrassed to utter in face-to-face situations. He found it difficult to praise people in personal meetings, but he could write them handsome compliments. Wilson found it especially hard to act warmly toward colleagues whom he disliked, but on ceremonial occasions he could laud them eloquently. Professor Ely, toward whom Wilson had been cool when they were at the Johns Hopkins, was amazed many years later by the handsome tribute that Wilson paid him at a dinner in Ely's honor. Significantly, while Ely remembered the glow that Wilson's words gave him, he could not recall their substance.[24] Rather than confront political opponents and critics directly, Wilson often preferred to answer them in the rhetoric and metaphors of public speech.

Some of Wilson's most dramatic metaphors were those of the life processes—the growth and functions and malfunctions of the human body, and their relationships to nature. He spoke of political entities as if they were living organisms. "The State," he wrote in 1899, "is an abiding natural relationship. . . . It is an . . . embodiment of a form of life higher than that of the individual."[25] "Like health," he maintained five years earlier, "the harmonious correlation of forces that make up political liberty depend on a nice balance of functions."[26] He included the development of the human spirit and progress toward democracy in his conception of evolution. Such language had a strong appeal to a generation which sought to combine the teachings of religion and science in order to achieve a better world. Wilson could

[23] Robert K. Root, "Wilson and the Preceptors," in William Starr Myers, ed., *Woodrow Wilson: Some Princeton Memories* (Princeton, N.J., 1946), pp. 14-15.

[24] Ely, *Ground Under My Feet*, p. 110.

[25] "Notes on Statesmanship," Wilson notebook, c. June 5 to September 5, 1899, *ibid.*, Vol. 11, p. 125.

[26] Notes, *ibid.*, Vol. 11, 125.

make an audience feel that political policy was a part of God's unfolding plan for the perfection of mankind. Wilson had a deep emotional attachment to metaphors related to the physiology of the cardiovascular, respiratory, and digestive systems. His favorite word was "heart." This organ "beat faster," "bled," "expanded," "stood still," "ached," and even "breathed." He and Ellen searched for the "unspeakable heart word" which would express their love most exquisitely. He made frequent references to the circulation of the blood. "The Western frontier population," he once wrote, "felt the very keenest throbs of the nation's life. . . . Their blood flowed to them directly from the veins of the older communities."[27] In moments of emotional stress, he condemned the financiers who squeezed workingmen so that blood oozed through their fingers.[28] Not only could people absorb the principles of democracy by breathing the fresh air; they could also be overcome by the noxious gases emitted by politicians, especially Republican ones.

Wilson liked contrasts of light and darkness and sunlight and shade. He was fond of images of the landscape and the water—uplands and valleys, streams, rivers, and the sea. When he talked of commerce, he spoke often of ships plying the seven seas. He expressed his affection for Walter Bagehot when he described Somersetshire, Bagehot's birthplace, as "that land of golden light, with sea on either side, and the sunlight [which] remained in his soul during his whole life."[29] Wilson constantly referred to Europe as "across the water." He spoke of a "clear mountain current" and of "the great stream of freedom."[30] He compared the rivulets forming a river to the streams that fertilize the consciousness of men. Wilson was attached to springs and fountains— "exquisite fountains of English," "fountains of friendship," "fountains of knowledge," and used the word no less than fourteen times in a baccalaureate address. Other favorite words were "quick," in the sense of live, "pulses," "processes," "counsel," used both as a verb and noun, "visions," and "voices."

The content of the metaphors and other figures of speech, preferred in states of emotional stress, is determined by custom and culture, the nature of the problem, and the way in which symbolic theme has been a source of identity and a channel of social relatedness. These features are represented in Wilson's use of gastrointestinal figures of speech.

[27] "Anti-Slavery History and Biography," *ibid.*, Vol. 8, p. 297.
[28] Address in Denver, October 7, 1912, *ibid.*, Vol. 25, p. 373.
[29] Lecture in Lancaster, Pa., January 16, 1896, printed in the Lancaster, Pa. *Daily Intelligencer,* January 16, 1896, and *ibid.*, Vol. 9, p. 382.
[30] "Leaders of Men," *ibid.*, Vol. 6, p. 647.

In the society in which he grew up, digestive metaphors were commonly applied to the difficulties of teaching the young and were among his father's favorite expressions. Wilson used them particularly during periods of emotional disturbance when he was having trouble with his bowels. His Scotch-Irish ancestry served as a symbol of his courage and fighting spirit. In the Wilsons' cultural milieu, as we have seen, a variety of problems were represented in the vocabularies of religion and morality.

Experiences that are originally traumatic may evolve into forms of adaptation to stress. The child who overcomes his fear of dogs by crawling on all fours and barking provides a simple example. Wilson's adolescent play and fantasy life about the Royal Navy, and his later fondness for images and poetry of the sea, may have been related to the fear of the water instilled in him by his mother. References to Europe as "across the water" were very common, but Wilson used the expression invariably. One can also speculate on the connection between his emphasis on health and disease and his mother's chronic invalidism and the fears about illness that she transmitted to him. Such metaphors may have had a particular quality of validity by virtue of the way in which the language was symbolic of the intensely intimate emotional relationship between mother and son.

The history of Wilson's attitudes toward automobiles, and the ways in which he used cars as symbols, provide a well-documented illustration of the relationship between stressful emotional experience and metaphorical speech. Initially, he disliked automobiles intensely. He had no interest in their novelty and mechanical aspects, abhorred their noise and fumes, and resented the manner in which motorists interfered with his bicycling.[31] He declared in a speech delivered in 1906: "I think that of all the menaces of to-day the worst is the reckless driving in automobiles. In this the rights of the people are set at naught. When a child is run over the automobilist doesn't stop, but runs away. Does the father of that child consider him heartless? I don't blame him if he gets a gun. I am a Southerner and know how to shoot.[32] Would you blame me if I did so under such circumstances?"[33] Wilson was delighted when the one automobile in Bermuda broke down and there was no mechanic on the island to repair it. In 1910, after the Wyman bequest precipitated Wilson's humiliating defeat in the graduate col-

[31] WW to Mary Allen Hulbert Peck, May 12, 1909, *ibid.*, Vol. 19, p. 193.

[32] As a boy, Wilson may have shot rabbits or squirrels, but there is no evidence that he had any skill with firearms.

[33] "The Young Man's Burden," speech reported in the *New York Times*, February 28, 1906, printed in *ibid.*, Vol. 16, p. 320.

lege controversy at Princeton, he made the statement that he hated automobiles because of the rich, empty-headed people who, for the most part, rode around in them.[34] When Wilson entered politics, he regularly used the metaphor in his speeches. He charged that cars were infernal machines and that their use by the rich would cause the spread of socialism, and he compared the heads of great business corporations who practiced abuses to reckless automobile drivers. During his first presidential campaign, after he had changed his views about the regulation of corporations, he used the same theme in an opposite context. By the time that he was elected President, motoring had become his favorite form of outdoor relaxation; the metaphor disappeared altogether from his political repertoire.

Wilson loved to play with symbols: he enjoyed puzzles and conundrums and took pleasure in reciting nonsense rhymes and limericks. Throughout his life he retained the sense of the romance of names and titles which he had had as a child. In Washington, he amused himself on automobile rides by reading aloud the inscription FREDERICK WILLIAM AUGUSTUS BARON VON STEUBEN every time his car went around the statue.[35] Wilson liked secret codes and nicknames. In the days when he aspired to be a writer of fiction, he used "Axson Mayte" as a pseudonym. At Wesleyan, he sent the essays of students competing for the history prize to his friend, J. Franklin Jameson, under the fictitious designations of "Sam," "Grotius," "Victim," and "McGinty." In his cabinet, Secretary of State William Jennings Bryan was "Primus," Secretary of the Navy Josephus Daniels was "Neptune." He was superstitious about the number thirteen. He was the thirteenth president of Princeton, and he told Dr. Grayson that one winter he and his family had consulted thirteen specialists.[36] He also observed that the names WOODROW WILSON and GEO. WASHINGTON each had thirteen letters.[37]

Like his father, Wilson had a great store of jokes and anecdotes. He was an excellent mimic and relished telling his stories in Scotch, Irish, and Negro dialects. He would often give his yarns an autobiographical flavor, such as "An old darkie who worked for my Uncle James" or "There was a former Confederate colonel who lived across the street from us in Wilmington."[38] Wilson was embarrassed by jokes about

[34] Interview with Jacob N. Beam, September 24, 1942, Bragdon Collection.

[35] Axson Memoir.

[36] The Diary of Cary T. Grayson (December 3, 1918 to September 27, 1919), MS. in the possession of Cary T. Grayson, May 13, 1919; hereinafter cited as the Grayson diary.

[37] William B. Hale, *The Story of a Style* (New York, 1920) p. 76.

[38] Interview with William F. Magie, July 13, 1941, Bragdon Collection.

sex,[39] but he occasionally told one which was mildly risqué.[40] Unlike Dr. Wilson, he was not hopelessly addicted to puns, but he was not completely above them. When he heard that Senator Carter Glass was an important figure in the Methodist Church, Wilson expressed surprise that the Methodists would raise a glass so high. As has been mentioned, he liked to joke about his minor ailments, particularly his gastrointestinal complaints. As his story of his encounter with Dr. Delafield indicates, he made a point of trying to get laughs out of his doctors.[41]

Wilson had much spontaneous wit. Once, when he read a paper on sovereignty to the Princeton Faculty Club, President-Emeritus McCosh was in attendance. When Wilson finished, McCosh commented, "Umph! I have always understood that sovereignty is derived from God." Wilson smiled and answered, "So did I, Dr. McCosh, but in this paper I was not going back that far."[42] On another occasion, some Princeton alumni banded together to build the Princeton Inn as a public benefit and petitioned for a liquor license. *The Voice*, a prohibition paper, objected to serving beer to students. Two of the petitioners lived in Morven,[43] the Revolutionary estate of Richard Stockton, who was one of the signers of the Declaration of Independence. Wilson commented that Morven had produced three signers, one for liberty and two for license.[44] Wilson enjoyed telling jokes about himself, but was less appreciative when they were told by others. While Governor of New Jersey, he had difficulties with the Republican-controlled Senate in 1912, mainly because he traveled about the country campaigning for the presidency. It was customary for the senators to give a dinner for the Governor toward the close of the legislative session. The menu at the 1912 dinner took the form of a cleverly done railroad timetable. Wilson was not amused.[45]

When the environment becomes less stable, orderly, and predictable in settings of stress, often there is a compensatory increase in metaphor and other forms of experiential symbolism. Words are more apt to express feelings, establish rapport, and maintain identity than desig-

---

[39] Reid, *Woodrow Wilson*, p. 73; Axson Memoir.

[40] A favorite one was about a woman who became embarrassed at a circus in which a performer could see through a board, and presumably clothing as well. "Let me get out of here," she said, "me with these thin things on."

[41] Axson Memoir.

[42] Baker, II, 18-19.

[43] Now the residence of the Governor of New Jersey.

[44] Axson Memoir.

[45] James Kerney, *The Political Education of Woodrow Wilson* (New York and London, 1926), pp. 205-206.

nate reality referentially. Symbols become more stereotyped, more condensed, and more self-referential. Thus descriptions of events, people, and places become, to a greater degree, representations of the speaker's own motivations. We have seen these processes in operation in Wilson's essays on Bismarck, Chatham, and Bright; in his poetry to Hattie Woodrow; and in his story about John Hart.

As has been noted, when Wilson wrote *George Washington*, he was under severe physical, emotional, and financial strain. By any literary or scholastic standard, the book is his most mediocre work. It is a mixture of fact and fancy—in this respect like any other popular biography of its day. Contemporary critics were surprised that someone of Wilson's eminence should have descended to writing a potboiler. In fact, Harper and Brothers, the publishers, claimed that the book would put Wilson into the first rank of novelists. Later biographers of Wilson have condemned or dismissed it. William Bayard Hale, who became a bitter enemy of Wilson, regarded *George Washington* as evidence of Wilson's deterioration as a scholar.[46] The important fact about the book is the way in which Wilson used it self-referentially to express his own political beliefs and symbolize his needs and aspirations.

George Washington was the apotheosis of the gospel of order which Wilson was preaching in the late 1890s.[47] Washington, he wrote, led the American armies against England, not primarily to oppose a legally established government, but to assert the rights of the colonists as Englishmen. After the Revolution, in the absence of effective national government under the Articles of Confederation, Washington was almost the only hope for stability and law. Wilson took pride in Washington's Virginian birth and breeding. The Old Dominion, he wrote, had been founded by freedom-loving Englishmen, who, aghast at the death of Charles I on the scaffold, had come to the New World because their political rights had been suppressed under the tyranny of Cromwell. The air of Virginia had liberated her public men from local prejudices and given them a vision of statesmanship that representatives of other regions lacked.[48]

[46] Hale, *The Story of a Style*, pp. 77-78. An amusing feature of Hale's book is its listing of Wilson's many linguistic affectations. It is noteworthy for students of language and personality as one of the first attempts at content analysis in the English language. Unfortunately, the book is marred by unsophisticated use of psychoanalytic terminology and some nonsensical ideas about "mental degeneration."

[47] Dr. Wilson told Woodrow, "You are preaching a gospel of order, and thus of safety, in the department of political morals and conduct." JRW to WW, March 6, 1889, enclosed in EAW to WW, March 8, 1889, *PWW*, Vol. 6, p. 137.

[48] Woodrow Wilson, *George Washington* (New York, 1897), p. 261.

Wilson used the book to air his own sentiments about Southerners, New Englanders, and the practice of law. New England delegates to the first Continental Congress had expected to see rustic squires from the South; instead, they found men of elegance and learning. While the men from the cities of the North had studied law for the narrow purposes of trade and litigation, Virginians had learned the law in order to administer their great estates. Written at a time when Wilson was strapped for money, parts of the book exude an atmosphere of wealth. The contrast between the aristocratic Virginians and the simple inhabitants of Massachusetts was to be shown in a suggestion that Wilson made to his illustrator, Howard Pyle: "On the eleventh day of December, 1775, Mrs. Washington, with escort of horsemen, arrived at her husband's headquarters in Cambridge in a coach and four, the horses ridden by black postilions in scarlet and white liveries. What a scene, of Virginian display and ceremony, for the somewhat bucolic and very democratic volunteers from the farms of New England, no doubt standing by with open, and leering, mouths, the stately commander-in-chief receiving the *little* [author's emphasis] lady, etc. What could you *not* make of it! It has taken great hold upon my fancy."[49]

The description of Washington's personality bears a close resemblance to Wilson's self-image. George was a model son, but he was not tied to his mother's apron strings. Like Jessie Wilson, George's mother prudently kept him from going to sea when he was fourteen. There are many references to Washington's good looks. As a youth, he was high-strung and "manly," with a passion for high achievement. Wilson described him as having strong sexual drives, as possessing "the blood of a lover beyond his fellows," which he had to fight to control.[50] Washington was self-disciplined in everything that he did, possessed a strong sense of duty, and followed the right because it was right.[51] He might seem cold and distant at times, but he was warm and sympathetic underneath. While fair in all things, he could be exacting to the point of harshness and had small patience with those who breached an agreement. Wilson does not fail to mention Washington's health, noting that he had a good digestion.[52] Another self-reference may be Wilson's account of how General Washington's friends, out of deep uneasiness about his health, urged him not to attempt a new campaign, and how Washington retired from the field only after he was sure that he had done his duty.[53]

[49] WW to Howard Pyle, February 4, 1896, *PWW*, Vol. 9, 402.
[50] *George Washington*, p. 101.
[51] *Ibid.*, p. 111.   [52] *Ibid.*, p. 77.   [53] *Ibid.*, pp. 94-95.

Wilson tried to write *George Washington* in the style of the eighteenth century, as a contemporary might have written.[54] The book contains many archaisms such as " 'tis" and " 'twas." The term "out of," as in "out of England," is used to indicate provenience. Martha Custis was "six-and-twenty" when Washington met her. The Old Dominion "made shift" to do without towns. By the end of the seventeenth century, the inhabitants of New England "mustered a full hundred thousand strong."[55] Interestingly, Wilson, during the period when he was writing *George Washington*, added " 'twas" and " 'twould" to his lecture on Edmund Burke.[56]

George Washington contains many physical descriptions of people and scenes, as if Wilson were typecasting and making stage settings. Among the dramatis personnae are "hardy frontiersmen" and "wily Indians," "shrewd fur traders" and "dauntless priests," Virginians with "the hottest blood of the Cavaliers," the "dark and distant" Lord Dunmore, Governor of Virginia, and the "truculent" General Braddock. There is a colorful description of Washington's campaigns against the French and Indians and Braddock's defeat. Interestingly, when Washington first faced the French in the open field, he was fighting in "manly" fashion. Later, when, in a similar situation, he advised Braddock to take cover, he was showing good judgment.

The book was a huge commercial success and went through several large printings. Wilson received many admiring letters from readers, and publishers vied for his services. His loyal Princeton classmates gave him a testimonial dinner at which they presented him with a replica of Houdon's bust of George Washington. The biography gave Wilson a popular image linked with that of a great American. The very features of language which, after *Division and Reunion*, made Wilson a superficial historian helped to make him a successful politician.

[54] Edward Ireland Renick to WW, January 13, 1896, *PWW*, Vol. 9, p. 379.
[55] *George Washington*, pp. 6, 11, 16, 99.
[56] Editorial Note, "Wilson's First Lecture on Burke," *PWW*, Vol. 8, 315.

CHAPTER IX

The First Strokes

WILSON'S FIRST KNOWN STROKE, in 1896, manifested itself in a weakness and loss of dexterity of his right hand, a numbness in the tips of several fingers, and some pain in the right arm. Aside from the pain, which was transitory, the symptoms and manner of onset indicate that he had suffered an occlusion of a central branch of the left middle cerebral artery. This vessel supplies the regions of the left cerebral hemisphere that control movement and sensation for the contralateral extremities. The subsequent course of the disease suggests that the branch was blocked by an embolus from the left internal carotid artery. (See Chapter 10.) The stroke of 1896 may not have been Wilson's first. In 1891, he had what he described as "a temporary illness (slight but immediately concerning my nerves)" that made it painful for him at the time to write even a letter.[1] The usual cause of strokes in young persons is hypertension, which Wilson later showed; however, in 1896, accurate measurement of blood pressure was not yet a part of the medical examination.

The question of whether emotional stress (such as that which Wilson underwent in 1895 and 1896) has a connection with high blood pressure and strokes is an enormously complicated one. While many clinicians, from their experience, believe that there is a relationship, there are no verified prospective studies to support this belief. The problem in large part is a methodological one, since it is difficult to define and quantify stress and to find an adequate control population, which will take all variables into account. The occurrence of Wilson's stroke in 1896, after a prolonged period of intense stress, appears more than coincidental. In contrast, subsequent episodes in 1904 and 1906 came at times of relative contentment.

In 1896 Wilson consulted Dr. William Williams Keen of Philadelphia, one of the foremost surgeons in the country. However, Dr. Keen probably did not recognize the nature of Wilson's problems, or, if he did, regarded it as not serious enough to postpone or cancel Wilson's planned trip to Great Britain. Wilson, accordingly, sailed for Glasgow, aboard *S.S. Ethiopia* of the Anchor Line. The course of his condition

[1] WW to Albert Bushnell Hart, August 21, 1891, *PWW*, Vol. 7, p. 274.

can be traced in his letters to his wife, which he wrote with his *left* hand.[2] While the abnormal sensation wore off, the lack of dexterity and weakness persisted; it was not until the middle of September (after his return to Princeton) that he was able to use his right hand for even an occasional signature. After this he wrote with his right hand only briefly and sporadically, including a notation in his desk diary on dining with Theodore Roosevelt on January 21, 1897. He mainly typed; on one occasion, he wrote the last paragraph of a letter to his wife with his right hand because "to do anything else would be too much like *kissing* you by machinery."[3] Wilson did not write consistently with his right hand until April 1897.

Wilson was able to write with his left hand almost immediately. He sustained the stroke on or about May 27 and sailed on May 30. Not knowing what the duration of his disability would be, and probably hoping that it would be short-lived, he probably did not practice writing with his left hand while still ashore. Aboard ship, in his first letter to his wife, he complained that he had had no opportunity to practice with his left hand.[4] Yet his left-handed script is perfectly legible, with well-formed characters. The difference between Wilson's normal right-handed penmanship is mainly in the slant of the letters. There is a slight deviation from the horizontal baseline, and the left-handed writing is more ornamental and old-fashioned with elaborate loops on the d's, g's, and l's.[5] Wilson's feat of ambidexterity is remarkable, neurologically. The left limbs of patients with right-sided paralysis following a stroke are usually very clumsy in contrast to the way in which a person who has lost the use of his right arm through a fracture may become rapidly dexterous with his left hand. The reason, according to Dr. Norman Geschwind,[6] is that a lesion in the motor region of the dominant left hemisphere interferes with the control by the right hemisphere of learned movements of the left arm. It is likely that Wilson's accomplishment was made possible by his bilateral cerebral representation of language and graphological skills.

Wilson's attitude toward his disability differed markedly from his reaction to past psychosomatic symptoms. These were manifestations of tension; he had complained openly, often dramatically, of his head-

[2] WW to EAW, June 9, 1896, *PWW*, Vol. 9, pp. 512-13.

[3] Wilson diary, January 21, 1897; WW to EAW, January 29, 1897, *ibid.*, Vol. 10, pp. 120, 124.

[4] WW to EAW, June 9, 1896, *ibid.*, Vol. 9, pp. 512-13.

[5] Karl Aschaffenburg of Princeton, N.J., kindly made the handwriting analysis.

[6] Norman Geschwind, "The Apraxias: Neural Mechanisms of Disorders of Learned Movement," *American Scientist*, LXIII (March-April 1975), 188-95.

106 High St., Middletown, Ct,
16 December, 1888

My precious father,

My thoughts are full of you and dear 'Dode' all the time. Tennessee seems so far away for a chap as hungry as I am for a sight of the two men whom I love. As the Christmas seers approaches I realize, as I have so often before, the pain there is in a season of holiday and rejoicing away from you. As you know, one of the chief things about which I feel most warranted in rejoicing is that I am your son. I realize the benefit of being your son'

Wilson's normal right-hand script

THE GRAND HOTEL,
CHARING CROSS,
GLASGOW.

[June 11, 1896]

My own sweetheart

Here I am in Glasgow. We got in at about two this morning, had breakfast at six on the boat, and got up to the hotel about 8:30. = I am very well. The voyage did me good for all it was so tedious. We did not learn of the savage gale that caught the "Umbria" (Cunarder) in the n. Atlantic till we reached Londonderry yesterday, tho. we had very rough weather on the same days, catching, no doubt, the outer edge of the storm. The U. left the same day but went further north.

When I say "we" reached the hotel I mean my delightful southern friends of the voyage and I.

I called on the Sec'y of the University faculty this afternoon, but he was out. To-morrow I call

---

Letter written left-handed by Wilson soon after his stroke of 1896

again; and rest.

Your sweet 1st. letter came to-day, and fills my heart with a love and tenderness unspeakable. Ah, my love, my Eileen, how can I stay away from you!

I must not drive this hand further. Love to Mrs. Brown. Ask Hibben to make out the check for interest in your name. Write to father.

I would give my trip and everything else to be in your arms!

Your own

Woodrow.

aches and "colds" and joked about his digestive troubles. In contrast, he now ignored, denied, and minimized the paralysis of his arm and showed no overt sign of anxiety or depression. When his cablegrams, which announced his arrival at various points on his itinerary, contained no news of his health, his worried wife had to wire back for information.[7] He gave highly optimistic reports in his letters. Not only was he well, he told Ellen, but he was *very* well."[8] Actually, the only things he complained about on his trip were his "useless left hand" and his hemorrhoids—"these wretched piles."[9] Commenting on his attendance at the anniversary celebration of Lord Kelvin's tenure at the University of Glasgow, he called it "as hard a thirty-six hours' work as a able-bodied man would want."[10] Although his syphon broke and he had to discontinue his stomach lavage for two weeks, there were no ill effects on his digestion.[11]

Nor did Wilson complain of the severe loneliness that had hitherto been an accurate indicator of depression. He thoroughly enjoyed his summer in England and Scotland. Despite his clumsy hand, he took long bicycle trips and visited Oxford and Cambridge and the shrines of his heroes. He went to Adam Smith's grave, saw the church in which Burke was buried, and was enchanted by Langport in Somersetshire, the birthplace of Bagehot. In Edinburgh, he went to Greyfriars Church, a building that he had so often envisioned. Throughout his journey, he met interesting traveling companions. He felt especially close to Ellen when he went through the Wordsworth country and spent an afternoon at the National Gallery in London.

Wilson returned to Princeton in September with a vigor and aggressiveness that surprised Stockton Axson.[12] He immediately set to work on his address, "Princeton in the Nation's Service," for the Princeton sesquicentennial celebration, at which he was to be the principal speaker. He typed the first eleven pages of his manuscript with his left hand before turning the work over to others. He went on, over the subsequent months, to work at his usual pace, typing notes and letters or having Mrs. Wilson write them in longhand. He

[7] EAW to WW, June 18, 1896, *PWW*, Vol. 9, p. 520.

[8] WW to EAW, June 11, 1896, *ibid.*, p. 513.

[9] WW to EAW, June 9, 11, 13, and 14, 1896, *ibid.*, pp. 512-15.

[10] WW to EAW, June 17, 1896, *ibid.*, p. 519.

[11] WW to EAW, July 13, 1896, *ibid.*, p. 538.

[12] WW to EAW, June 13, 19, 21, 23, 26, 28, 29, July 20 and 26, August 12, *ibid.*, pp. 514, 521-22, 523-24, 526, 527, 528, 542, 547, 565. On greeting Wilson, Axson asked him how he had liked England. Wilson replied that it had made him a better American. His next remark was an attack on William Jennings Bryan and the "Cross of Gold" speech. Axson Memoir.

apologized to some of his friends for typing rather than writing, saying that he had been "threatened" with an attack of "writer's cramp"— another aspect of his denial of the seriousness of his condition.[13] According to Baker, Wilson was so reticent to let many of his friends know about his trouble that they felt aggrieved by his apparent neglect of them.[14]

The stroke was a far more stressful experience for Wilson than his psychosomatic ailments had been. His digestive disturbances and headaches had been self-limited and manageable: they appeared when he was lonely, depressed, and under pressure, and they had departed promptly with relief of tension. The weakness of his arm, however, did not clear up even after many months of rest. Wilson's psychosomatic symptoms had rarely interfered with his work, while his affected arm handicapped him considerably. Wilson may not have known that he had had a stroke, but he must have been distressed by a condition which had appeared so suddenly and unexpectedly and which persisted so relentlessly.

Wilson's denial and minimization of his illness was an integral part of his personality and the expression of an important cultural value. People with so-called "anosognosic,"[15] or denial personalities, tend to conceive of the manifestations of incapacity in terms of principles and values which transcend the intrinsic physical features of the situation. They regard health and illness as moral issues and believe that the maintenance of health is a matter of personal duty and responsibility. Like the inhabitants of Samuel Butler's *Erewhon* (where illness was a crime) they react to incapacity with feelings of embarrassment, shame, and guilt. To admit impairment is to lose status and self-respect. Wilson's father had taught him that one remained well by following the laws of right living and fulfilling one's obligation to God, so that becoming ill represented some moral weakness or dereliction of duty (a common Protestant understanding in the late nineteenth century). Denial thus became a means to avoid anxiety and depression and to preserve one's sense of personal integrity.

Denial of illness is closely linked to attitudes toward work and accomplishment. People who deny and minimize their disabilities are

[13] "Princeton in the Nation's Service," October 21, 1896; WW to Francis Henry Smith, October 13, 1896; WW to Charles William Kent, November 11, 1896; WW to Albert Shaw, November 16, 1896, *PWW*, Vol. 10, pp. 11, n.1, 6, 49, 54.

[14] Baker, *Wilson*, II, 31.

[15] From the Greek, anosognosia means "lack of knowledge of disease." For a fuller description, see Edwin A. Weinstein and Robert L. Kahn, *Denial of Illness: Symbolic and Physiological Aspects* (Springfield, Ill., 1955), pp. 71-84.

usually highly work-oriented. They are generally described by their relatives and colleagues as highly conscientious and compulsive about work. They are punctual and orderly, stubborn, and insistent on being "right." By reason of their intelligence, drive, and sense of responsibility, they—men, particularly—are often quite successful in business and the professions. Even when ill, they continue to work and tend to avoid consulting doctors. Paradoxically, they may attribute symptoms to overwork. When idle, they tend to become restless and anxious. While they ignore or rationalize manifestations of illness in themselves, persons with denial personalities are apt to be very solicitous of others. They are usually leaders of the family and are seen as practical, reserved, and controlled. They are conventional in tastes and habits, rarely artistic or creative.

The mechanisms of denial are strengthened by the tendency of persons with "anosognosic" personalities to regard the manifestations of illness as detached from the real self and capable of carrying on an existence of their own. Thus, after Wilson's stroke in 1906, when he became almost blind in his left eye and weak in his right hand, he wrote to his sister: "I am puzzled what to report about myself. I have never *felt* as if there were anything the matter with me, you know, except for the eye."[16] Like Wilson, patients are apt to refer to a disabled part of the body not as "my eye" or "my arm," but rather as "the eye" or "that arm."[17] For Wilson, the body was the servant of the spirit, and he believed that the mind could control the body. After his loss of vision, he told his wife that he would train the eye to behave. Woodrow Wilson did not regard his behavior as a denial of reality stemming from culturally derived imperatives.[18] Rather, he probably saw himself as manly and courageous, considerate of his family, and unwilling to admit defeat by unknown forces.

According to Stockton Axson, there was a change in Wilson's behavior after his stroke. He became more energetic and purposive and

[16] WW to Annie Wilson Howe, August 2, 1906, *PWW*, Vol. 16, p. 432.

[17] A letter from Franklin D. Roosevelt to one of his doctors provides a striking example of this dichotomy. He wrote: "*My* own legs continue to improve," but "I cannot get rid of the brace on *that* left leg yet. It is still a mystery to me as to why *that* left knee declines to lock." (Italics mine.) Burns, *The Lion and the Fox,* p. 88.

[18] Reid, *Woodrow Wilson,* p. 94. Denial of illness is still common, but probably less so than fifty years ago. Among the factors associated with the change are advances in medical science, lessening of fear of doctors, weakening of the work ethic and the ideal of "rugged individualism," and a diminution of the social stigma attached to certain diseases and the romanticizing of others. One might compare the public recording of the illnesses of Presidents, beginning with Dwight D. Eisenhower, with the concealment of the illnesses of his predecessors.

less relaxed. He became more critical of people and was more reluctant to offer praise. He appeared "all business" and took little or no time for recreation. He gave up billiards and bicycling for pleasure, and only occasionally dropped into the Nassau Club for conversation and gossip. He systematized his work schedule further so that he lectured only on Mondays and Tuesdays, in order to leave the rest of the week free for writing and out-of-town activities. Axson also believed that, before 1896, Wilson had paid relatively little attention to the revolutionary changes that had been going on in American education. However, after his stroke, beginning with his sesquicentennial address, he became more interested in the relationship of liberal education to national affairs. The crisis, Axson thought, "freshened his sense of mission in the world.[19]

The increase in concentration may have been responsible for a recurrence of his digestive troubles. In 1898 he consulted Dr. William W. Van Valzah of New York, probably the first physician who understood the nature of Wilson's gastrointestinal problem. Dr. Van Valzah took him off the stomach tube and put him on a diet. The details are not specified, but the doctor probably lightened Wilson's habitual regimen of fried chicken, green beans cooked in heavy grease, gravies, corn, and rice and substituted some green vegetables and fruit. The change was successful. Put another way, Wilson's digestion was good when he was calm enough to observe his diet.[20] When he appeared under tension, in 1899, his wife and friends persuaded him to spend the summer abroad, and he went on a tour of Scotland and England with Stockton Axson. He took up golf, probably under protest. He eventually found that the game relaxed him and that, by concentrating on his shots, he could shut out his problems. When his right arm bothered him, he played left-handed. In 1900, he had a recurrence of the left facial twitching that had so alarmed his father in 1896. It seems likely that it was a nervous tic rather than a sign of any organic brain involvement, since Wilson noted that the movements came on only when he was upset or overtired.[21] He had some persisting weakness of his right upper extremity, or possibly it was another stroke. He considered hypnosis,[22] and took some exercises guaranteed by a

[19] Axson Memoir.

[20] WW to EAW, July 13, 1899, PWW, Vol. 11, p. 165.

[21] WW to EAW, August 9, 1899; WW to William B. Pritchard, July 5, 1900, ibid., pp. 213-17, 553-54. Wilson probably took up golf sometime during late 1898. See the Daily Princetonian, April 12, 1899, which noted that he would take part in the Spring Handicap Tournament on April 12, 1899, with a handicap of sixteen.

[22] Henry Mills Alden to WW, October 8, 1900, PWW, Vol. 12, p. 22.

notorious quack, Alois B. Swoboda, to strengthen his arm.[23] It is unlikely that either Swoboda's exercises or the prescription of drinking four pints of water a day had any effect, but Wilson had no further neurological manifestations until 1904.

Wilson's health during the period after his recovery from his stroke may have been better than his wife's. Early in 1896, she had an episode of nausea, abdominal pain, and fever. Dr. Wikoff suspected typhoid fever or peritonitis and kept her in bed for a week.[24] There is no record of a urine analysis, so it is possible that she had had another attack of pyelonephritis. The following year she developed a soreness in the region of the appendix and again was in bed.[25] She consulted Dr. Van Valzah, who decided, after several examinations, that her symptoms were due to nervousness.[26] However, she continued to feel sick at her stomach and had a "loathing" for food.[27] Wilson, at this time, was in Baltimore and eager for Ellen to visit so that she could meet Mrs. Reid. Her courage failed her when one of the children cut an eyelid, but Woodrow urged that she not let "one little accident" rob her of her self-possession.[28] Later, she was reluctant, partly because she was not feeling well, and partly because she thought the atmosphere was too sophisticated for a "country-bred wife" like herself. She cited Dr. Van Valzah's opinion that a "week of social engagements" would be too much for her. Wilson and Mrs. Reid insisted and, as the day of her departure approached, she woke up with a violent sick headache.[29] After postponing the visit several times, Ellen went and evidently had a good time.

Ellen's symptoms may also have been related to the strain she was experiencing over her husband's health and her inability completely to reveal her fears to him. She wrote to her confidante, Anna Harris, after the death of a mutual friend: "I cannot somehow shake off for a moment the weight it has laid upon my spirits, all the more so perhaps because for Woodrow's sake I must not show it. He is almost terribly dependent on me to keep up his spirits and to 'rest' him as he says. So I dare not have the 'blues.' If I am just a little sky-blue he immediately becomes blue-black!"[30]

[23] Alois P. Swoboda to WW, October 2, 1901, *ibid.*, pp. 190-91.

[24] EAW to WW, January 24 and 25, 1896, *ibid.*, Vol. 9, pp. 388-89.

[25] Wilson diary, January 17, 1897, *ibid.*, Vol. 10, p. 119.

[26] EAW to WW, February 3, 1898, *ibid.*, p. 374.

[27] EAW to WW, February 5, 1898, *ibid.*, p. 376.

[28] EAW to WW, February 8, 1898; WW to EAW, February 9, 1898, *ibid.*, pp. 380, 383.

[29] EAW to WW, February 20, 1898, *ibid.*, p. 404.

[30] EAW to Anna Harris, January 31, 1899, *ibid.*, Vol. 11, p. 102.

The sesquicentennial of the founding of Princeton, elaborately organized by Andrew Fleming West, Professor of Classics, was a magnificent three-day affair. The participants included outstanding academic figures from the United States and Europe who, gowned and
hooded, formed the most brilliant academic procession ever seen in
America. Unfortunately, the brilliance of the celebration was not
matched by Princeton's advance toward becoming a major university.
The growing discontent of the younger faculty over the lack of progress
centered on the continuing low standards of scholarship, loose discipline, and the failure of the administration to establish a graduate
school. The first trustees' committee on the graduate school could not
raise an adequate endowment, and President Patton was able to prevent further action until 1900. At that time the trustees formally established the graduate school, with West as its dean. In the same year
the faculty created the University Committee on Scholarship, or "Vice
Committee," under the chairmanship of Professor William Francis
Magie. Two years later it made recommendations for drastic reforms.
Again, Patton, a master of delay, was able to sidetrack the report by
having it resubmitted to the committee.

However, changes were on the way. The alumni moved successfully
to gain direct representation on the board of trustees. The first alumni
trustees were elected in 1901. Unlike the older trustees, who accepted
Dr. Patton's guidance and were content with the status quo, the newer
members (including those among the charter trustees) were in close
touch with Wilson and other faculty members and were well aware
of the state of affairs at Princeton. Moreover, they were wealthy men,
who could help to implement progress in a material way.[31]

Wilson shared the unhappiness of his associates. He was particularly
distressed when Patton and conservative Presbyterians on the board
of trustees persuaded a majority of the board to turn down his strong
recommendation of Frederick Jackson Turner for a chair in history
because Turner was a Unitarian. (Turner probably would have come
to Princeton.) Wilson seriously considered resigning and accepting an
offer to become the first President of the University of Virginia (the
University had heretofore been governed by a faculty committee).
However, he remained at Princeton when Cyrus Hall McCormick and
other trustees appealed to his Princeton loyalties and provided him
with a supplement of $2,500 to his annual salary. When Dr. Patton
appointed an ineffectual supporter to be Dean of the Faculty, Wilson

[31] Editorial Note, "The Crisis in Presidential Leadership at Princeton," *ibid.*, Vol. 12,
pp. 289-93.

showed his displeasure by resigning from the Discipline Committee. Yet, Wilson, a superb academic politician, was not one of Patton's more active critics. He did not join the "Vice Committee," since he knew that he was in line for the presidency and did not want to antagonize Patton's supporters.[32]

The anti-Patton trustees had gained control of the board by 1902. A group of them informed Dr. Patton that he must either resign or else allow the university to be run by an executive committee. Wilson was asked to draw up a plan for the transition. Generous financial provisions for Patton were made; it was agreed that he could retain his professorship and that his son should be promoted to full professor; and Patton resigned. After he had strongly advised against the selection of Dean West (his most active critic), Patton nominated Wilson as his successor. In a move to forestall a possible contest, the trustees suspended a bylaw that required a day's interval between the resignation of one president and the election of another. Woodrow Wilson was unanimously elected the thirteenth President of Princeton on June 9, 1902.[33]

Dr. Wilson lived to rejoice in his son's election, but his mental capacity and physical health declined markedly in the last years of his life. He became petulant and irritable, and his celebrated wit ran at times to the puerile.[34] He developed frequent episodes of severe abdominal pain and required opiates for relief. Periods of "rigor" were followed by stupor, probably sequelae to the convulsive seizures.[35] The burden of nursing fell on Ellen, since Sister Annie was abroad in 1901-1902 with her son, George, who was studying in Germany. Wilson gave up his sabbatical year to be with his father and spent long hours with him talking, reading, and singing the old man's favorite hymns.[36] Dr. Wilson died on January 21, 1903, a few weeks short of his eighty-first birthday. The cause of death, Wilson wrote to a family friend,

[32] Bragdon, *Wilson*, p. 275.

[33] Cyrus Hall McCormick to David Benton Jones, April 16, 1902; David Benton Jones to Cyrus Hall McCormick, May 31, 1902; minutes of the board of trustees of Princeton University, June 9, 1902, *PWW*, Vol. 12, pp. 342-43, 385, 398-402.

[34] Dr. Wilson never lost his sense of humor. After he had lapsed into a stupor several weeks before his death, the family was summoned to Woodrow's house. By the time that a relative had arrived, Dr. Wilson had recovered consciousness but was still confused. He did not recognize the relative and asked what he was doing in the house. The visitor replied that he had just "dropped in," whereupon the old man commented, "I am a little dropsical myself." Axson Memoir.

[35] James Sprunt to WW, January 12, 1901, *PWW*, Vol. 12, p. 72; WW to EAW, July 18, 1902; EAW to Mary E. Hoyt, December 15, 1902, *ibid.*, Vol. 14, pp. 24, 294.

[36] Axson Memoir; Baker, *Wilson*, II, 142.

was "thickening of the arteries, which resulted in a slow clogging of the action of the organs, and resulted finally in blood poisoning."[37] The deterioration of Dr. Wilson's mental faculties and the seizures are compatible with cerebral and renal arteriosclerosis; the episodes of abdominal pain may have been the result of occlusion of mesenteric (intestinal) blood vessels; and the "blood poisoning" is suggestive of uremia.

Wilson's presidency of Princeton University began auspiciously. He was in good health, and his election was widely acclaimed in the academic world. A committee of the faculty, of which Dean West was a member, drew up a resolution of general approval. His classmates gave him a "coronation banquet," the program of which showed a cartoon of Wilson dancing on a pier in the embrace of an exultant Princeton tiger. Floating away in the stream were top hats with the initials of the reputedly unsuccessful candidates. Wilson's inauguration in October, an event of national significance, was attended by scholars, literary men, politicians, and business leaders.[38] From the women's colleges came representatives of Mount Holyoke, Wellesley, and Radcliffe, but none from Bryn Mawr. Among the messages of congratulations was an invitation from Theodore Roosevelt to visit the White House. The only dissenting voice was that of J. McKeen Cattell, editor of *Science*, who regarded Wilson as hostile to science.[39]

As Wilson prepared to assume his office, he felt confident, relaxed, and involved. He had none of the sense of detachment that had accompanied his achievements in the past. From his summer vacation retreat in New England, he wrote to his wife: "Yesterday I had a snug snooze of a couple of hours, the fruit of sheer laziness. . . . I think a good deal about college affairs these quiet hours, but not to fatigue. The right to *plan* is so novel, the element of vexation, the sense of helplessness we had for so long, is so entirely removed, that it is a pleasure to think out the work that is to be done. If it did not have the incalculable money element in it, there would be no touch of worry about any of it."[40] He saw his old friends Heath Dabney and Bliss Perry and visited Junius S. Morgan, the nephew of J. P. Morgan and

[37] WW to Mrs. Christian S. Baker, April 20, 1903, *PWW*, Vol. 14, p. 417.

[38] The guests included Booker T. Washington, Mark Twain, William Dean Howells, J. Pierpont Morgan, Henry C. Frick, Robert T. Lincoln, and Thomas B. Reed, Speaker of the House of Representatives. See the account in the *Princeton Alumni Weekly*, III (November 1, 1902), 83-86, printed in *ibid.*, pp. 191-95.

[39] Theodore Roosevelt to WW, October 18, 1902; WW to Bridges, July 17, 1902, *ibid.*, pp. 147-48, 21-22, n.2.

[40] WW to EAW, August 6, 1902, *ibid.*, p. 57.

a Princeton trustee, at his estate on the Maine coast. There Wilson enjoyed a fishing trip, an activity that he had not liked as a young man in Wilmington. He concluded his vacation by spending a week in New Hampshire with friends from Princeton, the John Grier Hibbens and John Howell Westcotts. Edith Gittings Reid thought that he was happier and gayer than he had ever been or was to be.[41]

On his return to Princeton, Wilson presented to the board of trustees a report on the financial state of the university, with an estimate of the cost of the programs he hoped to implement. It included introduction of a preceptorial (or group tutorial) system, the development of the graduate school, the creation of schools of jurisprudence and electrical engineering, and the establishment of a museum of natural history. The total cost of these undertakings amounted to $12,500,000, four times the existing endowment of the university. Staggering as the sum was, Wilson believed that it could be raised from interested and wealthy alumni. In explaining the need for the preceptorial method, Wilson pointed out that students were not learning through the lecture system. The lecture, he said, should stimulate students to seek further information, and the preceptors would supervise their reading and discuss it with them. Examinations would not, as in the past, be on lectures alone, but on the subject as a whole. Wilson emphasized the importance of scientific research and the necessity of building up the physics and biological laboratories, and he dwelt upon the place of theoretical scientific knowledge in liberal education.[42]

These proposals marked a radical change from Wilson's previous attitudes and practices. Lecturing had been the basis of his teaching, and his examination questions had been taken from the material of his dictated notes. In his article on Adam Smith, he had eloquently extolled the virtues of the old-style lecture.[43] In his sesquicentennial address of 1896, he had deprecated the laboratory in favor of "the world of books" and had attacked science for breeding "a spirit of experiment and a contempt for the past."[44] The changes indicate what Wilson had learned about education over the intervening six years. They also illustrate the difference between self-referential, metaphor-

[41] WW to EAW, August 12, 13, 16, 17, and 19, 1902, *ibid.*, pp. 76-77, 79-80, 89, 89-90, 93; Reid, *Woodrow Wilson*, p. 87.

[42] Report to the board of trustees of Princeton University, October 21, 1902, *PWW*, Vol. 14, pp. 150-161.

[43] Fragment of a draft of a lecture on Adam Smith, c. November 20, 1883, *ibid.*, Vol. 2, pp. 543-44.

[44] "Princeton in the Nation's Service," October 21, 1896, *ibid.*, Vol. 10, pp. 29-30.

ical speech, which served as a mode of adaptation to stress, and a more explicit referential style of communication.

At the time of his sesquicentennial address, Wilson was suffering from the effects of his stroke. He still had literary ambitions and was defending himself against charges of lack of scholarship. His criticism that science would destroy the spirit of literature and history was largely a defense of his own methods, and he represented literature and science in highly rhetorical fashion. Literature, Wilson said, walked "within her open doors in quiet chambers with men of olden time, storied walls about her, and calm voices infinitely sweet; here 'magic casements, opening on the foam of perilous seas, in fairy lands forlorn.' " On the other hand, he had given a gloomy lifeless image of "calm Science seated there, recluse, ascetic, like a nun, not knowing that the world passes, not caring, if the truth but come in answer to her prayer."[45] In 1902, Wilson thought that the "closeted scholar should throw his windows open to the four quarters of the world" and, aside from a scattering of references to "fresh air," "sunlight," and "quickening of the pulses,"[46] there are no vivid metaphors or quotations of poetry.

Wilson proceeded to build up a strong faculty as quickly as possible. He had received from the board of trustees authority to dismiss incompetent professors without cause, but he used this power only occasionally and tactfully in his first few years.[47] He turned to the eminent biologist, Henry Fairfield Osborn, for guidance in the organization of the biological sciences and the establishment of the museum of natural history.[48] He put Henry Burchard Fine, his new Dean of Faculty, to work recruiting mathematicians and physicists. The mathematical physicist James Hopwood Jeans came from Cambridge University in 1905; a year later, he was followed by Owen Willens Richardson, who was to win a Nobel Prize for his work at Princeton. When John Huston Finley resigned as Professor of Politics in June 1903 to accept the presidency of the College of the City of New York, Wilson replaced him with Harry Augustus Garfield, the son of the former President, who had made a great reputation as a municipal reformer in Cleveland. Garfield, with Wilson's blessing, went on to become President of Williams College. When Edward Samuel Corwin was interviewed for

[45] *Ibid.,* p. 31.

[46] "Princeton for the Nation's Service," October 22, 1902, *ibid.,* Vol. 14, pp. 174, *passim.*

[47] WW to Charles William Leverett Johnson, April 7, 1903, *ibid.,* Vol. 14, p. 404.

[48] Henry Fairfield Osborn to WW, September 10, 1902, *ibid.,* pp. 126-29.

a position as a preceptor in political science, he was surprised to learn that Wilson had not read Henry Jones Ford's distinguished *Rise and Growth of American Politics*. Wilson promptly read the book and brought Ford in as a professor of political science.[49] Wilson's refusal to be influenced by religious preference was shown when he engaged Frank Thilly as Professor of Psychology, after having been told by Thilly that he was not a member of a church and that he was concerned about conflicts between science and revealed religion.[50] Wilson himself continued to teach a course each semester.

The new administration soon stiffened entrance requirements and academic standards. In 1902 it was announced that students must pass over half their courses or be dropped. In 1903 over a quarter of the applicants for admission were refused; after mid-year examinations forty-six students, including some athletes, were asked to leave college. This Draconian policy, as the *Princeton Alumni Weekly* called it,[51] created unhappiness among students and their parents, but it had the desired effect. Professors upgraded their courses, and a senior song memorialized one easy marker:

> He had to make his courses hard
> Or he couldn't play in Woodie's yard.[52]

The new rigor produced a sharp drop in undergraduate disciplinary offenses, and the measures taken had the strong backing of the faculty and trustees. Wilson spoke frequently to the alumni and won their support.[53] Wilson and Dean Fine also kept in touch with the students through communications in campus publications and consultation with the elected Senior Council. Nor were the rules enforced arbitrarily. In a message to the *Daily Princetonian*, Wilson, in explaining an exception that had been made, stated that no penalty would be attached to conditions acquired retroactively.[54]

The Committee on the Course of Study, with Wilson as its head, achieved the first thoroughgoing reorganization of the curriculum in Princeton's history. Previously, the University had been divided be-

[49] Interview with Edward S. Corwin, June 9, 1959, Bragdon Collection.

[50] WW to Frank Thilly, February 1, 1904, *PWW*, Vol. 15, p. 152.

[51] *Princeton Alumni Weekly*, III (March 7, 1903), 355, printed in *ibid.*, Vol. 14, p. 383.

[52] Quoted in Bragdon, *Wilson*, p. 288.

[53] See, for example, accounts of such addresses before alumni at Harrisburg, Pa., February 20, 1903; Pittsburgh, March 8, 1903; and Newark, N.J., May 16, 1903, *PWW*, Vol. 14, pp. 362, 385, 462.

[54] WW to the Editor of the *Daily Princetonian*, February 28, 1903, printed in *ibid.*, p. 379.

tween the Academic Department and the School of Science. The admission requirements of candidates for the B.S. degree did not include Greek, and the variety of subjects that could be substituted had led to the admission of poorly prepared students. Moreover, they could choose from a wide range of academic subjects, so that, in effect, the School of Science was often graduating men with little training in science. Under the new plan, the alternatives to Greek were limited, and the course of study centered on science and mathematics. For men who wanted a liberal arts program without having to take Greek, the Bachelor of Letters degree was instituted. Upperclassmen were required to concentrate their studies in a single department, and the number of elective courses for them, which had proliferated during the Patton years, was markedly restricted.[55] Wilson noted that the new plan of study was not quite the scheme he had proposed at the outset, but a much better one.[56] Wilson also reorganized the administrative structure of the university, which under the Patton regime had been chaotic. The Department of Philosophy had included not only moral and mental philosophy (psychology), but also history and politics. Each professor had been directly accountable to the President. Wilson created eleven departments corresponding to subjects and appointed a head of each to handle its administration.[57]

Working closely with alumni and trustees, Wilson took an active part in fund raising. He frequently addressed alumni clubs and kept them informed about developments and plans. Under Wilson's leadership, Princeton was the first university to organize the solicitation of funds from its alumni on a systematic basis. Wilson personally wrote to designated alumni and to other prospective donors. Among them was Andrew Carnegie, who, Wilson hoped, would give a liberal endowment to the best "Scottish" university in America. Instead, Carnegie donated a lake. Despite Wilson's disappointment over receiving cake when he had asked for bread (as he reputedly said to Carnegie),[58] he and the steel master gave delightfully witty speeches at the dedication of Lake Carnegie.

As he had done at the beginning of previous years, Wilson kept a diary briefly in 1904. Its contents reveal the relative informality of his official schedule,[59] the ready approval of his actions by the faculty, his

[55] Editorial Note, "The New Princeton Course of Study," *ibid.*, Vol. 15, pp. 277-92.
[56] WW to EAW, April 26, 1904, *ibid.*, p. 296.
[57] WW memorandum, c. November 20, 1903, *ibid.*, pp. 55-56.
[58] Howard Russell Butler, "The History of the Lake," *Princeton Alumni Weekly,* V (April 29, 1905), 489-92.
[59] An entry for Sunday, January 3, reads: "West came in at noon for a little chat, and

enjoyment of his social activities, and his close friendship with John Grier and Jenny Davidson Hibben.[60] Hibben had come to Princeton as Professor of Logic in 1897, and he and his wife became the Wilsons' closest friends. The two men saw each other almost daily and corresponded when they were separated. Hibben was not a noted scholar or teacher but a very pleasant person who was universally liked. Wilson had complete confidence in him and would designate him as acting president when he was away.[61] Hibben was appointed to so many committees that faculty members regarded him as Wilson's personal representative.[62] Wilson may have been even more devoted to Jenny Hibben, whose conversation he enjoyed and who wrote him many admiring and affectionate letters. Interestingly, despite their close friendship, Wilson in his courtly fashion, at least in their correspondence, never addressed her by her first name.

Until 1904, nothing happened to disturb Wilson's harmonious relationships with the faculty and trustees. He remained active in the Nassau Club, and he and Mrs. Wilson entertained regularly at "faculty dinings" at Prospect, the President's house.[63] In faculty meetings, he was occasionally arrogant and sarcastic when opposed, but he was open to persuasion and would change his mind if good reasons were shown to him.[64] One day in a faculty meeting, after he had given a long involved explanation, Wilson's good friend, George McLean Harper, Professor of English, accused him of quibbling. Wilson became angry and gave Harper a verbal scorching. Walking home, depressed by the incident, Harper felt a hand on his shoulder. It was Wilson who said, "Don't let this little spat spoil our friendship."[65]

Wilson had another episode of weakness of his right hand in the summer of 1904. Neither the date of onset or duration of disability is clear, but the episode probably began some time after May 27, at which time Wilson wrote a letter to his wife in longhand, as was his custom.[66] He first mentioned his weakness in a typed letter to Jack Hibben on July 23.[67] An example of adaptation and denial was Wilson's apology to a friend for the use of "the typewriter." He wrote:

---

after him Hibben and [Joseph Heatley] Dulles." Wilson diary, January 3, 1904, *PWW*, Vol. 15, p. 117.

[60] Wilson diary, January 4, 1904, *ibid.*, p. 117.

[61] Axson Memoir.

[62] Undated interview with William F. Magie, Bragdon Collection.

[63] Axson Memoir.

[64] William B. Scott, *Some Memories of a Paleontologist* (Princeton, N.J., 1939), p. 258.

[65] Interview with George M. Harper, July 1, 1939, Bragdon Collection.

[66] WW to EAW, May 27, 1904, *PWW*, Vol. 15, pp. 350-51.

[67] WW to John Grier Hibben, July 23, 1904, *ibid.*, p. 420.

"I find real difficulty now-a-days in using the pen, because of an immoderate use of it in the past."[68] Ordinarily, Wilson, in referring to the pen, would have used the first person possessive. The degree of incapacity was probably less than he had experienced in 1896 and 1897, but the period of disability in 1904 was associated with several incidents which show Wilson acting in an impulsive, oversensitive, and highly arbitrary fashion. The first involved Wilson's dismissal of Arnold Guyot Cameron, Professor of French. Cameron, an erratic person, was well known for his bizarre behavior in the classroom. Although he seldom taught any French, he amused his students and had three times been voted the most popular professor. Because of Cameron's idiosyncrasies, Wilson had appointed Williamson Updyke Vreeland, Cameron's junior in rank, as head of the Department of Romance Languages as part of his administrative reorganization. Wilson had long regarded Cameron as a "charlatan" and a "mountebank," but he did not take definite action until Cameron told a class of students that women were good only for raising bread, babies, and hell. This remark, Wilson felt, "went beyond the bounds of decency." He consulted John Lambert Cadwalader, an alumni trustee, and pondered Cadwalader's advice to proceed with the dismissal. Two or three weeks before commencement, Wilson met with Cameron at Prospect; he asked him to resign and offered him an additional year of employment. Cameron became excited and, in the heat of the discussion, said something that made Wilson feel that he had been insulted in his own home. Deeply offended, Wilson ordered Cameron out of the house and withdrew his offer of an extra year of employment.

The Cameron affair had a long history. Guyot Cameron was a member of an old Princeton family; he was the son of Henry Clay Cameron and the nephew of Arnold Guyot, both of whom had taught Wilson. The elder Cameron had been secretary of the faculty for many years, and Wilson, as a faculty member, had been as critical of the way he kept the minutes as he had been of the manner in which Cameron had taught Greek in Wilson's undergraduate years. Wilson's criticism had extended to Cameron family affairs. Wilson was shocked when, after young Cameron's marriage, his father and mother had refused to speak to the bride. In his turn, Guyot Cameron disliked Wilson. He was reputed to be the source of a story in the New York *Evening Sun*, which accused Wilson of unscrupulous conduct in the resignation of President Patton, and had circulated the article on the campus.[69]

[68] WW to Fannie Bayle King, October 20, 1904, *ibid.*, p. 522.
[69] Interview with Jacob N. Beam, December 19, 1939, Bragdon Collection.

Hearing of Cameron's dismissal, Wilson Farrand, a classmate and close friend of Cameron, and later a Princeton trustee, attempted to intercede. He guaranteed Guyot's good behavior and told Wilson that he would induce the students to call off their planned parade of protest if Wilson would permit Cameron to stay another year. Wilson refused, but Farrand persuaded the students not to march and wrote a letter of apology which Cameron signed. Wilson accepted it and granted the additional year. During this period Cameron behaved himself, but Wilson did not retain him. The incident had unfortunate consequences for each man. Farrand became an active enemy of Wilson; Cameron, who did not have independent means, never found another teaching position. He continued to live in Princeton in penury and was so embittered that it is said that he never again set foot on campus or permitted any of his seven children to do so.[70]

Just what Cameron said that so incensed Wilson is not recorded. Knowing Wilson's sensitivities, Cameron's tendency for off-color remarks, and the strong family feelings of both men, one might guess that Cameron made what Wilson considered an improper reference to his family. It is likely that Wilson had planned for some time to dismiss Cameron, but he could not have summoned him to Prospect at a more inopportune time. He may have already sustained his stroke, or had premonitory signs, and he was lonely. His wife was away on a tour of Italy, her return delayed because Jessie had developed diphtheria. The Hibbens, to whom Wilson might have turned for advice, had also gone abroad. Wilson was so upset by the Cameron interview that he sent two letters to Jenny Hibben in one day.[71] This combination of factors contributed to Wilson's loss of control of his feelings in an area in which he was particularly sensitive. It was the first time in his administration that he had allowed his emotions to dictate an official action.

In the second incident, Wilson again had trouble in separating his public and personal roles. Before leaving for a family vacation in Canada in July 1904, he ordered the construction of an iron fence around the grounds of Prospect. Wilson's explanation was that the barrier was needed to protect the gardens from the intrusions of "excursionists from Trenton" (a trolley line between Princeton and Trenton had recently been built). Many students were outraged when they returned in September. An editorial in the *Daily Princetonian* criticized the fence as "unnecessary and unsightly" and as detracting from the

[70] For the details of the Cameron affair, see WW to Arnold G. Cameron, November 18, 1903, *PWW* Vol. 15, p. 52, n.1.

[71] Jenny Davidson Hibben to WW, June 28, 1904, *ibid.*, p. 395.

beauty of McCosh Walk, "a spot which has been the pride of under-graduates since the days when it was customary to see President McCosh taking his daily walk there." The editorial understood the administration's reason for the construction, but it suggested that privacy could be achieved by the erection of "a temporary, portable" barrier during those seasons when intruders might come.[72] The *Nassau Literary Magazine* ran a defiant editorial,[73] and the editor-in-chief of the *Daily Princetonian* personally urged Wilson to make his explanation public. Wilson flatly refused, saying that when a man was right he need not make explanations.[74]

Another Battle of Princeton was drawn. One night, undergraduates dragged freshmen out of their beds, armed them with picks and shovels, and had them dig out a portion of the concrete-imbedded fence. Wilson promptly had it repaired but took no other action. The *Daily Princetonian* condemned the vandalism, but a week later the senior class put on its annual "horse peerade" in which the students, in grotesque costumes, bore placards satirizing Wilson's action. In their midst, they dragged a pig on a cart—a symbol of Wilson's selfishness. Several days later unknown persons broke the glass in several windows of 1879 Hall, a dormitory, tore down a chandelier, and chipped the steps in one of the entries from top to bottom. After this depredation, two trustee friends, Cornelius Cuyler Cuyler and Moses Taylor Pyne, advised Wilson that, in view of loud complaints from prominent alumni, it would be well to move the portion of the fence skirting McCosh Walk. To save face for Wilson, Cuyler inserted a notice in the *Daily Princetonian* which explained that the fence had been erected by the Grounds and Building Committee and had been authorized by the trustees.[75]

Possibly neither the Cameron nor the fence incidents would have occurred, at least in the form they took, had not Wilson had his stroke in 1904. Each episode illustrates also, how, in situations of stress, Wilson became very sensitive to the sexual implications of events, particularly as they affected his family. In the summer of 1904, Margaret was eighteen and Jessie was seventeen, and the girls were receiving attention from students. Nell, the least serious and most vivacious, was about fifteen. According to Madge Axson, Wilson was

[72] *Daily Princetonian*, October 1 and 3, 1904, printed in *ibid.*, p. 503, n.2.

[73] *Nassau Literary Magazine*, XL (November 1904), 171-72.

[74] Bragdon, *Wilson*, p. 303.

[75] *Daily Princetonian*, October 3 and 13, 1904; *New York Herald*, October 9, 1904; Cornelius Cuyler to WW, October 11, 1904, *PWW*, Vol. 15, pp. 503, 507-508, 509, n.2.

very interested in their callers. He entertained the ones he liked and ignored those he did not. Although he liked most of the young men, he invariably turned against them if the girls showed any sentimental interest in them.[76] If one recalls how upset Wilson had been in 1892 by the thought of young girls' being exposed to the temptations of a college town, the fence may have been a symbolic chastity belt. A year or so later, Christian Gauss, then a young preceptor, lent one of the girls the poems of Edward de Vere, Earl of Oxford, who celebrated love too lustily for Presbyterians. Wilson discovered the volume and burned it.[77]

In 1907, after Wilson's stroke of the year before, and during the crisis over the quadrangle plan, a similar episode occurred. Wilson heard that one of the doctors attending students in the infirmary was telling his patients dirty jokes. Wilson concluded that the morals of the students were being corrupted and ordered that only the university physician, Dr. John McDowell Carnochan, be permitted to visit students. Dr. Carnochan became ill in 1909 and was unable to see a boy who developed a serious case of pneumonia. Local physicians would not come, and physicians had to be called from Trenton and Philadelphia. The rule was not rescinded until after Wilson left the university.

By December 1904 Wilson had completely recovered the power of his right hand and entered the Presbyterian Hospital in New York for a physically unrelated condition, a hernia. Dr. Andrew J. McCosh, the son of the former president, performed a successful repair, but the patient developed a postoperative complication, a phlebitis in his left leg. He spent several more weeks in the hospital, then convalesced for five more weeks in Palm Beach in the company of his wife. He returned to Princeton on February 15, 1905, feeling fit and looking well.[78] He promptly set about staffing and setting up the preceptorial system. However, continued concern with his health seemed to be expressed in his baccalaureate address to the Class of 1905, for he emphasized the importance of good physical health and the saving health of moral sanity. The modern struggle for wealth, he told the graduates, was more like a consuming fever than a right function of health.[79]

The preceptorial system was launched successfully in 1905, but

[76] Elliott, *My Aunt Louisa*, pp. 184-85; McAdoo, *The Woodrow Wilsons*, p. 81.
[77] Interview with Edmund Wilson, November 1961, Bragdon Collection.
[78] WW to Bridges, December 9, 1904, *PWW*, Vol. 15, p. 571, n.1; WW to Walter Hines Page, February 24, 1905; WW to Azel Washburn Hazen, February 24, 1905, *ibid.*, Vol. 16, pp. 12-13.
[79] Baccalaureate address, June 11, 1905, *ibid.*, pp. 122-27.

tragedy struck the family in that same year. On April 24 Edward Axson and his family were accidentally drowned. After graduating from Princeton in 1897, Eddie had studied chemical engineering at M.I.T. and, in 1905, had become superintendent of a mining company in Georgia. While crossing the swollen Etowah River on a ferry, the horses of his carriage took fright and plunged into the river. Ed, his pregnant wife, and infant son were swept away in the swiftly flowing stream while Eddie tried to save his family. Ellen was heartbroken, and it was weeks before she could resume her normal activities.[80] She probably never got over the loss of her "darling boy," whom she had reared as a son. Wilson was so affected that even a year later his voice choked and his eyes filled with tears when he spoke of Ed.[81]

Stockton Axson's mental illness, for which he was hospitalized for a number of months, was another trial. Axson had joined the Princeton faculty in 1899 as Professor of English and was highly regarded by his colleagues and students. He had a sensitive, introspective, and perceptive temperament. His memoir shows a great deal of insight into the characters of both Joseph Ruggles and Woodrow Wilson. He never married and remained extremely close to his sister and brother-in-law.[82] Since his youth, he had suffered recurrent episodes during which he felt hopeless and inadequate and was unable to face people.[83] Ellen was filled with sympathy for her brother and also tormented by the fear, in view of their father's melancholia and suicide, that the condition might be hereditary.

While Wilson was devoted to Stockton, he had little understanding of and evidently a great fear of mental illness. Once, at Wesleyan, when discussing the statistics of suicide, he told Axson: "You see how the number of people who commit suicide annually is practically constant in proportion to the growing population of the country. You might say that this implies that a certain number of people in the United States are compelled to commit suicide each year. But you know perfectly well that it is within our own will and choice whether you or I shall make one of that number next year."[84] Mary Hoyt thought him "a bit hard-hearted in regard to anything that implied

[80] McAdoo, The Woodrow Wilsons, p. 87.

[81] Hardin Craig to RSB, July 5, 1927, Baker Papers.

[82] Wilson dedicated Mere Literature to him. The inscription reads: "To Stockton Axson, by every gift of heart a friend, this little volume is affectionately dedicated." Mere Literature and Other Essays (Boston and New York, 1896).

[83] ELA to WW, March 27, 1885, PWW, Vol. 4, p. 419; Stockton Axson to WW, October 22, 1896, ibid., Vol. 10, p. 33.

[84] Axson Memoir.

lack of self-control.''[85] Wilson disparaged psychology and told an audience in Chicago: "Whenever a man is studying anything queer he calls it sociology (laughter). I guess that what is normal is good enough for me (laughter). . . . These people who call themselves alienists are at one of the centers of sociological inquiry (laughter)."[86]

The Wilsons were also troubled by their daughter Margaret's "nervous collapse," which led her to withdraw from the Baltimore College for Women (now Goucher College) and to study music at home.[87]

Wilson never wavered in his certainty about God, but Ellen had less belief in the dogmas instilled into her during her childhood. Her intellectual curiosity and need for assurance had led her into the reading of philosophers, notably Kant, Hegel, and Fichte. Characteristically, she tried to avoid self-pity and to conceal her grief. Wilson insisted that they spend the summer at Lyme, Connecticut, so that she could join the artists' colony and take her long postponed lessons in landscape painting. It would, Wilson thought, be good therapy for her.[88] She was depressed throughout the year and developed what Wilson described as "a painful stiffness in the back and limbs, which has made constant massageing necessary and has held her off from a great many of her ordinary activities."[89] Wilson believed that the illness was a result of the strain she had experienced. The symptoms and situation suggest that they were of psychosomatic origin, rather than a manifestation of another episode of kidney disease.

Baker states that in the winter of 1905-1906 Wilson seemed "suddenly to have awakened to a fresh and powerful realization of the real conditions in the country, and a renewed sense of his own futility in meeting them."[90] Affairs at Princeton were going very well, and, whether it was because patriotic duty called, or he was looking for new worlds to conquer, or he was reacting to depression at home, Wilson launched into a series of public addresses outside the university and the alumni, which brought him into added national prominence. Whatever serious ambitions he might have had came seemingly to an abrupt end when, in the morning of May 28, 1906, he awoke blind in his left eye.

[85] When an artist at Lyme was unable to work because of melancholia, Wilson said, "Cousin Mary, it is possible to control your thoughts, you know." Mary E. Hoyt, memorandum on Wilson, October 1926, Baker Papers.

[86] "The Relation of University Education to Commerce," address to the Commercial Club of Chicago, November 29, 1902, PWW, Vol. 14, p. 240.

[87] EAW to Anna Harris, February 12, 1907, ibid., Vol. 17, p. 34.

[88] Stockton Axson to RSB, February 8, 10, 11, 1925, Baker Papers.

[89] WW to Arthur W. Tedcastle, April 10, 1906, PWW, Vol. 16, p. 357.

[90] Baker, Wilson, II, 194.

CHAPTER X

A Major Stroke and Its Consequences: The Quadrangle Plan

THE CLINICAL NEUROLOGIST would say that Wilson's stroke in 1906 and his previous history clearly defined the nature of his illness. The combination of sudden blindness in one eye and episodes of weakness and paresthesia (sensations of tingling or numbness) in the opposite upper extremity is characteristic of disease of an internal carotid artery. This vessel, a main supplier of blood to the brain, originates just below the neck. It gives off a first branch, the ophthalmic artery, to the eye on the same side, and goes on to supply most of the cerebral hemisphere. When the artery becomes sclerotic and narrowed, ulcerations form, and when blood platelets come into contact with the ulcerated surface, a chemical change occurs and platelets aggregate. Bits break off and are swept along in the blood stream to lodge in smaller branches. The symptoms are determined by which vessels are blocked. In Wilson's earlier strokes anterior branches of the left middle cerebral artery—itself a continuation of the internal carotid—were occluded and resulted in weakness and impaired sensation in the opposite arm. In 1906 the left ophthalmic artery was also blocked. The weakness of the right hand cleared, but, after some initial improvement, there was permanent visual loss in the left eye.[1]

Although stenotic carotid artery disease was recognized early in the nineteenth century, its nature and course has been clearly defined only since the introduction of cerebral angiography, approximately forty years ago.[2] The course of the disease is highly variable, with frequent episodes and remissions during which the patient is apparently well. Episodes of weakness last from minutes to months, while blindness is usually permanent, and the ultimate course is progressive. Overall duration may be very long, with periods of up to twenty-five years elapsing from the initial manifestations to final incapacity. Most pa-

---

[1] Wilson probably had a scotoma or blind spot. After a time, he compensated for it and was not aware of the blotting out of part of the visual field.

[2] Angiography is a method in which the injection of a radio-opaque dye delineates on X-rays the vessels supplying the brain.

tients with carotid artery disease have high blood pressure, a condition that may predispose vessels to sclerotic change.

Accompanied by Jack Hibben, Wilson went to Philadelphia to consult Dr. George de Schweinitz, a noted ophthalmologist, and Dr. Keen. De Schweinitz told him that he had sustained a blood clot in the eye and that the event was part of a more generalized condition. The Doctor advised Wilson to give up active work.[3] Eleanor Wilson recalled her father's return from Philadelphia. While the family was engulfed in panic and despair, Wilson was "calm, even gay."[4] Years later, Wilson told Cary Grayson how deeply depressed he had been. Stockton Axson asked Hibben not to report any bad news to his sister, but Ellen was a sharp questioner and elicited the facts.[5] The gloom spread from the Wilson household into the community. Moses Taylor Pyne was highly agitated after a visit and told Axson what a disaster it would be for Princeton if Wilson were to be permanently disabled.[6]

Several weeks after he had consulted Dr. de Schweinitz, Wilson was examined by Dr. Alfred Stengel of Philadelphia, an internist, who gave a more favorable prognosis. Ellen quoted the following from his cautiously worded report:

"I find a very moderate grade of arterial trouble and of a character that does not suggest any progressive course as likely in the near future. You were fortunate in having the local (ocular) trouble because it called attention to the general condition which would otherwise have passed unnoticed. I feel entirely confident that a rest of three months will restore you fully. Of course 50 year old arteries do not go back to an earlier condition, but I expect that you will be as well as you need be for any work you can reasonably wish to undertake next Fall. The warning simply indicates that excess of work is dangerous. You have doubtless done too much in the last few years."[7]

Even with this somewhat more reassuring opinion, Ellen Wilson was still distressed. She wrote to her cousin:

"I know now more exactly than I did then what is really threatening Woodrow. It is hardening of the arteries, due to prolonged high pressure on brain and nerves. He has lived too tensely. It is, of course, the thing that killed his father; as a rule it is the result of old age. Mr. Adams, there in Balt., died of it,—'premature old age' they called it in his case. Of course, it is an awful thing—a dying by inches, and

---

[3] EAW to Mary E. Hoyt, June 12, 1906, *PWW*, Vol. 16, p. 423.
[4] McAdoo, *The Woodrow Wilsons*, p. 93.
[5] Axson Memoir.
[6] *Ibid.*
[7] EAW to Florence S. Hoyt, June 27, 1906, *PWW*, Vol. 16, pp. 430.

incurable. But Woodrow's condition has been discovered in the very early stages and they think it has already been 'arrested.' "[8]

Ellen searched for evidence that would bear out the Doctor's opinion that her husband's stroke had been brought on by strain and overwork. She blamed it on Wilson's having to take over Dean Fine's duties for the several weeks that Fine had been abroad.[9] She determined to follow Dr. Stengel's advice to the letter and resolved never to permit anything to happen that might upset Woodrow. The trustees also agreed that the stroke had been caused by overwork and passed the following motion, introduced by Grover Cleveland and seconded by Pyne:

"RESOLVED that we desire to express our solicitude on account of the condition of President Wilson's health which deprives him of active participation in our Commencement activities. And in recognition of the fact that this condition is the direct result of close application and unremitting devotion to his labours in behalf of the University, we request, and especially enjoin it upon him, that he prolong his vacation to such an extent, as to time and manner of enjoyment, as may promise the complete restoration of his health and vigor."[10]

The Wilsons sailed for Europe on June 30. Despite lack of further improvement in vision and the persisting weakness of his arm, Wilson's letters, as after his stroke in 1896, were optimistic and reassuring. As has been said, he tended to regard the impaired functioning of his left eye as something apart from him; in his letters he emphasized his excellent general health and told of having tramped fourteen miles a day.[11]

Wilson consulted an ophthalmologist in Edinburgh, Dr. George A. Berry, and an internist, Dr. Francis D. Boyd. He reported to his wife that Dr. Berry had found "the eye" in excellent condition and was permitting him to read. Dr. Boyd found his blood pressure to be "very little off," and Wilson wrote that the Doctor thought that it would probably be better for a man of his temperament "to go back to (moderate) work" than to lead an aimless and perhaps anxious year in Great Britain.[12] Whether or not Wilson was quoting Dr. Boyd's advice verbatim, it seemed to correspond exactly with his own opinion.

Wilson returned to Princeton in the autumn, filled with energy and determined to overcome his handicaps and press ahead with his plans

---

[8] *Ibid.*, 429-30.

[9] EAW to Mary E. Hoyt, June 12, 1906, *ibid.*, pp. 423-24.

[10] Minutes of the board of trustees of Princeton University, June 11, 1906, *ibid.*, p. 422.

[11] WW to Annie Wilson Howe, August 2, 1906, *ibid.*, p. 432.

[12] WW to EAW, August 31 and September 1, 1906, *ibid.*, pp. 444, 445.

for Princeton. Because of the persisting weakness of his right hand, he used a pen holder, two or three times normal size, and had a rubber stamp for his signature made.[13] Consistent with his belief that the body was the servant of the spirit, he told his wife that he would train his eye "to behave."[14] He did make some concessions to the doctors' warnings and his wife's anxieties. For the first time, he acquired a full-time secretary and moved his office from Prospect to the tower room of 1879 Hall. To the annoyance of some of the faculty, he saw people only by appointment and tended to meet socially with members of the Princeton community only at official functions. He took regular naps and learned to put himself to sleep at will. Unfortunately, on account of his poor vision, he had to give up golf, and this deprived him of exercise and relaxation.[15]

Wilson's next project was a proposal for the social reorganization of the university, to become known as the quadrangle plan. It called for the establishment of residential colleges, or quadrangles, in which all undergraduates would live together under the guidance of unmarried faculty members.[16] Wilson regarded the quad plan as the logical extension of the preceptorial system. He had been impressed by the quadrangles at the University of Virginia and at Oxford, and he seems to have envisaged the kind of tutelary relationship that he had enjoyed with his father and uncle. As early as 1897 or 1898, he had told Stockton Axson that, if he ever attained power at Princeton, he would reform the curriculum, adopt the Oxford tutorial system, and reorganize the social life of the university so that freshmen would not be cut off from contact with upperclassmen and instructors.[17]

The plan called for radical changes in the club system. The eating clubs had been an inconsequential feature of college life in Wilson's undergraduate days, but, under the benevolent regime of President Patton, they had proliferated and become the most important social institutions on the campus. In the McCosh era, an undergraduate's primary loyalty had been to his class—an identification strengthened by hazing and class rivalries—and to Whig or Clio. As campus violence and class spirit decreased, and as debating was supplanted by inter-

[13] Baker, *Wilson*, II, 208; Hardin Craig to RSB, July 5, 1927, Baker Papers.
[14] Reid, *Woodrow Wilson*, p. 94.
[15] *Princeton Alumni Weekly*, VII (October 20, 1906), 63, printed in *PWW*, Vol. 16, pp. 463-64; WW to Mary Allen Hulbert Peck, July 25, 1909, *ibid.*, Vol. 19, p. 318.
[16] The plan was not original. Charles W. Eliot, President of Harvard University, had proposed it twice, and Professor Harper had urged its adoption at Princeton. Bragdon, *Wilson*, p. 316.
[17] Interview with Stockton Axson, March 15 and 16, 1927, Baker Papers.

collegiate athletics, the students turned to their clubs. With the increase
of wealth, these had become more and more elitist; they furnished not
only luxurious eating and recreational facilities for upperclassmen, but
were also festive gathering places and housing for returning alumni.
By 1906, from two-thirds to three-fourths of the upperclassmen belonged to clubs. Competition for membership was keen. For many
students—and their parents—the success or failure of their college
careers depended upon election to a particular club. No freshman or
sophomore was permitted to walk on Prospect Avenue, where the
clubs were situated. Thus they (as well as non-club members) were
entirely excluded from the social life of the university. The period
during which elections took place, known as bicker week, was described as an annual frenzy which prevented sleep and destroyed
friendships. In addition, there were freshmen and sophomore clubs
which acted as feeders. Sophomore club members wore distinctively
colored hats and bands to indicate their status. Arrangements for
freshman club membership were made in some of the larger preparatory schools, such as Lawrenceville and St. Paul's, so that a social
hierarchy was already in existence at matriculation.

There had been widespread criticism of the clubs and unsuccessful
attempts to reform them. Most of the criticism centered on the richer,
older clubs—Ivy (1879), Cottage (1886), Tiger Inn (1890), and Cap
and Gown (1891). A committee of the trustees, headed by M. Taylor
Pyne, a member of Ivy, had made an investigation in 1903 and concluded that, on the whole, the clubs were a good influence. Yet, a year
later, an editorial in the *Daily Princetonian* charged the clubs with
trying to break up the freshman commons.[18] The club members themselves had agreed to forbid clandestine early solicitation, and each
sophomore, on election to a club, was required to sign a statement
that, on his word of honor, he had made no prior commitment to join.
However, the temptations, for the weaker clubs especially, to approach
prospective members in advance of the agreed date often proved to
be too strong. Also, the interclub treaty, as the compact to reform the
system was known, not only did not improve the situation; it also
increased the barriers between underclassmen and upperclassmen. A
club member seen talking to a freshman or sophomore would be
suspected of proselytizing. Some club members themselves were eager
for a change. Donald G. Herring, of Cap and Gown, later estimated

---

[18] Moses Taylor Pyne, report to the board of trustees of Princeton University, c. June
8, 1903, *PWW*, Vol. 14, pp. 479-84; *Princeton Alumni Weekly*, IV (March 19, 1904),
386-87, printed in *ibid.*, Vol. 15, pp. 199-200.

that at least 40 percent of the members of the interclub treaty committee favored abolition of the clubs.[19]

Wilson saw the clubs—as McCosh had regarded the fraternities—as anti-intellectual and divisive influences. A year earlier, Wilson had suggested, in an address to an alumni group, that the existing clubs "be made the nuclei of small educational communities."[20] Abroad in September, he had written to Cleveland Dodge that the summer had "brought to maturity the plans for the University which have for years been in the back of my head but which never before got room enough to take their full growth."[21] Wilson formally presented his plan to the trustees at their meeting in December 1906. He began by stating that, while the changes he was suggesting were "radical," they were "the fruit of very mature consideration." He detailed the abuses of the clubs, which, he declared, were causing a decline in the democratic spirit of the university and were "incompatible" with "a true republic of letters and of learning." He proposed that the university be divided into colleges, each complete with living facilities. The larger, wealthier clubs would themselves become colleges, with graduate members contributing the funds for the necessary expansion. Each college would be under the guidance of a resident faculty member, appointed by the university. The residences would be arranged in quadrangles which would contain all social facilities.[22] It is important to note that the plan did not call for the abolition of the clubs but for their transformation.

Wilson's plan took the board completely by surprise, as it had been thought that the next step for the development of Princeton would be the building of a graduate college. Wilson and the board had given a commitment to that effect to Dean West in October 1906.[23] Taken aback by the suddenness and unexpectedness of Wilson's proposal, and in accord with their habit of unfailing acquiescence in his measures, the trustees made neither objection nor protest. They appointed Wilson head of a committee to investigate the problems involved in the proposed reorganization of the university. In line with his program for adequate rest, Wilson sailed for a month's vacation in Bermuda after the meeting.[24]

[19] Interview with Donald G. Herring, April 12, 1939, Bragdon Collection.

[20] Address to Princeton Alumni Association of the Oranges, reported in the *Newark Evening News*, November 10, 1905, printed in *PWW*, Vol. 16, p. 218.

[21] WW to Cleveland H. Dodge, September 16, 1906, *ibid.*, p. 453.

[22] A supplementary report to the board of trustees of Princeton University, c. December 13, 1906, *ibid.*, pp. 519-25.

[23] See pp. 199-201.

[24] Minutes of the board of trustees of Princeton University, December 13, 1906, *ibid.*,

Wilson did very little to recruit support for the quadrangle plan. He did not mention it in talks to the alumni organizations of Philadelphia, Baltimore, and Pittsburgh in the spring of 1907.[25] There were no formal faculty discussions until April 15, when Wilson met with Harry Fine, Harry Garfield, and Paul van Dyke, Professor of History. Wilson stated that he had originally considered that the quad plan would take twenty-five years to accomplish, but that now it seemed immediately obtainable. He showed blueprints around and asked for opinions. Fine favored the plan, as did Garfield, who thought it timely since the clubs were not as deeply rooted at Princeton as at other colleges. Van Dyke, one of the founders of Ivy, thought that the plan would stir up trouble and break up the club system.[26] Wilson, however, received strong encouragement from a trustee, David Benton Jones, who warned him that if he did not act the university would become only the academic and artistic background for the clubs. Although Hibben had expressed doubts, Jones assured Wilson that he could count on his friend's support.[27]

Wilson submitted the report of his committee, which he of course wrote himself, to the board of trustees at their meeting on June 10, 1907. He proposed that each club vest its property in the hands of a small board of trustees, of its own choice, which, in association with university authorities, would administer it for the university. The clubs would thus be absorbed into the university by the natural process of becoming residential quads. Wilson called on the club members to show their devotion to Princeton by this supreme act of self-sacrifice.[28] The board adopted the report by a vote of fourteen to one and authorized Wilson to take such steps as might "seem wisest for maturing this general plan, and for seeking the cooperation and counsel of the upper-class clubs in its elaboration." The board also authorized Wilson to devise detailed plans for the future consideration of the board, "so soon as such plans can be perfected by common counsel among all concerned."[29] The expressions, "so soon as" and "common counsel,"

---

p. 526. For an account of Wilson's departure for Bermuda, see the *Daily Princetonian*, January 11, 1907, printed in *ibid.*, p. 559.

[25] WW notes for an address to the Philadelphia alumni, February 14, 1907, *ibid.*, Vol. 17, p. 38; news report of WW speech to Baltimore alumni, Baltimore *Sun*, February 19, 1907, printed in *ibid.*, pp. 43-45; John A. Wilson to WW, March 9, 1907, *ibid.*, p. 64, n.1.

[26] Baker, *Wilson*, II, 226-27.

[27] David B. Jones to WW, May 15, 1907, *PWW*, Vol. 17, pp. 147-48.

[28] "Report on the Social Coordination of the University," c. June 6, 1907, printed in *ibid.*, pp. 176-77, 180-86. See "President Wilson's Address to the Board of Trustees," *Princeton Alumni Weekly*, VII (June 12, 1907), 606-15.

[29] Link, *Wilson*, I, 48.

two of Wilson's favorite phrases, make it almost certain that Wilson wrote the resolution. He regarded the board action as tantamount to acceptance of the quadrangle plan.

The publication of the plan in the *Princeton Alumni Weekly* on June 12 set off a storm of protest from faculty members and alumni. Henry van Dyke,[30] in a rejoinder in the *Alumni Weekly* criticized the plan extensively. He complained that the proposal had never been brought before the faculty as a whole, stated that quadrangle cliques would inevitably develop, claimed that the regulations of the academic communities would impair the students' self-reliance, and charged that the heavy expense would postpone the building of a graduate college.[31] Dean West was furious. "If the spirit of Princeton is to be killed," he wrote to Wilson, "I have little interest in the details of the funeral." He also accused Wilson of acting immorally.[32] There was a general outpouring of alumni opinion, and, as the summer progressed, it became clear that an overwhelming majority in the Northeast were opposed. The Philadelphia alumni, while recognizing the evils of the clubs, were against the quad plan because of the cost and the belief that the divisions into colleges would destroy class spirit.[33] Harold Griffith Murray, secretary of the Committee of Fifty, Princeton's fundraising organization, stated that opposition among the New York alumni was so strong as to put the university in financial jeopardy.[34]

As the tide of alumni protest increased, compromises were offered. Bayard Henry, a trustee from Philadelphia, proposed that a single model quadrangle be built.[35] Henry Burling Thompson, a trustee friendly to Wilson, suggested that all freshmen and sophomores be put into separate refectories in order to break up the sophomore clubs.[36]

However, even the counsel of Wilson's closest friends failed to move him. When Stockton Axson asked him if he would be satisfied with a plan to be effective in five years, Wilson replied that he would be

[30] Henry van Dyke, Princeton 1873, a brother of Paul, was also a graduate of Princeton Theological Seminary and an ordained Presbyterian minister. He served as a Professor of English Literature from 1900 to 1923 and was a distinguished and widely read author, poet, and speaker. Wilson appointed him Minister to the Netherlands and Luxembourg in 1913.

[31] Henry van Dyke, "The 'Residential Quad' Idea at Princeton," *Princeton Alumni Weekly*, VIII (September 25, 1907), 4-7, printed in *PWW*, Vol. 17, pp. 276-79.

[32] Andrew F. West to WW, July 10, 1907, *ibid.*, p. 271.

[33] Bayard Henry to Henry B. Thompson, July 13, 1907, *ibid.*, pp. 304-305.

[34] Harold G. Murray to Andrew C. Imbrie, September 12, 1907, *ibid.*, pp. 381-83.

[35] Bayard Henry to WW, August 16, 1907, *ibid.*, pp. 347-48.

[36] Henry B. Thompson to Cleveland H. Dodge, September 10, 1907, *ibid.*, p. 380.

"greatly disappointed" if the quad plan was "not in operation long before that period had elapsed."[37] Cleveland Dodge, who had under- written most of the cost of the preceptorial plan, and who had always been one of Wilson's strongest supporters, tried to persuade him to go more slowly.[38] After Jack Hibben had warned him of the negative sentiment among the faculty and alumni, Ellen Wilson told Hibben that the information "had merely disheartened" Woodrow for the fight.[39] When Henry van Dyke suggested to Wilson that the advice he was receiving was not a sign of disloyalty, but was meant to protect him against the gathering hostility of the alumni, Wilson reportedly replied (quoting Oliver Wendell Holmes), "The Truth is no invalid!"[40]

Wilson spent the summer with his family in Keene Valley in the Adirondacks.[41] He indicated his state of mind and degree of emotional commitment in a long letter to Hibben. (Hibben had written to warn of the dangers ahead and to tell Wilson that he could not support him.) Wilson began by insisting that he could not yield the principle that the clubs must be absolutely controlled by the university. He continued:

"It is true that what you have told me of the attitude of the trustees, the alumni, and the faculty (above all the faculty) has 'deprived me of hope.' I can only hope that you are mistaken. If what you suppose to be the prevailing sentiment and purpose should turn out to be so indeed, I shall stand isolated and helpless. But before I accept that conclusion I must do everything in my power that is honourable and legitimate,—everything that a gentleman and a lover of our dear alma mater may do,—to convince all upon whom I depend for support of the wisdom and necessity of what I propose. They have most of them made up their minds before hearing me, before two-sided debate, instead of after it. Two-sided debate there shall be, of the frankest and most genuine sort. The Faculty shall know in the autumn, whatever they may now believe to the contrary, that I am ready to put myself in their hands. They may refuse to support me in this matter, and if

[37] Winthrop M. Daniels to John G. Hibben, August 9, 1907, *ibid.*, p. 343.

[38] Cleveland H. Dodge to WW, July 2 and August 6, 1907, *ibid.*, pp. 243, 341.

[39] John G. Hibben to WW, July 8, 1907, *ibid.*, p. 263-64.

[40] J. Duncan Spaeth, "Wilson As I Knew Him and View Him Now," in Myers, ed., *Wilson: Some Princeton Memories*, p. 82.

[41] During the summer of 1907, Madge Axson discovered a Ouija board when the Wilsons were in the Adirondacks. After several unsuccessful trials, Wilson summoned up the spirit of James McCosh. They talked at some length of the old days in Princeton, and then Wilson asked, "What do you think of Andrew West, Doctor?" "West will burn in hell to the greater glory of God." was the reply. Elliott, *My Aunt Louisa*, p. 230.

they do I shall with no bitterness whatever, I hope and believe, accept their decision as a definitive defeat. I say without bitterness because I shall believe that many of them are moved by the same high, unselfish motives that move you, my dear, dear friend. I cannot conceal from you the deep anxiety and sadness that fills me in view of the whole situation. I cannot for the present think of Princeton without a deep pang of realization of what may be the consequences of this agitation; but I should feel a mere contempt for myself should I lose courage or falter: for I never had a clearer sense of duty. I should feel myself faithless and utterly blind to what the performance of my duties as president has brought to light were I to draw back. Mistakes of judgment are, of course, possible even in a measure so deliberately and anxiously conceived as this; and failure is bitter, how bitter it would be impossible to say, for a man convinced of duty as I am; but worse than either, infinitely worse, is it to shirk. To shirk would kill me; to fail need not."

Then, Wilson concluded in one of the most poignant passages that he ever penned:

"This, my dear Jack, is the whole matter, as I would speak it to my own heart. You have done your duty, and I love and honour you for [it]; I shall try to do mine, and so win your love and respect. You would not wish me to do otherwise. And our friendship, by which I have lived, in which I have drawn some of the most refreshing, most renewing breath of my life, is to be as little affected by our difference of opinion as is everything permanent and of the law of our hearts. Do not, I beg of you, torture yourself in any way about it all. A struggle is ahead of me,—it may be a heartbreaking struggle,—and you cannot stand with me in it; but we can see past all that to the essence of things and shall at every step know each other's love. Will not that suffice?"[42]

On his return to Princeton, Wilson seemed to Henry B. Thompson to be "nervous and excitable," although in control of his emotions.[43] At a faculty meeting on September 26, 1907, Henry van Dyke offered a motion to sidetrack the quadrangle plan. To Wilson's astonishment, Hibben seconded the motion. While Wilson knew Hibben's views, he had never imagined that his dearest friend would take an active part against him. Several days later, Van Dyke's motion was defeated eighty to twenty-three. All but one of the fifty preceptors supported Wilson; West, both Van Dykes, Magie, and Patton were against him. However, Wilson would have won without the support of the preceptors.

[42] WW to John G. Hibben, July 10, 1907, *PWW*, Vol. 17, pp. 268-69.
[43] Henry B. Thompson to Cleveland H. Dodge, September 10, 1907, *ibid.*, p. 379.

At Paul van Dyke's request, Wilson then addressed the group. With an unusual show of emotion, he reiterated that the quad plan was the necessary sequel to the preceptorial method and affirmed that the purpose was not social but intellectual.[44] A week later, when he again addressed the faculty, Wilson compared the relationship of instructor and student to the natural companionship of father and son. The clubs, Wilson declared, "estopp[ed] any plan for organic reorganization." Perhaps with the image of Henry V before Agincourt in mind, he concluded: "I beg of you to follow me in this hazardous, but splendid adventure."[45]

Despite Wilson's majority support among the faculty, Pyne, who had succeeded Cleveland as the leading member of the trustees, had decided to scuttle the quad plan. At a meeting of the board on October 17, Pyne moved that the trustees rescind their decision adopted in June and ask Wilson to withdraw his proposal. The motion was passed fourteen to one. To spare Wilson's feelings, Cleveland Dodge offered a resolution, seconded by Pyne, to the effect that the board recognized the President's convictions and had "no wish to hinder him" in his efforts to persuade the board, and Princeton men in general, of their validity. This resolution was adopted. However, Grover Cleveland's motion that the board cooperate with the President was voted down.[46]

Wilson's defeat left him distressed and bitter. Momentarily giving way to despair, he wrote out a letter of resignation in shorthand, but did not send it.[47] Instead, he decided to defy Pyne and continue the fight. In an interview with the New York *Evening Sun*, he said that he did not think that the trustees had opposed his plan "on principle," but had "merely reversed their former decision," because they thought that the members of the Princeton community had not been "sufficiently informed." He stated that he planned to outline his plan to the students and visit the alumni organizations and, when he had persuaded them of the plan's wisdom, he expected that they would immediately sanction its adoption.[48] Amazed and indignant, Pyne rushed to the President's office and threatened to withdraw his support from

[44] Minutes of Princeton University faculty, September 26 and 30, 1907; diary of William Starr Myers, September 30, 1907, *ibid.*, pp. 402-03, 408-09.

[45] Andrew F. West, abstract of Wilson's speech to the faculty, October 7, 1907, *ibid.*, pp. 422-24.

[46] Minutes of the board of trustees of Princeton University, October 17, 1907, *ibid.*, pp. 441-42.

[47] WW to board of trustees of Princeton University, October 17, 1907, *ibid.*, pp. 443-44.

[48] Interview with WW, New York *Evening Sun*, October 18, 1907, *ibid.*, pp. 444-45.

the university if Wilson resumed his campaign.[49] Wilson also expressed his views, symbolically, in a speech in which he evoked the spirit of George Washington, whose greatness, Wilson stated, consisted chiefly in never knowing "when he was beaten" and in fighting "harder after a defeat."[50] Whatever plans Wilson may have had to campaign immediately among the alumni were prevented temporarily by another stroke which he sustained in November.

While a number of factors were involved in Wilson's defeat, any consideration must include the effects of the stroke of 1906 on his behavior. In an apparent effort—strongly reinforced by his wife—to conserve his energies, he did not undertake the preparation of the faculty and alumni as he had done in instituting the reform of the curriculum and in the adoption of the preceptorial system. Also, the depression associated with his illness may have made him reluctant to meet with people aside from his family and closest friends, the Hibbens. Another factor was Ellen Wilson's attitude. While she always loyally supported her husband, she had formerly tried to point out all sides of a question. Now, afraid of upsetting him, she unquestioningly approved his actions. Once, after a Princeton dinner, at which Wilson had been particularly outspoken, Lawrence Crane Woods, a graduate of the class of 1891 and a supporter of the quad plan, told Axson that Wilson should be more conciliatory. When Axson reported the conversation, Wilson became angry, and Ellen said that Woods ought not to "instruct Woodrow." When Axson reminded them that, while Woods might be wrong, his intentions had been good, Wilson apologized.[51]

Even with his family, Wilson was sometimes irritable. The fears that he did not have long to live and that his mental faculties might deteriorate as his father's had probably contributed to Wilson's insistence on the immediate implementation of the plan. He was aware of the obstacles—the force of tradition, the loyalty of alumni club members, and the substantial money that would be necessary. However, in the emotional state following his stroke, Wilson did not think as much about these obstacles as he did about what he thought were the larger issues and ideals involved.

Much can be learned about Wilson's feelings and motives from the language in which he presented the quadrangle plan to the trustees in

[49] M. W. Jacobus to WW, Nov. 5, 1907, *ibid.*, p. 468; Moses T. Pyne to Andrew C. Imbrie, October 23, 1907; David B. Jones to WW, November 12, 1907, *ibid.*, pp. 453-54, 496.

[50] "The Importance of Singlemindedness," October 25, 1907, *ibid.*, p. 455.

[51] Interview with Stockton Axson, March 15 and 16, 1927, Baker Papers.

December 1906. He feared deterioration and death; hence he put emphasis on healing and the life processes. In his address to the board of trustees, Wilson repeatedly referred to the "disintegration" and demoralization of Princeton, and emphasized the need for reintegration, regeneration, and restoration. He talked of "drawing the scattered fragments of their undergraduate body together" and the regeneration of the whole body of the college. He concluded his remarks as follows: "The disintegration is taking place, a disintegration into atoms too small to hold the fine spirit of college life. We must substitute for disintegration a new organic process. The new body will have divisions, but all the parts will be organs of a common life. It is reintegration by more varied and more abundant organic life. This is the time to act, when the fluid mass trembles upon the verge of some sort of final crystallization."[52]

The way in which the effects of Wilson's stroke affected his judgment and his use of the symbolism of health and growth were shown in his speeches to the alumni in February 1907. In Philadelphia, according to newspaper accounts, he aroused great enthusiasm by announcing that Princeton was on the verge of receiving such donations as to make it the greatest seat of learning and research in the world.[53] Wilson may have had in mind promised gifts for laboratory buildings. However, four days later, in Baltimore, he stated that the reports from Philadelphia had been erroneous and that the receipt of such "munificent gifts" would cause a growth which "would not be healthy."[54]

Wilson's preoccupation with renewal and regeneration was also shown in his choice of a text for his baccalaureate address to the class of 1907. Wilson selected the passage from Romans 12:2 which reads: "And be ye not conformed to this world: but be ye transformed by the renewing of your mind, that ye may prove what is that good, and acceptable, and perfect will of God."[55]

This language suggests that Wilson was speaking experientially and self-referentially. The faults of the clubs notwithstanding, Princeton University was hardly on the verge of dissolution. Actually, under Wilson's administration, its academic standing had never been higher. In his address, he was consciously using his favorite metaphors of organic life processes to impart force and fervor to his ideas and also

[52] Supplementary Report to the board of trustees of Princeton University, c. December 13, 1906, *PWW*, Vol. 16, pp. 519-25.

[53] Philadelphia *North American*, February 15, 1907; Philadelphia *Public Ledger*, February 15, 1907, *ibid.*, Vol. 17, pp. 38-40.

[54] Baltimore *Sun*, February 19, 1907, *ibid.*, pp. 43-44.

[55] Baccalaureate address at Princeton University, June 9, 1907, *ibid.*, p. 187.

to heighten the sense of urgency. Less consciously, he may have been symbolically representing the threats of bodily and mental deterioration that his illness posed. These were projected outside of the self. It was *Princeton University* which was in danger of dissolution and the students who were threatened with mental stagnation. The clubs stood for the agents of evil and disease with which there could be no compromise. That Wilson was not completely carried away by his symbolism is indicated by some favorable comments that he made about the clubs, and a certain ambivalence in advocating their complete elimination.

Thus the quadrangle plan was the symbol of Wilson's physical, moral, and mental integrity. "The fight is on," he told Cleveland Dodge, "and I regard it, not as a fight for the development, but as a fight for the restoration of Princeton. My heart is in it more than it has been in anything else, because it is a scheme of salvation."[56] At one point, Wilson was so intent on the quad plan that he was willing to drop the preceptorial system. It had become a test of his courage, and the emotion that it aroused touched on two of his deepest sources of identity. In accepting an LL.D. degree from Harvard in June 1907, he declared:

"I cannot help thinking, as I sit here in this hall, that it is dedicated to men who thrashed the men that I most loved. I come from a more ancient Commonwealth than the Commonwealth of Massachusetts, namely, the Commonwealth of Virginia, and I am one of those who are of the seed of that indomitable blood, planted in so many parts of the United States, which makes good fighting stuff,—the Scotch-Irish. The beauty about a Scotch-Irishman is that he not only thinks he is right, but knows he is right. And I have not departed from the faith of my ancestors."[57]

The private character of Wilson's symbolism led to difficulties in communication. While most of the trustees thought in terms of alumni unrest and financial contributions—the cost of the quad plan was estimated at $2,000,000, the preceptorial system was still not paid for, and the Panic of 1907 had made money tight—Wilson talked of regeneration and revitalization. Wilson's language also confused some of his own followers. Unaware of the symbolism involved, they made proposals to reform and democratize the clubs—all of which Wilson turned down. Even so, Wilson might have won had he followed the advice of David B. Jones and another trustee, Melancthon Williams

[56] WW to Cleveland H. Dodge, July 1, 1907, *ibid.*, pp. 240-41.
[57] Address at Harvard University, June 26, 1907, *ibid.*, p. 226.

Jacobus, to make his case openly on the legitimate issue of elitism and social snobbery. Yet over and over, Wilson insisted that his aim was not "social, but academic and intellectual."[58]

Wilson's new stroke may possibly have been precipitated by the turmoil of 1907. The exact date of onset is not recorded. He first mentioned weakness and numbness in his right arm, which interfered with his writing, in a letter of late November 1907.[59] By the middle of December he had recovered sufficiently to write with his right hand and to return to work. His wife blamed the illness on the emotional distress caused by the break with the Hibbens. She, along with Pyne and Dodge, urged him to go to some sunny place where he could rest and get his mind off Princeton matters. He returned to Bermuda for the month of January.[60]

Wilson relaxed in Bermuda and worked on lectures to be delivered at Columbia University in 1908 and to be published in 1909 as *Constitutional Government in the United States*. He also renewed his friendship with Mary Allen Hulbert Peck, an attractive grass widow whom he had met the previous year. Back in Princeton, he continued to criticize the clubs in his talks with students[61] and speeches to the alumni.[62] A committee, made up of Wilson supporters, proposed that no additional clubs be formed, that sophomores be admitted to the existing clubs, that club members encourage social relationships between themselves and faculty members, and that a university club, open to the three upper classes, faculty, alumni, and trustees, be established.[63]

While Wilson retained the respect of the faculty, his authority, for the first time, had been shaken. He and Pyne remained on a first-name basis and Pyne continued to be solicitous of Wilson's health, but their old intimacy and complete confidence in each other had ended. Grover Cleveland, as his fatal illness progressed, sided increasingly with West,

---

[58] WW to Andrew C. Imbrie, July 15, 1907; WW to Albridge C. Smith, Jr., July 15, 1907; WW to Arthur H. Osborn, July 17, 1907, *ibid.,* pp. 282-83, 286-87.

[59] WW to Mabel K. Fentress, November 26, 1907, *ibid.,* p. 523.

[60] Moses T. Pyne to WW, December 17, 1907; Cleveland H. Dodge to WW, December 18, 1907; WW to EAW, February 4, 1908, *ibid.,* pp. 562, 563, 611-13.

[61] In the spring of 1909, Wilson listened to Dr. Patton deliver an attack, in Biblical parable, on the quad plan at the Cottage Club. Wilson responded in similar fashion and demolished Patton. Brown Rolston to Bragdon, January 22, 1945, in Bragdon, *Wilson,* p. 355.

[62] He tried later to obtain funding for the quad plan from Carnegie and John D. Rockefeller, but did no active campaigning.

[63] Thompson *et al.* to the board of trustees of Princeton University, April 8, 1908, *PWW,* Vol. 18, pp. 236-41.

and he and his wife, Frances, became bitter personal enemies of Wilson.[64] The most painful sequel of the quad fight was the break between the Wilsons and the Hibbens. Wilson remained convinced that his best friend, whom he had loved and trusted completely, had betrayed him.

[64] After Wilson remarked, "After all, what does Grover Cleveland know about a university?" Cleveland wrote to a friend that the President of Princeton lacked professional honesty. Walworth, *Wilson*, I, 115.

CHAPTER XI

"Dearest Friend":
The Story of Mrs. Peck

WILSON'S FRIENDSHIP with Mary Allen Hulbert Peck affords deep insight into his personality and motivations. Their relationship affected his domestic life, influenced his behavior during the graduate college controversy, and played an important role in his political career.[1]

Mary, the daughter of Charles Sterling Allen and Anjennet Holcomb Allen, was born on May 26, 1862, in Grand Rapids, Michigan. She related in her autobiography that, soon after her birth, she was considered dead, but that her grandmother revived her with mouth-to-mouth resuscitation. She grew up in Grand Rapids and in Duluth, Minnesota. Her family had moved to the latter city to live near her maternal grandparents because of financial difficulties. In October 1883 she married Thomas Harbach Hulbert, the son of Edwin J. Hulbert, a wealthy friend with whom she played piano duets. She recalled the marriage as a happy one, although the couple spent relatively little time together during the six years before her husband's death. Young Hulbert, who was a mining engineer and prospector like his father, worked out of Port Arthur, Ontario, a Lake Superior harbor and terminus for several railroads. Mrs. Hulbert found that conditions in Port Arthur were unsuitable,[2] and the couple, except for occasional visits, lived together only in Duluth during the winter, when mining operations could not be carried out. After two years of marriage, Mrs.

---

[1] The following account of Mrs. Peck's life is taken largely from her anecdotal and melodramatic autobiography, *The Story of Mrs. Peck: An Autobiography* (New York, 1933), which she wrote at age seventy-one.

[2] In her autobiography, Mrs. Peck gives the impression that Port Arthur was a rough mining camp. Actually, it was a settled community with many social amenities. The Canadian census of 1881 lists a population of 699 males and 576 females. The town was the seat of a district court and had police and fire departments. It had a newspaper, public high and parochial schools, and Presbyterian, Methodist, and Roman Catholic churches. Mrs. Hulbert's musical interests would have been served by a brass band, a pipe band, choir services, and a Philharmonic Society. See *ibid.*, p. 58, and compare with Charles E. King, *From the Landing to Modern Port Arthur* (Port Arthur, Ont., 1927).

Hulbert spent six months abroad with her husband's parents in Munich, Venice, Florence, and Rome. She later related that on the ocean voyage to Europe, where she met the first of many famous people she was to know, she had sat at the captain's right, opposite D'Oyly Carte and Sir Arthur Sullivan, who invited her to England to meet the Prince of Wales.[3] Apparently her father-in-law thought that this trip abroad was better for her husband, for, had she remained in Duluth, Tom would have "eaten his heart out" thinking of her "so near and yet so far."[4]

The couple had one child, Allen Schoolcraft Hulbert, born in September 1888. The next year Tom Hulbert died suddenly, apparently of a cerebral hemorrhage. Mrs. Hulbert then went to Italy to live with her recently widowed father-in-law and his woman companion whom he later adopted. The young widow enjoyed the cosmopolitan society of Rome in which she met artists and literary figures and was courted by handsome and titled men. After two years, the *ménage à trois* was interrupted when Mrs. Hulbert had to return to the United States for an operation to correct injuries sustained in childbirth. She wrote that the Italian doctors had told her that the operation was highly dangerous and, without it, she had only a year to live.[5] Much to her surprise, she survived the operation.[6] She was left with limited funds and found that men considered a young widow "legitimate prey."[7] In December 1890 she married Thomas Dowse Peck, a widower with two daughters.

The couple lived in Pittsfield, Massachusetts, where Peck was the president of a woolen manufacturing company. Almost from the beginning, the marriage was unhappy, and they became increasingly estranged. Mrs. Peck claimed that her husband was cruel, unsympathetic, and penurious. She wrote that he refused to give her the money to visit her ill father, so that she had been unable to see him before his death.[8] During her second winter in Pittsfield, she developed melancholia of such severity that she had to be carried downstairs from her bedroom for an examination.[9] On the advice of her "wise and beloved" physician, she spent winters after 1892 in Bermuda—away from her husband. There her health improved splendidly. She became

---

[3] Hulbert, *The Story of Mrs. Peck*, pp. 59-61.

[4] *Ibid.*, p. 59.

[5] *Ibid.*, p. 92. The nature of the operation, performed at St. Luke's Hospital in Chicago, is not known. Usually procedures to correct injuries sustained in childbirth involve relatively minor surgery and minimal risk.

[6] *Ibid.*, p. 96.   [7] *Ibid.*, p. 99.

[8] *Ibid.*, p. 123.   [9] *Ibid.*, p. 124.

a prominent member of society, a friend of the Governor, Lieutenant General Sir Walter Kitchener, of Admiral Sir John Arbuthnot Fisher, Commander of the North Atlantic Fleet, of Mark Twain, and of other celebrities. In spite of Mr. Peck's stinginess, she dressed fashionably,[10] entertained well, and collected Queen Anne and Georgian furniture, glass, and china. She was able to travel to Bermuda with her own maids and to rent luxurious historic houses.

When Wilson met Mrs. Peck in 1907, she was a vivacious, witty, sophisticated, and talented woman of forty-five; a gourmet cook, a pianist, and an excellent dancer. Wilson was attracted to her immediately. After dinner with her[11] on the evening before his departure from the island, he came on the following day to tell her goodby; and, before he returned to Princeton, he wrote to tell her how keenly disappointed he had been that he had not found her at home.[12] He sent her a copy of Bagehot and a volume of his own essays.[13] Mrs. Peck must have told Wilson about her marital unhappiness because, in her answer to his letter, she thanked him for having given her strength and courage to go on when her spirit had faltered.[14] In his reply, Wilson expressed delight that his friendship had given her pleasure and hope; he also commented on the "instinctive sympathy" that seemed to have arisen between them.[15]

Their friendship blossomed during Wilson's second visit to the island in January and February 1908. She introduced him to her friends, and he escorted her to teas and dances; while she danced, he sat on the veranda and listened to the music. On long walks along the beaches, he read to her from the *Oxford Book of Verse*. He told her of his boyhood and made many wry comments about his plain face.[16] He confided to her about his troubles at Princeton and his ambitions for

[10] Mrs. Peck seems to have remembered every dress worn on a festive occasion since, as a child, she had been chosen Queen of the May. The description of the trousseau for her first wedding fills two pages of her autobiography. See *ibid.*, pp. 21-22.

[11] Mrs. Peck entertained Wilson at Inwood, still one of the oldest and most famous houses in Bermuda. It has a vast lawn, a formal garden, a rose garden, stables, and a two-storeyed servants' house! Hudson Strode, *The Story of Bermuda* (New York, 1932), pp. 292-96. Her heart was broken, Mrs. Peck wrote, when her husband would not buy a home for her in Bermuda. Hulbert, *The Story of Mrs. Peck,* p. 108.

[12] WW to MAHP, February 6, 1907, *PWW*, Vol. 17, p. 29.

[13] WW to MAHP, February 20, 1907, *ibid.,* p. 48. When Wilson later asked Mrs. Peck how she had liked Bagehot, she replied enthusiastically, "Oh, I loved it!" "Yes, yes," he replied, "I notice you have not cut the pages." Charles C. Cutler, Jr., "Dear Mrs. Peck," *American History Illustrated,* VI (1971-72), 5-9, 46-48.

[14] MAHP to WW, February 25, 1907, *PWW*, Vol. 17, p. 50.

[15] WW to MAHP, March 27, 1907, *ibid.,* p. 94.

[16] Hulbert, *The Story of Mrs. Peck*, pp. 144, 164, 166, 172.

high political office. Whereas Ellen, because of her fears for his health, had hesitated to encourage his hopes, Wilson's new friend expressed what he later recalled as a "serene, unreasonable faith" in his future.[17] By February 1908 he was deeply smitten. On the reverse side of a petition, which he had drawn up to ban automobiles from the island, he wrote "My precious one, my beloved Mary."[18]

The development of Wilson's devotion to Mrs. Peck can be measured by comparing his letters to his wife in 1907 with those in 1908. There was no diminution in the expressions of love for Ellen. However, whereas he had had to "fight with myself to keep from going back" on the next steamer[19] in 1907, he was much less lonely in the subsequent year. His letters of 1907 contained many interesting descriptions of Bermuda, while his correspondence in 1908 centered on Mrs. Peck, her family, and their friends. During his initial stay he spent mornings writing his lectures, but in 1908 he did just enough work, he said, to keep his blood moving.[20] In 1907 he gave a talk to young people at a church and preached a sermon, but he apparently did not attend divine services[21] in 1908. On his first trip, he twice wrote Ellen that she must come with him the next year for a second honeymoon; he seems to have given up the idea in 1908.[22]

Ellen Wilson undoubtedly suspected the depth of her husband's attachment to Mrs. Peck. He went to great lengths in 1908 to suggest that their friendship was platonic. Shortly after his arrival in Bermuda, he wrote: "Of course I am seeing a great deal of Mrs. Peck. She is fine and dear. But I am remembering your injunction. There is quite a household, all of whom I enjoy: her mother, a fine old lady with the breeziness of the West about her, her step-daughter [Harriet Peck], a perfectly charming young person of twenty-two of whom she has had charge since she was four, and who is enough like her to be her own daughter, her son by her first marriage, for the sake of whose throat and lungs she stays down here, the tutor who is preparing him for college (for which he is a good deal belated), a very attractive young product of sober college training, and another youngster who is her son's most intimate friend and whose modesty and good sense prove her son's good taste in choosing chums. . . . It is a lively and most

[17] WW to MAHP, September 28, 1913, PWW, Vol. 28, p. 337.

[18] C. February 1, 1908, ibid., Vol. 17, p. 611.

[19] WW to EAW, January 26, 1907, ibid., p. 14.

[20] WW to EAW, February 4, 1908, ibid., p. 612.

[21] See Wilson's notes for a sermon at Christ Church, Warwick, Bermuda, February 3, 1907, ibid., pp. 27-28. Mrs. Peck was a Presbyterian but not a churchgoer. Hulbert, The Story of Mrs. Peck, pp. 173-74.

[22] WW to EAW, January 26 and 30, 1907, PWW, Vol. 17, pp. 15, 27.

engaging household, in which one can never be alone, and in the midst of which your husband is as young and gay as the youngest member, never, unless expressly challenged to it, saying a single serious word. They are nearly out of the woods: they have heard nearly all my stories! I brought two pictures of you with me: a small copy of the drawing and the photograph which I keep in an oval frame, and Mrs. Peck is so charmed with them that she insists upon keeping one of them on the mantelpiece in her drawing room, so that it sometimes seems almost as if my darling were there. You can imagine how delightful it is for me to have such a young and jolly circle to resort to."[23] Wilson was also impressed by Mrs. Peck's interesting mind, frank disposition, and motherly attention to the young officers of the garrison.[24]

Ellen evidently was not convinced that her husband had been spending all of his time frolicking with the children, and, at some time during the next months, there was a confrontation over Mrs. Peck. Its nature is not recorded,[25] but Mrs. Wilson did not accompany her husband to Great Britain as she had done in 1906. None of her letters to him over the summer have survived—possibly they were destroyed by Wilson himself, or by a member of his family after his death. Wilson expressed his feelings of guilt and repentance in a highly emotional letter from the Lake District: "Oh, how my heart *aches* for my dear ones, and how much sharper the pain will be there! I never in my life longed for *you*, my sweet, sweet darling, as I do now or realized more entirely all that you mean to me, everything that sustains and enriches life. You have only to believe in and trust me, darling, and *all* will come right, what you do not understand included. I know my heart now, if ever I did, *and it belongs to you.* God give you the gracious strength to be patient with me! 'Emotional love,'—ah, dearest, that was a cutting and cruel judgment and utterly false; but as natural as false; but I never blamed you for it or wondered at it. I only understood—only saw the thing as you see it and as it is *not,* and suffered, am suffering still, ah, how deeply!—but with access of love, constant access of love. My darling! I have never been worthy of you, but I love you with all my poor, mixed, inexplicable nature, with everything fine and tender in me. Suffering and thinking over here by myself, *I know it!*"[26]

[23] WW to EAW, February 4, 1908, *ibid.,* pp. 612-13.

[24] WW to EAW, January 26, 1908, *ibid.,* pp. 607.

[25] There is no existing Peck-Wilson correspondence during the seven months following his return from Bermuda.

[26] WW to EAW, July 20, 1908, *PWW,* Vol. 18, pp. 371-72.

Wilson may also have projected feelings of guilt in his comments on receiving the news of the death of Grover Cleveland. With reference to the former President's support of Dean West, he told his wife that Cleveland had been West's "dupe and tool." Cleveland's death was "not untimely," he then wrote, because "the degree and the manner in which some of his early moral weaknesses[27] had returned might soon have become generally known."[28]

Wilson described his arrival at the home of Frederic Yates—a portrait painter whom the Wilsons had met and liked in 1906—in painstaking detail (apparently to assure his wife that he was not engaged in another affair). "I knocked at the door, Mrs. Yates opened it, and we faced one another with delight. She almost embraced me. Yates himself was in the garden up the hillside, putting in some lettuce, and, before my greetings with Mrs. Yates were over, I had him, too, by the hand. Mrs. Yates drew us both into the house, one arm about her husband, the other for a moment about me."[29] When he later told Ellen about his stay, he quite gratuitously referred to the "quite hopeless New England limitations" of Mrs. Yates's mind.[30]

Wilson's high level of emotional excitement was indicated by particularly vivid visual imagery and some remarkable memory phenomena. "At every turn," he wrote Ellen, "I came upon some tree or nook or sweet outlook that you had admired and loved. I could almost hear your dear voice at my elbow and feel the touch of your dear hand on my arm."[31] A mountain reminded him of "some great nourishing breast."[32] He had either recurrent dreams or hypnagogic hallucinations.[33] "I saw your face as clearly as if you had actually been within touch of my lips the other night in a dream. It has come to me again and again of late, but this time it was so real, so vivid, so dear, that it brought me wide awake and I could have cried with longing for you."[34]

On the day of his debarkation in Glasgow, he had a vivid panoramic memory: "Like the creature of habit I am, I have come to the Grand Hotel, the hotel I came to twelve years ago, when I first came over alone for a bicycle trip, and here I sit in the writing room where I then

[27] Wilson was referring to Cleveland's illegitimate child; the following remark is mysterious.
[28] WW to EAW, June 29, 1908, PWW, Vol. 18, p. 346.
[29] WW to EAW, July 16, 1908, ibid., p. 365.
[30] WW to EAW, August 24, 1908, ibid., p. 411.
[31] WW to EAW, July 16, 1908, ibid., pp. 364-65.
[32] WW to EAW, July 20, 1908, ibid., p. 371.
[33] Visions or illusions occurring in states of light sleep.
[34] WW to EAW, July 10, 1908, PWW, Vol. 18, p. 358.

laboriously wrote my first letter to you with my left hand! The moment
I entered the room the whole thing came over me again, with startling
vividness; and, with that, every other detail of the trip [of 1896], for
I have not stopped at this hotel since and so nothing has intervened
here to blur or supplant those first associations. I remember how we
parted in New York, how you went to the 23rd St. car with me and
there left me, of course without a parting kiss; how I watched your
dear figure as long as I could see it, with an intolerable lump in my
throat. I remember the dress you had on as if I had seen it yesterday.
And then the novel voyage and all that followed! There is no dear Mr.
Woods[35] this time, alas! sitting here with me in the writing room and
I am desperately lonely."[36]

A month later, on entering Ambleside, a village where the Wilsons
had stayed in 1906, he had a comparable experience, this time with
a déjà vu quality.

"It would be quite impossible for me to describe my feelings," he
wrote. "No walk in Princeton, not even the road from our gate to our
door at Prospect, could have been more familiar to me than was every
foot of that way, or could have stirred deeper feelings, more varied
or vivid memories. I hurried a bit; I did not *wish* to stop at any one
point. I did not scrutinize the cottage: I only glanced at it. It seemed
as if I did not have to *look* at anything. A singular warmth came into
my veins, such as has always come into them when I was conscious
of *you*, the warmth of comradeship and solace and love and close
sympathy, the warmth of a sort of permanent romance, the source of
all my happiness, the warmth of being your lover in every fibre of me,
in every drop of my blood! In the midst of my acute loneliness, I was
intensely happy."[37]

Déjà vu phenomena and panoramic memories are manifestations
of excessive neural discharge from the temporal lobe, a region of the
brain where memory, time sense, perception, and some of the components of dreaming are integrated. In a panoramic memory, time is
condensed; events, which originally had been experienced over hours
or days, seem to reoccur in seconds. In a déjà vu episode, there is an
overwhelming sense of familiarity even though the subject has never
before witnessed the scene. Moreover, the person feels not only that
he has "already seen," but that he knows exactly what will unfold
next. Each phenomenon may be accompanied by intense emotion, and

[35] The Charles A. Woods, of Marion, S.C., who had met Wilson on their way to
Great Britain in 1896.
[36] WW to EAW, June 29, 1908, *PWW*, Vol. 18, p. 345.
[37] WW to EAW, July 27, 1908, *ibid.*, p. 379.

there is often a transcending sense of reality and of heightened clarity of perception. Déjà vu and panoramic memory experiences may occur as part of a convulsive seizure, but there is no evidence that Wilson had seizures. They are much more common in states of great emotional stress—like the experience of seeing one's life pass before him when facing death.

When Wilson fell in love with Mary Peck in 1908, he was at a low point in his fortunes—deeply discouraged over the defeat of his quadrangle plan,[38] distressed over the defection of Jack Hibben, and worried about the new stroke that he had suffered the previous November. Mrs. Peck had an antidepressant effect on him. "Your affection," he wrote her later, "seems in some way to restore my tone, to set the courses of my blood straight again, and give me a strange mastery of myself in the midst of distressing circumstances."[39] Several years later he recalled, "I had some delicious hours in that dear little house with the bougainvillia (?) on the road to the South Shore, hours when I lost all of the abominable self-consciousness that has been my bane all my life, and felt perfectly at ease, happily myself, released from bonds to enjoy the real freedom of my mind."[40]

Mary Peck's autobiography and her letters indicate that she had a good understanding of her friend. She thought that, because he had denied himself any play for so long, he was attracted to her by her "zest for the joy of living." She could joke with him in a way in which Ellen and the serious-minded faculty wives in Princeton could not. She teased him about his devotion to fried chicken, corn and beans, and southern cooking, and laughed at his remark that he had never smoked because he could not kiss his loved ones with the taste of tobacco on his lips.[41] The fact that she smoked seemed to make her more daringly glamorous. She was an enchanting figure in the fairyland of Bermuda.

Ellen Wilson's ambivalence was another factor which furthered the romance. After the stroke of 1906, she wanted her husband to have any pleasure that might relax him. She had encouraged him to meet women like Nancy Saunders Toy and Edith Gittings Reid, whom she believed were more interesting and "gamesome" than she. "Since he has married a wife who is not gay," she told her cousin Florence Stevens Hoyt, "I must provide him with friends who are."[42] Wilson urged her to go to Bermuda with him in 1907, but she refused[43] (as

[38] He joked to Mrs. Peck that he had lost the quads and gotten the wrangles.
[39] WW to MAHP, February 21, 1910, PWW, Vol. 20, p. 150.
[40] WW to MAHP, January 10, 1911, ibid., Vol. 22, p. 325.
[41] Hulbert, The Story of Mrs. Peck, pp. 164-65, 178.
[42] Interview with Florence S. Hoyt, October 1926, Baker Papers.
[43] Elliott, My Aunt Louisa, p. 197.

had been the case when Wilson wanted her to come to Baltimore in 1892). Ellen might have felt that she would not feel comfortable in the idle and sophisticated society of Bermuda. She was upset by the tense situation at Princeton, worried over the recurrent nervous breakdowns of her brother Stockton, and still grieving for Eddie Axson. She might have felt that Woodrow would enjoy himself more without her. From what we know of her character, she might have reacted to Wilson's involvement with Mrs. Peck with self-reproach. She regarded it her duty to accept any humiliation for his sake. In the last year of her life, Ellen told Cary Grayson that the Peck affair was the only unhappiness that Woodrow had caused her during their entire marriage.[44]

Ellen carried out the amenities. After Woodrow's return from abroad, she went with him to visit the Pecks in Pittsfield and invited Mrs. Peck to Prospect. Madge Axson recalled Mrs. Peck's stay in Princeton. "She was gay and entertaining and interested in our doings, a woman of the world, not beautiful, but giving the effect of beauty. The women of Princeton at that time were not smart looking, and Mrs. Peck was nothing if not smart. She wasn't accustomed to faculty circles and the difference between their clothes and hers made her vaguely uncomfortable. Dressing for a tea one afternoon, she called me into her room. 'Do you think this frock is too extreme?' she asked with a touch of anxiety that I thought very appealing."[45] Eleanor Wilson remembered Mrs. Peck as a fascinating, charming woman with great intelligence and humor. "We all enjoyed her immensely, but her constant suggestions about improving our appearance got on our nerves at last. She insisted that Jessie would be more attractive with a sleek coiffure and long dangling earrings, an idea that horrified us all."[46]

Wilson's letters to Mrs. Peck in the autumn of 1908 took on the

---

[44] Breckinridge Long wrote in his diary: "Cary and I have several points in interest of mutual nature—horses and Woodrow Wilson. We soon got on the subject of Wilson and he told me—briefly—of several incidents I did not know much about. 'Mrs. Peck' was the subject of one. It seems W. W. has talked to Cary several times about her. He used to write her letters—many of them. Mrs. Wilson—the first—also talked about her to Cary and among other things said that the 'Peck' affair was the only unhappiness he had caused her during their whole married life—not that there was anything wrong— or improper—about it, for there was not, but just that a brilliant mind and an attractive woman had some-how fascinated—temporarily—Mr. Wilson's mind and she (Mrs. Wilson) did not want to share his confidence or his inner mind with anyone." The Diary of Breckinridge Long, MS. in the Papers of Breckinridge Long, Library of Congress, Jan. 11, 1924; hereinafter cited as the Long diary.

[45] Elliott, *My Aunt Louisa*, p. 198.

[46] McAdoo, *The Woodrow Wilsons*, p. 131.

tone of those to a relative or long-time family friend. He wrote of the trials of a college president and of university and family activities. Jessie made a trip to Pittsfield, and Wilson wrote to Mrs. Peck, telling her how charmed Jessie had been by her. Similarly, he was pleasantly surprised by an unexpected visit from Allen Hulbert.[47] There is no surviving correspondence for the winter 1908-1909, but the first letter that we have (dated April 13, 1909) indicates that Wilson had again become deeply involved emotionally with her problems. Also, he addressed her no longer as "Dear Mrs. Peck," but as "Dearest Friend." The letter was apparently in response to one of hers in which she had told Wilson how upset she had been by his advice to get a separation rather than a divorce. Wilson asked her forgiveness for wounding her with apparently cold counsel.[48] When she wrote two weeks later that Allen had left her to take a job in New York,[49] he consoled the doting and bereaved mother: "I know what it will cost you, your 'boy' gone, a man substituted to whom you can play mother only in your heart, by yearning solicitude, tender counsel, a word now and again when the dear chance of seeing him comes, all the sweet intimacy and dependence gone, your baby gone out of your arms, and in great part out of your ken; and my heart is heavy for you. I know how desolate you will feel—how the sense of loneliness will thicken like something that chokes your faculties, weakens your sense of reality—of identity even—and makes all your life seem strange and disconnected from memory. I never had a son, but I *was* a son and had a mother whom I devotedly loved and in whom I saw all these things when I was separated from her for life. She lived long enough to be very proud of her son's success, and he loved her always as he had loved her when he was a lad, but he had gone from the household, his call was not in her ear, the days went by without him. I am sorry, so sorry, and wish I knew the right words of comfort with which to wing my words of deep, affectionate sympathy. Perhaps you will go to live with him— and the years bring you the love of new friends of whom I am proud to be one."[50] Through Mrs. Peck, Wilson thus replayed the drama of his own separation from his mother, and movingly described the experience of loneliness.

As the pressures of the graduate college controversy mounted in the spring of 1909, Wilson grew more lonely for his dearest friend. As he was ready to leave with Mrs. Wilson to deliver the Phi Beta Kappa

---

[47] WW to MAHP, October 25, 1908, *PWW*, Vol. 18, pp. 471-72.
[48] WW to MAHP, April 13, 1909, *ibid.*, Vol. 19, pp. 160-61.
[49] Allen Hulbert had given up his plan to go to college.
[50] WW to MAHP, April 28, 1909, *PWW*, Vol. 19, p. 175.

oration at Harvard, he wrote that his thoughts played constantly about her.[51] He asked his friend how he could have the holiday spirit if his thoughts were filled with "anxious conjecture" about those he loved.[52] The Wilsons spent the summer in Lyme, Connecticut. When Wilson was unable to visit Mrs. Peck while he was on a trip to New York (she had taken an apartment there with her mother after her separation), he wrote that he had thought of her "a thousand times."[53] Wilson was upset when Mrs. Peck considered an invitation to be the guest of the Governor of Bermuda, a bachelor with whom local gossip had linked her romantically.[54]

There was an intensification of their relationship during the great crisis in the graduate college controversy, which preceded Wilson's departure for Bermuda in February 1910. Mrs. Peck was unable to spend the winter there because she was short of money, but Wilson visited her at her apartment before he left. Aboard ship, about to sail, he wrote: "Here I am—sad, lonely, homesick, friendsick—but well and deliberately cheerful."[55] An excerpt from her first letter indicates how intimate they had become. She wrote: "I have just returned from spending the weekend with Mrs. Roebling,[56] and glad I am to be back in my own little nest on the housetop. . . . Before I write another word, I want to tell you—best beloved—of a small habit you have, which may cause you to be misjudged. You will laugh when you hear it. Do *not* leave your spoon in your cup when you drink your tea. It's a crime in the eyes of some, no less. You do not mind my telling you? *I* would not care if you lapped it up with your tongue. The king can do no wrong. I am so tired I can hardly write—but want to send you just a line and the addresses you wish. The papers announce that you left for Bermuda—*silent*. How does this happen. Write me a *long* letter— tell me of our blessed isles. Ah! If only I were there. Rest every moment of the day and night—and come back *soon*."[57]

From Bermuda, Wilson wrote letters of equal frequency, length, and warmth to his wife and to his devoted friend.[58] He told them of his

---

[51] WW to MAHP, June 26, 1909, *ibid.,* p. 271.

[52] WW to MAHP, July 25, 1909, *ibid.,* p. 317.

[53] WW to MAHP, July 18, 1909, *ibid.,* p. 312.

[54] WW to MAHP, September 12, 1909, *ibid.,* p. 383.

[55] WW to MAHP, February 12, 1910, *ibid.,* Vol. 20, p. 122.

[56] Cornelia Witsell Farrow (Mrs. Washington Augustus) Roebling, who lived in Trenton, N.J.

[57] MAHP to WW, February 15, 1910, *PWW,* Vol. 20, p. 127.

[58] Wilson even indicated divine approval of the romance. He wrote Mrs. Peck: "God was very good to me to send me such a friend, so perfectly satisfying and delightful, so *delectable*." WW to MAHP, February 21, 1910, *ibid.,* p. 150.

affection and loneliness, and they responded in characteristic fashion. When he complained to his wife that he was "intensely lonely" because the steamer had not brought a letter from her, she replied that she was "horribly distressed and ashamed" to have disappointed him.[59] Ellen described her activities in Princeton and urged him to prolong his vacation, while Mary told him how depressed she was away from Bermuda and how much she missed him in "this hateful place."[60] When Wilson told his wife how deeply affected he had been by the abuse heaped on him at Princeton, she replied that it was well that he was having a rest from it.[61] Mrs. Peck, on the other hand, not without a touch of humor, fed his self-righteousness and emphasized her own martyrdom. She wrote: "Of *course* you feel the hurt of things said and done, and you may have more to bear, but you have not that hardest thing—regret at having been untrue to yourself and your ideals. 'Blessed are ye, when men shall revile you, etc' (That 'etc.' does not look very respectful in that quotation, does it?) but you know what I mean. The *best* are on your side, but unfortunately they are sometimes in the minority. I think I understand the meaning of *infinite* patience and of love better than I ever have before, now that we can, by the great inventions of this time see the world whole—as we never have before. And know it in all its meanness—and sordid selfishness."[62]

Although Wilson told his wife that he missed her with "an almost unendurable longing" and pictured the joy of holding her in his arms "close, close, close, until your sweetness fairly enters my blood and makes me over,"[63] he restrained his longing in planning his homecoming schedule. He told Ellen that, because of the delays at quarantine and customs, it was likely that he would miss the morning train to Princeton, but that he would be home by dinner time.[64] However, on the same day he wrote rather more enthusiastically to Mrs. Peck: "Next steamer I come myself! Heaven send the good old Bermudian [to] get me in at such time as will enable me to see my dear, dear friend before I must start for Princeton. It would be heartbreaking to have to wait still longer, when my thought has been waiting, waiting, waiting for the happy moment when I should be in your presence again and have one of the hours with you that means so much to me!"[65]

[59] WW to EAW, February 20, 1910; EAW to WW, February 24, 1910, *ibid.*, pp. 144, 172.

[60] MAHP to WW, February 18, 1910, *ibid.*, p. 142.

[61] EAW to WW, February 17, 1910, *ibid.*, p. 134.

[62] MAHP to WW, February 18, 1910, *ibid.*, p. 142.

[63] WW to EAW, February 25, 1910, *ibid.*, pp. 175-76.

[64] WW to EAW, February 28, 1910, *ibid.*, p. 184.

[65] WW to MAHP, February 28, 1910, *ibid.*, p. 185.

Several days later, he assured her that, should the fates be against him, he would be back to see her in a day or two.[66]

What the fates decreed for Wilson is not recorded, but his passions soon cooled. When he courted his second wife, Edith Bolling Galt, in 1915, he confessed to what he called the contemptible error and madness of a few months that had left a stain upon his whole life.[67] Although Wilson and Mary Peck apparently had no further amorous relationships, they continued to correspond and remain devoted friends until he fell in love with Mrs. Galt. Over this period, he described to Mrs. Hulbert in intimate fashion his feelings about his last days at Princeton and his reactions to the exciting events of his governorship and presidency. Some of her letters were gay and witty over these years, but more and more often they dealt with her unhappiness. She became a pathetic figure following her divorce in July 1912 and her resumption of Hulbert as her legal surname. She experienced economic difficulties due largely to extravagant living and her son's ill-starred business ventures and problems with alcohol. She lapsed into periods of vaguely defined ill health and depression, which even Bermuda failed to remedy. Wilson was unfailingly sympathetic; he helped her to find jobs, and he aided her financially. One factor in Wilson's devotion may have been the fear that Mrs. Hulbert, in her impoverished state, might sell his letters and ruin his career—she refused offers from his political enemies—but this was hardly a primary consideration.

Wilson's attachment to her had many of the features that had bound him emotionally to his mother. He empathized with her ailments and misfortunes as he had identified himself with his mother's ill health and unhappiness. On campaign trips, he was more apt to report fatigue and stomach upsets to Mrs. Hulbert than to his wife. He idealized Mary Hulbert as uncritically as he had his mother. He saw behind the gay facade of a woman of fashion a thoughtful, noble, courageous, and uncomplaining person. Many of Mrs. Hulbert's virtues, however, existed only in Wilson's fancy. Along with her wit and charm, she was a histrionic, self-indulgent, flirtatious[68] woman, dependent on the

[66] WW to MAHP, March 4, 1910, *ibid.,* pp. 210-11.

[67] WW to Edith Bolling Galt, September 21, 1915, Wilson Papers.

[68] Mrs. Peck recalled in her autobiography that, when she was in Rome during her first marriage, men courted her in the Continental fashion. "Madame Glacée, I call you," one of her admirers said, "for when I even try to touch your lovely hair, you are one iceberg." In Bermuda, when Governor Kitchener was escorting her in the rain to her carriage, she exclaimed that her gold slippers would be ruined. When the gallant Governor offered to carry her, she said, "Yes, and utterly swamp your dignity as Governor, possibly your reputation, to say nothing of mine." Hulbert, *The Story of Mrs. Peck,* pp. 69, 111.

pleasures of society and the attentions of important men. While Wilson admired her devotion to her son, others might have thought that Allen was spoiled. Wilson's sense of chivalry was outraged when a gossip writer commented on her cable bills to Bermuda and her fad of designing new monographs for her cigarettes.[69] He solicitously cautioned her not to overdo as she had during the "twenty heartbreaking years" of her marriage to Peck.[70] Once he told her that she had worn herself out by a "*life*-time of moral effort."[71] He strongly reinforced her image of herself as a wronged, betrayed, and long-suffering martyr. Never did he suggest that she might have brought some of her troubles on herself.

Mary Hulbert became part of Wilson's self. He told her that he was "singularly lonely," and that he could follow her moods and thoughts and participate in her experiences.[72] The charm of her letters, he wrote, seemed to come out of some past life of his own.[73] When he felt hemmed in by responsibilities, he called her a free creature, a "veritable child of nature." Thoughts of her brought feelings of freshness and freedom into his life. "There is an air about you like the air of the open, a directness, a simplicity, a free movement that link you with wild things that are yet meant to be taken into one's confidence and loved. And so you have seemed part of the day to me ever since morning."[74]

Mary Hulbert played an important role in Wilson's life. While his wife complemented his more rational self, his "dearest friend" continued to fulfill emotional needs. Particularly in times of stress, his evocation of romantic images of her compensated for her physical absence.

[69] WW to MAHP, August 1, 1909, *PWW*, Vol. 19, 322, 324, n.2.
[70] WW to MAHP, March 12, 1912, *ibid.*, Vol. 22, p. 500.
[71] WW to MAHP, March 17, 1912, *ibid.*, Vol. 24, p. 250.
[72] WW to MAHP, January 10, 1911, *ibid.*, Vol. 22, p. 324.
[73] WW to MAHP, February 19, 1911, *ibid.*, p. 439.
[74] WW to MAHP, September 19, 1909, *ibid.*, Vol. 19, p. 385.

CHAPTER XII

The Graduate College Controversy

THE ORIGIN of the graduate college controversy goes back to 1900, when Andrew F. West was chosen to be dean of the new Princeton Graduate School. West's election was part of the revolt against President Patton's do-nothing regime, and, lest Patton block the school's development, West was given extraordinary powers. He had authority to set policy, appoint faculty members, and award degrees. This control made him virtually independent of the President and subject only to the board of trustees.

In his inaugural address, Wilson set a new residential graduate college as one of the priorities of his administration. He said:

"We mean, so soon as our generous friends have arranged their private finances in such a way as to enable them to release for our use enough money for the purpose, to build a notable graduate college. I say 'build' because it will be not only a body of teachers and students but also a college of residence, where men shall live together in the close and wholesome comradeships of learning. We shall build it, not apart, but as nearly as may be at the very heart, the geographical heart, of the university; and its comradeships shall be for young men and old, for the novice as well as for the graduate. It will constitute but a single term in the scheme of coordination which is our ideal. The windows of the graduate college must open straight upon the walks and quadrangles and lecture halls of the *studium generale*."[1]

Wilson and West were agreed upon a plan for graduate students to live in a great quadrangle, with their own conference rooms, under a master whose residence, after the manner of an English college, occupied one corner of the quadrangle.[2] In August 1902 West went to Europe for four months to study graduate education and spent most of his time at Oxford and Cambridge. His seventeen-page report, put out in a handsome brochure, emphasized architecture: it included sketches of Magdalen College and photogravures of cloisters, halls,

---

[1] "Princeton for the Nation's Service," October 25, 1902, *PWW*, Vol. 14, pp. 182-83.

[2] Report to the Board of Trustees of Princeton University, October 21, 1902, *ibid.*, pp. 157-58.

and gardens. West recommended Gothic-style buildings and a location on campus on the site of the present McCosh Hall.[3] His vision was that of an Oxford college transplanted to Princeton.

President Wilson and the board of trustees approved West's report, but little was done to implement it. Wilson was applying the funds of the university to new buildings, recruitment of faculty, and to the preceptorial plan; and he vetoed West's request to solicit an endowment from the alumni. West was disappointed, but he continued to support Wilson's program. West's fortunes looked up in 1904, when Grover Cleveland, a close friend, became chairman of the trustees' Committee on the Graduate School. One year later, West obtained a temporary home for the graduate college at Merwick, a spacious estate bought by Moses Taylor Pyne and situated half a mile off the campus on Bayard Lane. Wilson, in his commencement address of 1905, praised the beauty of Merwick and stated that it gave the graduate college the prospect of early realization under the influence of Dean West.[4] This prospect appeared close at hand when, in March 1906, Josephine Swann died and left about $275,000 for the construction of a graduate college, to be named for her first husband, John R. Thomson, and to be located on the grounds of Princeton University.

As the struggle over the graduate college became so highly personalized, it is important to note the background of Wilson's major antagonists, West and Pyne, and Wilson's chief supporter on the faculty, Henry Burchard Fine. West, born in 1853, was, like Wilson, the son of a Presbyterian minister. His father, like Joseph R. Wilson, was contentious. After attending Centre College in Kentucky, Andrew F. West matriculated at Princeton and graduated in the Class of 1874. He held a fellowship in classics for two years and taught in a secondary school until 1881, when he studied in Europe for several months. On his return he became principal of Morris Academy (New Jersey). In 1883 he was given an honorary Ph.D. degree from Princeton and appointed to a professorship of classics. West published a Latin grammar, translated the plays of Terence, wrote articles on Alcuin and other medieval scholars, and was the author of a book on the rise of Christian schools in the Middle Ages. He was awarded the degree of D.Litt. on the occasion of his visit to Oxford. West was a gifted writer of light verse and epigrams in English, Latin, and Greek. After Wilson, he was probably the most sought-after speaker among the Princeton

---

[3] Andrew F. West, *The Proposed Graduate College at Princeton University* (Princeton, N. J., 1903), pp. 14-20.

[4] News account of Wilson's commencement address, *Daily Princetonian*, June 14, 1905, in *PWW*, Vol. 16, pp. 140-41.

faculty. He was a brilliant organizer of ceremonies: he arranged both the Sesquicentennial celebration and Wilson's inaugural festivities.

"Andy" West had a gregarious disposition, with a genial arm-around-the-shoulder manner. He suffered a personal tragedy when, after the birth of their only child, his wife became psychotic and was permanently hospitalized. He is said to have visited her every week of her life and was compassionate with people in trouble. He took a fatally ill colleague and his family into his home and cared for the man until he died. West was a noted *bon vivant* and led a social, bachelor's life. He was a delightful conversationalist and had a remarkable ability to win the friendship of the famous and the wealthy.[5] West invited Grover Cleveland to the Sesquicentennial, and the President was so charmed that he settled in Princeton after his retirement and named his estate "Westland." In tribute to West's reputation as a fund raiser, Cleveland inscribed in a copy of his *Defense of Fishermen*: "Andrew F. West who like the disciple Andrew discovers those with loaves and fishes."[6] West was an interesting teacher and was popular with un-dergraduates, but he was criticized for cutting classes and showing favoritism toward the sons of wealthy families.[7]

Despite West's gracious personal qualities, he was ill-equipped to be the head of a modern graduate school. He had been neither a graduate student nor an instructor of graduate work. West had little academic knowledge outside his field of classics; he knew little of science or of research. His ideas of education were elitist: Princeton had entrance examinations, but West wanted graduates of certain private schools admitted by certificate.[8] Bound by Presbyterian ortho-doxy, he had opposed the election of Frederick Jackson Turner to the faculty.

Life at Merwick was idyllic. Work in the morning followed a late and leisurely breakfast. Afternoons were devoted to long walks in the country and to sports—mainly tennis on the Merwick court. Food was excellent; dinners were splendid occasions, with students in academic gowns; and the master said grace in Latin. On Wednesday evenings, the students, wearing evening clothes under their gowns and bearing lighted candles, escorted West across the lawn from his residence on

[5] The verse in the "Faculty Song" devoted to West ran:
   Here's to Andy three million West
   Sixty-two inches round the vest
   At getting money he's the best.
[6] Perry, *And Gladly Teach*, p. 146.
[7] Interview with David Magie, June 6, 1939, Bragdon Collection.
[8] Walworth, *Woodrow Wilson*, I, 102.

the other side of the street. Usually, there was a guest who spoke after dinner.[9] The new graduate college was to be a place where raw youths would be turned into cultured gentlemen, and the lost art of conversation would be rediscovered.[10] Yet West was not, as some of his critics later charged, primarily interested in wealth and show. West's vision was that of a many-spired Gothic edifice, steeped in monastic medieval traditions, which would imbue students with the spirit of Christian learning—and of himself presiding over the high table intoning Latin graces. The ideal of such a graduate college became an all-consuming passion with West. To realize his dream, he worked skillfully, industriously, and indefatigably.

Moses ("Momo") Taylor Pyne, like the other major participants in the graduate college controversy, was wholly dedicated to Princeton. A graduate of the Class of 1877, he became a trustee in 1885, and never missed a meeting of the board for thirty-five years. He became chairman of the Committee on the Graduate School on the death of Grover Cleveland in 1908. Pyne had inherited great wealth, and he and his family had contributed lavishly to the university. While he maintained an office in New York, he lived on a large estate, Drumthwacket, located on the outskirts of Princeton, in order to be closer to the university. Pyne was responsible for the formation of the alumni associations in the 1890s and was one of the founders of the *Princeton Alumni Weekly*. He was Princeton's most respected and influential alumnus.[11] "Momo" Pyne took a proprietary interest in Princeton. Until they disagreed over the quadrangle plan, Pyne figuratively worshiped Wilson.

Henry B. Fine graduated as valedictorian of the Class of 1880, after having succeeded Wilson as managing editor of *The Princetonian*. He received the Ph.D. degree from the University of Leipzig in 1885 and was appointed Professor of Mathematics at his alma mater in 1891. Wilson made him Dean of the Faculty in 1903. Fine was not only a distinguished mathematician, a founder and later president of the American Mathematical Association, but he also had broad scientific and educational interests. As has been said, he played a major role in

[9] Edward Capps *et al.*, Supplementary Memorandum, January 10, 1910, enc. in Henry B. Fine *et al.* to WW, January 11, 1910, *PWW*, Vol. 19, pp. 755-56; J. D. Davies, "The Lost World of Andrew Fleming West," *Princeton Alumni Weekly*, LX (Jan. 15, 1960), 10-14.

[10] Interview with Edward Capps, March 23, 1943, Bragdon Collection.

[11] On Pyne's birthday in 1907, just after the final defeat of Wilson's quad plan, West wrote a poem to him elegantly printed and bound and inscribed with a Greek phrase that translates "Keep young, dear soul." Walworth, *Woodrow Wilson*, p. 120, n.4.

the development of the scientific departments at Princeton during the Wilson administration. He took an active part in the arduous task of reforming the curriculum and in the enforcement of academic standards and discipline. A man of stern demeanor and unquestioned fairness, he was highly respected by the students.[12] Fine made independent judgments and, despite their personal friendship, he did not hesitate to express his critical views firmly and directly to Wilson. Throughout the quadrangle plan and graduate college controversies, he was Wilson's most vigorous advocate on the faculty, sometimes pushing him further than Wilson was willing to go at the time.

Wilson, although he was on friendly terms with West, had been wary of his political tactics. Shortly after his inauguration, he told Bliss Perry: "If West begins to intrigue against me as he did against Patton, *we must see who is master!*"[13] West, however, did not openly oppose Wilson until the spring of 1906. They had their first disagreement when Wilson proposed the Bayles Farm, a tract of university-owned land adjacent to the campus, as the permanent site of the graduate college. West, although he had previously declared for a location on campus, now came out for Merwick. Because of his stroke, which occurred on May 28, Wilson was unable to attend the meeting of the board of trustees in June and asked Jack Hibben to represent him. He charged Hibben to emphasize that geographical separation was out of the question and that it was important for professors to be able to meet with their students outside of regular courses, in small, intimate groups.[14] It was evident to the members of the board that West was bidding for autonomy; in Wilson's absence, they deferred a decision.

The meeting of the board of trustees on October 19, 1906, held a few days after Wilson's return from his convalescence abroad, was one of the most dramatic and decisive events of the whole graduate college controversy. On October 6, the day after Wilson sailed from Glasgow, West received an offer of the presidency of the Massachusetts Institute of Technology. The choice of West, a classicist with no experience or interest in scientific matters, was surprising.[15] Two factors,

[12] His verse to the "Faculty Song" ran:
  Here's to Harry our brand new Dean
  His bones are long and his legs are lean
  Gives the students all fair play
  He's doing well so let him stay.
[13] Perry, *And Gladly Teach*, p. 158.
[14] WW to John G. Hibben, draft of a letter, June 4, 1906, *PWW*, Vol. 16, pp. 413-14.
[15] It was so surprising that a rumor spread that M.I.T. had meant the offer for Dean

however, had led to his selection by the corporation of M.I.T. The school was expanding and moving its campus from within the city of Boston, and the executive board must have been impressed with West's reputation as a money raiser. Secondly, President Charles W. Eliot of Harvard was putting pressure on M.I.T. to enter a merger which would make M.I.T. the science department of Harvard, and West was known as a strong opponent of Eliot's educational imperialism.[16] West made the offer public, but Wilson was probably ignorant of it until his arrival in Princeton.

West was asked to announce his decision at the trustees' meeting. According to his own account, he stated that he was attracted by the M.I.T. position because he was discouraged by the long delay in the construction of the graduate college, and that he did not want to be identified indefinitely with an unsuccessful enterprise. He said that, despite his loyal support of Wilson's programs, he and the President had not hit it off. Then the Dean listed numerous examples of what he regarded as Wilson's unfairness and asked the President directly if he had said anything that was untrue. If so, West recalled, he said that he wanted any misstatement pointed out. Then, according to West's account, Wilson sat silent for a long time with his head bowed and said only, "I am bound to say that you have a remarkable memory."[17]

In retrospect, Wilson made a great mistake in not permitting West to go to M.I.T. Undoubtedly, Wilson already had the quad plan in mind, and he may even have considered that a school of jurisprudence took precedence over a West-controlled graduate college. The least Wilson could have done was to have made it clear under what conditions he and West could work together at Princeton. Then and there he could have resolved the questions of site and West's independence. Instead, Wilson offered the following motion:

"Resolved: That the Board learns with the utmost concern of the possibility that Professor Andrew F. West may accept a call which would take him away from Princeton. The Board would consider his loss quite irreparable. By his scholarship, by his ideals, by his fertility

---

Fine, but the emissary to Princeton, asking for "the Dean's house," had been misdirected to West's home. Actually, Fine was approached by M.I.T. soon after but he refused, reportedly because he felt that he should remain at Princeton to guide Wilson. Bragdon memorandum of interviews with Jacob N. Beam, March 29 and May 3, 1941, Bragdon Collection.

[16] See Prescott, *When M.I.T. Was Boston Tech*, pp. 193-203, for an account of M.I.T.'s growing pains.

[17] Andrew F. West, "A Narrative of the Graduate College of Princeton University . . . ," mimeographed MS., Princeton University Archives.

in constructive ideas, he has made himself one of the chief ornaments and one of the most indispensable counsellors of the place. The Board has particularly counted upon him to put into operation the Graduate College which he conceived and for which it has planned. It begs to assure him that he cannot be spared and that the Board trusts that, should he remain, its hopes and his may be the sooner realized because of this additional proof of his devotion."[18]

The resolution was adopted unanimously, and West and other members of the board interpreted it as a vindication of his position and a promise of full and prompt support.

The effects of Wilson's stroke should be taken into account in trying to understand his behavior. He was, as has been noted, not in good physical shape. He was left with poor vision in his left eye and persisting weakness in his right arm.[19] The weakness was so marked that, after he had written the first four lines of his resolution extolling West, he typed the rest. Despite Wilson's cheery pronouncements about his health during the summer, he was basically depressed, frightened, and ashamed of his incapacity. In this state he may have felt that he could not afford the loss of prestige that admission of the truth of West's charges would have caused. Wilson's inordinate praise of West indicates the intensity of his concealed anger, and Wilson may have avoided a confrontation for fear of losing emotional control and perhaps precipitating another stroke. Aside from these considerations, Wilson, with the assurance gained from previous successes, may have believed that he would continue to outmaneuver West.

For the next year and a half, discussions about a graduate college were overshadowed by the events of the quad plan battle. In April 1907 a committee consisting of Wilson, the ailing Cleveland, and another trustee, Edward W. Sheldon, recommended that the new graduate college be built on the grounds of Prospect and the land adjacent to it. West countered with a delay of his building specifications and a report to the trustees that to place the college on campus would create diversions from study. This was a specious argument, but West evidently felt that he was justified in using it because he believed that Wilson had broken a commitment to him when he introduced the quad plan. Imagery and language may have played a role in keeping West and Wilson set on their divergent courses. West's original report had called for a building on campus; he had envisaged undergraduates

[18] C. October 20, 1906, *PWW*, Vol. 16, p. 467.
[19] WW to Charles W. McAlpin, July 19, 1906; WW to Annie Wilson Howe, August 2, 1906; WW to West, August 20, 1906; WW to EAW, August 24, 1906, *ibid.*, pp. 431, 432, 435, 438. See *ibid.*, p. 468, for facsimile of resolution.

passing by it on their daily walks.[20] But, in the stress of battle, the romantic image of a sheltered, monastic retreat may have taken over. The inspiring qualities of the word, "heart," as in the "geographical heart" and the "very heart" of the university, may have helped to commit Wilson to a narrow strategy.

In contrast to the refusal of alumni to contribute to the quadrangle plan, and to the meager endowment of the Graduate School, almost a million and a half dollars had been contributed for laboratories of physics, chemistry, biology, and geology. Wilson recruited such new faculty members as Edwin G. Conklin, a biologist from the University of Pennsylvania; Edward Capps and Frank F. Abbott, classicists from the University of Chicago; and James H. Jeans from Cambridge University. They came with the understanding that graduate instruction would be a major share of their duties. They were well trained and experienced in graduate programs, and their presence pointed up West's inadequacies. They were highly disturbed by the Dean's arbitrary methods and his emphasis on the social amenities, and, along with Fine and Winthrop More Daniels, urged Wilson to limit West's powers. In February 1909 Wilson proposed that West, as an ex-officio member, should work with a faculty committee on the Graduate School composed of Fine, Capps, Conklin, Daniels, and Hibben. When West objected that Wilson's action was inconsistent with his pledge of 1906, Wilson is alleged to have replied: "I wish to remind the Dean, somewhat grimly, that he must be digested into the processes of the University."[21]

Although the board approved the curbing of West's control, events did not go well for Wilson in the spring of 1909. The divisions of the quad plan fight remained, and the trustees were still not wholly committed to the Prospect site.[22] There were rumors of another donation for a graduate college, and there was disagreement over whether to go ahead and build with the Swann money or to wait for a possible addition. West and the other committee members were at odds on the architectural plans, with the Wilson supporters advocating a smaller and less luxurious facility. Alumni opposed to Wilson were backing an antiadministration candidate for alumni trustee, Wilson Farrand— the defender of Guyot Cameron. Wilson was also engaged with Harry Fine in a dispute over the preceptorial system.[23]

[20] West, The Proposed Graduate College, p. 14.

[21] West, "A Narrative," p. 44.

[22] Melancthon W. Jacobus to WW, March 26, 1909, PWW, Vol. 19, p. 122.

[23] Fine argued for a greater representation for the sciences and for a review of the efficacy of the entire system. Wilson gave in by increasing the proportion of science preceptors and by having a thorough five-year review in 1910.

West's answer to his demotion and apparent defeat was the famous Procter letter. William C. Procter, scion of the wealthy Cincinnati soap manufacturing family, was a Princeton alumnus who had been a high-school pupil of West's and later a personal friend. At the trustees' meeting on May 10, 1909, West handed Wilson a letter addressed to him (West) in which Procter proposed to give Princeton $500,000 to build a graduate college, provided the university raised a like amount. Procter, in addition, stated that the Prospect site was not suitable and that his offer was contingent upon the choice of a site satisfactory to himself.[24] Wilson, West, Pyne, and two other trustees were appointed as an *ad hoc* committee to negotiate with Procter. Wilson, temporarily concealing his anger over having been bypassed, wrote Cyrus McCormick that he was hopeful that a satisfactory site could be arranged. However, in a speech at St. Paul's school two weeks later, Wilson expressed his actual feelings.

The address was not recorded verbatim, but Wilson reportedly said that wealth was a danger to education. He said that he was sorry for the lad who was going to inherit money, since it was no longer distinguished to be rich, and the wealthy youth was doomed to obscurity. Resorting to what was to become one of his favorite alimentary metaphors, he then said: "So far as the colleges go, the sideshows have swallowed up the circus, and we don't know what is going on in the main tent and I don't know that I want to continue as ringmaster under those conditions." He also stated that all the education that took place in a school or college took place outside the classroom, and warned that schools like St. Paul's and Princeton would pass out of existence unless they adapted themselves to modern life.[25]

The speech was picked up by the Associated Press and caused a sensation. Interviewed by the *Princeton Alumni Weekly*, Wilson expressed his mortification that his old familiar doctrines had been so "misrepresented." He denied any radical intent and charged that the reporter, with "devilish ingenuity," had taken a few "whimsical illustrations" as the whole substance of his address.[26] It was true, of course, that Wilson was not expressing any radical intent, nor had he meant to attack education as a whole. Rather, he was expressing his anger at Procter for trying to dictate the site of the graduate college.

Wilson may well have known of the Procter offer before West presented it. In an address on May 6 to the Newark alumni, he launched

[24] William C. Procter to West, May 8, 1909, *PWW*, Vol. 19, pp. 189-90.

[25] Reported in the Concord, N. H., *Evening Monitor*, June 3, 1909, printed in *ibid.*, pp. 227-28.

[26] *Princeton Alumni Weekly*, IX (June 9, 1909), 551; WW to Lawrence C. Woods, June 10, 1909, *ibid.*, pp. 238, 239.

an attack on men who were using their wealth for predatory purposes. Repeating the word "criminals," he charged that covert, ingenious criminals, unschooled in the field of statesmanship, served themselves by patronizing their government and thought that they were uplifting the country. They were the country's greatest enemies.[27]

Wilson's correspondence with Mrs. Peck during the spring of 1909 reflected his state of mind. Although he was in good physical health, his repeated complaints of fatigue and the large amount of sleep he was getting suggest that he was depressed. But he told her that, as "a Scots-Irishman who will not be conquered," he was determined to win.[28] During the summer in Lyme, he rested, slept a lot, played golf, and wrote Mrs. Peck that he expected to go back to Princeton "with normal nerves and a stiffened purpose, while my opponents show signs of weakening if they should be hard pressed a little longer."[29]

Prior to his departure for vacation, Wilson and his supporters had won a victory when they defeated a motion to rescind the board's previous choice of a campus site. They again prevailed in committee sessions in the autumn of 1909. However, their success was unavailing, because Pyne had come to an agreement with Procter that the golf links, situated a mile off campus, was a suitable site. The question as to whether the golf links was legally "on the grounds of the University" was still unsettled, but the board, on October 21, voted to accept the Procter gift provided that the legality of the new site could be established. Wilson was now in a position similar to the one in which he had found himself, two years before, when the board had voted to withdraw its approval of the quad plan.

Wilson expressed his indignation in a letter to Mrs. Peck. The board, he told her, had accepted the plan of "that arch-intriguer," West, because the money overshadowed his, Wilson's, counsel. The board, he explained, did not trust West any more than he did and would be glad to get rid of him, but they wanted the money. Twice now on important questions, he complained, the board had failed to follow his counsel because money talked louder. His intrinsic thought was to resign and turn to a new field, but he would not disappoint the men on the faculty and on the board who had backed him. On a more intimate note, he told Mrs. Peck that the certainty of her love freshened his powers. "It is," he wrote, "a greater comfort than I know how to estimate to have you with your perfect sympathy and understanding

[27] News report of an address to the Newark alumni, reported in the *Newark Evening News*, May 6, 1909, in *ibid.*, pp. 186-88.

[28] WW to MAHP, April 13, 1909, *ibid.*, p. 162.

[29] WW to MAHP, August 29, 1909, *ibid.*, p. 356.

to turn to. I shall have to be careful not to overburden you with my own untoward fortunes, to dwell on them just enough to help you for a little to forget your own."[30]

In response to his frustration, Wilson turned to political activity and gave a number of speeches on national affairs and the state of the Democratic party. He also considered accepting the presidency of the University of Minnesota.[31] Wilson's troubles did not affect his health; his old Hopkins friend, Albert Shaw, found him looking "strong and well."[32] For a time it seemed as if the struggle might be settled amicably by acceptance of the golf links site and by stripping West of authority. Pyne wrote Wilson a conciliatory note recalling their long friendship and intimate association. He expressed his willingness to forget personalities and pledged himself to support Wilson in any way consistent with his oath as a trustee.[33] In December, Procter visited Princeton and, at a reception given for him at Merwick, Wilson and the other guests, all with a good word for Procter, mingled in friendly fashion over sandwiches and beer.[34]

The truce came to an end in late December. Wilson presented Pyne with a proposal to build two graduate colleges—one on the campus, according to the terms of the Swann bequest, the other on the golf links with the Procter money. Wilson told Pyne that the plan had the enthusiastic support of colleagues such as Capps and Daniels, and that Sheldon and other trustees would approve. Pyne did not regard the offer worth considering, as he did not believe that Procter would be willing to permit the $300,000 which he intended to put into endowment to go toward the building of dormitories and common rooms.[35] Wilson went to New York to talk with Procter on December 22. According to the account of the conversation which was given by Procter in a letter to West, Wilson said that "he had thought of another obstacle in Mrs. Swa[n]n's will": her provision for a building with a dining room and kitchen. Wilson suggested that the terms of her will would be fulfilled and money could be saved by building a smaller dining room than the elaborate one that Procter was planning as a memorial to his mother. Procter thought that a more "dignified" dining

---

[30] WW to MAHP, October 24, 1909, *ibid.*, pp. 442-44.

[31] Wilson received a letter from "Dr. Will" of the Mayo Brothers urging him to accept. William J. Mayo to WW, November 23, 1909, *ibid.*, p. 532.

[32] Albert Shaw to WW, December 15, 1909, *ibid.*, p. 606.

[33] Moses T. Pyne to WW, November 30, 1909, *ibid.*, p. 540.

[34] Howard C. Butler to Pyne, December 22, 1909, *ibid.*, p. 621.

[35] Pyne to Joseph B. Shea, December 18, 1909; WW to Pyne, December 21, 1909, *ibid.*, pp. 608-09, 611-12.

room was necessary. Mrs. Swann had specified that if all the rooms in the college were not occupied by graduate students, they should be rented to undergraduates. Wilson told Procter that the expected enrollment would exceed the facilities of the golf links and that Mrs. Swann's intent would be carried out if there were buildings on campus to house both graduates and undergraduates. Procter did not agree. In the ensuing discussion, Wilson became indignant when Procter (foolishly, Procter admitted to West) mentioned that $100,000[36] of Princeton's matching contribution would be spent for the non-revenue-producing Cleveland Memorial Tower. Wilson told Procter that not more than ten percent of the faculty favored the golf links site.[37] Procter replied that the trustees had accepted his offer and that he had nothing to do with differences among the faculty. Then, Procter reported, Wilson rose "abruptly from his chair, saying he was in despair over the situation, that he was worried to death about it and could see no solution." When Procter commented that Wilson should get a new board of trustees, Wilson replied, "No, I think they had better change their President."[38]

The Wilson-Procter interview has been given in some detail because of the dramatic events that followed. When he returned to Princeton late in the day, Wilson, from the Jersey City railroad station, wrote a brief penciled note to Pyne which seemed to threaten resignation if he could not have his way. It read:

My dear Momo:
   I spent an hour and ten minutes with Mr. Procter this afternoon. He is unwilling to adjust the terms of his offer to my suggestion.
   The acceptance of this gift has taken the guidance of the University out of my hands entirely, and I seem to have come to the end.

Affectionately yours, Woodrow Wilson[39]

The almost suicidal tone of the note indicates that Wilson was in the grip of some emotional crisis. Several days later he wrote to Thomas D. Jones: "I found myself in the grip of a conviction which I could not escape, and which I could not delay obeying. A decision made

[36] It was to cost $200,000.

[37] George M. Harper estimated that, at the time, four fifths of the faculty supported Wilson. George M. Harper to Wilson Farrand, February 3, 1910, PWW, Vol. 20, p. 74.

[38] Procter to West, December 28, 1909; WW to Pyne, December 25, 1909, ibid., Vol. 19, pp. 652-54, 628-30.

[39] WW to Pyne, December 22, 1909, ibid., p. 620.

now may possibly save the University from demoralization: a delayed decision might come too late, when everything had crystalized against it. To come to any other conclusion would have been to risk the loss of some of the most valuable men in the Faculty and an impossible situation under West, who must now be entirely eliminated, administratively." Wilson, in a letter to Pyne on Christmas Day, made it clear that the trustees would have to choose between him and the Procter offer and West.[40]

This episode raises some questions. How could Wilson have conceived such an impractical scheme as two graduate colleges, and why was he plunged into such deep despair when Pyne and Procter rejected it? The plan, if executed, would have meant duplication of buildings and a deepening of the schism. Wilson would have had his quad, but West would have had his graduate college. Why did Wilson tell Pyne that the idea had the "enthusiastic support" of his colleagues when, in all probability, he had not consulted them? There is no evidence that he had talked to Fine, Capps, or Daniels; in two letters from Daniels at the time, the matter was not mentioned.[41] He notified his allies on the board of trustees only after he had spoken with Pyne. It was precisely because Wilson was taking precipitate action without consultation that Cyrus McCormick later proposed a special committee to advise him.[42] One wonders, most of all, why Wilson could not have waited to get home before writing his letter of December 22 to Pyne. It was the only time in his and Ellen's life together (with the exception of his firing of Cameron, when she was in Italy) that he had made an important decision without consulting his wife.

The answer may lie in the intensity of Wilson's reaction to his relationship with Mrs. Peck. There is virtually no preserved correspondence for November, December, and January—probably the few months of madness to which he referred in his confession to Mrs. Galt. The brief notes between Wilson and Mrs. Peck that have survived from this period[43] and the passionate manner of Wilson's leave-taking for Bermuda show that they were in close touch. Wilson was in the habit of visiting Mrs. Peck when he was in New York on business; he was in or near the city at least six times during November and

[40] WW to Thomas D. Jones, December 27, 1909; WW to Pyne, December 25, 1909, ibid., pp. 633-34, 628-31.

[41] Winthrop M. Daniels to WW, December 20 and 21, 1909, ibid., pp. 610, 613.

[42] Cyrus H. McCormick to Edward W. Sheldon, March 4, 1910, ibid., Vol. 20, p. 213.

[43] WW to MAHP, January 2, 1910, ibid., Vol. 19, p. 704; WW to MAHP, February 8, 1910; MAHP to WW, February 10, 1910, ibid., Vol. 20, pp. 87, 118.

December. Interestingly, Mrs. Peck's apartment at 39 East 27th Street was only five blocks from the house where Dr. Wilson had received Mrs. Grannis's "loving ministries." Wilson may have been struck by the coincidence since, on December 9, in a speech in Summit, New Jersey, he stated that the most important effect that a college should have on a young man was to make him as unlike his father as possible.[44] The fact that Wilson's mind was on sex during this period is suggested also by letters written about two Princeton undergraduates who had been disciplined for being intoxicated and harassing a landlady. In each letter, Wilson stated that, among undergraduates, the only offense of greater moral turpitude than intoxication was sexual impurity.[45]

One can appreciate the degree of Wilson's emotional turmoil when one considers his behavior against the background of his previous attitudes toward sex—his prudery,[46] his jealousy of young men attracted to his daughters, and his fear that he might not be able to control his erotic drives. He had been particularly sensitive to any suggestions of marital infidelity. Stockton Axson relates an example. At Wesleyan, he and Wilson had attended a lecture by Professor Winchester on Robert Burns in which Winchester said, "Even one who was not a poet or lover felt the inspiration of the scene." The remark provoked Wilson into exclaiming, "The idea! When he said he was neither a poet nor a lover he as much as said he is no longer in love with Mrs. Winchester." Axson demurred, but Wilson insisted, "A husband should never forget he is a lover and if I said that Ellen would have a right to think I was no longer her lover."[47] In a conventional sense, Wilson's affair with Mrs. Peck was a reversal of conduct, but psychologically, it marked a breakdown, under conditions of stress, of his defenses against his sexual drives.

It is likely that, on the day of his talk with Procter at the Holland House, Wilson visited Mrs. Peck at her apartment. The agitated state in which he wrote his note to Pyne may have stemmed more from his amorous experience than from anything that Procter had told him. It is also possible that Wilson's liaison with Mrs. Peck may have motivated his ephemeral two-colleges plan. With his great capacity for

[44] Address at Summit, N.J., December 9, 1910, reported in *Newark Evening News*, December 10, 1909, printed in *ibid.*, Vol. 19, pp. 599-601.

[45] WW to Stephen Baker, December 3, 1909; WW to Adolf F. Schauffler, December 3, 1909, *ibid.*, pp. 546, 547.

[46] Mrs. Peck described Wilson's shock when a woman guest at a dinner performed the Spanish cigarette makers' dance. Mary Allen Hulbert, "The Woodrow Wilson I Knew," *Liberty: A Weekly for Everybody*, I (December 20, 1924), 8.

[47] Axson Memoir.

symbolization, he may have, unconsciously, represented the dichotomy in his emotional life—Ellen in Princeton and Mary in New York—in the form of a legitimate establishment near Prospect and an illegitimate one on the golf links.

Pyne now planned a maneuver to undermine Wilson's argument that the site of the graduate college was vital. He induced Procter to write him a letter accepting Wilson's two-colleges proposal,[48] which Wilson was no longer advancing. As the January 1910 meeting of the trustees' Committee on the Graduate School approached, both sides had prepared their strategy. The Wilson forces would introduce a motion to reject the original Procter offer, and Pyne would spring the new Procter letter.[49]

Pyne called the meeting to order in his Wall Street office at 10 a.m. on the morning of Wednesday, January 12. The brief minutes state only: "On the motion of President Wilson the Committee adjourned to meet in the Faculty Room in Princeton at half past ten Thursday morning, January 13th, to consider a recommendation to the Board of Trustees concerning the acceptance of Mr. Procter's gift."[50] According to Melancthon W. Jacobus, one of Wilson's strong supporters, the adjournment was made at Pyne's request on the plea that he had not yet made up his mind about what should be done.[51] Actually, Pyne wanted the postponement because he had not yet received Procter's letter. It arrived that afternoon. Wilson may have made the motion because a free morning in New York would have given him an opportunity to see Mrs. Peck.

The resumed committee meeting was disastrous for Wilson. Pyne was late and presented the Procter letter only ten minutes before the meeting of the full board of trustees began. Wilson was infuriated and declared that any further dealing with Procter was impossible. When he was questioned, Wilson admitted that the proposal for two graduate colleges was the same one that he himself had suggested and that, he said, had had the enthusiastic support of members of the faculty. Wilson then said that the members of the faculty now did not approve the plan, although he had earlier supposed that they did. When asked

[48] Procter to Pyne, January 12, 1910, *PWW*, Vol. 20, p. 3. Apparently, Pyne wrote this letter. See Procter to Pyne, January 22, 1910, *ibid.*, p. 47.

[49] Editorial Note: "Wilson at the Meeting of the Board of Trustees of January 13, 1910," *ibid.*, pp. 6-9.

[50] "Princeton University. Minutes of the Standing Committee of the Board of Trustees on the Graduate School, from 1901 to 1946," bound minutebook, University Archives, Princeton University, p. 265.

[51] Jacobus to Sheldon, January 27, 1910, *PWW*, Vol. 20, p. 62.

why he had proposed the two establishments in the first place, Wilson allegedly replied, "I did not know what else to suggest."[52]

Wilson entered the meeting of the full board severely shaken. The account of events that followed is based upon the testimony of Wilson Farrand, a strong opponent of Wilson. After the reading of the Procter letter, Wilson said that the trustees, in their debates about the site of the graduate college so far, had avoided the real issue. He reportedly said, "The question is one not of geography but of ideals. If the Graduate School is based on proper ideals, our Faculty can make a success of it anywhere in Mercer County." Wilson then read aloud from Procter's letter to West of May 8, 1909, in which Procter had approved the ideas set forth by West in *The Proposed Graduate College of Princeton University*. Subsequently, Wilson reportedly held up a copy of West's brochure and declared: "There, gentlemen, in that book is the real reason why the Procter gift must be declined. That book contains Professor West's ideals for the Graduate School. . . . The fundamental difficulty with Mr. Procter's offer is that it is specifically intended to carry out the ideals of that book. A graduate school based on those ideals cannot succeed." Wilson also read a biting memorandum from Dean Fine and the other majority members of the Faculty Committee of the Graduate School. It accused West of having "dilettante ideals."

James Waddel Alexander, who was urged on by Pyne, then asked Wilson why he had written a laudatory preface to West's brochure. Wilson rejoined that he had not read the book when he wrote the preface. At this point, Farrand asked him if the book was published before or after Wilson and the trustees had persuaded West to decline the presidency of M.I.T. Wilson responded that the book was published for private circulation only; however, he did admit that it appeared prior to West's call in 1906.

Wilson then signaled to Jacobus to present the motion withdrawing the earlier conditional acceptance of the Procter gift. The Rev. Dr. John De Witt at this point stated that Procter's letter of January 12 embodied Wilson's own plan for two graduate colleges, and he asked Wilson to provide a clearer explanation of why he proposed to decline the Procter offer. Wilson replied that he had advanced the two-colleges proposal "in perfect good faith," but that, when he told his friends in the faculty about his action, they had persuaded him that "the plan was unworkable and unwise." Farrand also recalled that another of

[52] West, "A Narrative," p. 77.

1. Janet Woodrow Wilson

(All photographs from collections in Princeton University Library or Archives)

2. Joseph Ruggles Wilson

3. Woodrow Wilson in 1879

4. Ellen Axson Wilson in the 1890s

5. Woodrow Wilson as a Professor at Princeton University in the 1890s

6. Stockton Axson

146 N. Charles St.,
Baltimore, Oct. 14th /83

My own sweet Ellie,

I have not forgotten that
scarcely two days have elapsed since
I wrote you a twelve-page letter: I
am quite conscious, on the contrary, that
I am carrying this matter of letter
writing beyond all bounds of reason.
But, then, I don't intend this to be a
twelve-pager, and I feel justified in
writing on this particular day because
it is a sort of mensiversary: just four
weeks ago to-day you were sweet and
imprudent enough to promise to marry
a certain respectable person whose life
has been brightened beyond measure by
that promise, and who has felt every
Sabbath afternoon since that memorable
16th that he had cause for special thanksgiving that He who ordereth all things
had given him the love of such a woman

7. Woodrow Wilson to Ellen Louise Axson

S.S. Ethiopia 9th June, 96

My own darling,

This has proved an exceptionally slow and tedious voyage,—12 days instead of 10,—not because of rough weather, but because of an excessively old and slow tho. safe boat. I have fared famously, with only a very few qualms; and have found some delightful companions,—southern people, of course (?)

There are so few conveniences for writing, or for any sort of privacy, that I have not practiced this useless left hand at all. It is already tired out.

I am perfectly well, and love you tragically.

Your own

Woodrow

[Over

8. Woodrow Wilson to Ellen Axson Wilson written with his left hand

9. John Grier Hibben—Andrew Fleming West

10. Mary Allen Hulbert Peck

11. President Wilson at his desk in the Oval Office of the White House in 1920

12. Edward Mandell House

13. Cary Travers Grayson

14. The President meets his Cabinet in April 1920

15. Mr. and Mrs. Wilson leaving their home on S Street in Washington in 1921

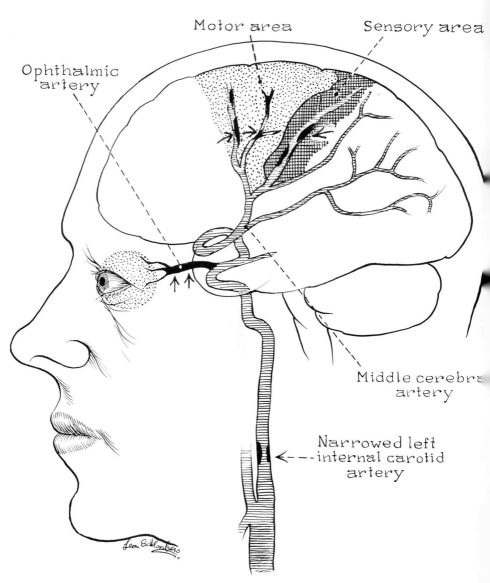

Motor area   Sensory area

Ophthalmic
artery

Middle cerebral
artery

Narrowed left
internal carotid
artery

16. Diagram of carotid circulation indicating sites of vessel narrowing and occlusion
(Provided by Dr. Edwin A. Weinstein)

the ministers, Simon John McPherson, indicated his belief that the situation "did not appear to comport with standards of strict honor." Wilson vigorously resisted this suggestion, but McPherson maintained his position. The adoption of a resolution calling for a committee to confer with Procter brought the meeting mercifully to a conclusion.[53]

Wilson had been hoist on his own petard. He had not only seen West's report but had edited the manuscript with handwritten annotations before it went to the printer.[54] With an ill-advised scheme and a few ill-chosen words Wilson had destroyed his major thesis—that a central location was necessary for the Graduate College to be the energizing force of the university. He was soon to reassert it, but by then irreparable damage had been done.

Pyne and his allies now began a campaign to force Wilson to resign. Procter would be asked to withdraw his original offer with the understanding that it would be renewed under a new administration; West would also resign as dean, while retaining his professorship. In his letter of resignation, West would say that he was acting because the administration did not desire the building of the Graduate College. This scheme, Pyne told Farrand, would put their side in a strong position by showing up the "crookedness" of their opponents.[55] On another front, Farrand, Alexander, and Jesse Lynch Williams, editor of the *Princeton Alumni Weekly*, surreptitiously circulated pamphlets denigrating Wilson and ridiculing him in satirical verse.[56] The conflict spread into the metropolitan press: both sides inspired articles and denied responsibility. Wilson, in private correspondence, supplied material to the *New York Times* for an editorial which described the issue as one between special privilege and democracy. Wilson told Hiram Woods that he was in no way responsible for the editorial but had merely repeated things that he had said in public to correct misrepresentations.[57] Wilson had once stated that "the truth is no invalid," but at Princeton it had developed some alarming symptoms.

The struggle dragged on, with Pyne and Wilson each implacably set on having his own way. Even though most legal opinions, including

[53] Wilson Farrand, undated MS. about the graduate college controversy, Farrand Papers, cited in Editorial Note: "Wilson at the Meeting of the Board of Trustees," *PWW*, Vol. 20, pp. 8-9.

[54] West to Matthew C. Fleming, March 21, 1910, *ibid.*, p. 277.

[55] Pyne to Farrand, January 25, 1910, *ibid.*, pp. 56-57.

[56] Bragdon, *The Academic Years,* pp. 372-73, n.53.

[57] See editorial, the *New York Times*, February 3, 1910; WW to Hiram Woods, March 23, 1910, *ibid.*, pp. 74-76, 286.

that of the executors, considered the golf links to be part of the university grounds, Wilson insisted that the expenditure of any of Mrs. Swann's money for a building there went against his conscience and "would be a very serious breach of the moral obligations of the Board."[58] Wilson was determined to get rid of West at all costs, and Fine and his other advisers deterred him with difficulty. They pointed out that to make a martyr of West would play into the hands of the opposition.[59] Pyne found it hard to comprehend the "vagaries" of Wilson's mind,[60] while Henry B. Thompson called Pyne's mental condition "almost impossible."[61]

Spring was a season of indecision and frustration for Wilson, and his thoughts dwelt on politics as much as on academic affairs. Despite a growing interest, he gave an evasive answer to Colonel George Harvey's request that he commit himself on the New Jersey gubernatorial nomination.[62] At Princeton, Wilson's strategy was to submit the whole question of the Graduate College to the faculty, where he was sure of a majority. However, the board of trustees defeated the motion by a vote of 14 to 13 on April 14, with five of the six ministers among the majority.[63]

Two days later Wilson broke all restraint in a shockingly intemperate speech to the Pittsburgh alumni. He made a broadside attack on the universities, the churches, and the leaders of both national parties. Princeton, he charged, was being maintained for pleasure rather than for the service of the country. He completely reversed his previously expressed views and claimed that Abraham Lincoln was a better leader because he had not gone to college. "The great voice of America," he declaimed, "does not come from the seats of learning, but in a murmur from the hills and the woods and the farms and the factories and the mills, rolling on and gaining volume until it comes

---

[58] WW to Daniels, April 5, 1910, *ibid.*, p. 319.

[59] Henry B. Fine to WW, February 24, 1910, *ibid.*, pp. 173-75.

[60] Pyne to Charles Wood, January 18, 1910, *ibid.*, p. 29.

[61] Henry B. Thompson to Sheldon, March 14, 1910, *ibid.*, p. 241.

[62] Harvey, according to one account, asked Wilson if he would accept the gubernatorial nomination of New Jersey's Democratic party if it was offered to him "on a silver platter." Wilson replied, "If the nomination for governor should come to me in that way, I should regard it as my duty to give the matter very serious consideration." William O. Inglis, "Helping to Make a President," *Collier's Weekly*, LVIII (October 7, 1916), 37, cited in Editorial Note: "Colonel Harvey's Plan for Wilson's Entry into Politics," *ibid.*, p. 147. See also below, p. 224.

[63] Minutes of the Board of Trustees of Princeton University, April 14, 1910; Thompson to Dodge, April 15, 1910, *ibid.*, pp. 357, 361.

to us the voice from the homes of the common men." In an obvious reference to his quad plan and Graduate College defeats, he declared that America would not tolerate the seclusion of students from the rough and tumble of college life. He still smarted from the adverse votes of the clerics on the board and assailed the churches because they had dissociated themselves from the people and were serving the classes, not the masses. Wilson, carried away on the wings of cardio-vascular and hematological metaphor, claimed that political leaders had "thrust their cruel hands into the very heartstrings of the many, on whose blood and energy they are subsisting," and warned: "If she loses her self possession America will stagger like France through fields of blood before she again finds peace and prosperity under the leadership of men who understand her needs." The political parties, he stated, were going to pieces and needed moral regeneration.[64]

The Pittsburgh speech reflected the depths of Wilson's despair. He had told his host, Lawrence C. Woods, that his life had been a failure, and that, in taking the moral position that his conscience dictated, he had not only failed to realize his educational ideals but had also put his family in a precarious financial position.[65] He also seemed despondent to a trustee, Joseph B. Shea.[66] On his return to Princeton, Wilson admitted that he had made a "stupid blunder."[67] However, he fought even more stubbornly against any compromise. In May, Sheldon enthusiastically advanced a settlement by which the Thomson and Procter buildings would be built on the golf links, once the legal issues had been decided by the New Jersey Court of Chancery; West would resign and the administration of the Graduate School would be put in the hands of the faculty committee; and West would be relegated to the position of provost, or master, of the Graduate College, and ex-officio member of the faculty committee.[68] Pyne reluctantly accepted the arrangement, but Wilson asked for time to consider it. He added that to ask him to accept West in any administrative capacity would be to ask him to forego his "most fundamental judgment in the whole matter of education." With West at the Graduate College,

[64] See accounts of Wilson's speech in the Pittsburgh *Gazette Times,* April 17, 1910, and the *Pittsburgh Dispatch,* April 17, 1910, printed in *ibid.,* pp. 363-68. For a text of this speech that was approved by Wilson, see the *Princeton Alumni Weekly,* X (April 20, 1910), 467-71, printed in *ibid.,* pp. 373-76.

[65] Walworth, *Woodrow Wilson,* p. 139.

[66] Shea to Pyne, May 16, 1910, *PWW,* Vol. 20, p. 458.

[67] WW to Isaac H. Lionberger, April 28, 1910, *ibid.,* p. 399.

[68] Sheldon to McCormick, May 9, 1910, *ibid.,* pp. 427-28.

he wrote, "The atmosphere of the college will be the atmosphere breathed by the school. It has never been possible to *govern*[69] West in any respect."[70]

Meanwhile, Dean West had not been preparing himself for a sacrificial role, but had discovered another of "those with loaves and fishes." While Wilson's head may have been full of thoughts of his "dearest friend," West had cultivated Isaac Chauncey Wyman of Salem, Massachusetts, a wealthy alumnus of the class of 1848.[71] West persuaded Wyman to leave his estate, estimated by West at from $2,000,000 to $4,000,000,[72] for the building of a graduate college along lines recommended by the Dean, who became one of the two executors of the will. Wilson had known about Wyman. While on vacation in 1902 he had gone to Wyman's home in Salem, but the old man had been out. In June 1909, after Wyman's lawyer had called on him at Prospect to convey Wyman's good will, Wilson "ventured" to write to extend his "very warm expressions of regard and appreciation" and his hope that, on some early occasion, he could pay his respects in person.[73] Wyman died on May 18, 1910. West went to attend the funeral to lay a sprig of ivy from Nassau Hall on the casket and to file the will in court. From Salem he exulted to Pyne: "TE DEUM LAUDAMUS. NON NOBIS DOMINE."[74]

Although he had lost control of policy, Wilson did not resign. He told Hiram Woods that to do so would be "small and petulant";[75] Wilson considered it his duty to stay at the helm to prevent the demoralization of Princeton.[76] He presided graciously over the surrender: he officially announced the Wyman bequest, withdrew his objection to the golf links site, acquiesced in the Procter offer, and stated that it was eminently desirable that West should be included in the university's councils.[77] Wilson's gracious demeanor, however, concealed

---

[69] Author's emphasis. This word choice possibly related to Wilson's thoughts of running for Governor of New Jersey.

[70] Pyne to Procter, May 10, 1910; WW to Sheldon, May 16, 1910, *ibid.*, pp. 431-32, 457.

[71] Wyman's father, also an alumnus, had fought under George Washington at the Battle of Princeton. See West to Pyne, May 22, 1910, *ibid.*, pp. 465-66.

[72] The actual amount eventually realized by the university came to $622,606.50. See John M. Raymond and West to WW, telegram, May 22, 1910, *ibid.*, p. 464, n.3.

[73] WW to EAW, August 9 and 10, 1902, *ibid.*, Vol. 14, pp. 67, 70; WW to Isaac C. Wyman, June 1, 1909, *ibid.*, Vol. 19, p. 225.

[74] West to Pyne, May 22, 1910, *ibid.*, Vol. 20, pp. 465-66.

[75] WW to Hiram Woods, May 28, 1910, *ibid.*, p. 482.

[76] Link, *Wilson*, I, 89.

[77] WW to Thomas D. Jones, May 30, 1910, *PWW*, Vol. 20, pp. 483-85.

feelings of rejection and a longing to be loved. He described them to Mrs. Peck:

"Yesterday the celebrated Mr. Procter was here in Princeton, spending the day with West. . . . It is always West or Pyne he comes to see, never me. I have never been part of the University in his mind! The now complacent West gave him a lunch, to wh. the whole of his crowd (the opposition crowd) was invited, their beloved Mrs. Cleveland at their centre once more, returned fresh and more beautiful than ever from her year in Europe. Not a member of the Faculty who is known to have sympathized with me in my brutal lack of appreciation of Mr. Procter's generosity was favoured with an invitation. I was bidden and thought it best to go; but moved amongst those dames and gentlemen like a man trying not to overhear their thoughts or to show any consciousness of the complacent triumph and condescension in their bearing,—or of their whisperings apart and air of being a 'party,' each in the confidence of all. It was a trying experience for your humble servent [servant]; but he trusts he came through with a calm front."[78]

Wilson did not admit to Mrs. Peck that he had been defeated. He told her that, despite the great ovations he had received at the commencement exercises, he had been mortally afraid that he might sound like a man who had surrendered. He assured her that he had yielded what he did only because it had been the unanimous opinion of his friends that he do so. His enemies, he wrote, seemed so "deeply irritated" as to make him feel that the "real advantage" rested with him. In a vein similar to that in which he and his mother had denigrated the rivals of his youth, Wilson wrote of the Dean of the Graduate School: "West, by the way, was made nothing of at Commencement. His real character seems to have been devined [divined] during the recent controversy very shrewdly and on all hands. Nobody trusts him or thoroughly believes in him."[79] Even to his closest friends, Wilson evidently needed denial to avoid feelings of failure and shame.

Despite, or possibly also because of, his feelings of rejection, Wilson could never free himself of the bonds of love and hate that tied him to Jack Hibben. In a revealing letter to Mrs. Peck, written after he, then Governor of New Jersey, attended a function at which Hibben presided as acting president, he agonizingly wondered: "Why will that wound not heal over in my stubborn heart? Why is it that I was blind and stupid enough to love the people who proved false to me, and cannot *love*, can only gratefully admire and cleave to, those who are

[78] WW to MAHP, June 5, 1910, *ibid.*, p. 500.
[79] WW to MAHP, June 17, 1910, *ibid.*, pp. 535-36.

my real friends by the final, only conclusive proof of conduct and actual loyalty, when loyalty cost and mean something?" He continued: "My best course, the course I instinctively follow most of the time, is to think always of my new job, never of my old, and to relieve my heart by devoting all its energies to the duties which do not concern friends but that great mass of men to whose service one can devote himself without thought of the rewards of personal affection or friendship. Perhaps it is better to love men in the mass than to love them individually!"[80]

Wilson's grievous sense of loss of love, hurt and betrayal was activated again by the chance—perhaps more than chance—occurrence of renting a house in Princeton next door to the Hibbens. He expressed his feelings to his friend:

"I am somehow made aware at every turn of how the University, for which I spent the best thoughts and aspirations and energies that were in me, has turned away from me, and of how full the place is of spiteful hostility to me. It is a dreadful thing to be hated by those whom you have loved and whom you have sought to serve unselfishly and without fear or favour! It sickens the heart and makes life very hard. I went about from familiar place to place with a lump in my throat, and would have felt better if I could have *cried*. But I did my duty, feared no man and no thing, and the event is in the hand of God! What a comfort, what a delight it is to think of you in the midst of such memories, of your true heart and generous friendship and perfect comradeship!"[81]

It is difficult to evaluate the respective roles of so-called psychogenic and organic factors in Wilson's changed conduct after the strokes of 1906 and 1907. Alterations in social and emotional behavior appear following strokes, but they endure only if there is extensive brain damage. Wilson's clinical history indicates that his pathology was confined to a limited area in the left cerebral hemisphere. It is possible that such focal lesions may produce generalized biochemical effects in the brain, but these are transient and reversible. When Wilson entered politics in 1910, he had not had a stroke for almost three years, and, aside from diminished vision in his left eye, and perhaps some residual weakness of the right arm, he was in good neurological condition.

[80] WW to MAHP, February 2, 1911, *ibid.*, Vol. 22, p. 426.
[81] WW to MAHP, October 8, 1911, *ibid.*, Vol. 23, p. 425.

CHAPTER XIII

The New Morality

WILSON'S NAME was first seriously mentioned for the presidency of the United States in February 1906, when Colonel George Brinton McClellan Harvey, an editor and publisher with close ties to eastern financial circles, proposed Wilson as the candidate of the conservative, anti-Bryan wing of the Democratic party. Wilson did not commit himself but showed great interest.[1] Two months later he affirmed his conservative credentials in a Jefferson Day address to the Democratic Club of New York, in which he transformed Jefferson from a French-oriented radical into a Cleveland free-enterprise Democrat. Wilson reversed his earlier opinion and now described Jefferson as a typical American—a product of the Virginia frontier, who had the same wide view of national affairs as George Washington. Jefferson, Wilson said, had only two firm principles: the right of the individual to unhindered opportunity and the right of a people to develop freely. Jefferson's philosophical theorizing, Wilson explained, was mere literary dress not expressed in action. His spirit, not his tenets, ruled, and the spirit was the introduction of plain, everyday morality into the conduct of the business of the nation. For this, Wilson said, corporations were necessary. The country did not need laws regulating the corporations, but only laws to find the dishonest men responsible for abuses. The government should serve only as an "umpire" between competing groups. He paraphrased the Sage of Monticello to the effect that there should be as little government as possible and called on men to show their moral muscle by not expecting anyone but God and themselves to take care of them.[2]

The role of corporate business was a paramount issue in American politics, and Wilson's belief that the remedy for abuses lay in prose-

---

[1] Harvey's speech proposing Wilson for the presidency, February 3, 1906, is found in *Speeches at the Lotos Club*, arranged by John Elderkin *et al.* (New York, 1911), pp. 309-12, and printed in *PWW*, Vol. 16, pp. 299-301. See Wilson's reply to Harvey, February 3, 1906, *ibid.*, p. 301.

[2] Address at the annual Jefferson Day dinner of the National Democratic Club of New York, April 16, 1906, National Democratic Club, *Annual Dinner on Jefferson Day April the Sixteenth One Thousand Nine Hundred and Six, at the Waldorf-Astoria* (n.p., n.d.), printed in *ibid.*, pp. 362-69.

cuting dishonest individuals was highly acceptable to conservatives. Not only would it be difficult to ferret out the culprits in the corporate maze, but criminal judgments against men of wealth were also almost impossible to obtain in the courts at that time. Wilson's view that the conduct of business was a moral problem was shared by progressives, but their solutions were radically different. William Jennings Bryan proposed to break up the "trusts." President Theodore Roosevelt regarded the existence of large corporations as inevitable and necessary and advocated regulating them through national legislation.

Wilson's problems at Princeton after his strokes of 1906 and 1907 were dramatically expressed in an exposition of his political views in November 1907, soon after the board of trustees withdrew its approval of the quadrangle plan. His self-referential language, "third-person" projections, inappropriate metaphors, and inaccuracies and contradictions indicate the intensity of his emotional stress and possibly some transitory alteration in brain function. In an interview with a reporter from the *New York Times*, Wilson charged that governmental restrictions upon the railroads' ability to borrow money[3] had precipitated the Wall Street panic of the previous month. In a metaphor that must have made Colonel Harvey wince when he read it, Wilson compared the directors of corporations and "trusts" to groups of "burglars, legally organized" for purposes of "plunder." Even fines and criminal actions could not be effective, he declared, because the jury system made it next to impossible to imprison a man of influence. Possibly motivated by his anger over the private negotiations among Pyne, West, and Procter, he proposed that reports of meetings of corporation directors be filed with state governments. In order to correct abuses, he advocated moral force and a common council—a sort of people's forum under the chairmanship of J. Pierpont Morgan.[4] He stated erroneously that the Texas legislature had passed a law forbidding the sale of any goods manufactured by a "trust." When the interviewer asked Wilson if "trusts" were violating the Constitution, he replied, "There is nothing in the Constitution that forbids the accumulation of business; on the contrary, it demands protection for life, *limb*,[5] and

---

[3] The Hepburn Act of 1906, which gave the Interstate Commerce Commission the power to set railroad rates upon complaint by shippers.

[4] Wilson may have been hoping for a contribution for the quad plan. At various times he approached John D. Rockefeller, Andrew Carnegie, and Thomas Fortune Ryan, New York traction and utilities magnate.

[5] Author's emphasis. Nowhere does the Constitution require protection of "limb"; Wilson was perhaps unconsciously and symbolically representing the weakness of his arm.

property, but behind the enormous growth of corporate power is the American social spirit that insists upon a moral basis of human life, as distinguished from a selfish, inhuman greed."

Wilson criticized Bryan for making political propositions that he, Wilson, termed "absurd," but he refused to list them. He attacked President Roosevelt for not thinking before he spoke. While he fell short of accusing Republican Governor Charles Evans Hughes of New York of a lack of political integrity, he charged that the Governor had not specified the names of the men involved in the recent insurance frauds in his state.[6] Wilson and Hughes had been on the speakers' platform together on July 4, 1907 at the Jamestown Exposition. Wilson told the New York Times reporter that, when he had heard Hughes's address, he had been forced to change the entire plan of his speech and interrupted it to ask the Governor what the transactions were and how they could be avoided. According to Wilson, Hughes had turned red in the face and said nothing.[7]

Wilson's recollection was inaccurate. He had, in fact, delivered his planned speech. When he had stopped in a discussion of the greed of the "trusts" to ask what remedy an aggressive governor like Hughes would apply, a voice from the rear thundered, "He'll bust the trusts— and we're going to make him the next President," and the crowd burst into applause for Hughes. Wilson was unable to continue for ten minutes, while Hughes sat quietly behind him, smiling, but showing no other recognition of the demonstration.[8]

Immediately after the interview in the New York Times appeared, Wilson complained that the writer had singularly heightened "the color" of his views. While he admitted that the body of the interview was accurate, Wilson denied that he had stated that corporations should file the minutes of their meetings with a public official. He said that his remark about burglars was only a "playful illustration," and that he did not believe that corporations had been conceived in a "predatory" spirit. He had not meant, he wrote, to suggest the appointment of a "common council." Rather, he had meant to say that the leaders simply should take "common counsel." Wilson objected particularly to the Times' headline, which proclaimed that he had

---

[6] In 1905, Hughes had exposed the illegal financial manipulations of the officers of major insurance companies and their attempts to gain political influence through large contributions to the Republican National Committee.

[7] Interview in the New York Times, magazine section, November 24, 1917, printed in PWW, Vol. 17, pp. 513-21.

[8] New York Times, July 5, 1907, printed in ibid., pp. 247-48.

made a "scathing arraignment" of political and industrial conditions.[9] Very likely he had been more angry about the misdeeds of the Princeton board of trustees than he was about those of corporation directors.

Colonel Harvey was not discouraged by his protégé's intemperate performances and continued to work diligently for him. He persuaded Joseph Pulitzer, publisher of the New York *World*, the leading Democratic newspaper in the country, to back him, and continued to enlist support among conservatives and wealthy Democrats.[10] When, in the spring of 1908, it became evident that Bryan would again be the Democratic candidate, Wilson, as he had done in 1896, refused to support him.[11] He also specifically stated that under no circumstances would he accept nomination for Vice-President.[12] Harvey's strategy now was to secure the New Jersey governership for Wilson in 1910 and to seek the presidency in 1912.

In March 1908 Wilson restated his conservative position in a speech to the Commercial Club of Chicago. He was in a calmer mood, and his language showed much less evidence of stress. He had largely recovered from his stroke—his arm tired only after he wrote a good deal—and the Graduate College situation was temporarily favorable to him. As he had stated previously, he declared that it was the individual wrongdoers, not the businessmen of the country, who should be punished. Morality, Wilson declared, was individual; there was no such thing as corporate morality. He opposed governmental commissions as socialistic in principle and denounced the "perfect mania for regulation that has taken hold of us." He stated that the chief things that were wrong were specific abuses like overcapitalization and stock-market manipulation. These, in his opinion, should be dealt with by the courts, not by the executives of government. In closing, he declared: "We must recover by one process or another the ancient principles of morality, the ancient principles of public spirit, the ancient principles of common purpose, and then there will be no difficulty in putting a

[9] After the publication of the interview on November 24, Wilson sent a letter to the editors of the *Times*. The newspaper did not print his letter but instead sent a reporter to interview Wilson. On November 27, 1907, the *Times* printed a statement, approved by Wilson, which purportedly corrected the misrepresentations and inaccuracies contained in the first interview. See WW to the editor of the *Times*, dated November 24, 1907, and Wilson's statement, published on November 27, 1907, printed in *ibid.*, pp. 521-23, 524-27.

[10] Inglis, "Helping to Make a President," p. 67.

[11] WW to Henry J. Forman, April 10, 1908, *PWW*, Vol. 18, pp. 258-59.

[12] Baker, "Memorandum of a Conversation with Stockton Axson," March 12, 1925, Baker Papers.

stop to the things which are against the public welfare."[13] Wilson reiterated these positions in a talk in Pittsburgh two weeks later.[14] However, by the time that he returned to the political stage after his emotional crisis over the summer, his views of morality and politics had changed dramatically.

Wilson, before 1908, had conceived of morality as a personal matter closely tied to religion, family, and social relationships, with little bearing on politics and government. In a series of lectures given in 1894, he had defined morality as the science of relationships between men and between men and God. Personal morality, he had said then, was a set of immutable rules, established for all time by the coming of Christ. Political morality, on the other hand, had no standard but expediency and was determined by such actions as would further the progress of society.[15] Wilson shared the popular indignation over frauds in business and corruption in politics, but he had remained outside the great current of social reform that was sweeping the Protestant churches and the country. He did not believe that the inequalities of wealth and the working and living conditions resulting from the rapid industrialization of the country were proper concerns of government. He had criticized professional reformers for their self-righteousness[16] and called them an "unmitigated nuisance."[17] He even had a good word for political bosses; he told a group of northern New Jersey Princeton alumni that, while the bosses had to go, they had provided a necessary human connection between the people and the lawmakers.[18] To a considerable degree, as has been said, Wilson had thought of morality in terms of personal character, sexual purity, and the sanctity of the home.[19]

[13] "The Government and Business," an address before the Commercial Club of Chicago, March 14, 1908, *PWW*, Vol. 18, pp. 35-51.

[14] "The Government and Business," an abstract of an address to the Traffic Club of Pittsburgh, April 3, 1908, *ibid.*, pp. 221-25.

[15] "Political Liberty, Political Expediency, and Political Morality in the Democratic State," July 2, 1894, *ibid.*, Vol. 8, p. 607.

[16] Address at alumni dinner at East Orange, N. J., November 10, 1905, reported in the *Princeton Press*, November 11, 1905, and printed in *ibid.*, Vol. 16, p. 217.

[17] Address to the Princeton Alumni Association of Tennessee at Memphis, November 9, 1907, in the *Princeton Alumni Weekly*, VIII (November 20, 1907), 138-41, printed in *ibid.*, Vol. 17, p. 484.

[18] Address at alumni dinner at East Orange, N. J., November 10, 1905, *ibid.*, Vol. 16, p. 217.

[19] Wilson was critical of child psychologists; he charged that it was "absolutely immoral" to experiment on a child. Address at the Barnard Club, Providence, R. I., reported in *Providence Journal*, November 12, 1905, printed in *ibid.*, p. 221.

Even before he went abroad for the summer in 1908, Wilson, unhappy over the threatened loss of his wife's complete devotion as a consequence of his involvement with Mrs. Peck, felt less certain of his formulation of morality. For his baccalaureate address to the class of 1908, he chose the theme of righteousness: "Let no man deceive you: he that doeth righteousness is righteous, even as He is righteous." He told the graduating class that the world had changed and that there were now confusing circumstances and conflicting standards. The difficult questions of the day were the moral questions, he said, and moral judgments had never been simple. They had "always been complicated by a thousand circumstances" which puzzled the will. He recognized that men were inevitably part of organizations and that the issues of individual conscience and composite judgment were complex. Yet, he insisted that it was men, not societies, who were bad, and that wrong was conceived in the individual heart. What laws of nature govern our moral lives, he asked, except the laws operative in our own wills? Righteousness, he concluded, might be facilitated by social arrangements and encouraged by law, but society would find its reforms, not in law, but in the individual conscience.[20]

Soon after Wilson returned from England, he dealt further with the issues of morality and conscience in a speech in Pittsfield, where he and Ellen were visiting the Pecks. The talk, entitled "Public Affairs and Private Responsibility," adverted to the participation of citizens in politics, the relations of capital and labor, and governmental regulation of business. However, the major portion of the address clearly referred to the problems of his attachment to Mrs. Peck. According to the press report, Wilson's keynote statement was: "He must have a bad conscience who devotes himself to private affairs to the exclusion of public concerns." He reportedly said, "It is dangerous to concentrate moral forces upon self. The way to do right is to do in the best way possible duty as it is perceived. Character will take care of itself." After discussing the need for standards of honor in business as well as in the home, Wilson allegedly declared: "If there is a place where we must adjourn our morals, that place should be in what we call the private life. It is better to be unfaithful to a few people than to a considerable number of people. I do not say we can afford to adjourn our morals in either case. I simply assert that we can better afford to adjourn them in private life. Yes, there are so many men who are good in their private lives who are unwise in public affairs and purposes. Men who are saints in private life may be poor leaders."

[20] Baccalaureate address, June 7, 1908, *ibid.*, Vol. 18, pp. 323-33.

After referring to the undesirability of voting for someone simply because he was agreeable, Wilson declared: "After perfect agreement comes supineness. The American government originated in the biggest kick on record. When I look at the flag I think of it as strips of parchment. The blue represents the principles that have been the guiding stars through all the years. The red represents the blood that has been shed that those principles might be confirmed."[21] The white of purity was conspicuously absent and had apparently been absorbed by the new morality. It was not to reappear until 1916, after he had confessed his sin to Edith Bolling Galt and obtained forgiveness and assurance of her love.[22]

The central thesis of the new morality was that public duties took precedence over private ones. Wilson restated the principles of the new morality in his baccalaureate sermon to the class of 1909. The text— "We are unprofitable servants: we have done that which was our duty to do" (Luke XVII:10)—had occurred to Wilson while he had been listening to a Scottish sermon during the tempestuous summer of 1908.[23] Wilson told the graduating students: "In our social relations we will remember the loyalty and affection we owe our loved ones at home, and the watchful and thoughtful service we owe our partners in business and all who have honoured us with their confidence, but we will add to these things which manifestly bind us the service which no law can exact of us. We will be thoughtful citizens, not for the protection of our families or the benefit of our business, but for the benefit of our neighbors and of the country which nourishes and sustains us all. Here is our field of final and supreme test, in which it will inevitably appear whether we have been bred to the true spirit of our alma mater or not. She has meant us to be men of such kind: we will remember her in all that we do." The profitable servant, Wilson went on to say, was one who did more than fulfill his bond. Wilson attacked businessmen, who, while honestly keeping their legal obligations, piled up great wealth and debauched the country; he castigated students content to get by with doing as little work as possible; and he criticized trade-union members who only conformed to the required standards of work.[24]

Wilson may have practiced some of the principles of the new morality during a conversation with Dean West. According to the rec-

---

[21] Address in Pittsfield, Mass., reported in the Pittsfield, Mass., *Berkshire Evening Eagle*, October 9, 1908, printed in *ibid.*, pp. 441-43.

[22] See below, p. 293.

[23] WW to EAW, July 10, 1908, *PWW*, Vol. 18, p. 358.

[24] Baccalaureate address, June 13, 1909, *ibid.*, Vol. 19, pp. 246-51.

ollections of Professor William F. Magie, Wilson's classmate and an opponent in the Graduate College controversy, West asked Wilson if he meant to keep his personal promises. Wilson answered that the larger interests of the college demanded that he be relieved of his personal promises to West. He allegedly added, "There are after all two moralities, public and private." Whereupon, West is alleged to have asked, "Which one are you going to use on me?"[25]

Wilson preached the doctrine of the new morality to a nationally representative audience for the first time in October 1908, just before he left for Pittsfield. He told the American Bankers' Association in Denver that a standard of business morality was necessary which measured, not the interest of individual enterprises, nor of the commercial or manufacturing classes of the country alone, but the interests of the nation and people as a whole. He warned that the only remedy that would save America from the extremes of socialism and monopolistic capitalism was the general acceptance of a new morality, which he vaguely defined as a social reunion and "social reintegration which every man of station and character and influence in the country can in some degree within the scope of his own life set afoot."[26]

In his speeches over the next year, Wilson did not forsake individual morality and also stated that it was necessary to adjust it to the organization of society. In January 1910, at the height of the Graduate College crisis and his involvement with Mrs. Peck, he told a group of New York financiers, which included J. Pierpont Morgan, that banking was founded on a moral and not a financial basis.[27] In the following May he carried the new gospel to the bankers of New Jersey. Morality, he informed them, was no longer a matter of separate individual choice but of corporate arrangement. "Therefore," he said, "we have to reckon men's morality now as if they were fractions and not as if they were integers,—not as if they were units, but as if they were subordinate parts of great complicated wholes."[28]

The new morality can be viewed as the means by which Wilson expiated the sin of his affair with Mrs. Peck; indeed, he said precisely

[25] Interview with William F. Magie, July 13, 1941, Bragdon Collection.

[26] Quoted in Link, *Wilson*, I, 121.

[27] Morgan reportedly looked glum and puffed his cigar "energetically" during the talk. See the New York *Evening Post*, January 18, 1910; New York *World*, January 18, 1910, *PWW*, Vol. 20, pp. 23-25.

[28] Address to the New Jersey Bankers' Association, Atlantic City, N. J., May 6, 1910, in *Proceedings of the Seventh Annual Convention of the New Jersey Bankers' Association Held at Hotel Chelsea Atlantic City, New Jersey May 6 and 7, 1910* (n.p., n.d.), pp. 81-87, printed in *ibid.*, pp. 414-21.

this to Mrs. Galt in 1915. No longer pure in his personal life, he would devote himself to the service of others and to purifying politics. As the metaphors of revitalization and regeneration of Princeton had served to resolve his concern about his stroke of 1906, so the dogmas of the new morality enabled him in 1908 to cope with the problems of conscience and guilt. Moreover, some of the language which Wilson had originally used symbolically to represent his sexual problems and the frustration of his plans for Princeton had a favorable impact on audiences, who took his statements in a more referential context. The emotion that generated his words gave his public delivery a particular warmth and earnestness.

Wilson's passage from conservatism to progressivism cannot be attributed wholly to the new morality. His conversion was not unique. The great majority of the reformers of 1908 had been conservatives in the 1890s, and most of the Democrats among them had not voted for Bryan in 1896.[29] Rather, the new morality provided Wilson with the emotional fervor and feeling of righteousness with which he expressed his political views. Nor had the new doctrine completely absolved him of his secret sin. He continued, even after he began to advocate governmental legislation to control corporations, to insist on punishment for the guilty individuals. Also, his condemnation of secrecy in government may have been self-referential. In a private context, when Wilson was threatened with the loss of his wife's love in the summer of 1908, the new morality may have saved him from an emotional breakdown.

[29] George F. Mowry, *The Era of Theodore Roosevelt, 1900-1912* (New York, 1958), p. 87.

CHAPTER XIV

Political Apprenticeship

NEW JERSEY, in 1910, was a boss-ridden, corporation-controlled state, dominated by the railroads and a public utilities monopoly.[1] Republican governors had been elected since 1896, but the corrupt alliance of business and politics flourished no matter which party was in power. However, throughout the years reformers such as George Lawrence Record, an outstanding progressive Republican, had kept the issues before the public. The Democratic bosses, particularly James Smith, Jr., of Newark, hoped to regain control by permitting a liberal platform which they could disregard, and by choosing a prominent citizen whom they could control as their candidate for governor.

Wilson was nominated with Smith's support on the first ballot by the Democratic state convention in Trenton in September 1910. In his acceptance speech, Wilson immediately declared his independence of the party machine and declared that the nomination had come to him unsolicited and that, if elected, he would have no obligations except to the people of the state. He committed himself to specific measures for which reformers had been fighting for a decade—the direct primary, workmen's compensation legislation, a corrupt practices act, and a commission to regulate the rates and services of public utilities and railroads. He called for a renaissance of public spirit and a return to the great age in which democracy was set up in America. At the end of his formal address, he turned to the flag over the speaker's stand and exclaimed: "When I look upon the American flag before me I think sometimes that it is made of parchment and blood. The white in it stands for parchment, the red in it signifies blood—parchment on which was written the rights of men and blood that was spilled to make these rights real. Let us devote the Democratic party to the recovery of these rights."[2] Wilson had exchanged the white of purity for devotion to the rights of men.

[1] For a fuller account of New Jersey politics and Wilson's campaign for governor, see Ransom E. Noble, Jr., *New Jersey Progressivism Before Wilson* (Princeton, N. J., 1946); David W. Hirst, ed., *Woodrow Wilson, A Documentary Narrative* (Princeton, N. J., 1965), and Link, *Wilson*, I, 131-307.

[2] Impromptu remarks to the Democratic State Convention, reported in the Trenton *True American*, September 17, 1910, printed in *PWW*, Vol. 21, p. 120.

Wilson's first campaign speech, delivered in Jersey City, was a disappointment to the progressives. He seemed to have abandoned his role as a progressive leader and to have forgotten the promises of reform which he had made at Trenton. Stockton Axson, who was present, recalled that Wilson stammered and hesitated and that he tried to hold his audience with inappropriate anecdotes.[3] He expressed reluctance to ask for votes and attempted to hang a tasteless joke on the word "gall." He disclaimed any particular qualifications for office beyond a desire to serve the people and stated that he would say nothing against the Republican party. His audience was made up largely of workingmen, and he declared that he had always been a poor man, close to the plain people. He took up none of the issues, such as election fraud and the corrupt relationship between business and government.

Instead, he launched into a succession of metaphors. He asserted: "Every great state is like a great tree. It does not receive its nourishment and renewal from its fruit and branches. It is received from its root, and every great state is rooted in that great soil, which is made up of all the vast body of unnoticed men, the great masses of toilers." He returned to his old view that corporation lawlessness could not be controlled by legislation, but only by punishing the guilty individuals. He compared corporations to motor boats whose crews should not be sheltered from the waves; then he used the example of a car with a reckless driver, and ridiculed the idea that the automobile should be locked up. He further compared the corporation to a gun which was harmless unless someone fired it. Wilson used an image of the sea to oppose regulatory legislation; he stated that he did not think that the lawyers could supply the ship of state with the ballast necessary to carry the canvas. He further drew an analogy between a proposed increase in the powers of the Interstate Commerce Commission and a cancer: "Now, I do not want the interstate clause of the constitution to be a cancer, but I do want that clause in the constitution . . . to be a progressive growth, and I call myself, on that account, a conservative, a conservative because a progressive."[4]

Wilson's performance seems to have been a compound of poor preparation, anxiety, and indecision. However, he soon recovered his poise and direction and, two days later in Newark, declared that he stood "absolutely and unequivocally" for every point in the Democratic platform. Yet the way that he contradicted himself when he used

[3] Axson Memoir.

[4] Speech at St. Peter's Hall in Jersey City, N. J., September 28, 1910, PWW, Vol. 21, pp. 181-91.

his favorite automobile metaphors suggests that he was still uncertain about the major issue of how to deal with corporations. On the one hand, he said that he was not critical of the automobile, but only of the man at the wheel; on the other hand, he said that touring cars had become too big for the city streets. He closed his address with an appeal for the purification of the politics of the country and called for vast reforms to increase the happiness of mankind.[5] Several days later, he asserted that, although political corruption existed in both parties, most of the Democratic party throughout the nation had been "purified by the very air that vibrates the country itself."[6] When he preached the doctrines of the new morality, he called on people to accept the responsibilities of citizenship and appealed for a common national purpose which was superior to personal, family, and class loyalties.

As the campaign progressed, Wilson combined his rhetoric with a clear exposition of the issues, homely illustrations, and humor. He commented that philanthropy should be extended so that corporation officers who broke the law should not be deprived of the "moralizing effect" of jail.[7] He joked that the Republican party was like an automobile which, when the crank was turned, trembled all over, but did not move an inch. He told a story, in Negro dialect, in which he compared the Republican party to a mule on a Mississippi River boat which had eaten its destination tag so that no one knew where it was going.

Wilson also spoke humorously about his looks. His explanation to a reporter of his refusal to have a photograph taken was that he had inherited a dislike for "pictorial publicity" from his mother.[8] On another occasion, he converted his idiosyncrasy into an effective political thrust. He had been informed, he told an audience, that his Republican opponent had the advantage of him in looks. "Now," he added, "it is not always the most useful horse that is most beautiful. If I had a big load to be drawn some distance I should select one of those big, shaggy kind of horses, not much for beauty, but strong of pull."[9] After former Republican Governor John William Griggs referred slightingly to him as a schoolmaster, Wilson replied that he wished that some of the gentlemen opposing him had attended school so that they might not have appropriated school funds for their political purposes.[10]

[5] Speech in Newark, N. J., September 30, 1910, printed in *ibid.,* pp. 202-212.
[6] Address in Trenton, N. J., October 3, 1910, printed in *ibid.,* p. 237.
[7] Speech in Newark, N. J., September 30, 1910, printed in *ibid.,* p. 210.
[8] Interview in *Philadelphia Record,* October 2, 1910, printed in *ibid.,* p. 225.
[9] Speech in Red Bank, N. J., October 1, 1910, printed in *ibid.,* p. 217.
[10] Speeches in Cape May Court House and Wildwood, N. J., October 8, 1910, reported in the *Philadelphia Record,* October 9, 1910, printed in *ibid.,* p. 283.

On a notable occasion, Wilson's quick rejoinder got him into what, for a time, appeared to be a difficult situation. He was stung by Griggs's taunt that he was a "man of the library," unacquainted with practical politics or the business of the state, and rashly declared that, although an amateur, he would welcome any politician in the state to debate any public issue. The challenge, to the dismay of the regular Democrats, was immediately accepted by Record, who was running for Congress on the Republican ticket. Record not only knew far more about New Jersey politics than did Wilson; he was also in a position to ask embarrassing questions about the Democratic machine. Wilson and James R. Nugent, chairman of the Democratic state committee, tried to avoid the debate and to exploit the differences between Record and the regular Republicans. The Republican state chairman, Frank Obadiah Briggs, however, told Nugent that he regarded Record as qualified to answer the challenge.[11]

Wilson's conservative supporters urged him not to meet Record, while the reformers told him that a refusal to answer Record would mean the loss of the votes of the progressive Republicans and independents. Wilson solved the problem neatly. He wrote to Record and stated that, because Briggs's letter had been "so evasive and inconclusive," they (he and Record) would have to deal with each other "as individuals and not as representatives of any organization of any kind." Then Wilson gave the implausible excuse that he would not be able to debate with Record in public because he, Wilson, had authorized the Democratic state committee to fill every available campaign date. Wilson suggested that Record submit a list of written questions, which he would answer for Record to publish. He and Record were in essential agreement on the issues, Wilson added, and he said that a frank interchange of letters was preferable to public debate.[12]

Record could easily have taken personal advantage of Wilson's refusal to meet him on the debating platform. However, he regarded the passage of reform legislation and the defeat of the political machine as paramount. Moreover, he admired Wilson. Accepting the latter's proposal, Record wrote: "You convey the impression . . . that our views are fundamentally the same. . . . I hope this is so, because I know of no one in this State who exceeds you in ability to reason, or in power of statement, while your great and justly earned reputation gives weight and authority to whatever position you take." Record's letter was a primer on the boss system in New Jersey and throughout

[11] Frank O. Briggs to James R. Nugent, October 8, 1910, *ibid.*, p. 291.
[12] WW to George L. Record, October 11, 1910, *ibid.*, p. 296.

the country. He put nineteen questions to Wilson. One was whether Wilson would denounce the Democratic "Overlords" as well as the Republican "Board of Guardians." Evidently with his tongue in his cheek—or possibly because he had taken Wilson literally—he called attention to Wilson's statements that the Democrats had been regenerated, reorganized, purged, and purified. How had this come about, Record inquired. Had the party changed leaders; or, if the leaders were the same, how and when had the Democratic bosses become purified?[13]

Wilson responded to all but one of Record's questions in concise fashion. He affirmed his agreement with the progressive program and joined with Record in denouncing the corrupt bosses of both parties. He evaded only the item of the regeneration and purity of the Democratic party. He stated that he did not remember that he had made the statement; he recalled only that he said that the party was seeking reorganization and was therefore at the threshold of a new era.[14] The evasion had no political consequences; the publication of the Wilson-Record correspondence won over hitherto undecided progressives. Psychologically, Wilson's original statement and later misrepresentation of what he had said reveals the intensity of his emotional investment in purity.

Wilson ended his campaign with a speech in which he reached the heights of imagery and identified progressivism with the redemption of mankind. He asserted that the people needed a leader who, with the aid of public opinion, would purify politics. He closed his address with all the fervor with which his father had lifted the spirits of men and brought the presence of God into their hearts:

"We have begun a fight that may be will take many a generation to complete—the fight against special privilege, but you know that men are not put into this world to go the path of ease; they are put into this world to go the path of pain and struggle. No man would wish to sit idly by to whistle a tune and lose the opportunity to take part in such a struggle. All through the centuries there has been this slow, painful struggle forward, forward, up, up, a little at a time, along the long incline, the interminable way, which leads to the perfection of force, to the real seat of justice and of honor. There are men who have fallen by the way, blood without stint has been shed, men have sacrificed everything in this sometimes blind, but always instinctive and constant struggle; and America has undertaken to lead the way.

[13] Record to WW, October 17, 1910, *ibid.*, pp. 338-47.
[14] WW to Record, October 24, 1910, *ibid.*, pp. 406-11.

America has undertaken to be the haven of hope, the opportunity of all men.

"Don't look forward too much. Don't look at the road ahead of you in dismay. Look at the road behind you. Don't you see how far up the hill we have come? Don't you see what those low and damp miasmatic levels were from which we have slowly led the way? Don't you see the rows of men come, not upon the lower level, but upon the upper like the rays of the rising sun?

"Don't you see the light starting, and don't you see the light illumining all nations? Don't you know that you are coming more and more into the beauty of its radiance? Don't you know that the past is forever behind us, that we have passed many kinds of evils that are no longer possible, that we have achieved great ends and have almost seen the fruition of free America. Don't forget the road you have trod, but remembering it and looking back for reassurance, look forward with confidence and charity to your fellow men, one at a time as you pass them along the road, and see those who are willing to lead you, and say: 'We do not believe you know the whole road. We know that you are no prophet; we know that you are no seer, but that you can see the end of the road from the beginning, and we believe that you know the direction and are leading us in that direction, though it costs you your life, provided it does not cost you your honor.'

"And then follow your guide, trusting your guides, imperfect as they are, and some day when we are all dead, men will come and point at the distant upland with a great show of joy and triumph and thank God that there were men who undertook to lead in that struggle.

"What difference does it make it we ourselves do not reach the uplands? We have given our lives to the enterprise, and that is richer and the moral is greater."[15]

Wilson won a great victory at the polls. The Democrats gained an overwhelming majority in the Assembly, while the Republicans retained control of the Senate by a small margin. The Governor-elect, however, could not rest on his laurels, because the issue of the election of a United States senator came up immediately. Until the ratification of the Seventeenth Amendment in 1913, senators were chosen by the state legislatures. Primaries were held, but the legislature was not bound by the popular vote. No Democrat of standing had entered the primary because, before Wilson's nomination, the election of a Republican legislature had seemed assured. Accordingly, James Edgar Martine, a nonentity, had been persuaded to run and had defeated

---

[15] Address in Newark, N. J., November 5, 1910, *ibid.*, pp. 575-76.

Frank McDermit, a Newark criminal lawyer with a shady reputation. With the Democrats in control, James Smith, Jr., Democratic boss of Essex County, now indicated his desire to run for the Senate.

Political necessities left Wilson no alternative but to support Martine and oppose Smith. Wilson explained his decision to make Smith the first casualty of the battle for the new morality in a letter to Colonel Harvey. While the progressive opposition to Smith was unjust, it was unalterable, and he would have to sacrifice his erstwhile and highly esteemed benefactor to the public good. Ridiculous as it undoubtedly was, he would have to stand by Martine. It was not only a state issue, Wilson noted, but a national one, because, if Smith was nominated, disappointed independents throughout the country would return to the Republican fold.[16] In a series of interviews and statements to the press, Wilson praised Martine as an able and honest man and declared that support of him was "an absolute moral obligation which the Democratic party was bound to carry out if it kept faith with the people."[17] When a reporter asked if he would have regarded it as obligatory to support McDermit, had he won the primary, Wilson brushed the question aside.[18] When it was suggested that Martine had been chosen by a relatively small proportion of the electorate, Wilson asserted that "absolute good faith in dealing with the people, an un- hesitating fidelity to every principle avowed, is the highest law of political morality under a constitutional government."[19] Wilson con- ferred with every Democratic legislator and attacked Smith in two dramatic public addresses. In Jersey City he compared the present struggle to the "bloody angle" at Gettysburg.[20] In Newark he identified his cause with that of God and liberty, and pictured how, as at Jericho, the shouts of free men caused the enemy's stronghold to collapse.[21] Martine was elected overwhelmingly by the legislature. When the members offered Wilson their congratulations, he said: "Why con- gratulate me? It is the people who are to be congratulated. All you have to do is to tell them what is going on and they will respond."[22]

[16] WW to George B. M. Harvey, November 15, 1910, *ibid.*, Vol. 22, pp. 46-48.
[17] Interview in the New York *Evening World*, December 21, 1910, printed in *ibid.*, p. 236.
[18] *Ibid.*
[19] Statement, December 8, 1910, in Trenton *True American*, December 9, 1910, printed in *ibid.*, p. 153.
[20] Address in St. Patrick's Hall, Jersey City, N. J., January 5, 1911, printed in *ibid.*, p. 302.
[21] Link, *Wilson*, I, 232-33.
[22] News account in the *Philadelphia Record*, January 26, 1911, in *PWW*, Vol. 22, p. 367.

Wilson put through his reform program over the opposition of the Smith faction and the conservative Republicans. He summed up his accomplishment in a letter to Mrs. Peck.

"I wrote the platform, I had the measures formulated to my mind, I kept the pressure of opinion constantly on the legislature, and the programme was carried out to its last detail. This with the senatorial business seems, in the minds of the people looking on little less than a miracle in the light of what has been the history of reform hitherto in this State. As a matter of fact, it is just a bit of natural history. I came to the office in the fulness of time, when opinion was ripe on all these matters, when both parties were committed to these reforms, and by merely standing fast, and by never losing sight of the business for an hour, but keeping up all sorts of (legitimate) pressure *all the time*, kept the mighty forces from being diverted or blocked at any point."[23]

Although Wilson's evaluation was historically accurate, he might have added that Record wrote several of the bills and personally gained crucial Republican votes.

Wilson's relationship with Smith was highly ambivalent. When the two men met, Wilson was favorably impressed with the pleasant and urbane politician; Smith in turn, had long admired Wilson and had sent his three sons to Princeton. After Smith's defeat in 1911, Wilson expressed his sympathy in a letter to Mrs. Peck:

"I pitied Smith at the last. . . . The minute it was seen that he was defeated his adherents began to desert him like rats leaving a sinking ship. He left Trenton (where his headquarters had at first been crowded) attended, I am told, only by his sons, and looking old and broken. He wept, they say, as he admitted himself utterly beaten. Such is the end of political power—particularly when selfishly obtained and heartlessly used. It is a pitiless game, in which, it would seem, one takes one's life in one's hands—and for me it has only begun."[24]

However, Smith's retirement proved to be brief; in the autumn of 1912 he indicated that he would again seek the senatorial nomination. Even before Smith announced that he would enter the senatorial primary, Wilson interrupted his presidential campaign to denounce him. In Link's phrase, "no unhappy Orestes was ever pursued by the Fates more relentlessly than was Smith."[25]

Wilson's implacability was not only politically expedient but very personal. To justify his actions on moral grounds, he had to suppress

[23] WW to MAHP, April 23, 1911, *ibid.*, pp. 581-82.
[24] WW to MAHP, January 29, 1911, *ibid.*, p. 392.
[25] Link, *Wilson*, I, 498.

any feelings of affection or gratitude (Smith had handed him the gubernatorial nomination on a silver platter) and replace them with negative emotions. The events also reveal Wilson's difficulty in separating personal loyalty from political support and his failure to understand codes of honor and friendship other than his own. Smith's followers were dispersed, but they lived to fight another day, not only for Smith, but also for Wilson. During the latter's presidency, the Essex County machine, headed by James Nugent, Smith's successor, backed him strongly. Wilson later expressed pleasure at the thought that Nugent had been big enough to forget the crushing blows of the intervening years.[26]

Wilson enjoyed the amenities of the Governor's office. He had an inner circle composed of Joseph P. Tumulty, his secretary, Martin Devlin, a liberal politician, James Kerney, editor of the *Trenton Evening Times*, and William W. St. John, a newspaperman. They provided political intelligence and social relaxation. They lunched together at a nearby hotel and took walks along the banks of the Delaware and Raritan Canal.[27] Like the others, Devlin, born in Scotland of Irish Catholic descent, delighted in swapping Scottish stories with the Governor. To overcome the impression of members of the legislature that Wilson was stiff and formal, his associates arranged a picnic supper with the senators, whose antics, along with his own, he described amusingly in a letter to Mrs. Peck.[28] Visitors to Trenton were cordially received and, in the early months of his term, the Governor literally kept his door open to callers.[29] The difference between the confident, resourceful leader of 1911 and the dejected defeated Princeton president of 1910 is striking.

Wilson's election as Governor of New Jersey in 1910 was part of a progressive sweep across the country. For the first time in sixteen years, the Democrats won control of Congress; and the rift in the Republican party between conservatives and insurgents gave hope for Democratic success in 1912. The dominating influence of William Jennings Bryan in the Democratic party had declined as a consequence of his defeats in 1896, 1900, and 1908. By May 1911, when Wilson embarked upon a speaking tour of the West, he was the leading contender for the Democratic presidential nomination in 1912.

During his western tour, Wilson made abundant use of his favorite

[26] Kerney, *The Political Education of Woodrow Wilson*, pp. 471-72.

[27] See, for example, Joseph P. Tumulty, *Woodrow Wilson as I Know Him* (Garden City, N. Y., 1921), p. 80.

[28] WW to MAHP, April 2, 1911, *PWW*, Vol. 22, p. 532.

[29] Baker, *Wilson*, III, 150.

homilies and metaphors, often when he referred to issues about which he did not have detailed knowledge and for which he did not offer specific solutions. Problems of labor and capital, he stated, should be solved in the spirit of free men who had the interests of the country at heart. He once again compared liberty to the smooth functioning of parts of an engine.[30] Wilson frequently used metaphors of roots and growth. He closed a speech at the University of Wisconsin by saying that the schoolhouses of the nation "will some day prove to be the roots of that great tree of liberty which shall spread for the sustenance and protection of all mankind."[31] The roots of democracy, he often stated, lay in the soil of the common people. Referring to corrupt political machines, he vowed to lay the ax to the roots of every pestiferous jungle growth so that the liberties of mankind could find a pathway.[32] When a statement about using an ax to clear the jungle of growth of uncontrolled wealth received only "some applause," he explained that he would leave the large and useful trees but clear out the underbrush and weeds.[33]

Wilson repeatedly told audiences that the main purpose of a university was to make young men as unlike their fathers as possible.[34] It will be recalled that Wilson first made this statement in December 1909, when, at the height of his passion for Mrs. Peck, he may have noted the proximity of her apartment to the scene of his father's liaison with Mrs. Grannis. When taken in a political context, however, Wilson's declaration indicated his ideas about liberal education and freeing the younger generation from their fathers' conservative prejudices. Wilson's use of the theme may provide another illustration of the way in which he could transform feelings of guilt and shame into expressions of concern for the public good.

Although Wilson carried the gospel of progressivism, with its com-

---

[30] April 13, 1911, PWW, Vol. 22, p. 567.

[31] Address in Madison, Wisc., October 25, 1911, in *Bulletin of the University of Wisconsin*, Serial No. 470 (Madison, Wisc., 1911), pp. 3-15, printed in PWW, Vol. 23, p. 488.

[32] After-dinner address at the Burlington County Democratic Club, Burlington, N. J., April 5, 1911, in the *Newark Evening News*, April 6, 1911; address in Indianapolis, April 13, 1911, printed in *ibid.*, Vol. 22, pp. 537, 561.

[33] Address before the Association of Commerce of St. Paul, St. Paul, Minn., May 25, 1911, reported in the *St. Paul Pioneer-Press*, May 25, 1911, printed in *ibid.*, Vol. 23, p. 89.

[34] Address in Indianapolis, April 13, 1911, in *Indianapolis News*, April 14, 1911, in *ibid.*, Vol. 22, p. 558; remarks at dinner in Denver, May 8, 1911, reported in the Denver *Daily News*, May 8, 1911; address to the Association of Commerce of St. Paul, May 25, 1911, printed in *ibid.*, Vol. 23, pp. 22, 88.

mitment to the regulation of business, a recurring metaphor suggests
that he had not abandoned his conservative inclinations. On the day
that the Supreme Court announced its decision dissolving the Standard
Oil Company, he condemned the financiers who took "joy rides" in
corporations and asserted that, instead of "punishing the lawless
chauffeurs," the court was "trying to wreak vengeance by destroying
the machines."[35] Wilson actually never got over the idea of individual
responsibility and personal guilt. "Guilt is always personal and we
shall never get at the root of these things by changing merely the size
and organization of the business corporations," he told an interviewer
at the end of 1911.[36]

Stockton Axson was struck by Wilson's physical vigor during his
gubernatorial campaign,[37] but his efforts to function as both governor
and national campaigner brought a recurrence of his gastrointestinal
symptoms. In March 1911 his wife wrote to a friend that he was
working under fearfully high pressure.[38] Moreover, she complained,
he was "very wilful."[39] The return of his alimentary disturbances seems
to have coincided with the appearance of metaphors of digestion in
his speeches. For example, he told a luncheon group in Pasadena: "No
man should allow his stomach to become so squeamish that he does
not allow himself to know the facts. The standpatter does not want
to know the facts and when the dish is passed to him he says he does
not like it."[40] In Portland, Oregon, Wilson stated that he did not think
that a scandal over corruption was a disease, but a treatment—"evi-
dences of the awakening of the public conscience." He went on: "The
world for years suffered from inflammation of the bowels, but one
day a doctor discovered that it was due to appendicitis. Now hundreds
of lives are saved yearly and when you are cautiously opened and the
difficulty is removed there is no trouble thereafter. It is the same with
us; these outbursts are only the evidence of the recrudescence of the
public conscience."[41] Otherwise, Wilson was in good health during his
trip; his wife wrote that she was amazed at his "powers of endurance."[42] He injured, possibly may have fractured, his thumb, but,

---

[35] Address in Berkeley, Cal., May 17, 1911, in *San Francisco Chronicle*, May 17,
1911, *ibid.*, p. 59.

[36] Interview in the New York *World*, December 24, 1911, printed in *ibid.*, p. 613.

[37] Axson Memoir.

[38] EAW to Anna Harris, March 20, 1911, Wilson Papers.

[39] EAW to John W. Wescott, February 23, 1912, *PWW*, Vol. 24, p. 190.

[40] Luncheon speech in Pasadena, Cal., reported in the *Pasadena Star*, May 13, 1911,
ibid., Vol. 23, p. 48.

[41] Address in Portland, Ore., reported in the Portland *Morning Oregonian*, May 20,
1911, in *ibid.*, p. 75.

[42] EAW to WW, May 15, 1911, *ibid.*, p. 52.

characteristically, he did not inform his wife, who read of the accident in the newspapers.[43]

In the autumn of 1911, Wilson, still the leading contender for the nomination, came under virulent personal attack.[44] He also suffered a defeat in a campaign for commission government in New Jersey; the Smith-Nugent forces won primary elections in Essex County; and the Republicans regained control of the legislature. Predictably, Wilson had another recurrence of digestive troubles. A "bilious attack" put him to bed for a day in September.[45] The *Newark Evening News*, which in 1910 had commented on his stamina and good health, noted in October 1911 that he showed signs of fatigue.[46]

In December Wilson had an episode of impairment of function in his right hand; in a letter to Mrs. Peck, he complained of a cramped hand and difficulty in holding a pen.[47] The symptom was of brief duration, and one week later he wrote in his normal handwriting. He may possibly have had a cramp, but it is more likely that he had another minor stroke. The language of his Annual Message to the legislature in January 1912 suggests renewed concern with illness. In recommending a variety of measures, Wilson used the imperative "must" twelve times, and in each instance it was with reference to health, sanitation, mosquito and housefly control, dissemination of poisonous gases from factories, sewerage and garbage, and conservation. (When Wilson spoke of conservation of resources he invariably included men.)[48] The following month, while speaking at Harvard, he commented that he had had an episode of dizziness; jokingly, he told his audience of students that he attributed the spell, not to his liver, as his physician had surmised, but to the high praise of him by his introducer.[49] A visit to Dr. Stengel showed that his blood pressure was normal,[50] but Wilson may have experienced a transient ischemic episode.

Whatever his diagnosis, no doctor would have prescribed the program of activities in which Wilson was to engage over the next few months. His campaign had almost foundered for want of money, and,

[43] *St. Paul Dispatch*, May 25, 1911; EAW to WW, June 1, 1911, *ibid.*, pp. 93, 112.

[44] Link, *Wilson*, I, 347-80.

[45] WW to MAHP, September 17, 1911, *PWW*, Vol. 23, p. 329.

[46] See the *Newark Evening News*, October 24, 1910; October 7 and 12, 1911, in *ibid.*, Vol. 21, p. 412; Vol. 23, pp. 411, 443.

[47] WW to MAHP, December 17, 1911, *ibid.*, Vol. 23, p. 597.

[48] Annual Message to the Legislature of New Jersey, January 9, 1912, in *ibid.*, Vol. 24, p. 23.

[49] News report of speech, January 28, 1912, *Boston Post*, January 28, 1912, printed in *ibid.*, p. 94.

[50] EAW to John W. Wescott, February 23, 1912, *ibid.*, p. 190.

in response to the rise of the candidacies of Champ Clark of Missouri, Speaker of the House of Representatives, and Representative Oscar W. Underwood of Alabama, he was on the road almost constantly for the rest of the winter. The trips were not only physically and emotionally exhausting, but his frequent absences from the state made his relations with a Republican legislature difficult. Again, Wilson came under vitriolic personal attack. The most extreme Underwood spokesman, Tom Watson, Populist candidate for President in 1908, charged that Wilson favored Catholics, Jews, and Negroes and was an enemy of the workingman and farmer. William Randolph Hearst, whom Wilson detested and even refused to meet, came out for Clark in March. The Hearst newspapers, with their large foreign-born readership, featured the pejorative comments about immigrants from southern and eastern Europe in Wilson's *History of the American People*. Clark supporters spread rumors about Mrs. Peck; in April Wilson's hotel room in Chicago was entered and his briefcase stolen in an obvious attempt to obtain private correspondence.

The factual content of Wilson's speeches and interviews in the winter and spring of 1912 shows that he had learned a great deal about the workings of business. Yet his continued references to "joy riding" and individual guilt[51] indicate that he had not yet arrived at a program of dealing with the trusts. As the race grew keener and as evidence appeared that a stop-Wilson agreement had been made by his rivals, Wilson's language became more dramatic. He repeatedly evoked the symbolism of the flag, omitting, as usual, the white of purity.[52] In April and May, while Clark was winning primary after primary, and Underwood was gaining strength in the South, Wilson often closed his addresses with a plea for mankind to emerge from the dark valleys of despair and reach the uplands of light and justice. The disease of the body politic, which Wilson had once diagnosed as appendicitis, now had developed into a malignancy which could be removed by a careful Democratic surgeon.[53] Although in May 1912 his managers and his new friend, Colonel Edward M. House, considered his cause

[51] In one speech, Wilson declared that, in dealing with the trusts, it was necessary to "cherchez la femme." Address in Nashville, February 24, 1912, *ibid.*, p. 198.

[52] Address at the Light Guard Armory, Detroit, January 18, 1912, reported in the *Detroit News*, January 19, 1912; after-dinner address to the Real Estate Men of Boston, January 27, 1912; address to the General Assembly of Virginia and the City Council of Richmond, in Richmond, February 1, 1912, *ibid.*, pp. 53, 92, 103.

[53] Address in Frankfort, Ky., February 9, 1912, reported in the Louisville *Courier Journal*, February 10, 1912; address in Chicago, February 12, 1912, in *ibid.*, pp. 145, 159.

Wilson, in the fall presidential campaign of 1912, envisioned himself performing the

to be hopeless, Wilson continued to express confidence. There were rumors that he had suffered a nervous breakdown; he told Heath Dabney that he had simply gone to bed to cure a cold.[54] One month later, however, when it appeared likely that Clark would come to the convention with a majority of delegates, he conceded to Mrs. Peck that he had "not the least idea of being nominated."[55]

The exciting story of how Wilson won the nomination at the convention in Baltimore need not be repeated here.[56] Wilson himself told Mrs. Peck that it was "a sort of political miracle."[57] It was hardly that. Wilson won because his supporters were fanatically loyal to him and, most important, because the Wilson and Underwood delegates stood firm and prevented Clark from attaining the then necessary two-thirds majority.

Wilson's thinking about the control of corporations was profoundly influenced by Louis Dembitz Brandeis. This Boston lawyer, the outstanding progressive authority on monopoly and railroad regulation, converted Wilson to the proposition that competition and free enterprise could be restored by controlling competition itself. Wilson revealed this new approach, popularized as the New Freedom, in an address on Labor Day. He told a crowd of workingmen that the new Progressive party, which had nominated Theodore Roosevelt, wanted to legalize monopoly, and that eventually monopoly would control the government. He warned that such a government would bring about a state of politics in which open revolt would be substituted for the ballot box. "I believe," he declared, "that the greatest force for peace, the greatest force for righteousness, the greatest force for the elevation of mankind, is organized opinion, is the thinking of men, . . . and I want men to breathe a free and pure air." He then affirmed his new approach in a radically altered metaphor:

"And I know that these monopolies are so many cars of Juggernaut which are in our very sight being driven over men in such ways as to crush their life out of them. And I don't look forward with pleasure to the time when the Juggernauts are licensed. I don't look forward with pleasure to the time when the Juggernauts are driven by com-

surgery. "I have imagined myself what I am not, a skillful surgeon. I have imagined myself about to perform an operation upon a patient for the most part perfect, lusty, and well, but troubled with growths upon the vital parts, which have to be cut with such a nice and discriminating skill that no healthy fiber will be touched or damaged." Speech in Montclair, N. J., October 29, 1912, *ibid.*, Vol. 25, p. 471.

[54] Link, *Wilson*, I, 422; WW to Dabney, May 13, 1912, *PWW*, Vol. 24, p. 398.

[55] WW to MAHP, June 9, 1912, *PWW*, Vol. 24, p. 466.

[56] The most complete account can be found in Link, *Wilson*, I, 431-65.

[57] WW to MAHP, July 6, 1912, *PWW*, Vol. 24, p. 541.

missioners of the United States. I am willing to license automobiles, but not Juggernauts, because if any man ever dares take a joy ride in one of them, I would like to know what is to become of the rest of us."[58]

It was now time, Wilson had decided, to lock up the machine.

It was soon evident that President Taft would not be reelected, and the contest would be a duel between the two progressive leaders, Wilson and Theodore Roosevelt. Roosevelt was flamboyant and impulsive; Wilson was deliberate and controlled. Wilson himself made the contrast: "He is a real, vivid person, whom they have seen and shouted themselves hoarse over and voted for, millions strong; I am a vague, conjectural personality, more made up of opinions and academic prepossessions than of human traits and red corpuscles."[59] Actually, the two men resembled each other in their self-centeredness and combativeness and in their ability to control public opinion to assert the potential power of the presidency. Roosevelt's success in his two terms of office had strongly influenced Wilson's views of leadership.[60]

Gossip arose again about Mrs. Peck (now Mrs. Hulbert), and for a time it appeared that a scandal was in the making. Wilson heard that Elihu Root[61] knew of a letter connected with the Peck divorce which might implicate him. Alarmed, Wilson wrote to Mrs. Hulbert that, even if such a letter were subsequently discredited, it would ruin him utterly. There were "great issues . . . of life and death" at stake, he told her, and he expressed the hope that the people who believed and trusted in him would be suffered to continue to do so by his "malevolent foes."[62] It may or may not have been coincidence that Wilson, who had previously avoided ad-hominem attacks, now assailed Roosevelt personally.

In Denver, in the same auditorium where, a year and a half before, he had given an inspiring address on the Bible, Wilson delivered the most dramatic speech of the campaign. He began by charging that Roosevelt, as President, had sat by helplessly while special interests had gained an overwhelming degree of power and influence in the

[58] Address before United Trades and Labor Council, Buffalo, N. Y., September 2, 1912, *ibid.,* Vol. 25, pp. 73-74.

[59] WW to Mary Allen Hulbert, August 25, 1912, *ibid.,* p. 56.

[60] Link, *Wilson,* II, 147.

[61] Republican Senator from New York, former Secretary of War and Secretary of State. He was prominent in the international peace movement and won the Nobel Peace Prize in 1912.

[62] WW to MAH, September 29, 1912, *PWW,* Vol. 25, p. 285.

federal government. After he had spelled out in detail the methods by which the trusts stifled competition, Wilson declared:

"I have seen these giants close their hands upon the workingmen of this country already, and I have seen the blood come through their fingers. And I am not hopeful to believe that they will relax their grasp and lift these victims into the hopeful heavens. Ah, ladies and gentlemen, when you are starting out on a program, when you are starting out on a journey, look beneath you and see the beast you are riding. You cannot get to any goal by that vehicle. Why, I was saying today that I had an image in my mind of the great trusts of this country, impersonated as you please, standing upon a great stage. There would not be so many of them as there are on this stage, and in front of them Mr. Roosevelt leading them in the Hallelujah Chorus. I don't know whether he thinks he can teach them the tune or not, but I think I see the cynical smile on their faces as they would try to learn it from him. Leave the government and the industry of the United States under the control and in the possession in which it now is, and the Hallelujah Chorus will sound like bitter mockery in our ears."

Concluding, Wilson exclaimed: "When I look at this great flag of ours, I seem to see in it alternate strips of parchment and of blood. On the parchment are inscribed the ancient sentences of our great Bill of Rights, and the blood is the blood that has been spilled to give those sentences validity. And into the blue heaven in the corner has swung star after star, the symbol of a great commonwealth—the star of Colorado along with the star of ancient Virginia. And these stars will shine there with undiminished luster only so long as we remember the liberties of men and see to it that it is never again necessary to shed a single tear or a single drop of blood in their vindication."[63]

Wilson told a friend that he did not have the strength of a bull moose,[64] but he remained, aside from an occasional headache and digestive upset, "astonishingly well."[65] A few evenings before the election, he sustained a bloody four-inch scalp laceration. He received treatment, went home to bed, and his family learned of the accident only at the breakfast table the next morning. Characteristically, Wilson refused to pose for a picture; he joked to reporters that his plastic patch was private property.[66]

Although he failed to gain a popular majority, Wilson defeated

[63] Address in Denver, October 7, 1912, *ibid.*, pp. 371-74, 377.
[64] WW to Frank P. Glass, September 6, 1912, *ibid.*, p. 113.
[65] WW to MAH, August 17, 1912, *ibid.*, p. 46.
[66] See accounts in the *Trenton Evening True American*, November 4, 1912, and in the *Newark Evening News*, November 4, 1912, printed in *ibid.*, pp. 508-11.

Roosevelt decisively. He had a margin of 435 to 88 in the electoral college, while Taft ran a poor third. The voters also returned Democratic majorities to the House and Senate.

The President-elect set forth his ideas for his administration in two speeches delivered shortly after he had returned from a vacation with his family in Bermuda. He appealed to a group of financiers in New York to regard themselves as trustees of the economic interests of the nation and promised "a gibbet as high as Haman" for anyone who tried to set off a financial panic.[67] Wilson gave one of the most delightfully intimate addresses of his career—free of automobiles, roots, blood, and diseases—at a celebration in Staunton, Virginia, commemorating his fifty-sixth birthday. As he spoke from the steps of Mary Baldwin Seminary, he recalled playing in the yard of the manse across the street[68] and picking flowers there but, in deference to present company,[69] he would not say with whom.[70]

It was not with a light heart of a happy Christmas spirit, Wilson said, that he looked forward to the responsibilities of his great office. The wine of prosperity, he went on, had made men drunk enough to forget for a while that America's mission was not to pile up great wealth, but to serve mankind in humanity and justice:

"All the world, I say, is turning now as never before to this conception of the elevation of humanity, of men and women, I mean, not of the privileged few, not of those who can by superior wits or unusual opportunity struggle to the top, no matter whom they trample under foot, but of men who cannot struggle to the top and who must therefore be looked to by the forces of society, for they have no single force by which they can serve themselves. There must be heart in a government. . . . And men must look to it that they do unto others as they would have others do unto them. This used to be, and has long been, the theme of the discourse of Christian ministers, but it has now come to be part of the bounden duties of ministers of state."

Wilson saw himself as the instrument of the people, who would bring the North and the South together, and he told the story of the Confederate soldier, trudging home after the surrender, who was heard to mutter to himself: "Well, I'm not sorry I went in. I believe I was right. I would do it again because I love my country; but I'll be hanged if I'll ever love another country!" Although he honored the emblem of the sword, Wilson declared, he looked forward to the day when

---

[67] Address to the New York Southern Society, December 17, 1912, printed in *ibid.*, p. 602.

[68] The manse where he was born.

[69] His wife.   [70] Harriet Woodrow.

service could be rendered without the spilling of blood. He closed with a tribute to Thomas Jefferson, who, looking from his "coign of vantage" at Monticello, had seen far beyond the fertile fields of Virginia and had tried to divest his mind from the prejudices of race and locality and speak for the permanent issues of human liberty—the only things that rendered life on this globe immortal.[71]

Although Wilson had been able to convert personal weaknesses into political assets, one of his idiosyncrasies had unfavorable public consequences. As has been said, he had always been embarrassed to ask for money.[72] The New Jersey constitution explicitly stated that, when the Governor was out of the state, both his duties and his emolument were to be taken over by the president of the Senate. Wilson, on returning from campaign trips, was required by the state controller to make over his checks to the acting Governor, who would endorse them back. He believed that the controller, Edward Irving Edwards, with whom he had been friendly, had gone out of his way to inconvenience him. When Edwards, a banker and progressive Democrat, sought election by the legislature to the position of state treasurer, Wilson intervened to block him. In a private confrontation, he admitted to Edwards that he had been a good Wilson man but refused to say so to the press. Instead, he issued a public statement that it was "unwise and inexpedient for a banker to be State Treasurer."[73]

By the time that Wilson took office as the twenty-eighth President of the United States on March 4, 1913, he had demonstrated remarkable capacities for political leadership. He had shown himself a charismatic figure; he had inspired multitudes; and he had dramatized the goals for which progressives had been fighting for a generation. Wilson, aided by his command of language, had translated what otherwise would have been personal feelings of failure and guilt into ideas

[71] Address at Mary Baldwin Seminary, Staunton, Va., December 28, 1912, in *PWW*, Vol. 25, pp. 628-32.

[72] Margaret Axson Elliott wrote: "Woodrow was no earthly good at it. He insisted that the obligation of raising funds belonged properly to the [Princeton] trustees, while the president should be left free to run the college. Moreover, in addition to his convictions as regards the duties of a college president, he was temperamentally unfitted for the task of raising money. Normally a man of easy gracious manners, when confronted by a possible donor, he became shy, ill at ease, as embarrassed as though he were about to ask for money for himself." Elliott, *My Aunt Louisa*, pp. 190-91.

[73] Wilson's action weakened the progressive cause. After he indicated that he would not support Edwards, Nugent, to embarrass the Governor, backed the Controller. Wilson was then obliged for a time to continue his opposition to Edwards. Later, as United States senator from New Jersey, Edwards was a strong Wilson supporter. Kerney, *The Political Education of Woodrow Wilson*, pp. 253-55; Link, *Wilson*, II, 32.

of moral and social uplift. With his conscience bolstered by the new morality, he had been able, in what he believed were the interests of the mass of the people and the cause of progressivism, to discard men and policies whose purposes had been fulfilled. While taking a high moral stand, he had recognized that patronage—handled in New Jersey by Tumulty and Kerney—was necessary for the execution of a political program. He had learned from both radicals and party regulars. He had broadened his contacts beyond upper-class Protestantism; indeed, he enjoyed working with Irish politicians and was at ease with audiences of workingmen, immigrants, and unsophisticated people. His victories had confirmed his belief that he was close to the people and that he understood them. Most important, he had grown committed to a humane view of the functions of government and of the role of executive power in the service of all people.

CHAPTER XV

An Untimely Blow:
The Death of Ellen Axson Wilson

THE THEMES of Wilson's first inaugural—one of the briefest on record—were restoration and the rightings of wrongs. "Our duty," he declared, "is to cleanse, to reconsider, . . . to purify and humanize every process of our common life without weakening or sentimentalizing it." He stated that there had been "something crude and heartless and unfeeling" in the nation's haste to be great, and that government must serve humanity by safeguarding the people's health and welfare. "The feelings with which we face this new age of right and opportunity," he added, "sweep across our heartstrings like some air out of God's own presence, where justice and mercy are reconciled and the judge and the brother are one." He proclaimed a day, not of "triumph," but of "dedication," and he summoned all "honest," "patriotic," and "forward-looking men" to "counsel and sustain him." Some of Wilson's words may have been self-referential, since his wife had shown signs of the illness which resulted in her death and for which Wilson blamed his presidential ambitions.[1]

On the evening of his inauguration, at a dinner given in his honor by the Class of 1879, Wilson expressed his resolve to overcome personal weaknesses and avoid past errors. Among those present were the members of the old Witherspoon gang—Bridges, Talcott, Godwin, Lee, Webster, and Woods. Wilson confessed that he had sometimes been too strong in his likes and dislikes, and that he had been too harsh in pursuing a course of action dictated by his principles. He admitted that he had always had the ambition to hold high office, but, now that he held the highest executive office in the world, he did not feel happy. There had been a moment of joy, perhaps, when he actually took the oath, but on the return from the Capitol, down Pennsylvania Avenue, he had felt frankly frightened by what faced him and by his own inadequacy. He hoped that his class would always stand by him, and he added that he would drop anything that he was doing at any

---

[1] Inaugural address, March 4, 1913, *PWW*, Vol. 27, pp. 148-52.

time to see any of them, because he knew he could trust them to tell him the truth.[2]

It was one of the few times that Wilson admitted that he had made mistakes at Princeton.

The brilliant achievements of Wilson's first term in office have been amply documented elsewhere.[3] Under his active and resourceful leadership, Congress fulfilled the major pledges of the Democratic platform. Wilson set the tone for his administration when, at the suggestion of a reporter,[4] he delivered his message on the tariff in person to a joint session of Congress. He worked closely with committee chairmen in preparing the tariff and the Federal Reserve bills, kept control of the Democratic majority by a combination of persuasion, pressure, and patronage, and won support from progressives and insurgent Republicans. Wilson also influenced legislation by making his views known through the press; his public denunciation of special-interest groups during the tariff fight led to an investigation which broke the power of a well-financed sugar lobby. After making concessions on the tariff, he issued an ultimatum which brought remaining congressional dissidents into line. While he was obliged to make compromises over banking and currency reform, the basic features were preserved, and the Federal Reserve Act of December 1913 is regarded as a great legislative accomplishment. In the first months of 1914, Wilson showed what Link calls "one of the most extraordinary displays of leadership of his entire career" when he induced a rebellious Congress to repeal the act giving free passage to American coastwise ships using the Panama Canal.[5]

Wilson maintained outstanding leadership and good rapport with his cabinet. He gave his officers a great deal of freedom, but took overall responsibility and backed them when he considered that they had been unfairly attacked. Wilson intervened in matters of patronage only on rare occasions. He appointed William Jennings Bryan as Secretary of State in recognition of the Nebraskan's long service in the

---

[2] David Lawrence, "The Inauguration of President Wilson," *Princeton Alumni Weekly*, XIII (March 5, 1913), 421; interview with Charles Presbrey, September 14, 1942, Bragdon Collection; Abraham Woodruff Halsey to WW, March 5, 1913, *PWW*, Vol. 27, p. 154, n.1.

[3] See Link, *Wilson*, II and V, *passim*.

[4] The reporter was Oliver Peck Newman, who pointed out that Washington had read his first message to Congress and that Jefferson had discontinued the practice because he was a poor speaker. David Lawrence, *The True Story of Woodrow Wilson* (New York, 1924), pp. 81-83. Wilson appointed Newman to the Board of Commissioners of the District of Columbia.

[5] Link, *Wilson*, II, 310-14.

party and in order to insure Bryan's support for his domestic program. Bryan's loyal cooperation gratified Wilson, and the two men worked harmoniously until 1915, when Bryan resigned over differences concerning American policy toward the German submarine campaign. Wilson was particularly fond of Josephus Daniels, his Secretary of the Navy. Daniels, a North Carolinian and a close friend of Bryan, had worked for Wilson before Baltimore. He was a progressive force in the cabinet and a vigorous proponent of the supremacy of civilian over military authority. Daniels became unpopular and a subject of ridicule when he abolished the drinking privileges of naval officers and tried to raise the educational level of enlisted men. Wilson defended Daniels against his critics and effectively discouraged efforts to remove him from office. William G. McAdoo, Secretary of the Treasury, who married Eleanor Wilson, was the ablest and most ambitious of the group. Wilson opened cabinet sessions with a joke or anecdote, after which he introduced a topic for discussion. Afterwards he summarized what he thought had been the sense of the meeting. Wilson rarely argued or criticized; he listened patiently to even long and verbose speeches. Secretary of the Interior Franklin K. Lane and Secretary of Agriculture David F. Houston both noted Wilson's consideration for the feelings of the members.[6] In 1913 and 1914, the events which prompted Secretary of War Lindley Miller Garrison to call him a man of high ideals and no principles lay in the future.[7]

When Wilson entered politics, he had promised his wife that he would not allow himself to become emotionally involved as he had done at Princeton. He was mindful of the anguish he had suffered when friends had turned against him and was cognizant of the way in which his partiality toward Jack Hibben had contributed to his downfall. As his talk to his class on the evening of his inaugural indicates, he also had insight into his own failings. As President, he leaned over backward to avoid any show of favoritism. Daniels wrote that, at each cabinet meeting, Wilson would ask a different member to present departmental business first, in order to avoid creating any impression that he thought one man's work was more important than another's.[8] A prominent feature of Wilson's personality, already noted, was the belief that one should be able to master his thoughts and feelings, and he was determined to control any anger and irritation.

[6] House diary, April 29, 1914, *PWW*, Vol. 29, p. 536; David F. Houston, *Eight Years with Wilson's Cabinet, 1913-1920*, 2 vols. (Garden City, N. Y., 1926), I, 88-89.

[7] Interview with Lindley M. Garrison, November 30, 1926, Baker Papers.

[8] Josephus Daniels, *The Wilson Era: Years of Peace, 1913-1917* (Chapel Hill, N. C., 1944), p. 137.

Houston remembered that Wilson would avoid meeting men rather than reproach them or quarrel with them.[9] These traits led to one of Wilson's greatest political weaknesses—his extreme reluctance to dismiss men who were incompetent or who actively opposed his policies.[10]

As a corollary to his habit of self-scrutiny and the feeling of detachment that he often felt, Wilson often perceived himself as a private individual, apart from his office. During his campaign, he remarked to a reporter that he could not quite believe that he was the same fellow whose name was on the banners. He told his old friend, Nancy Toy, that, when he talked on the telephone, he could not bring himself to say, "This is the President" but instead always said, "This is Wilson."[11] The various forms of presidential protocol embarrassed him; he wanted to treat his guests as a gentleman would in his own home.[12] He had been upset when he saw Theodore Roosevelt go through a door ahead of a lady. Unlike other Presidents, Wilson had no home other than the White House, and he believed that he was entitled to as much privacy as any other citizen. Maintenance of privacy became a major cause of his difficulties with the press. Wilson had got along well with reporters as Governor of New Jersey and candidate for the presidency, but he was quite unprepared for the public curiosity about the doings of a presidential family. Only occasionally did dinner or overnight guests include others than relatives, family friends, and such virtual members of the household as Dr. Grayson, Joseph P. Tumulty, Wilson's secretary, and Colonel Edward Mandell House, his most intimate friend and adviser. In southern fashion, Wilson regarded the White House domestic staff as his family's servants, and he treated them with exceptional courtesy and generosity. He felt especially warmly toward Irwin Hood "Ike" Hoover, the head usher.[13] Hoover was devoted to the President, and Wilson referred to him as "the faithful Hoover, whom I shall always love and value."[14]

During Wilson's tenure, the White House had none of the trappings of a court, such as the Executive Mansion had acquired under Theodore Roosevelt. In contrast to his predecessor, Wilson never used what he considered his home for political purposes. For example, Roosevelt

[9] Memorandum of interview with David F. Houston, December 1, 1928, Baker Papers.

[10] Secretary of State Robert Lansing and Walter Hines Page, Ambassador to Great Britain, were striking examples.

[11] Diary of Nancy Saunders Toy, January 4, 1915, *PWW*, Vol. 32, pp. 12-13.

[12] McAdoo, *The Woodrow Wilsons*, p. 82.

[13] Hoover oversaw the maintenance staff and served as a general manager and expediter. Eleanor McAdoo called him "the most quietly efficient" man she had ever known. *Ibid.*, p. 214.

[14] WW to Edith Bolling Galt, August 19, 1915, *PWW*, Vol. 34, p. 259.

had created a stir when he invited Booker T. Washington to dinner at the White House, an act inconceivable for Wilson on social and racial grounds. Wilson permitted segregation in two governmental departments, but, to judge from other political acts concerning Negroes, he would not have allowed such a miscarriage of justice as Roosevelt's summary dishonorable discharge in 1906 of three companies of Negro soldiers for allegedly provoking a riot in Brownsville, Texas.

Wilson appeared to be in particularly good health and spirits when he entered the White House. His daughter Eleanor recalled: "Father looked extraordinarily well and vital during these first weeks. When I saw him come out of his study and stride down the hall toward us, I noticed that his walk had acquired more than its usual buoyancy. His eyes were strikingly clear and bright, and there was a sort of chiseled keenness in his face. He was finer looking in those days than ever before in his life."[15]

Wilson's medical record, as President, began benignly enough. On the Sunday following his inauguration, he experienced a gastrointestinal upset for which he was treated by Dr. Grayson. The Doctor recalled that his patient "got the drop" on him by telling him the story of Dr. Delafield and the stomach tube. In characteristic fashion, Wilson joked throughout the examination. He referred to his complaints as "turmoil in Central America," and, when Grayson ordered him to bed, he said that the Doctor was forcing him to set a bad example for the American people by not going to church.[16]

Wilson could hardly have found a physician better suited to his temperament than Cary Grayson. Wilson must have been impressed by the Doctor's ancestral credentials. The earliest Grayson in America was of Scottish extraction and had been a colonel on George Washington's staff. Cary Grayson, born in Culpeper County, Virginia, on October 11, 1878, was the grandson of a physician, and the son of Dr. John Cooke Grayson, who had served in the Confederate Army.[17] Cary Grayson was also a connection by marriage of Presley Marion Rixey, Surgeon-General of the Navy and White House physician to Roosevelt and Taft. Grayson's parents died while he was still a boy, and Doctor Rixey took an interest in his career.[18] After an internship

[15] McAdoo, The Woodrow Wilsons, pp. 240-41.

[16] Grayson, An Intimate Memoir, pp. 2-3; Baker, Wilson, IV, 22.

[17] "Cary Travers Grayson," National Cyclopaedia of American Biography, 58 vols. (New York, 1928-40), XXVIII, 132-33.

[18] Presley Marion Rixey, The Life Story of Presley Marion Rixey: Surgeon General, U.S. Navy 1902-1910 (Strasburg, Va., 1930), p. 391.

at the Columbia Hospital for Women in Washington, Dr. Grayson received a naval commission and served at the Naval Hospital after which he was assigned to *USS Maryland* in the cruise of the Great White Fleet around the world. After his return, he joined the medical staff of the White House. Dr. Grayson went on to serve in the Taft administration, and Wilson appointed him White House physician on Taft's recommendation.[19]

Grayson recognized the nature of Wilson's psychosomatic symptoms and their relationship to stress. He was sparing with drugs and encouraged his patient to take regular exercise, which included deep breathing, calisthenics, and golf.[20] Wilson became devoted to the game and played almost daily; he found that if he concentrated on his shots he could keep troubling thoughts out of his mind. He even practiced with a red ball in the snow. Motoring became a passion. Wilson had never owned a vehicle grander than a bicycle, and there were six cars at his disposal at the White House. On his first full day in office, he took his wife and his friend, Fred Yates, out for rides.[21] Grayson was far more interested in horses than he was in automobiles, and Wilson liked to tease him about his fondness for the race track. Like Wilson, the Doctor was an excellent story teller, and the men enjoyed exchanging anecdotes. They developed a close friendship far exceeding the usual doctor-patient relationship.

Wilson's health problems as President have been attributed erroneously to overwork. He completed his daily duties in from five to six hours and had plenty of time for recreation. He rose at eight, had a breakfast of two raw eggs in fruit juice—like swallowing a newborn baby, he said—oatmeal, and coffee. He dictated from nine to ten and then saw visitors until one. After lunch with his family, he returned to his office for an hour or two. He took an automobile ride in the afternoon and worked during evenings only in times of great crisis.

[19] Dr. Grayson's first patient during the Wilson administration was Wilson's sister, Annie Wilson Howe, whom he treated for a minor injury sustained when she slipped on the White House stairs at the inaugural reception.

[20] Like most golfers, Wilson had an explanation of why his shots were less than perfect. "My right eye is like a horse's. I can see straight out of it but not sideways. As a result I cannot take a full swing because my nose gets in the way and cuts off my view of the ball. That is the reason I use a short swing." Lawrence, *The True Story of Woodrow Wilson,* p. 129. If the reader will look to one side and then cover the eye on the side of the direction of gaze, he will find that his sight is impeded by his nose. Because of Wilson's loss of vision in his left eye, he saw his nose when he tried to converge on the ball. This is a variety of the neurological phenomenon of visual extinction.

[21] Frederic Yates to Emily C. M. Yates, March 5, 1913, *PWW,* Vol. 27, p. 156.

"Ike" Hoover, who served many Presidents, regarded Wilson as the most intelligent and the most satisfactory one with whom to work.[22] Wilson worked with incredible speed and intensity because he could write so rapidly in shorthand. He usually made shorthand drafts of important letters, state papers, diplomatic notes, etc., and would then dictate them to his personal secretary, Charles L. Swem, or type them himself. He answered communications within forty-eight hours and dictated letters once without later drafts or corrections. The impressions of overwork obtained by biographers seem to have come from his family's and friends' worries about him and his letters to Mrs. Hulbert and others in which he apologized for not having written because he was hard-pressed and tired.

Wilson had been in office barely a month when he had a recurrence of his neurological condition. On April 11 he sustained a probable stroke affecting, this time, his left upper extremity. He minimized its severity to Mrs. Hulbert in characteristic fashion: "I have been lying in bed all day, not only because it was Sunday and I was tired and *could* rest, but because for the last forty-eight hours there has been a threat in my left shoulder of my old enemy, *neuritis*, as nasty a beast as ever attacked poor human flesh,—and a mean coward, besides, for the sneak comes only when a fellow is worn out and there is no fight in him. Maybe, this time, it is only a touch of cold. At any rate, this evening it is better and I am cheerful enough. This slight ailment of mine does not interest me as much as your own health."[23] Wilson's "touch of neuritis,"[24] as he termed it, lasted for at least several weeks.[25]

Wilson reacted to his affliction as he had to his blindness in 1906— with a transient euphoria followed by depression. Colonel House, who lunched with him on April 12, noted that he was unusually cheerful: "We laughed the hour away." Wilson's heightened mood was tinged with irritability as he complained to House that some members of the cabinet bothered him by taking up his time threshing out matters with him instead of presenting them in condensed fashion.[26] House recorded on April 15: "I went to McAdoo's and together we went to the White House to see the President. The President looked so worn and tired that I broke up the conference almost immediately."[27] Three days later

---

[22] Irwin H. Hoover, *Forty-Two Years in the White House* (Boston, 1934), p. 244.

[23] WW to MAH, April 13, 1913, *PWW*, Vol. 27, p. 298.

[24] "I have had a touch of neuritis in my left shoulder," he wrote to his brother. WW to JRW, Jr., April 14, 1913, *ibid.*, p. 307.

[25] Helen Woodrow Bones to Jessie Bones Brower, c. May 3, 1913, *ibid.*, Vol. 29, p. 557.

[26] House diary, April 13, 1913.   [27] *Ibid.*, April 15, 1913.

the diarist reported: "The President seemed depressed and I tried to brace him by telling him that everything was in splendid condition excepting himself; that was the only thing troubling me."[28]

The episode which affected Wilson's left arm was particularly ominous from a clinical standpoint. The most likely diagnosis is that he had developed an ulcerated plaque in his right carotid artery from which an embolus had broken off. This meant that the cerebral circulation has been impaired on the right, previously unaffected, side of the brain. This evidence of bilaterality of involvement not only increased the risk of further strokes, but also created the possibility that enduring changes in behavior, based upon insufficient blood supply and impaired oxygenation of the brain, might eventually occur. Over the next six months, Wilson voiced occasional complaints of "neuritis," which were probably transient ischemic attacks.[29] Grayson's statement to Colonel House in October that Wilson was in good health indicates that the Doctor was not aware that his patient had arterial disease of the brain.[30]

Despite the severity of his stroke, Wilson, in his usual fashion, carried on his work as if nothing had happened. His distress, however, seems to have been a factor in some inconsistent political actions. On April 12 he declared that he would sign a bill exempting labor unions from the provisions of the antitrust laws, a form of flagrant class legislation which violated a major tenet of the New Freedom. Congress took Wilson's cue and proceeded to pass the bill. After Wilson had signed it, he tried to evade responsibility by stating that he was merely supporting the opinion of Congress.[31]

The psychological and possible physiological effects of the new stroke may have been shown on a trip to New Jersey, which Wilson took on May 2 to confer with party leaders and to speak publicly in behalf of jury reform. Although the Democratic legislature expected his guidance, he talked to them in generalities and refused to advise any specific course of action. When he arrived in Jersey City for a public address, he appeared haggard, worn, and short-tempered.[32] His speech was rambling, and, considering the subject, extraordinarily impassioned. He called the State House a temple in whose corridors a "high priest of intrigue [Nugent]" lurked. He asked rhetorically,

---

[28] *Ibid.*, April 18, 1913, *PWW*, Vol. 27, p. 334.

[29] The diagnosis of neuritis at the time was a catchall, which included a wide variety of aches and pains and muscular weaknesses, as well as actual involvements of peripheral nerves. Grayson could hardly have been apprehensive of a second term on such a basis.

[30] House diary, October 14, 1913.   [31] Link, *Wilson*, II, 266-68.

[32] *Ibid.*, p. 47.

"Are you going to burn incense to his god, or are you going to burn incense to the God of mankind, the God of love and of justice and of purity and of righteousness?" "If there was ever anything to make a man's red corpuscles jump through his veins," he said, it was the fight for jury reform. Then, on what seems to have been a note of desperation, Wilson exclaimed: " 'Why go up and fight for a losing cause?' Well, I know my fellow citizens in New Jersey, and I deny that it is a losing cause. But suppose it was! I would rather have my body one of the first to fall by the wall than one of the last. Anybody can come on with the battalions that marshal millions strong before the war is over, but only men of sturdy courage can go with the little handful that starts the battle. And whether we win or lose, the battalions are coming on, and the eventual outcome of the day of battle is not in doubt. There is a God in the heavens, and all is well."[33]

Ellen Wilson had mixed feelings about her husband's entry into politics. She had certainly been eager to leave the depressing atmosphere of Princeton, but she had also feared that a political career would endanger her husband's health. She expressed her dilemma to her brother, Stockton, one evening after her return from a performance of *Macbeth* in New York. "It makes one pause and think: Lady Macbeth wanted Macbeth to have the crown because he wanted it, not because she wanted to become Queen of Scotland. Maybe these husbands ought not always to be encouraged to get the things to which their ambitions lead them, but how can wives who love them do anything except help them? Of course, I don't mean when the object of their ambition is something wrong as it was in Macbeth's case, but even when it is right, it may wear out their strength and health and spirits, and yet they will never be happy unless they get it."[34] Despite her reservations, she worked diligently in the gubernatorial campaign; she kept a file of clippings from newspapers which Wilson did not read, so that he could peruse them later. On the day when he was inaugurated in Trenton, she observed sadly to James Kerney, "This is all very glorious, but somehow I feel that it is the end of our happy home days."[35] As the wife of the Governor, she went beyond her own family to concern herself with the welfare and care of the inmates of state institutions.

During Wilson's campaigns for the presidency, she consulted Dr. Francis X. Dercum of Philadelphia, a neurologist, who had taken care

---

[33] Address in Jersey City, N. J., May 2, 1913, in *PWW*, Vol. 27, pp. 386-90.
[34] Axson Memoir.
[35] Kerney, *The Political Education of Woodrow Wilson,* p. 161.

of her brother in one of his emotional breakdowns.[36] Dr. Dercum assured her that Wilson's "neuritis" would respond to baking and a hot climate and that he could assume the office.[37] However, another eminent neurologist, Dr. Silas Weir Mitchell, predicted publicly that Wilson would not live through his term.[38] Wilson himself may have suspected as much when he wrote to Nancy Toy in 1913 that he expected his first year in office to be the period of his greatest efficiency, and that it was now or never.[39]

While Ellen occupied herself with Wilson's political career, her own health had begun to deteriorate. She had never fully recovered her spirits after the death of her brother, Eddie, and when, in the spring of 1912, Jessie and Eleanor noticed that she was less animated and had become slow in her movements, they attributed her condition to worry about Stockton, who was going through another depression. The girls were sufficiently disturbed to offer to stay at home with her, but, characteristically, she refused to hear of their interrupting their careers.[40] Shortly after the Wilsons returned from their Bermuda vacation in December 1913, Colonel House noted that, although Mrs. Wilson was a strong woman, she was beginning to show the effects of "over work."[41] While helping her mother to dress for the inaugural ceremonies, Eleanor Wilson was distressed to see her "so white and so helpless and so tiny."[42]

The subsequent course of Ellen Wilson's illness indicates that her lack of vigor and depression were related, not only to concern for Woodrow's health, but also to the progression of her chronic nephritis. Because of her indisposition, Wilson canceled the traditional inaugural ball. However, she carried on with other White House social duties and began a project to improve living conditions in Washington's Negro slums. In June, however, the New York Times reported that, although she was "not seriously ill," she had, on the advice of her physician, given up active philanthropic work.[43] Ellen spent the summer and early autumn in Cornish, New Hampshire, while Wilson remained in Washington, occupied with Congress and the Mexican situation. As his visits were "depressingly few,"[44] she made a trip to

[36] It was customary for neurologists to treat patients with emotional illnesses, or "neuroses." Psychiatrists, mainly in asylums, took care of the insane.

[37] Axson Memoir.   [38] Grayson, An Intimate Memoir, p. 81.

[39] Nancy S. Toy to WW, October 9, 1914, Wilson Papers.

[40] McAdoo, The Woodrow Wilsons, pp. 148-49.

[41] House diary, January 8, 1913, PWW, Vol. 27, p. 24.

[42] McAdoo, The Woodrow Wilsons, p. 201.

[43] New York Times, June 21, 1913.

[44] McAdoo, The Woodrow Wilsons, p. 253.

the city to reassure herself about his health. She remained in Cornish for several more months, and returned in mid-October to help in the preparations for Jessie's wedding to Francis Bowes Sayre. Wilson himself was laid up with a severe cold and bronchitis in December, and, on his recovery, the couple went for a vacation on the Gulf Coast of Mississippi. There she rallied temporarily.

Mrs. Wilson may have already been in kidney failure when she fell heavily in her room on March 1, 1914. It is probable that a fainting spell was the cause of Mrs. Wilson's fall. She stayed in bed for several weeks recovering from the soreness and stiffness; but she remained weak, lethargic, and anorexic, a triad of symptoms typical of chronic nephritis. She seemed to improve slightly after a stay at White Sulphur Springs and was able to hear Wilson's message to Congress on Mexico on April 20. However, at the wedding of Eleanor Wilson and William G. McAdoo on May 7, Stockton Axson was shocked to see how feeble his sister had become. He was, nevertheless, assured by Wilson that Dr. Grayson had expressed full expectation of her recovery.[45]

Ellen's condition did not improve through the spring. She ate poorly, despite Woodrow's coaxing, and spent most of her time lying on her sofa. On pleasant days, she sat outdoors amid her flowers and directed the gardeners from her wheelchair.[46] She never complained and refused to let her daughters even ask about her health.[47] She seemed more concerned that Woodrow would be upset. Although he was tragically aware that she was no better, he persisted in expressing the belief that she would get well. "There is nothing at all the matter with her organically," he wrote to Mrs. Hulbert early in June. "It is altogether functional; and the doctors assure us that all with care will come out right. But a nervous break down is no light matter and my heart is very heavy."[48] No one in the family could express their feelings of anxious dread. Eleanor McAdoo recalled, "We were hiding our secret fear about mother from one another—all stubbornly pretending that she would soon be well again; but I remember waking up one hot morning with a dreadful sense of oppression—of intense terror. I could hardly wait to dress and get over to the White House where I sat for hours outside her door as she slept. Then I saw father coming down the long corridor. His step had lost its swing and, when I saw his face, gaunt and gray, etched with deep lines, I spring up and ran and clung to him desperately. We sat hand in hand on the sofa near mother's

[45] Axson Memoir.
[46] Elliott, *My Aunt Louisa*, p. 270.
[47] McAdoo, *The Woodrow Wilsons*, p. 290.
[48] WW to MAH, June 7, 1914, *PWW*, Vol. 30, p. 158.

door, and he told me that he had not for a moment lost hope—that the doctors kept reassuring him; but in my heart I knew."[49]

Wilson persisted in his denial almost to the end. As late as July 28, a week before his wife's death, he claimed that there was nothing organically wrong and that it was only the weather that was holding her back.[50] Dr. Grayson could not steel himself to tell the family the truth, and it fell to Dr. Edward P. Davis, Wilson's classmate, to inform the President that Ellen had only hours to live. Wilson did not speak on receiving the news, and, for the first time in her life, Eleanor saw him weep.[51] Ellen died on August 6, two days after Great Britain declared war against Germany. Before losing consciousness, she drew Dr. Grayson to her and said, "Doctor, if I go away, promise me that you will take good care of Woodrow."[52]

Grayson was in an extraordinarily difficult position during Mrs. Wilson's illness. Grayson's status as a virtual member of the family— he was best man at the McAdoo wedding—made it difficult for him to act with professional detachment. He had been a confidant of Ellen and probably was the only person other than Woodrow to whom she had ever expressed her feelings about Mrs. Hulbert.[53] Grayson was probably aware that she was seriously ill, but he was a military medical officer, serving under, and primarily responsible for the health of, the President. With this duty in mind, he could not risk upsetting Wilson by trying to penetrate his denial system and possibly precipitate another stroke. In effect, he reinforced Wilson's denial. This attitude may have delayed the calling in of consultants until relatively late in the illness. Yet the President's affection for and confidence in his physician remained unchanged. A year later he recommended him for the position of Surgeon-General of the Navy.

Wilson's denial of the gravity of his wife's illness led to an angry attack on the press. When Mrs. Wilson did not recover promptly from her fall, there were reports that she was more seriously ill than the official announcements indicated. Wilson opened his press conference on March 19 by scolding the reporters for writing stories that his daughter Margaret was engaged to various men.[54] He went on to say

---

[49] McAdoo, *The Woodrow Wilsons,* pp. 296-97.

[50] WW to Edward P. Davis, July 28, 1914, *PWW,* Vol. 30, p. 312.

[51] McAdoo, *The Woodrow Wilsons,* p. 299.

[52] Memorandum of interview with Cary T. Grayson, February 18, 1925, Baker Papers.

[53] See p. 189, n.44.

[54] Margaret Wilson never married. After a singing career, she spent several years as a social worker and then went to India to spend the rest of her life as a member of a religious cult.

that, since his daughters had no brother to protect them, it was his obligation to defend the women of his household from annoyance. "Every day I pick up the paper and see some flat lie, some entire invention, things represented as having happened to my daughters where they were not present, and all sorts of insinuations. When they are told that the person who is nearest to me in all the world is not seriously ill and is steadily recovering from a fall, they go about to create rumors that something is being concealed."[55] Wilson may have unconsciously revealed his preoccupation with his wife's illness in an exchange with reporters a week earlier. When he was asked, in connection with diplomatic affairs, if the Monroe Doctrine still stood, he replied, "I haven't heard of its falling."[56] The President apologized for his outburst the following day in an address to the National Press Club in which he spoke of the difficulty of separating his private from his official self.[57]

The agonizing fear that his wife would not recover may have contributed to the breaking of Wilson's resolve to let bygones at Princeton be. At the thirty-fifth reunion of the Class of 1879, he gave vent to the insecurities and resentments, which, a year earlier, he had hoped to overcome. Robert H. McCarter many years later recalled that Wilson became upset by a request for a group photograph, complained that he was tired, and insisted on taking a nap. His picture had to be inserted later by the photographer. Wilson refused to shake hands with Parker Handy, a trustee who had voted to elect Jack Hibben[58] as President of Princeton University. Wilson began his speech at the class dinner graciously, but he soon launched into an account of the "grim things" that he had learned in his life. He said that he would never again be fool enough to make believe that a man whom he knew was his enemy was his friend. He knew the sheep from the goats, he declared, and he reminded the class that there would be an arrangement for goats in the next world. Having consigned the goats to their fate, Wilson spoke of the "natural brotherliness of men" and the "general love of the great human element that unites us all together."

[55] Press Conference, March 19, 1914, PWW, Vol. 29, pp. 353-54.

[56] Press Conference, March 12, 1914, ibid., p. 334.

[57] Remarks to the National Press Club, March 20, 1914, ibid., pp. 361-66.

[58] McCarter was one of Wilson's best friends when they were undergraduates, but he incurred Wilson's enmity when he opposed his plans for reorganization of the university. McCarter was eighty-one years old when he was interviewed by Henry Bragdon, and he died the following year. His advanced age may have caused him to be hazy on details, but it is unlikely that he fabricated the incident entirely. See interview with Robert H. McCarter, July 15, 1940, Bragdon Collection; WW to Dodge, June 17, 1914, PWW, Vol. 30, p. 189.

He seemed to reach back across the years to the quadrangle plan when he charged that the bad thing about having social classes was that they erected artificial barriers between people; and he expressed his desire for close, unaffected contact with all sorts of men. In a reference to the more recent events, Wilson attacked the press for its lies and stated that he had stopped reading newspapers. In closing, Wilson admitted that he had been wandering from point to point. What he had really wanted to say was that the day had refreshed him and renewed the delightful impression of the heart which had been the sources of spiritual and physical life. It was his privilege both to remember and forget what the intervening years had brought.[59]

Wilson's distress over his wife's illness may have been a factor in his bellicose action which almost led to war between the United States and Mexico. Wilson had been intent on deposing the Mexican usurper, General Victoriano Huerta, and on assisting Huerta's opponents, the Constitutionalists. An opportunity came on April 9 when Mexican military authorities at Tampico arrested some American sailors who had gone ashore without obtaining permission from the local Mexican commander. The Mexican general apologized and released the men, and Huerta issued written regrets to the American Chargé in Mexico City. Wilson, however, found the Mexican response unsatisfactory and backed Admiral Henry T. Mayo's demand that the Mexicans salute the American flag with twenty-one guns. When Huerta refused, Wilson ordered the Atlantic and Pacific fleets to Mexican waters and declared that he could no longer tolerate Huerta's insults to the American people. Huerta then offered to make the salute reciprocal. However, when Huerta would not give in unconditionally, Wilson broke off negotiations and went before Congress to ask for approval of punitive action. He greatly exaggerated two trivial incidents in an effort to prove that the Huerta government had adopted a deliberate program of provocation. The Republicans had long favored intervention, but Senators Elihu Root of New York and Henry Cabot Lodge of Massachusetts ridiculed Wilson's reasons. The resolution was, nevertheless, adopted overwhelmingly and on the following day Wilson, in order to intercept a shipment of arms to the *Huertistas*, directed the seizure of the customhouse at Veracruz. The Mexicans, to Wilson's surprise, resisted and, in the ensuing battle, nineteen Americans were killed. Huerta broke diplomatic relations and Wilson ordered troops to Veracruz and the border. The contending Mexican factions united in a wave of patriotic indignation, and American consulates were looted and burned.

[59] Remarks to the Class of 1879, June 13, 1914, *ibid.*, Vol. 30, pp. 176-80.

Wilson averted a full-scale war by promptly stopping military preparations. Overcome by guilt, he held himself personally responsible
for what had happened. "The thought haunts me that it was I who
ordered those men to their deaths," he told Grayson.[60] An observer
at the press conference which Wilson held soon after he received the
news from Veracruz observed: "How preternaturally pale, almost
parchmenty, Mr. Wilson looked when he stood up there and answered
the questions of the newspaper men. The death of American sailors
and marines owing to an order of his seemed to affect him like an
ailment. He was positively shaken."[61] While still in a state of shock
over Ellen's death, Wilson wrote to his Secretary of War that, whatever
the excesses of the Mexican Revolution, the United States had no right
to interfere with its course. "I speak very solemnly but with clear
judgment in the matter, which I hope God will give me strength to act
upon."[62]

During the four or five months which followed his wife's death,
Wilson went through a severe reactive depression. Along with his
intense grief and loneliness, he suffered feelings of guilt and hope-
lessness, and a loss of self-esteem. He told his family that if it were
not for his political ambitions, Ellen would still be alive.[63] "God has
stricken me almost beyond what I can bear," he wrote to Mary Hulbert,[64] but what emotions he may have experienced about their affair
were not revealed. He felt completely empty, like a machine which
had run down, he said; he had no heart for anything, and did not see
how he could get through the remaining years of his term. Complaints
of confused thinking and poor memory are common in depression;
Wilson told Colonel House that he was unfit to be President because
he could not think straight.[65] He felt that his life was over, and, in the
depths of his depression, he expressed the wish that someone would
kill him.[66] He told Mrs. Toy that he had hoped to escape from con-
templation of himself by dealing with the problems of the war with
"enhanced sympathy and quickened insight," but soon found that the
love of mankind and attention to the affairs of state were no substitute
for the intimacy of a dear one.[67] Although he complained of feelings

[60] Grayson, *An Intimate Memoir*, p. 30.

[61] H. J. Forman to RSB, undated, quoted in Baker, *Wilson*, IV, 330.

[62] WW to Lindley M. Garrison, August 8, 1914, *PWW*, Vol. 30, p. 362.

[63] Mary E. Hoyt to WW, August 22, 1914, Wilson Papers; Elliott, *My Aunt Louisa*,
p. 270; Grayson, *An Intimate Memoir*, p. 36.

[64] WW to MAH, August 7, 1914, *PWW*, Vol. 30, p. 357.

[65] House diary, November 6, 1914, *ibid.*, Vol. 31, p. 274.

[66] House diary, November 14, 1914, *ibid.*, p. 320.

[67] WW to Toy, October 15 and November 9, 1914, *ibid.*, pp. 157, 290.

of fatigue—another symptom of depression—he worked long hours to keep from thinking about himself. Wilson insisted that Jessie and Eleanor spend the summer in Cornish, but it took the repeated efforts of Dr. Grayson to induce him to take a short vacation there.[68] Throughout, he showed a remarkable capacity in his official dealings to conceal his feelings,[69] and, despite his emotional turmoil, there are no reports of further strokes.

Just as Wilson could not express his fears verbally to his daughters during the dark days of Ellen's illness, so he could not articulate his inner feelings about her for months after her death.[70] Had he been able to do so, the burden of guilt might have been eased. He was desperately lonely despite the visits of many relatives and old friends. Even the daily company of his favorite daughter Nell—"my dear baby," Wilson called her—did not cheer him. "No one can offer Cousin Woodrow any word of comfort, for there is no comfort," Helen Bones[71] wrote to a friend.[72] Wilson saw a great deal of his friend Colonel House. Dr. Grayson lived in the White House and sat by the President while he worked. Wilson played golf daily from mid-afternoon to sundown,[73] usually with Grayson. When the exhausted Doctor was obliged to take a vacation, Helen Bones walked around the course with Wilson. He went on automobile rides and took trips on the presidential yacht, Mayflower. Motoring gave occasion to a rare touch of humor. While Wilson encouraged the members of the household and the staff to use the White House cars for recreation, he insisted that everyone, including himself, strictly observe the speed limit, then twenty-two miles an hour. After his Secretary, Joe Tumulty, had been stopped by the police, the President would regularly ask at the dinner table, "Well, who's been pinched today?"[74]

Wilson sought to dispel his loneliness in letters to Mrs. Hulbert and Mrs. Toy. He told the former, "If I could see you your own irrepressible vivacity would, I think, draw something out of me."[75] He was as concerned as ever about Mrs. Hulbert's problems; he wrote that the news of one of Allen's financial disasters had been on his heart all day

[68] Cary T. Grayson to Edith Bolling Galt, August 25, 1914, *ibid.*, p. 563.

[69] Ray Stannard Baker interviewed Wilson and reported that he looked well and seemed thoughtful and confident. Baker, *Wilson*, V, 138.

[70] WW to Jessie Woodrow Wilson Sayre, March 14, 1915, *PWW*, Vol. 32, p. 370-71.

[71] Helen Bones had been Mrs. Wilson's personal secretary. She stayed on as Mistress of the White House.

[72] Helen Woodrow Bones to Agnes B. Tedcastle, November 16, 1914, Baker, V, 141.

[73] *Ibid.*, pp. 139-40.

[74] Walworth, *Wilson*, I, 416.

[75] WW to MAH, December 6, 1914, *PWW*, Vol. 31, p. 408.

"like a great chilling cloud."[76] Wilson helped her look for a job and did favors for several of her friends. After she had sent him a hand-written draft of her article, "Around the Tea-Table—Afternoon Tea," Wilson had the article typed, personally edited it, and sent it to a publisher.[77] Because Mrs. Hulbert was lonely in Boston, he suggested to Nancy Toy, who lived in Cambridge, that they meet.[78] Wilson and Mrs. Toy may have intensified their previously occasional correspond-ence at the suggestion of Helen Bones,[79] who constantly sought to divert him.

Mrs. Toy was an educated, independent-minded woman, interested in national affairs, with whom Wilson could discuss both his emotional and political problems. He also found that her letters had the "rare quality" of making him feel, after reading them, as if he had really seen her and talked with her "of many things."[80] For a brief time, Mrs. Toy shared the salutation of "Dearest Friend" with Mrs. Hulbert. Wilson was extremely pleased when she sent him a great horn spoon for Christmas. "I am Scots very deep down in me, and porridge in a horn spoon seems to me like a thing of (minor) religion," he wrote in appreciation of her gift.[81] Although Mrs. Hulbert had indicated that she was available, Wilson invited Mrs. Toy to visit the White House.

Wilson's invitation to Nancy Toy signaled a lessening of his severe depression. Colonel House, who came to Washington on December 3 to discuss Wilson's Annual Message, noted that he was more cheer-ful.[82] The improvement in Wilson's mood coincided with the exercise of more vigorous political leadership. Wilson had established the overall policies of strict neutrality and willingness to mediate between the belligerent sides, but, during the ensuing months, the initiatives

[76] WW to MAH, December 23, 1914, *ibid.*, p. 514.

[77] WW to Edward W. Bok, February 4, 1915, *ibid.*, Vol. 32, pp. 191-92.

[78] Wilson wrote, "I have a friend now living at 49 Gloucester St. in Boston whom I wish very much you might know. She has had a hard life, chiefly hard because it denied her access to the things she really loved and was meant to live by and compelled her to be (or to play at being until she all but became) a woman of the world, so that her surface hardened and became artificial while her nature was of the woods, of hearty unconventional friendships, and of everything that is sweet and beautiful: a born dem-ocrat." WW to Nancy S. Toy, December 12, 1914, *PWW*, Vol. 31, pp. 455-56.

[79] Evidence for Helen Bones's role comes from a letter to Wilson from Mrs. Toy in which she states that she is sending him an urgent message without writing to Helen to gain his consent. Nancy S. Toy to WW, January 22, 1915, Wilson Papers.

[80] WW to Nancy S. Toy, December 12, 1914, *PWW*, Vol. 31, p. 454.

[81] WW to Nancy S. Toy, December 26, 1914, *ibid.*, p. 532.

[82] "After dinner the President recited several new limericks, and read a whimsical poem or two, and then we settled down to work." House diary, December 3, 1914, *ibid.*, p. 384.

had come from Secretaries Bryan and McAdoo, Counselor Robert Lansing, and, particularly, Colonel House. In early December, however, the President came out strongly against the preparedness program, advocated by House and conservative Republicans in Congress, because he believed that it would arouse war spirit and aggravate dissensions between Allied and German sympathizers.

On January 2, 1915, the day of her arrival at the White House, Mrs. Toy noted in her diary: "He looked better than I have ever seen him physically and acknowledged later in reply to a question from Helen that he had never felt better in his life. But in his talk and manner the old buoyancy had gone and I missed it during my whole visit. Also there was more formality beneath the unvarying friendliness of voice and manner. Was it, as John Hay said about Roosevelt, 'the kingly shadow falling upon him?' "[83] Mrs. Toy also reported the shock that she received when she inadvertently brought up a newspaper story which ridiculed Daniels. "I have never seen the President angry before. I never want to see him angry again. His fist came down on the table. 'Daniels did *not* give the order that Tipperary should not be sung in the Navy. He is surrounded by a network of conspiracy and lies. His enemies are determined to ruin him. I can't be sure who they are yet but when I do get them—God help them.' "[84]

The clearing of a depression is often associated with the discharge of anger, and Wilson's rage found another outlet during the bitter struggle over the ship-purchase bill, a measure pushed by McAdoo to build up the merchant marine by the purchase of ships of foreign registry tied up in American harbors.[85] The bill was favored by the farmers of the South and West eager to export their produce, and opposed by most shipping and financial interests. Conservatives of both parties regarded it as socialistic, and some progressive Democrats, including Bryan, feared that acquisition of German ships would provoke a serious controversy with Great Britain. Senator Lodge, in a speech on January 6, 1915, linked the issue with Wilson's disastrous Veracruz venture.[86]

Infuriated by Lodge's taunt, and perhaps pricked by his own conscience, Wilson struck back two days later in a dramatic Jackson Day

[83] Diary of Nancy Saunders Toy, January 2, 1915, *PWW*, Vol. 32, p. 7.

[84] *Ibid.*, January 5, 1912, *ibid.*, p. 21.

[85] A fuller account of the struggle over the ship-purchase bill can be found in Link, *Wilson*, III, 81-91.

[86] The antagonism between Lodge and Wilson was of long standing. "A contemptible hypocrite" was the way Ellen Wilson had referred to the Senator in a letter written in 1894 (EAW to WW, February 17, 1894, *PWW*, Vol. 8, p. 491).

Address in Indianapolis. He was tired, he said, of staying in Washington and saying sweet things. He justified the bill on economic grounds and attacked the Republicans (they had not had a new idea in thirty years) and rebellious Democratic senators who were blocking passage of the ship purchase bill. Then he lashed out at the critics of his Mexican policy:

"With all due respect to editors of great newspapers, I have to say to them that I never take my opinions of the American people from their editorials. So that, when some great daily not very far from where I am temporarily residing, thundered with rising scorn against watchful waiting, Woodrow[87] sat back in his chair and chuckled, knowing that he laughs best who laughs last—knowing, in short, what were the temper and the principles of the American people."

Wilson also asserted: "You know, Jackson used to think that every man who disagreed with him was an enemy of the country. I have never gone quite that far in my thoughts, but I have ventured to think that they didn't know what they were talking about."[88]

Some of Wilson's closest friends criticized him for his intemperate remarks. However, he firmly believed that the struggle was not only a test of his leadership, but an out-and-out conflict between democracy and special interests. He expressed his anger to Mrs. Toy in language reminiscent of his battles at Princeton: "There is a real fight on. The Republicans are every day employing the most unscrupulous methods of partisanship and false evidence to destroy this administration and bring back the days of private influence and selfish advantage. . . . The struggle that is on, to bring about reaction and regain privilege is desperate and absolutely without scruple."[89] The filibusterers succeeded in killing the ship-purchase bill, and Wilson drafted a statement castigating them. On second thought, he decided not to issue it. Instead, he took his defeat in good grace, at least in public, and, at the close of the session, sent a message praising the work of the Congress.

Throughout his ordeal, Wilson was sustained by his religious faith. In a conversation with Mrs. Toy, who did not believe in a personal God, he declared: "*My* life would not be worth living if it were not for the driving power of religion, for *faith*, pure and simple." When she asked if he had never had a *Sturm und Drang* period, he replied, "No, never for a moment have I had one doubt about my religious beliefs. There are people who *believe* only so far as they *understand—*

---

[87] Wilson was officially reported to have said "Woody." Baker, *Wilson*, V, 125.
[88] Jackson Day Address in Indianapolis, January 8, 1915, *PWW*, Vol. 32, pp. 29-41.
[89] WW to Nancy S. Toy, January 31, 1915, *ibid.*, p. 165.

that seems to me presumptuous and sets their understanding as the standard of the universe."[90] Like many Americans, Wilson believed that he had been predestined to be President of the United States. The preservation of his life after his wife's death was to him a sign that God would not remove a man until his work was finished.[91] His greatest task, he now believed, was the preservation of American neutrality in order that the United States could bring peace to a war-torn world.

[90] Toy diary, January 3, 1915, *ibid.*, pp. 8-9.
[91] House diary, June 24, 1915.

CHAPTER XVI

"The Strangest Friendship in History"

COLONEL EDWARD MANDELL HOUSE—like Harvey's, his title was honorary—was a wealthy Texan who had been a power in state politics before he turned to the national scene. His great ambition was to make a President through whom he could guide the nation and have a voice in international affairs. House, a progressive Democrat but a financial conservative, had given William Jennings Bryan only nominal support. In 1910, he selected William Jay Gaynor, Mayor of New York, as a likely presidential candidate. However, after Gaynor rebuffed him, House became interested in the Wilson movement in the summer of 1911. He had a wide acquaintance among editors, businessmen, and politicians of all shades, and, through his connections with Walter Hines Page and William F. McCombs, Wilson's campaign manager in 1911-1912, arranged for Wilson to call on him at his New York hotel. To judge from House's description of their meeting in November 1911, it was love at first sight: "The first hour we spent together proved to each of us that there was a sound basis for a fast friendship. We found ourselves in such complete sympathy, in so many ways, that we soon learned to know what each was thinking without either having expressed himself. . . . A few weeks after we met and after we had exchanged confidences which men usually do not exchange except after years of friendship, I asked him if he realized that we had only known one another for so short a time. He replied, 'My dear friend, we have known one another always.' "[1]

What Wilson did not know was that the Colonel had prepared himself for many years for such meetings. During his apprenticeship in Texas, House had guided four governors into office and had acquired the reputation of never backing a loser. He refused office for himself and preferred to operate behind the scenes and work through a network of carefully cultivated personal relationships. House had been a close friend and neighbor of progressive Governor James Ste-

[1] Charles Seymour, ed., *The Intimate Papers of Colonel House*, 4 vols. (Boston and New York, 1926-28), I, 45.

phen Hogg and became the intimate friend and financial adviser of Hogg's successor, Charles Allen Culberson. When House heard that Bryan's daughter had been ill and wished to come south for the winter, he arranged for the Bryan family to live in a house on his property in Austin. House and Hogg took Bryan on a panther hunt, on which the Commoner bagged a panther. According to local gossip, the victim had been borrowed from a zoo and planted at a convenient site in the woods.[2] It was House's custom to find out as much as he could about the personality and hobbies of a man before he conferred with him. House preferred to hold the meetings in his own home and, when the guest arrived, he would find that his tastes in liquor and cigars had been anticipated by his host. Prior to their initial meeting, House had read Wilson's speeches and had made himself familiar with his difficulties at Princeton.

The House technique was evident during the presidential campaign of 1912. After an anti-third term fanatic had inflicted a bullet wound on Theodore Roosevelt, House immediately provided Wilson with a bodyguard, William J. ("Bill") McDonald, a well-publicized, elderly ex-Texas Ranger. McDonald was a political associate of House and, according to a House biographer, his instructor in the Texas art of the quick draw.[3] In addition to utilizing McDonald's strong-arm services at Texas conventions,[4] House had been instrumental in the publication of the former Ranger's autobiography. McDonald entertained the Wilson ladies with tales about his shooting exploits and impressed Wilson with stories of House's political prowess.[5]

House had a mild, unassuming, unobtrusive manner, and a confidential, intimate way with people. "Take my word for it," Senator Thomas P. Gore of Oklahoma said, "he can walk on dead leaves and make no more noise than a tiger."[6] In the tête-à-tête conversations which he loved, he listened attentively and gave his companion the feeling that he and House were in complete agreement. Members of Congress, cabinet officers, ambassadors, and American and foreign diplomats sought his advice. Sir Edward Grey, the British Foreign Secretary, wrote of House in 1915: "I found combined in him in a rare degree the qualities of wisdom and sympathy. . . . He had a way of saying 'I know it' in a tone and manner that carried conviction both

---

[2] Robert N. Richardson, *Colonel Edward M. House: The Texas Years, 1858-1912* (Abilene, Tex., 1964), pp. 228-29, 232-33.

[3] Arthur D. Howden Smith, *The Real Colonel House* (New York, 1918), p. 25.

[4] Richardson, *Colonel Edward M. House,* p. 54.

[5] House diary, November 8, 1912.

[6] Seymour, *Intimate Papers,* I, 93.

of his sympathy with, and understanding of, what was said to him."[7] In the winter of 1911, when Wilson was the leading candidate for the Democratic presidential nomination, House tried to gain Bryan's support for him; he explained to the Nebraskan that service in Wilson's cabinet would enhance his own chances for the nomination in 1916. Josephus Daniels thought that House was his friend and never knew that House had once participated in a cabal to drive him from office.[8] House was a strong Anglophile during the period of American neutrality in the First World War. However, he managed to convince the German Ambassador, Count Johann Heinrich von Bernstorff, that he was impartial. The Texan enjoyed the confidence of such bitter opponents as McAdoo and McCombs. Since House's conferees rarely compared their recollections of what had been said, he acquired the reputation of never betraying a confidence.

Charles Seymour, an admirer of House, and the editor of his papers, described his functions: "House set himself to the labor of innumerable interviews and multifarious correspondence, which might offset the criticism and lighten the burden of detail that weighs on every President. He intercepted importunates on their way to the White House and promised to arrange their business with the President more rapidly than they could themselves. He sifted applications for appointments. He discussed industrial relations with capitalists and labor leaders. He advised the chiefs of industrial corporations how to settle their difficulties with the Government. And, afterwards, reporting the gist of these interviews to the President, he brought him into touch with the currents of opinion and affairs."[9]

House had a creative mind, rich in ideas, and a keen sense of public relations, and he was adept at maintaining what today would be called the President's image. For example, after the shooting of Theodore Roosevelt, he advised Wilson to cancel his speeches until his opponent had recovered because it was the "generous, the chivalrous and the wise thing to do."[10] He was a flexible mediator, who could rise dispassionately above personal slights and grievances. He undertook many of the personal confrontations which Wilson found embarrassing or distasteful, and it was sometimes his task to tell people un-

[7] Sir Edward Grey, *Twenty-Five Years, 1892-1916*, 2 vols. (New York, 1925), II, 124-25.

[8] Link, *Wilson*, II, 95. Daniels' son commented: "House was an intimate man even when he was cutting a throat." Jonathan Daniels, *The End of Innocence* (Philadelphia, 1954), p. 89.

[9] Seymour, *Intimate Papers*, I, 128.

[10] House diary, October 5, 1912, *PWW*, Vol. 25, p. 421.

pleasant things. For example, after Wilson complained that some cabinet members were taking up too much of his time, House told them not to talk so much.[11]

One aspect of House's personality which contributed to his success in gaining the trust of people was his lack of "manliness." Because of his gentle, deferential, non-aggressive manner, men tended to see him not as a threatening competitor. Since House was not gallant with the ladies, they felt at ease with him. He won the confidence of Mrs. Wilson and her daughters in the same way in which he had become close to Mrs. Bryan. House advised the Wilson family on their personal finances, protocol, and even on ladies' dress for official occasions.[12] The Colonel was married and the father of two daughters, and Mrs. House (Loulie) seems to have been extraordinarily accommodating in adjusting her activities to her husband's schedule. When Wilson visited the Houses in New York and stayed overnight, she moved out of the apartment so that the men could talk together undisturbed. House disliked golf, so Loulie sometimes rode out to the course with the President. Once, when Wilson invited House to accompany him to church, he "compromised" by having his wife go in his place.[13]

In his diary, House describes the methods by which he sought to influence Wilson and control governmental policy. He did not usually offer advice unless Wilson personally asked him to do so, and, with rare exceptions, House did not come to Washington until he was summoned. He rarely disagreed openly, did not often argue, and confined any severe criticism of Wilson to his diary. With characteristic self-effacement, he often made it appear as if some suggestion had come from someone else—as indeed it might have, as a result of a House maneuver. He knew Wilson's dislike for men who sought office openly and blackballed at least one aspirant by telling Wilson that great political influence was being exercised in the man's behalf.[14] When he sought to persuade Wilson to follow a course of action, House emphasized that its achievement would assure Wilson a great place in history. In 1915, he told Wilson that, if their peace plan[15]

[11] House diary, April 14, 1913.

[12] House diary, January 8, 1913, PWW, Vol. 27, p. 20.

[13] House diary, November 8, 1914.

[14] House diary, January 21, 1914, PWW, Vol. 29, p. 159.

[15] House's plan was later embodied in the House-Grey Memorandum, which the Colonel and Sir Edward Grey, the British Foreign Secretary, drafted in late February 1916. The plan itself provided for British acquiesence in a peace conference which Wilson would convene. Should the Central Powers not agree to reasonable terms the United States would probably enter the war on the Allied side. For a fuller discussion of House's plan and its consequences, see Link, Wilson, IV, 101-41.

succeeded, the President would outrank any American who had yet lived.[16] The Colonel praised even routine political statements as great political documents and passed on the compliments paid by others. The most extravagant one was the opinion of a British diplomat, Sir William Wiseman, that the President's war message of 1917 could not have been more perfect had it been written by Shakespeare.[17] Significantly, this message was delivered by House at a time when his own influence with Wilson was waning.

Colonel House not only had a good understanding of Wilson's character; he also supplied many of the President's emotional needs. House recognized Wilson's yearning for assurances of affection and support from people in whom he had confided, and he regularly ended his letters with expressions of total love and devotion. House was very concerned about Wilson's health and performed a number of chores so that his chief could conserve his strength. Wilson, in turn, was deeply grateful for a friend who appeared totally uninterested in personal gain or favor, who asked for no reward other than the privilege of serving the country and its President, and who seemed to be utterly loyal. Wilson wrote to Mrs. Galt in 1915 that he believed that House would gladly give his life for him. As we have seen, Wilson was particularly dependent on House during the period of intense depression and loneliness after Ellen's death. Wilson visited House in New York several times and, when the Colonel came to Cornish, he occupied Mrs. Wilson's old bedroom and shared a bathroom with Wilson. When House left for England in January 1915 on a peace mission, Wilson told him, in lieu of explicit instructions: "There is not much for us to talk over for the reason we are of the same mind and it is not necessary to go into details with you."[18]

The legend of House's delicate health was an extremely important factor in his relationship with Wilson. Their friendship may not have been the strangest in history,[19] but House's illness was one of the strangest ever recorded. In a memoir, written in 1916, he relates that, at the age of twelve or thirteen, he fell from a swing and suffered a head injury which profoundly affected his entire life. "Brain fever ensued, and, for a long time, I hovered between life and death. Upon

---

[16] House diary, September 24, 1915, *PWW*, Vol. 34, p. 516.

[17] House diary, March 29 and April 2, 1917.

[18] *Ibid.*, January 24, 1915, *PWW*, Vol. 32, p. 117.

[19] Sir Horace Plunkett, the Irish land reformer and friend of House, called it "the strangest and most fruitful personal alliance in human history." As quoted in George S. Viereck, *The Strangest Friendship in History: Woodrow Wilson and Colonel House* (New York, 1932), p. 3.

my recovery, malaria fastened on me and I have never been strong since. The confining routine of an office was impossible."[20] He was also left with an inability to endure hot or cold weather and a dislike of crowds. He was sensitive even to the differences in temperature between New York and Washington.

There is no reason to doubt House's recollection that he had sustained a head injury or developed malaria. However, neither condition results in such lifetime sequelae, and there is no organic disease which could produce such a syndrome. Moreover, the condition did not come on until years later. Subsequently, House gave another story: he told a biographer that in early adult life he could work outdoors like a field hand, but that a heat stroke was responsible for his inability to stand hot weather.[21] Although House, a slender, tough, wiry man of medium height, thought of himself as physically frail, he actually was in excellent health. Indeed, he lived a very busy life until his death at the age of seventy-nine.

Colonel House's ailment was undoubtedly of emotional origin. His symptoms were probably a manifestation of phobic anxiety, a fear of what *might* happen to him in certain situations. He apparently believed that he would suffer irreparable damage to his health, or even die, if he were exposed to hot weather. House's idiosyncrasy controlled the migratory rhythm of his life. He went north to his summer home in Beverly, on the North Shore of Massachusetts, in the spring, spent part of each summer in Europe, and took a New York apartment, or returned to Texas, during the cold months. Although the day of Wilson's inaugural fell within House's allowable temperature range, he declined to attend the ceremony because of the crowds. Instead, he sent his wife while he "loafed around" the Metropolitan Club.[22] House's affliction had been associated with other signs of anxiety. In 1898 and 1899, he experienced a "nervousness so severe that he hated to think about it even in retrospect."[23]

Whatever the relationship between the voluntary and involuntary components of House's infirmity, he turned it into a political asset. In his early years in Texas politics, he endured the heat of several state conventions without ill effects. Later, when he found it preferable to conduct affairs *in absentia*, he escaped both the literal and figurative heat. The demands of his health also enabled him to avoid campaigning

---

[20] "Reminiscences of Edward M. House, 1858-1912," the Papers of Edward M. House, Yale University Library; hereinafter cited as "House Reminiscences."

[21] Smith, *The Real Colonel House*, pp. 43-44.

[22] House diary, March 4, 1913, *PWW*, Vol. 27, p. 152.

[23] Richardson, *Colonel Edward M. House*, p. 175.

for Bryan while retaining that perennial candidate's friendship. One of House's political maxims was that "men often destroy themselves by being too much in evidence."[24] Wilson was as sympathetic and solicitous about House's health as he had been about his mother's and Mrs. Hulbert's ailments. Wilson's first written expression of affection for House came after the latter let it be known that, because of sickness, he would be able to take only a limited part in the pre-convention campaign.[25] Actually, the state of the Colonel's health fitted in perfectly with his political strategy. Wilson's candidacy was experiencing difficulties, and House kept a low profile throughout the spring, when Wilson's defeat seemed likely. Prior to his departure for Europe, House informed Wilson that, although he was deeply interested in his success, he was physically unequal to the rigors of a national convention. He assured Wilson that his friends were in control of the Texas delegation and that he had arranged for any contingency.[26] Actually, House had played only a minor role in organizing the Texas Democrats, and the "immortal forty" would have stood by Wilson at Baltimore regardless of House's action. The Colonel, meanwhile, had kept his options open: three days after his letter to Wilson he wrote to Mrs. Bryan pledging his support should her husband be nominated.[27] In Wilson's reply to House, he thanked his friend for his thoughtfulness and expressed the hope that he would not risk his health by returning too soon.[28] When House returned from abroad, he went to his summer home in Beverly, whence he wrote to congratulate Wilson on his acceptance speech: "Altogether the best paper of the kind that has issued within my memory." He assured Wilson that, while he awaited cooler weather, he was "in touch with" and ready to take over the situations in Maine and Vermont.[29] (House was a master at hinting that there were powerful and secret forces at his command.) Wilson regretted that Beverly was not closer so that he could run up and see House, and he looked forward with eagerness to the time when his friend's hand could be beside his own on the "steering gear."[30] Significantly, the Colonel began his famous diary on September 24, 1912, just after the news

[24] *Ibid.*, p. 312.
[25] Wilson wrote: "Pray take care of yourself. If you will permit me to say so, I have come to have a very warm feeling toward you, and hope that in years to come our friendship will ripen." WW to House, January 27, 1912, *PWW*, Vol. 24, p. 81.
[26] House to WW, June 20, 1912, *ibid.*, pp. 489-90.
[27] House to Mary B. Bryan, June 22, 1912, House Papers.
[28] WW to House, July 17, 1912, *PWW*, Vol. 24, p. 556.
[29] House to WW, August 21, 1912, *ibid.*, Vol. 25, pp. 51-52.
[30] WW to House, August 22, 1912, *ibid.*, p. 52.

that William Randolph Hearst would support Wilson had made a Democratic victory almost certain.[31]

House described a conversation with Wilson before he, House, left for Europe for the summer of 1913: "I spoke to the President about conserving his strength, and suggested various means by which it could be done. I thought it was essential. He said it looked as if the people were trying to kill him, and he spoke of the lonliness of his position in a way that was saddening. He expressed again and again his regret at my departure. I said I felt like a deserter and that I would not go excepting that it had come to the point where I could no longer serve him, for I was broken down and it was absolutely necessary for me to get away for a few weeks. He thanked me warmly for all I had done, and said he would feel unhappy until I returned. I expressed my gratitude for his kindness and said it had been the greatest pleasure of my life to be associated with him. I spoke of his probable renomination and re-election."[32] On the eve of his sailing, House again explained that he was going only to conserve his strength so that he might serve the President better. "My faith in you," he wrote to Wilson, "is as great as my love for you—more than that I cannot say."[33]

With the World War beginning and Ellen sinking, Wilson longed to see his friend. House wrote to Wilson on August 1, 1914: "If I thought I could live through the heat, I would go to Washington to see you, but I am afraid if I reached there I would be utterly helpless. I wish you could get time to take the *Mayflower* and cruise for a few days in these waters so that I might join you."[34]

House's phobias probably had their origins in childhood. He was born in 1858, the youngest of seven children, six of whom were boys. His father, Thomas William House, was an English immigrant who made a fortune as a merchant, plantation owner, and land speculator. His store in Houston was one of the city's show places, and, during the Civil War, he prospered from blockade-running. Edward House tells an exciting story of growing up in an atmosphere of shooting and killing and having many narrow escapes from death. He was fascinated by his brothers' daring play and their reckless use of firearms. One of them was killed by a fall from a trapeze, and another had part of his face shot off. "Death was our constant playmate," he recalled.[35] House idolized the heroes of the Texas War for Independence, some of whom

---

[31] John T. Graves to WW, September 24, 1912, *ibid.*, p. 233.
[32] House diary, May 11, 1913, *PWW*, Vol. 27, p. 414.
[33] House to WW, May 21, 1913, *ibid.*, pp. 463-63.
[34] House to WW, August 1, 1914, *ibid.*, Vol. 30, p. 327.
[35] "House Reminiscences."

he met at his father's house. House wrote that his father had fought in the Texas revolution and had received a land grant for his services, but this, like a number of his other recollections, was a confabulation. According to the records of the Texas Land Office, the elder House got the land, not for fighting, but as an immigrant. The boy also identified himself with famous Texas desperadoes who killed so many men that they ceased to count their victims. In a self-referential way, he described them as "invariably polite, gentle, mild-mannered, mild-spoken and delicate looking men, actuated by the spirit of the Crusades with something fine and chivalrous about them."[36] Like Wilson, House had probably witnessed the disturbances of the Reconstruction period, but his account of desperadoes engaged in wholesale slaughter in broad daylight was probably fantasy. He grew up in a comfortable, if not a luxurious, home far from the lawless frontier.[37]

House's mother died when he was fourteen, and he was sent east to school in a remote part of Virginia, where his preoccupation with violence continued. Soon after his arrival, he warned off would-be hazers with his knife and six-shooter. He recalled how they would tie a boy's hands behind him and string him up over a limb until he grew purple in the face.[38] House managed to survive for three years. Then, at the age of seventeen, he entered the Hopkins Preparatory School in New Haven to prepare for Yale. He was, however, a poor student, and, since it appeared unlikely that he would be accepted at Yale, he was tutored and then admitted to Cornell. He continued to be indifferent to his studies but enjoyed practical jokes. Many of these involved the acting out of scenes of death and rescue. He and a chum took a candidate for a fraternity and tied him to a loose rail on a side track. Then, he and his friend, in the victim's hearing, speculated as to whether they would have time to remove him before the train came. When they heard the rumble and saw the headlight of the locomotive, House related, their fingers became all thumbs and they were unable to free the boy. As the train came, they jumped aside. The victim, fortunately, survived. On another occasion, House himself was placed blindfolded in a coffin and listened to a discussion of whether the lid should be screwed down and whether he would suffocate.[39]

[36] *Ibid.*

[37] House told a biographer that, because he had become so used to seeing desperadoes kill people in open daylight in the city streets, he was not as shocked as some people by the slaughter of the First World War. Smith, *The Real Colonel House*, p. 241.

[38] House Reminiscences, pp. 7-8.

[39] Edward M. House, "Memoirs of Colonel House," unpublished MS. Yale University Library, p. 19.

House also recalled a hunting trip in Texas on which he seems to have been constantly preoccupied with death. He traveled through country where Indians "might or might not have cut our throats as the spirit moved them."[40] He dressed himself in an old Confederate overcoat and took an assumed name in the belief that the disguise would make him less vulnerable to attack. Once he awoke to see a man standing four or five feet away from him holding a raised hatchet, only to find that he was chopping wood. During one night when he could not sleep, House raked the paw of his companion's dog down his master's back, so that the startled man awoke thinking that the dog had sensed danger. House feigned sleep as he enjoyed the scene.[41]

House also enjoyed hoaxes in which he could amuse himself at the gullibility of others and secretly enjoy a feeling of superior power. He told his roommate that he preferred a cold temperature and was letting the boy tend the stove as a special favor. He enjoyed playing pranks and, when they were discovered, he would act as an innocent bystander. A particular delight was to set boys quarreling and then step in as a peacemaker. House also recalled that he used to ask questions and get minute instructions how to do this or that thing, or how to play at games at which he was already more proficient than those who sought to teach him.[42]

House's memoir reveals little about his relations with his family, but it suggests that, as a child, he felt frightened and helpless, and that his fantasies and dramatizations of death and violence purged him of his fears.[43] In his play and fantasies he could abandon a weak and helpless self and transform himself into some powerful superior figure. The role of Texas gunfighter may have remained in his imagination— he carried a revolver with him on the streets of New York, and he found a substitute in politics. As a boy in preparatory school, he dreamed of becoming President; from New Haven he would go to New York and hang about Democratic headquarters. When he saw Samuel J. Tilden, he marveled that so frail a man could campaign for the presidency.[44] Through his chum, the son of Senator Oliver P. Morton of Indiana, the young House gained entry to the White House and the homes of high governmental officials. He was struck by the fact that the destinies of the country lay in the hands of so few men.

---

[40] *Ibid.*, p. 26.   [41] *Ibid.*   [42] *Ibid.*, p. 18.

[43] "Tragedy is thus the representation of an action that is worth serious attention, complete in itself and of some amplitude . . . by means of pity and fear bringing about the purgation of such emotions." Aristotle Poetics 6, 1449b in *The Oxford Dictionary of Quotations* (London, 1953), p. 12.

[44] Seymour, *Intimate Papers*, I, p. 14.

His academic performance was still undistinguished—he left college at the end of his second year—but his fascination with politics and power persisted. He soon recognized that his unprepossessing physical appearance and his lack of oratorical skill disqualified him from seeking the presidency, but his need to identify himself with some powerful person never left him. House wrote: "My physical handicaps and my temperament make it necessary for me to work through other men. I was like a disembodied spirit seeking a corporeal form. I found my opportunity in Woodrow Wilson."[45]

House states that he left Cornell in order to take care of his father, who had suffered a stroke. After the elder House's death, Edward moved from Houston to Austin for reasons of health and to be closer to the political scene. He also wanted quick access to the Texas Land Office. He augmented the considerable fortune left him by his father by buying and selling land and engaging in businesses, which included a large cotton farm. Although House was a very wealthy man with many sources of income, he tried to give the impression that he was not interested in money for himself. He wrote to the novelist Dorothy Scarborough: "During my Texas life I farmed almost exclusively as a means of livelihood."[46] In Texas, he gave money to colleges, schools, and a mental hospital. Although he was not a member of any denomination, he contributed to Methodist, Presbyterian, and Episcopal churches.[47] House refused any compensation for his services as presidential adviser and accepted travel expenses only because Wilson insisted that he do so.

In 1913 House put his fantasies into print in an anonymous novel, *Philip Dru, Administrator: A Story of Tomorrow*.[48] The hero, like House, was the youngest of seven children and his father's best-beloved son. Philip, described as not big or handsome, but as of medium height, slender, and toughly built, had been forced to leave the army because of a physical disability sustained as a result of exposure to the sun. While Dru had no desire to destroy or kill, he longed for action and battle. He led a revolution in which thousands perished in one great battle, when the spirit of love and brotherhood triumphed over the forces of defiant wealth and monopoly. (Significantly, House had shown his manuscript to Bryan and others before publication and rejected their advice that he omit the battle scene.) As dictator of the United States, after the President had been relegated to ceremonial

---

[45] House Memoirs.
[46] House to Dorothy Scarborough, cited in Richardson, p. 210.
[47] Richardson, p. 210.
[48] *Philip Dru, Administrator: A Story of Tomorrow* (New York, 1911).

functions, Dru instituted sweeping economic and social reforms before he turned over control to a constitutional government. Dru abhorred war, but during his administration the United States, by purchase or negotiation, acquired the whole of North America and the West Indies. A military invasion was necessary only in the case of Mexico. House, in his incarnation as Dru, envisaged a division of the world by the major powers into spheres of influence, and an American navy second only to that of Great Britain in order that the great English-speaking nations could maintain peace and freedom.

House's diary documents his grandiosity. He was ingenuous in his descriptions of his stratagems and manipulations in the belief that the magnitude of his endeavor justified such tactics. He unabashedly related how, when expedient, he advised Wilson to adopt a high moral tone. He was compulsively meticulous about detail, but he often omitted the scheming which led to a particular situation. The diary was obviously written for posterity. House professed to be shocked when Wilson said that he would lie if the public good required it or if the honor of a woman was involved. He wrote in 1917: "My whole life work has been directed toward the unfortunate many without equal opportunity, and their bitter struggle for existence. . . . I stood back of every liberal movement, both in Texas and the Nation."[49] The Colonel was an extremely resourceful politician. He usually gave Wilson excellent advice, and he was responsible for many of Wilson's accomplishments—and blunders; however, he often ignored the contributions of others. Although he praised the qualities of Wilson's mind and his courage, he gave the impression of his own superior capabilities.[50]

Lord Devlin observes that "there was no limit to his [House's] belief in his powers to put things in order and no territorial limit to his ambition."[51] Nowhere in his diary, after the account of his youth, does House express uncertainty or admit mistakes. In August 1915, he wrote to Walter Page: "I believe that if we could have started peace parleys in November [1914], we could have forced . . . a peace which would eliminate militarism both on land and sea."[52] In fact, the United States was in no position to use force against any major power, and under no conditions would Great Britain have yielded naval supremacy

[49] House diary, Mar. 17, 1917.

[50] House designated the President as Ajax and himself as Caesar in a secret code that he devised after America entered the war. House diary, May 30, 1917.

[51] Patrick Devlin, *Too Proud to Fight: Woodrow Wilson's Neutrality* (Oxford, 1974), p. 274.

[52] House to Page, August 4, 1915, in Seymour, *Intimate Papers,* II, p. 61.

or Germany military dominance. The Colonel implied that if Wilson had put him in charge of war mobilization, as he had urged him to do, all of the difficulties in the program would have been cleared up in a month.[53] House represented himself in public as merely the adviser and emissary of the President, but his yearning for fame did not lie completely hidden. Although he shunned publicity, the very air of mystery with which he surrounded himself drew attention. He deplored the extravagant compliments paid him, but duly recorded them in his diary. Even though he had written *Philip Dru* anonymously, a discerning reader could have recognized the book's authorship from the mention of meetings at "Mandell House."

House was among the few Americans who recognized the imminence of the Great War: he went abroad early in 1914 to try to reconcile the differences between England and Germany. He regarded the outbreak as an opportunity to exercise what he considered to be his greatest talent—peacemaking. In 1916 he confided to his diary: "The life I am leading transcends in interest and excitement any romance."[54] He saw diplomacy as a game in which he could coach the players and tease and tantalize them. He especially loved the atmosphere of intrigue and secrecy. In the codes through which he exchanged messages with Wilson, Germany was "Zadok"; Russia was "Winter"; the Kaiser was "Dante"; Konstantin Dumba, the Austrian Ambassador to the United States, was "Wisdom"; Sir Edward Grey was "White"; and Arthur Zimmermann, of the German Foreign Office, was "Black." Any bright ten-year-old could have broken the code; and, in fact, it was easily cracked by British Naval Intelligence in 1915. On one occasion, House abandoned the code and sent Grey two separately mailed letters which could be put together like a picture puzzle.[55] He induced Count von Bernstorff to write to him under the pseudonym of "Martin."[56] House and Grayson designated Wilson as "Thomas," and, in letters to his son-in-law, Gordon Auchincloss, he playfully referred to Wilson as "4U's."[57] The play was indeed the thing.

House usually followed Wilson's instructions and gave him accurate

---

[53] House diary, July 4, 1917. When rumors circulated that Wilson was about to appoint Bernard M. Baruch as chief purchasing agent for the United States and the Allies, House wrote in his diary, in a rare expression of pique and jealousy: "I believe Baruch is able and I believe he is honest, but I do not believe the country will take kindly to having a Hebrew Wall Street speculator given so much power." House Diary, May 27, 1917.

[54] *Ibid.*, March 10, 1916.

[55] Seymour, *Intimate Papers*, II, 90.

[56] J. H. von Bernstorff, *My Three Years in America* (New York, 1920), p. 270.

[57] Seymour, *Intimate Papers*, I, 386.

reports of his diplomatic conversations. However, he was often overly optimistic, and, as we shall see, gave selective and distorted versions when the situations involved his personal achievement. In these, he seems to have deceived himself as much as Wilson. He especially deluded himself in the hope that he could bring an end to the war through private, secret diplomacy. House, moreover, was not as immune to guile and flattery as he deemed himself and, on occasion, let himself be fooled when he thought he was manipulating others. The Colonel had a fertile imagination and an extraordinarily keen perception of human susceptibilities—other than of his own.

Any definition of personality is based on interactions among people, and the foregoing account of Edward House tells us a great deal about Woodrow Wilson and why their relationship was so intimate and exclusive.[58] House was invaluable to Wilson in providing him with information and attending to masses of detail. The Colonel served as buffer: even as President of the United States, Wilson was shy with people whom he did not know well, and of whose loyalty he was not certain. House did nothing more efficiently than to demonstrate his personal loyalty in ways in which more "masculine" men might have found embarrassing or even humiliating. Wilson loved House—as he had Hibben—as he loved a member of his family: such love in Wilson's code meant complete trust and denial of faults and limitations. Over the years of Ellen's depression and illness and in the months following her death, Wilson desperately needed a *confidant*. The intimacy of "the strangest friendship in history" began to wane when Wilson acquired a *confidante* in the person of Edith Bolling Galt.

[58] For other psychologically oriented analyses of the House-Wilson relationship, see the Georges' *Woodrow Wilson: A Personality Study* and Sigmund Freud and William C. Bullitt, *Thomas Woodrow Wilson: A Psychological Study* (Boston, 1967).

CHAPTER XVII

The Second Mrs. Wilson and the Break with Bryan

EDITH BOLLING GALT was an attractive widow of forty-two when she met Woodrow Wilson in March 1915. She came from a well-known but impoverished old Virginia family and, at the age of twenty-two, had married Norman Galt, a prosperous Washington jeweler. Galt died in 1908 and left his widow his store and a comfortable income. Mrs. Galt had little formal schooling and had not been concerned with politics: her major interests were friends, family, travel, and fashionable clothing. She was not as intellectual or as well read as Ellen Wilson had been and not as serious. Mrs. Galt was, on the contrary, independent, outgoing and vivacious—the first woman in Washington, she recalled, to drive her own car. Her connection with the White House had come about through Dr. Grayson, whom she may have met in 1903, when she was hospitalized at the Columbia Hospital for Women for a miscarriage. She and Grayson became closer in 1914 when the Doctor was courting Alice Gertrude Gordon, the daughter of an old friend of Mrs. Galt. Mrs. Galt consoled Grayson during his loved one's absences in New York, and the Doctor confided to Mrs. Galt his worries about the pitiful state of his bereaved patient in the White House.[1] Grayson introduced Mrs. Galt to Helen Bones, and the new friends went for walks and rides in Mrs. Galt's electric runabout. Few popular Wilson biographies have omitted Mrs. Galt's story of how the President and Grayson "happened" to end their golf game at the twelfth hole and "accidentally" encountered the ladies when they returned to the White House for tea. A less romantic but more likely version is that, after Wilson had recovered from his depression and the stormy session of Congress had ended, the Doctor and Helen decided that, with the groundwork laid, the time for Wilson's resurrection had come.

None of Dr. Grayson's prescriptions ever had a more salutary or instantaneous effect. Wilson entertained the ladies with conversation and limericks; Mrs. Galt remembered that he could hardly keep his

[1] Cary T. Grayson to Edith Bolling Galt, August 25, 1914, *PWW*, Vol. 31, p. 564.

eyes off her.[2] She properly refused an invitation to stay for dinner, and, several days later, when Helen called to take her for a drive in a White House car, she was "amazed" to see Wilson sitting in the front seat next to the chauffeur.[3] The party returned for dinner at the White House, and Wilson afterward read aloud and discussed books. Frequent dinners, readings, and evening drives followed, and, on May 4, Wilson proposed marriage. Although Mrs. Galt had responded warmly to his attentions, she obeyed the conventions of the time and refused the proposal. "It came to me as almost a shock," she recalled. "Not having given a thought to such a development, I said the first thing that came to my mind, without thinking it would hurt him: 'Oh, you can't love me, for you really don't know me; and it is less than a year since your wife died.' "[4] Wilson was too emotionally upset to recognize the *pro forma* nature of her refusal; the next day Helen Bones came to Mrs. Galt in tears and anger to tell her: "Cousin Woodrow looks really ill this morning. Just as I thought some happiness was coming into his life! And now you are breaking his heart."[5] Mrs. Galt said that she needed more time to think and sent the stricken Wilson assurances of her love: "I thrill to my very finger tips when I remember the tremendous thing you said to me tonight."[6]

Wilson's answer, which contained much underlining, many dashes, and eleven mentions of the word "heart," indicates the intensity of his feeling. He began: "I am infinitely tired to-night,—brain and body and spirit,—for it is still, for me, practically the same day on which I put my happiness to the test,—and I do not know that I can say anything as I would say it; but there are some things I must *try* to say before the still watches come again in which the things unsaid hurt so and cry out in the heart to be uttered. It was this morning—while I lay awake thinking of you in all your wonderful loveliness and of my pitiful inability to satisfy and win you, and to show you the true heart of my need, and of my nature,—that you wrote that wonderful note Helen brought me to-day, with its fresh revelation of your wonderful gifts of heart and mind,—the most moving and altogether beautiful note I ever read, whose possession makes me rich; and I must thank you for that before I try to sleep,—thank you from the bottom of a heart that your words touch as if they knew every key of it. I am proud beyond words that you should have thought of me in such

[2] Alden Hatch, *Edith Bolling Wilson: First Lady Extraordinary* (New York, 1961), p. 13.

[3] Edith Bolling Wilson, *My Memoir* (New York, 1938), pp. 56-57.

[4] *Ibid.*, pp. 60-61.   [5] *Ibid.*, pp. 61-62.

[6] EBG to WW, May 5, 1915, *PWW*, Vol. 33, p. 109.

terms and put the thoughts into such exquisite, comprehending words. God has indeed been good to me to bring such a creature as you into my life. Every glimpse I am permitted to get of the sweet depths of you I find them deeper and purer and more beautiful than I knew or had dreamed of. If you cannot give me *all* that I want—what my heart finds it hard now to breathe without—it is because I am not worthy."[7]

Wilson resumed his suit with quickened ardor. He saw Mrs. Galt several times a week, sent flowers daily, and spent hours each day writing letters to her. Many were written first in shorthand. "Ike" Hoover, who conveyed the messages, commented that the Library of Congress was hard put to the test of finding quotations in which he could express himself more eloquently.[8] Wilson composed a sonnet— always a sure sign of need and passion.[9] When the lovers were physically separated for more than a few hours, Wilson experienced the same pangs of loneliness which he had suffered when he had been away from Ellen. When Edith, who may have run out of ways to say "I love you," suggested that they not write every day, he was dismayed. Her letters, he wrote, brought her into his presence in all her "radiant loveliness." How else, he asked, could they show their inmost hearts to each other?[10] Wilson insisted that his happiness, health, and his very life itself depended on her entire love, and that only the knowledge that she was completely his could give him the strength to face the awesome tasks that confronted him.

Edith Galt, like Mary Hulbert, had had a loveless marriage. She told her chosen biographer—and presumably Wilson as well—that she had not been in love with Galt and had married him only after his persistent attentions had worn her down.[11] Although Edith does not seem to have dramatized her misfortunes as Mary did, Wilson nevertheless consoled her. "It grieves me that you should ever have been unhappy, that clouds should ever have shadowed you who are by nature and every sweet gift so radiant and full of the perfect light that shines in the heart of a completely gifted woman."[12] She had told him that her marriage had left her dead within, and he deemed it a "sacred enterprise" to free her wounded heart from its self-imposed cage.[13] Even though Edith was a robust woman of great vitality, Wilson, in

[7] WW to EBG, May 5, 1915, *ibid.*, p. 111.
[8] Hoover, *Forty-Two Years*, p. 64.
[9] See his poems to Hattie Woodrow and Ellen.
[10] WW to EBG, May 9, 1915, *PWW*, Vol. 33, p. 136.
[11] Hatch, *Edith Bolling Wilson*, p. 51.
[12] WW to EBG, May 6, 1915, *PWW*, Vol. 33, p. 118.
[13] WW to EBG, May 11, 1915, *ibid.*, p. 161.

his usual fashion, worried about her health. While she was away on a trip, he insisted that she report on her condition in each letter. He wrote, "When I think of anything happening [to] you you [*sic*] everything goes black before me!"[14]

Wilson's powers of fantasy could make his lover materialize. "As I lay between sleeping and waking you came and nestled close to me. I could feel your breath on my cheek, our lips touched, and there was all about me the sweet atmosphere that my Darling always carries with her."[15] It was not long before he experienced the ecstasy of his kisses on her eyelids, and the thrill of their arms around each other. One evening late in May, while they were riding in the back seat of the car with the curtains and divider drawn, Wilson may have made a further physical advance. If so, it evidently elicited more sexual stimulation than Edith was ready for, and she reacted with dismay and disapproval. Wilson was mortified and panic-stricken at the thought that she might leave him. The next morning, however, she reaffirmed her love, but made it clear that greater intimacies must await marriage. The forgiven lover was overcome with relief. "After many, many hours of deep depression and exquisite suffering, which brought on a sort of illness which I could not explain to the doctor and for which he could do nothing, the light has again dawned for me and a new certitude and confidence has come to me."[16]

Whereas Wilson had once urged Ellen to express her longing for him more explicitly, Edith gave him no cause for complaint. She wrote of her desires almost as passionately as he did of his. After a separation of a few days, he received the following: "The clock is striking midnight and I must go to bed. I have on my wrapper and am by the window. I also have on one pr. of the lovely white silk stockings [a gift from Wilson], and they are a joy—and make me feel so very rich[17] . . . and they look so pretty on that I think that is the reason I sat up to write tonight—instead of getting in bed as I usually do. A fond and very tender kiss my precious Woodrow, before *we* put out the light—and I feel your dear arms fold 'round me."[18]

The desperate intensity of Wilson's devotion was a reaction to months of loneliness and depression. It was also a recrudescence of

---

[14] WW to EBG, August 13, 1915, *ibid.,* Vol. 34, p. 192.

[15] WW to EBG, June 22, 1915, *ibid.,* Vol. 33, p. 442.

[16] WW to EBG, May 29, 1915, *ibid.,* p. 284.

[17] Mrs. Galt was fond of metaphors of gold; for example, "spires of gold," "tower of gold," "perfect flood of gold," "crock of gold," "vein of gold," and "tiny golden hearted roses."

[18] EBG to WW, August 16, 1915, *PWW,* Vol. 34, p. 225.

his lifelong fears of being abandoned. Wilson constantly needed assurances by women that he was admired and loved, and his panic over the possibility that Edith might not marry him replicated the fears which he had had about Ellen during the last months of their engagement. Also, as we shall soon see, the recurrence of his neurological symptoms and the prospect of limited time may also have been factors in his haste.

Wilson's romance began at a critical time in the nation's affairs.[19] The Germans had launched a submarine campaign against Allied shipping, and the British had retaliated by interdicting all trade to and from Germany. Wilson and Bryan had tried to avoid any action which might be interpreted as not neutral. They had not condemned the invasion of Belgium, lest it arouse war spirit in the country, nor had they protested when the British mined the North Sea and declared the entire area a war zone. Wilson and Bryan issued warnings that violations of American rights would not be tolerated, but, in general, they had acquiesced in the British maritime system and accepted submarine attacks on Allied ships, even though some American lives had been lost.

This policy of acquiescence was shattered when, on Friday, May 7, 1915, *Lusitania*, a British liner carrying hundreds of American passengers and a cargo of contraband, was sunk without warning off the coast of Ireland with great loss of life. Wilson was in a near state of shock at the news, but he controlled his emotions.[20] He carried on his routine of golf, motoring, and attendance at church over the weekend and saw only his family and Mrs. Galt. He worked alone on Sunday evening on a note to Germany and on a speech that he was to deliver the next day in Philadelphia. He remained in seclusion on Monday while he went over communications from Bryan and Counselor Robert Lansing and read the popular outpourings of indignation and sorrow. The great majority of the American people wanted to remain at peace, but they also looked to the President to uphold the nation's rights and prestige. Only a small minority, of which Roosevelt and Lodge were among the most vocal, demanded that the United States assert its right to trade with belligerents, even at the risk of war. Counsels within the administration were divided. House, in England, advised Wilson to break diplomatic relations with Germany, while Bryan urged that

[19] The following details of a political and diplomatic nature are drawn from Link, *Wilson*, III, pp. 57-73, 105-36, 171-90, 309-455.

[20] For an account of Wilson's severe emotional reaction to the sinking of *Lusitania*, see *ibid.*, pp. 379-83.

American citizens not be permitted to travel on ships carrying contraband.

Wilson saw Mrs. Galt on Monday afternoon, shortly before he left for Philadelphia. The meeting was a joyous one because Edith informed him that his "wonderful love" could indeed quicken what had for so long lain dead within her.[21] He arrived at Philadelphia in a state of ecstasy,[22] and delivered one of his most inspired speeches. To a large audience, which included several thousand newly naturalized citizens, he affirmed his belief in the ideals of America. Then came one of his most memorable utterances:

"The example of America must be a special example. The example of America must be the example, not merely of peace because it will not fight, but of peace because peace is the healing and elevating influence of the world, and strife is not. There is such a thing as a man being too proud to fight. There is such a thing as a nation being so right that it does not need to convince others by force that it is right."[23]

Although Wilson was in an exhilarated state, he did not speak impulsively; on the contrary, he voiced his deepest convictions. Wilson, Bryan, and most progressives believed that the war had resulted from the imperialistic and commercial rivalries of the great powers, and that the United States, by removing her own social and economic injustices and preserving peace, could serve as a model for the world. Three weeks earlier, Wilson had declared: "My interest in the neutrality of the United States is not the petty desire to keep out of trouble. . . . But I am interested in neutrality because there is something so much greater to do than fight: there is a distinction waiting for this nation that no nation has ever yet got. That is the distinction of absolute self-control and self-mastery."[24]

Uplifting as Wilson's "too proud to fight" speech was, it could hardly serve as the American answer to the *Lusitania* outrage, and the President stated the next morning that he had given only his personal opinion. The draft of his note to Germany, which he read to the cabinet, upheld the right of American citizens to travel on belligerent ships and expressed confidence that the German government would disavow the act of its submarine commander. Wilson expressed himself in humanitarian terms: the submarine war, he warned, could not be

[21] EBG to WW, May 10, 1915, *PWW*, Vol. 33, p. 146.

[22] WW to EBG, May 11, 1915, *ibid.*, p. 161.

[23] Address in Philadelphia to newly naturalized citizens, May 10, 1915, *ibid.*, pp. 147-50.

[24] Remarks to the Associated Press in New York, April 20, 1915, *ibid.*, pp. 39-40.

carried on without inevitable violations of the principles of justice and humanity.

Bryan approved the document reluctantly. The Secretary of State believed that, in order to maintain strict neutrality, the American government should, in similar fashion, condemn Allied violations of neutral rights. He suggested the inclusion of a statement that the United States would be willing to submit the matter to arbitration. Wilson agreed that such a statement might be given to the press and actually wrote it out. However, after strong objections from Tumulty, Lansing, and Garrison, Wilson decided not to issue it. At the same time, he rejected Lansing's advice that the language of the note be strengthened. Before he departed for a weekend cruise[25] on *Mayflower* to review the fleet, Wilson also asked Lansing to prepare a strong protest to London. Over the weekend, however, he again changed his mind and on his return informed the disappointed Bryan that it would not be wise to reproach Great Britain until he had received a reply to his *Lusitania* note.[26]

Wilson's reversal was in some degree influenced by one of Colonel House's overly optimistic reports. From England, House intimated that the British government might lift its embargo on foodstuffs if the Germans would abandon their submarine campaign and the use of poisonous gases. The British had previously rejected this *modus vivendi*—Bryan had suggested it—and House had no real evidence that they would accept it now. Wilson insisted that House approach the British Foreign Secretary, Sir Edward Grey. He would soon have to protest against British interference with American trade, Wilson told his adviser, and it would be a great stroke if England would resolve the situation for him. Grey, in London, listened sympathetically to House; he told him that he would personally support the proposal and present it to the British cabinet. Faint as Grey's encouragement was, House seized upon it and, on his own initiative, instructed Ambassador James W. Gerard to sound out Berlin. The Germans, who had complained about Britain's "starvation policy" for propaganda purposes, flatly refused the overture. The whole undertaking, Link

---

[25] Mrs. Galt recalled the cruise in a romantic vein. It was a clear night on the Potomac, and the river was like silver. She and Wilson stood alone by the rail, and he asked her if he should accept Bryan's resignation. She replied by relating the plot of a play in which a "boorish young lover" had quarreled with his fiancée and had refused her request that he kiss her and make up. Their dashing bachelor host, played by John Drew, then exclaimed, "Kiss her, sir, and [aside] thank God for the chance." Edith Bolling Wilson, *My Memoir*, pp. 63-64.

[26] WW to Bryan, May 20, 1915, *PWW*, Vol. 33, p. 224.

states, was an exercise in futility.[27] Wilson was embarrassed because the action had implicitly admitted what he was trying to avoid—that there was a connection between British and German violations of American rights. Moreover, the incident revealed to Bryan that negotiations were being carried out behind his back.

In the meantime, Wilson's note had achieved great success. It met with the approval of virtually the entire nation, and the German government, in reply to his appeal, promised that no neutral ships would be attacked. On the issue of *Lusitania* and the safety of Allied passenger ships, however, the German note was unresponsive, and the tension between the President and his Secretary of State mounted. In the cabinet meeting of June 1, at which the American answer to the German note was discussed, Bryan charged that some of his colleagues—and by implication Wilson—were unneutral in their attitudes. Wilson became angry and rebuked Bryan sharply; however, he soon regretted his action and sent Bryan a placating letter. He continued, however, to reject the Commoner's pleas for a softer tone toward the Germans. Wilson's strategy was revealed on the next day in an interview with Count von Bernstorff. In what the Ambassador described as a friendly conversation, the President suggested that, if the Germans gave up submarine warfare, he would press the British to ease their blockade. While Wilson and Bryan looked for a peaceful way out of the impasse, House, in London, predicted to his British friends that the United States would soon be in the war.

Wilson worked on his note late into the night of June 3 and read it to the cabinet on the following morning. It was, in effect, another appeal to the Germans to abandon their submarine campaign in the interests of humanity. Wilson appeared extremely fatigued during the discussion and for the next few days suffered from blinding headaches.[28] Bryan was under as much emotional strain. On June 5 he made one more attempt to persuade Wilson to adopt his suggestions—arbitration of the *Lusitania* dispute, action to prevent American citizens from traveling on ships carrying ammunition, and a protest to Great Britain—and he reminded Wilson that he had consented to the first and third points. In reply, Wilson expressed his regret that he could not agree. For Bryan, it was the end. After a sleepless night, he came to the White House on June 7 to offer his resignation. As Wilson tried to dissuade him, the Commoner became even more distraught and blurted out what he had for months believed, "Colonel House

---

[27] Link, *Wilson*, III, 392-94.   [28] *Ibid.*, pp. 418-424.

has been Secretary of State, not I, and I have never had your full confidence."[29]

Wilson greeted Bryan graciously when the latter visited the cabinet meeting next day to bid farewell, but within there was anguish and rancor. He confided to Mrs. Galt:

"The impression upon my mind of Mr. Bryan's retirement is a very painful one *now*. It is always painful to feel that any thinking man of disinterested motive, who has been your comrade and confidant, has turned away from you and set his hand against you; and it is hard to be fair and not think that the motive is something sinister. But I shall *wait* to think about *him* and put things to be *done* in the foreground. I have been deserted before. The wound does not heal, with me, but neither does it cripple."[30]

Two days later he added: "I have to admit (to the dear one I love most in all the world) that the defection touched me to the quick and the week has been one of the hardest in these hard years which have exacted such a tribute of sorrow."[31]

Edith responded with as much indignation as Jessie Wilson had expressed when she had denounced those who had treated her son unfairly. The hapless Bryan became in her eyes "that awful Deserter." When she heard that Wilson had made a courtesy call on his former colleague, she wrote: "If anything could make me hate him worse than I did before, this would accomplish it. And I will be glad when he expires from an overdose of peace or grape juice and I never hear of him again."[32]

Once again, Wilson believed he had been betrayed by someone he had trusted. He had appointed Bryan out of political necessity but had become personally very fond of him. Wilson had repeatedly expressed his appreciation of Bryan's loyalty and cooperation and his willingness to work for common goals while in a subordinate position. Wilson had overlooked Bryan's inadequacies—his tendency to offer simplistic solutions for complex problems, his frequent absences on the Chautauqua circuit, and his penchant for appointing "deserving Democrats" to diplomatic posts—and had defended him against ridicule.[33]

[29] House diary, June 24, 1915, *PWW*, Vol. 33, p. 449.
[30] WW to EBG, June 9, 1915, *ibid.*, p. 377.
[31] WW to EBG, June 11, 1915, *ibid.*, p. 384.
[32] EBG to WW, June 18, 1915, *ibid.*, p. 421.
[33] Bryan was the subject of much unflattering comment for his "grapejuice diplomacy"—State Department dinners and receptions without benefit of alcohol. For an interesting account of Bryan as a diplomat, see Richard D. Challener, "William Jennings

Wilson was also struggling against feelings of guilt. We have seen how strongly he had been swayed by Bryan's arguments, so recently his own. Wilson, by reason of his upbringing and culture and his hatred of militarism, was indeed pro-British in his sympathies, but he could not admit this to himself. Rather, he maintained his fundamental belief that he should be able to control his thoughts and feelings and *make* himself completely neutral. Ideally, Wilson might have recognized that Bryan had been consistent and aboveboard, that his desire for peace was as sincere as Wilson's own, and that the charge that he had been secretly shunted aside in favor of House was true. Instead, Wilson reacted with anger and self-righteousness. He soon regained his poise, however, and retained no personal animus. Although the Great Commoner continued to oppose some of his policies, the President expressed cordial feelings.[34] When Bryan campaigned strenuously for Wilson in 1916, the latter thanked him warmly.[35]

Another crisis arose in August when a German submarine sank the White Star liner *Arabic* without warning and with the loss of two American citizens. Wilson and Robert Lansing, who had succeeded Bryan as Secretary of State, issued a virtual ultimatum and elicited from the German government a promise not to attack any unarmed liners without warning and to make provision for the safety of passengers and crew. The pledge was accompanied by the Kaiser's demotion of leading advocates of unrestricted submarine warfare. After this diplomatic triumph, Wilson sent the long-delayed note to London condemning the illegalities of the British blockade. Although the United States thus announced its intention to uphold its rights against both belligerents, the less dramatic and hortatory language of the note to Great Britain reflected the belief of Wilson and many Americans that the destruction of life was a more serious offense than the confiscation of property.

Wilson's letters to Edith Galt tell us much of his feelings about the war and his methods of thought and work. "Certainly the Germans are blood-mad," he exclaimed after the *Arabic* sinking. In the same letter, he wrote: "The two things that are clear are that the people of this country rely upon me to keep them out of war and that the worst worst [sic] thing that could possibly happen *to the world* would be for the United States to be drawn actively into this contest,—to become one of the belligerents and lose all chance of moderating the results

---

Bryan," in Norman A. Graebner, ed., *An Uncertain Tradition* (New York, 1961), pp. 79-100.

[34] WW to Franklin P. Glass, November 10, 1915, Wilson Papers.

[35] WW to William Jennings Bryan, September 27, 1916, Wilson Papers.

of the war by her counsel as an outsider."[36] Another letter reads: "The fact is, I never have had any patience with 'ifs' and conjectural cases. My mind insists always upon waiting until something actually does happen and then discussing what is to be done about that. And so, to tell you the truth, I read only that portion of the discussion which Lansing had run a mark along the margin. He had given me all the essential points orally, and I am an impatient reader of *words*. But I wanted you to see how the minds of these men work, how dearly they love abstractions and fine-drawn legal points. The idea of spending their time debating the legal lodgement of *sovereignty* in Mexico! They are hopeless legalists,—and all legalists have a very vague and uncertain perception of facts, and no hold on them whatever."[37]

The letter indicates Wilson's distaste for theoretical discussion and his preference for major facts arranged in precise order. His dislike for detail and his "impatience with words" may have, as has already been suggested, stemmed from his slow reading. His intolerance of legalisms was also shown in the way he largely ignored the tangled legal issues of the *Lusitania* case. Wilson's policy at the time was to react only to provocations. Wilson himself joked that he would have to send the Kaiser a personal message to hold up the German reply to one of his diplomatic notes so that he could spend more time with his beloved.[38] The correspondence also reveals Wilson's lack of restraint in discussing matters of state with Edith. When she protested that she did not have the wisdom or information to advise him, he told her that, even if he were not in love with her, he would value her "clear-sighted counsel" above that of anyone else in the world, not excepting House.[39] He sent her many highly confidential documents, either conveyed by Hoover or mailed by ordinary post!

Wilson had continued to correspond with Mary Hulbert, but had not told her of his new interest. She may have had news of his romance, however, since in late May he was "startled" to learn that his "dearest friend" would visit him shortly.[40] Mrs. Hulbert arrived on the morning of May 31, and never did the White House entourage and transportation service function more efficiently. Mrs. Hulbert, Helen Bones, and Wilson went for a morning drive. After lunch, the women and

[36] WW to EBG, August 19, 1915, *PWW*, Vol. 34, pp. 257, 261.

[37] WW to EBG, August 18, 1915, *ibid.*, p. 241. Wilson was referring to hypothetical cases submitted by Latin American members of a conference to discuss the future of Mexico.

[38] WW to EBG, June 14, 1915, *PWW*, Vol. 33, p. 396.

[39] WW to EBG, August 13, 1915, *ibid.*, Vol. 34, p. 190.

[40] WW to MAH, May 23, 1915, *ibid.*, Vol. 33, p. 242.

Margaret Wilson went to Arlington Cemetery to hear Wilson speak. Mrs. Hulbert was then whisked to the railroad station in time to catch the four o'clock train to New York. Mary seems to have been at her most charming because Helen commented that Cousin Woodrow seemed "something of a goose" to be so titillated by her.[41] Mrs. Hulbert may have told Wilson of her intention to move to California, where Allen was planning to invest in an avocado ranch. Several weeks later, Wilson helped to finance the venture by purchasing, for $15,000, several mortgages which she held on property in New York.[42]

Wilson and Mrs. Galt spent six weeks of June and July in Cornish, where he continued to press his suit. Edith, early in July, consented to marry him, but only on the condition that he not serve a second term. To quiet the growing talk about their attachment, Mrs. Galt spent the month of August traveling with friends while Wilson remained in Washington. He took the separation badly and, on the first evening after her return, they went for a drive through Rock Creek Park. It seemed to her that he looked particularly tired and worried, and she withdrew her reservation: "I am proud to say that despite the fact that Mr. Murphy, of the Secret Service, and Robinson the chauffeur were on the front seat, and Helen beside me on the back seat, I put my arms around his neck and said: 'Well, if you won't ask me, I will volunteer, and be ready to be mustered in as soon as can be.'" However, she still thought that their engagement should last a year.[43]

While still in Cornish, Wilson consulted Colonel House, who, as usual, had kept himself well informed. He was mindful of the value of Wilson's public image as a bereaved widower, but Dr. Grayson had also told him that an early marriage was necessary for the President's health. House advised postponing the wedding until the following spring. Over the summer, rumors of the romance spread, along with the inevitable gossip about Mrs. Hulbert. Wilson had said nothing to members of his cabinet; at a secret session, they delegated Josephus Daniels to warn the President that an early marriage would alienate many voters, particularly women. Daniels declined the mission,[44] but McAdoo, perhaps with the connivance of House, came up with a

[41] Walworth, *Wilson*, I, 395.

[42] *PWW*, Vol. 34, pp. 39, 117.

[43] Edith Bolling Wilson, *My Memoir*, pp. 74-75.

[44] "I had never aspired to so exalted a place as Secretary of the Navy. Having been called to that by President Wilson I did not feel inclined to exchange it for the difficult and, perhaps, dangerous high and exalted position of Minister Plenipotentiary and Envoy Extraordinary to the Court of Cupid on a mission in which neither my heart nor my head was enlisted and in the performance of which my official head might suffer decapitation." Daniels, *The Wilson Era*, p. 454.

scheme to induce his father-in-law to discuss the problem. At lunch on September 18 McAdoo told Wilson that he had received an anonymous letter stating that Mrs. Hulbert had been showing his letters and was making it appear as if the $15,000 was a payoff.[45]

Wilson was severely shaken. He immediately sent a note to Mrs. Galt to ask if he could come to her home instead of her coming to the White House for dinner, as they had originally planned.[46] The tremulousness of his handwriting indicates how upset he was. He saw her alone, and his letter written early the next morning indicates that he confessed his affair with Mary Hulbert and offered to release her from her promise to marry him:

"You are more wonderful and lovely in my eyes than you ever were before; and my pride and joy and gratitude that you should love me with such a perfect love are beyond all expression, except in some great poem I cannot write. But I am equally conscious that it is anything but pride and joy and gratitude or happiness that the evening brought you: that it brought you, instead of a confirmation of your ideal of me, an utter contradiction of it, dismay rather than happiness, uneasiness in the place of confident hope,—the love that is solicitude and pity, not admiration and happy trust,—and that intolerable thought has robbed me of sleep. When it was the deepest, most passionate desire of my heart to bring you happiness and sweep every shadow from your path, I have brought you, instead, mortification and thrown a new shadow about you. Surely no man was ever more deeply punished for a folly long ago loathed and repented of,—but the bitterness of it ought not to fall on you, in the prime of your glorious, radiant womanhood, when you embody in their perfection, for all who know you, the beauty of purity and grace and sweet friendship and gracious, unselfish counsel. I am the most undeservedly honoured man in the world and your love, which I have least deserved, is the crowning honour of my life. I have tried, ah, *how* I have tried to expiate folly by disinterested service and honorable, self-forgetful, devoted love, and it has availed only to lead the loveliest, sweetest woman in all the world, for whom I would joyfully give my life, to mortification and dismay."[47]

Edith responded to Woodrow's distress by pledging herself anew.

---

[45] Edith Wilson was convinced of House's complicity. She reports that the Colonel confessed that he and McAdoo had planned the move together. Mrs. Wilson also quotes McAdoo as stating that it was entirely House's idea. Edith Bolling Wilson, *My Memoir*, p. 78.

[46] WW to EBG, September 18, 1915, *PWW*, Vol. 34, p. 489.

[47] WW to EBG, September 19, 1915, *ibid.*, p. 491.

"I will stand by you—not for duty, not for pity, not for honor—but for love—trusting, protecting, comprehending Love. And no matter whether the wine be bitter or sweet we will share it together and find happiness in the comradeship."[48]

In her memoir, written twenty-three years later, Mrs. Wilson gives a highly fictitious account of this whole episode. According to her version, Wilson could not bring himself to come to her home and dispatched Grayson instead. She relates that, after she sent her promise to stand by him, she did not hear anything from the White House for several days. Then the Doctor appeared in a state of great anxiety to say: "I beg that you will come with me to the White House. The President is very ill, and you are the only person who can help. I can do nothing." When she queried Grayson, he added: "If you could see him you would not hesitate. He looks as I imagine the martyrs looked when they were broken on the wheel. He does not speak or sleep or eat." Mrs. Wilson goes on to describe the scene which awaited her: "The curtains were drawn and the room dark; on the pillow I saw a white, drawn face with burning eyes dark with hidden pain. [Arthur] Brooks, the coloured valet, was by the bed. No word was spoken, only an eager hand held out in welcome, which I took to find icy cold, and when I unclasped it we were alone."[49]

Mrs. Wilson wrote her memoir approximately thirteen years after she had become a widow. It is likely that her amnesia about Wilson's visit to her home and her confabulation of a collapse brought on by love shielded her from the memory of the two most painful events of her life—Wilson's confession of his sin and the incapacity which followed his massive stroke of 1919. Her description of a white drawn face with burning eyes, no speech, and only an eager hand held out in welcome may have been the way that he appeared in the first days after his stroke. Confabulations are not only fictitious recollections of past events, but may be actual happenings displaced in space and time. As in myths and legends, an event, which at the time of its occurrence was catastrophic, may, with the passage of time, become anxiety-relieving when placed in another symbolic context.[50] The context in Edith Wilson's case was a romantic one.

Rather than languishing in bed, where Edith's fancy had him, Wilson was up and about and experiencing joyous feelings of liberation. He wrote:

[48] EBG to WW, September 19, 1915, *ibid.*, p. 490.

[49] Edith Bolling Wilson, *My Memoir*, pp. 76-78.

[50] Edwin A. Weinstein, Robert L. Kahn, and Sidney Malitz, "Confabulation as a Social Process," *Psychiatry*, XIX (November 1956), 383-96.

"Dearest,

"I slept last night because I had at last found my real self. As I look back I am amazed that I should have been so long about it. It was, I think, because my thoughts were going around instead of going straight. That talk with you yesterday—which is now one of the many, many things, generous and true and dictated by love, that have made me your debtor for the vital forces of life itself—did me a double service: it gave me a new insight into your love and it brought to me the startling, humiliating discovery that I was allowing myself to be dominated by fear and the desire to conceal something which no doubt everybody who has trusted and believed in me probably has a right to know, unless I am to play the hypocrite. That discovery set me free. I had not realized the real situation. I had looked at every other aspect of it except that, that I had [been] acting the part of coward. To realize that was an instant emancipation. I am not a coward,—that's the one thing about myself that I am certain of and have proved—and it's no great boast at best! I am mortified that I should have played the part. And now that I see straight I shall take steps to show what I really am. I suppose I dreaded the revelation which seemed to be threatened because I knew that it would give a tragically false impression of what I really have been and am,—because it might make the contemptible error and madness of a few months seem a stain upon a whole life. But now I know that to permit myself to live under the domination of such a fear and allow it to govern the whole course of my life in the matters of deepest concern to me—deprive me of happiness and peace of mind—would be even more inconsistent with my true character than the offence itself. The remedy is in my own hands and I will use it."[51]

Wilson's deliverance from sin and guilt was also commemorated symbolically by the return to the flag of the white of purity. "The stain of red which means the true pulse of blood, and that beauty of pure white which means peace of soul," he declared in a public address several months later.[52]

Mary Hulbert had had no intention of selling the letters of the man she still loved. Wilson notified her of his engagement, before the official announcement on October 6. "Dearest Friend," she replied, "I have kissed the cross. We are very very glad you have found happiness, and that you had time to think of us in the midst of it. I need not tell you again that you have been the greatest, most enobling influence in my life. You helped me to keep my soul alive, and I am grateful. I hope you will have all the happiness that I have missed. . . . *She* is very beautiful and some time perhaps I may meet her. . . . The cold peace of utter renunciation is about me, and the shell that is M.A.H. still functions. It is rather lonely, not even an acquaintance to make the air vibrate with the covering warmth, perhaps, of friendship. God alone knows—and, you, partly, the real woman Mary Hulbert—all her hopes and joys, and fears, and mistakes. I shall not write to you again thus intimately, but must this once."[53]

Wilson's attachment to Mrs. Galt meant a loosening of his emotional ties to Colonel House. Unlike Ellen, Edith would not share her husband's affection with another person. Moreover, she had little regard for politicians, especially when they tried to tell her when she should be married. She seems to have taken an immediate dislike to House, who struck her as weak. She considered Tumulty coarse. Wilson defended his advisers, and House, aided by the President, embarked on a campaign to win her over. Wilson described one of the Colonel's efforts: "But it was a joy to see House afterwards and talk to him about you. I never saw him so enthusiastic about anything as he was about you. He said he had not words in which to express his admiration for you,—that the sum of the matter was that you were a wonderful and delightful person and that it seemed to him that it was the best and most fortunate thing that could have happened, for me or for the country, that I had won such a partner and comrade and helper. I wish I could give you some impression of the way in which his face glowed when he spoke of you. . . . I love him more than ever— the true, loyal friend—because he has become, from the moment of seeing and knowing you, as much your friend and partisan as mine."[54]

Wilson was protesting too much, just as he was doing when, about the same time, he told House: "You are the only person in the world with whom I can discuss everything. There are some I can tell one thing and others another, but you are the only one to whom I can make an entire clearance of mind."[55] When a newspaper story was published to the effect that Wilson and his adviser had differed on Mexican policy, Wilson became so indignant that he asked the editor to withdraw the author of the report from the White House press corps.[56] Wilson and Mrs. Galt, after the announcement of their engagement on October 6, paid two visits to the Houses in New York

---

[53] MAH to WW, c. October 11, 1915, *PWW*, Vol. 35, p. 53.

[54] WW to EBG, September 25, 1915, *ibid.*, Vol. 34, pp. 519-20.

[55] Seymour, *Intimate Papers*, I, 116.

[56] Wilson relented later.

with attendant publicity. That the Colonel sensed the change is suggested by his notations in his diary of how close House had become to Mrs. Galt. On December 15, two weeks before House, at Wilson's insistence, was to go to England on a peace mission, he noted: "After dinner we went to see Mrs. Galt. She was alone and the three of us sat for a half hour in intimate personal conversation. She expressed regret that we were going to Europe and also that I was not to be at the wedding."[57] Woodrow Wilson and Edith Bolling Galt were married at her home on December 18.

Wilson's exhilaration over his personal fortunes and satisfaction from his diplomatic successes in 1915 were associated unfortunately with a worsening of his medical condition. In January 1915 Grayson informed House that the President's kidneys were not functioning well.[58] The Doctor did not specify the symptoms, but the same disease process which affects the vessels of the brain and retina may also involve the kidneys. Over the late spring and summer, Wilson reported numerous episodes of transient weakness of his right arm,[59] some of which he attributed to the exertion of golf. At the end of August, Wilson described such an episode and minimized it in characteristic fashion: "At this point on the sheet this hand of mine went back on me and I had to let it off from further struggles with the pen. It's all right this morning and I am *so* happy to be talking with you again! I think it must have been the rather hard game of golf I had had with the Colonel [Edward T. Brown] and the doctor that had tired my hand and arm,—for I am perfectly well and fit—fit as I shall ever be away from you. I shall keep my promise literally, Sweetheart, and tell you of even my little ailments, so that you need not have the least anxiety lest I am not well and you do not know it."[60] Along with this succession of probable transient ischemic attacks, Wilson had frequent headaches. He experienced four days of blinding headaches during the events which precipitated Bryan's resignation. Many observers noted Wilson's extreme fatigue.[61]

Medical evidence indicates that Wilson's headaches and fatigue may

[57] House diary, December 15, 1915, *PWW*, Vol. 35, p. 361.

[58] House diary, January 13, 1915, *ibid.*, Vol. 32, p. 67.

[59] WW to EBG, May 21 and 30, August 13, September 3, 1915, *PWW*, Vol. 33, pp. 234, 286; Vol. 34, pp. 192, 414.

[60] WW to EBG, August 23, 1915, *ibid.*, Vol. 34, p. 302.

[61] Walter H. Page to WW, March 10, 1915; EBG to WW, September 2, 1915; Oswald Garrison Villard to WW, September 14, 1915; WW to Villard, September 15, 1915; *ibid.*, Vol. 32, p. 363; Vol. 34, pp. 407, 466, 477; House diary, June 24, 1915; Walworth, *Wilson*, II, 18; Link, *Wilson*, III, 657, 662.

not only have been due, as in the past, to emotional tension, but also to his high blood pressure and the progress of his cerebral and retinal arterial disease.[62] Since his stroke of 1906, Wilson had been examined regularly by Dr. de Schweinitz. The Doctor measured his vision and, more importantly, observed the condition of his retinal blood vessels through the ophthalmoscope. Grayson discussed De Schweinitz's report of March 1914 with Colonel House, who noted: "I had a long talk with Dr. Grayson. He tells me everything concerning the President in the most minute detail in order to get my advice. He alarmed me somewhat by saying that the Philadelphia occulist, Dr. Swinehart [sic], who has had the President under his care for ten years or more, told him, Grayson, there was some indication of the hardening of the arteries. The President does not know this, neither does any member of his family."[63] Grayson voiced concern again in October. He told McAdoo that he did not think that Wilson would be able to go through another term of office.[64]

De Schweinitz next examined Wilson on the morning of August 20, 1915, and Wilson reported about the examination in a letter to Mrs. Galt: "The oculist pronounced my good eye as in *splendid* condition and its powers of vision even *above* the normal, and said that the bad eye was successfully holding it's own;[65] so that you need give yourself no anxiety on the score of my *eyes*, my precious One." Wilson left the Doctor's office in a carefree state, had a pleasant lunch at the Bellevue-Stratford Hotel, and enjoyed a walk down Walnut and Chestnut streets followed by a happy throng of people. "The journey back was comfortable and I felt more normal and more like myself, the real W.W., than I've felt on any journey since the 4th of March, 1913."[66]

Wilson's enthusiasm was ill-founded. The condition of his retinal blood vessels, rather than his visual acuity, was the important feature of the examination. The appearance of the retinal arteries is an indicator of the cerebral circulation, and good vision may exist along with arterial damage. Dr. de Schweinitz's original records have been destroyed, but Dr. Edward S. Gifford of Philadelphia, who was familiar with them, wrote the following to the author:

"When Dr. de Schweinitz died in 1938, his records passed to Dr.

---

[62] Headaches are not common in hypertension; they occur only with very high blood pressure.

[63] House diary, March 25, 1914, *PWW*, Vol. 29, p. 377.

[64] House diary, October 20, 1914.

[65] Note that it is "My good eye" and "*the* bad eye." See Chapter 9 for a discussion of the significance of this selective use of pronouns.

[66] WW to EBG, August 20, 1915, *PWW*, Vol. 34, pp. 258-59.

Alexander G. Fewell, who had assisted Dr. de Schweinitz in his office on Walnut Street every morning from 8 till 10 for many years. When Dr. Fewell retired in 1961, Dr. Fewell's records and practice came to me.

"But some time in the fifties Dr. Fewell destroyed Dr. de Schweinitz's records, which pained me considerably because I knew that those records contained historical material about many prominent people. Before destroying those records, however, Dr. Fewell read that of Woodrow Wilson and talked to me about it. According to Dr. Fewell, Woodrow Wilson suffered from a very high blood pressure and his fundi showed hypertensive vascular changes with advanced angiosclerosis [arteriosclerosis], angiospasticity [spasm of arteries], and exudates [white spots on the retina resulting from vessel damage and/or lipid deposits]. These observations were made while Wilson was president.

"Dr. Fewell died in 1965 and I know of no other source of information."[67]

Dr. Gifford does not state in which year this profound pathology appeared, and it probably had not reached such severity in 1915. The observations were, however, indicative of progressive impairment and, even in a milder form, were harbingers of cardiac, renal, and diffuse cerebral disease. De Schweinitz may not have held up this dismal prospect to his patient, but he undoubtedly communicated his findings to the referring physician.

[67] Edward S. Gifford to author, September 27, 1967.

CHAPTER XVIII

From Peace to War

THIS CHAPTER deals selectively with the remaining period of American neutrality from the point of view of Wilson's health, personal motivations, and relationships.[1]

One of Wilson's definitions of neutral rights emphasized the right of Americans to travel on belligerent passenger ships without the threat of death on account of unwarned underseas attacks. To acquire the power to protect this privilege, and in order to silence vehement Republican criticism of diplomatic weakness, Wilson reversed his previous defense policy and came out for preparedness. His action also indicates an intensely personal motive. Wilson had been fascinated by the sea ever since, as a child, he had heard the thrilling and frightening story of his mother's narrow escape from drowning. We have noted his boyhood fantasies of "Admiral Wilson" destroying pirates, and the intense romantic impact of Swinburne's description of Iseult crossing the stormy sea unafraid. The extraordinary anguish which he experienced on hearing the news of the sinking of *Lusitania* indicates how strongly he identified with the innocent people who had lost their lives. To be sure, the right of travel on belligerent ships was in accord with international law and American tradition, but so was the protection of citizens on foreign soil. Wilson, however—like Bryan—regarded Americans living and conducting business in revolutionary Mexico as doing so at their own risk.

Wilson's decision to build up the navy, increase the size of the army, and create a military reserve under federal control met with a mixed reception. For Bryan and the progressives of the West and South, and for urban liberals, preparedness was a code word for militarism. Advocates of state rights opposed the centralization of power in Washington and preferred a strengthening of the National Guard. Wilson's program was favored by conservative financial and manufacturing interests and by a number of intellectuals and academics, including the President of Princeton University. At one extreme were the big army and big navy enthusiasts, and at the other were the German-

---

[1] The following narrative relies principally upon Link, *Wilson*, III, IV, and V; Baker, *Wilson*, VI and VII; and Devlin, *Too Proud to Fight*, pp. 135-688.

American spokesmen and Anglophobic Irish Americans. Wilson tried to follow a middle course: he met personally with congressional leaders and attempted to allay fears of excessive federal control.

Since he faced the adamant opposition of the House Military Affairs Committee, Wilson took his case directly to the people, and, at the end of January 1916, left on a week's speaking tour of the Middle West, where opposition to preparedness was strongest. He asserted that his program would protect American shipping against both German submarines and British cruisers: only by preparing itself, he stated, could the country preserve peace and national honor. He received his greatest applause in St. Louis—a city with a large German-American population—when he declared that the United States should build "incomparably the greatest navy in the world."[2]

Wilson's appeal, however, did not break the deadlock between the administration and the House Military Affairs Committee, which was dominated by progressives and isolationist Democrats. Accordingly, Wilson modified his plan and accepted the committee's proposal to enlarge and federalize the National Guard. In so doing, he incurred the hostility of the military establishment and provoked the resignation of Secretary of War Garrison. Wilson more than had his way on the navy; in the end, a Senate measure, supported by the Republicans and calling for more spending than Wilson had originally requested was accepted by the House at Wilson's insistence.

Following Bryan's resignation, Wilson had appointed Counselor Robert Lansing to succeed him. The new Secretary of State, a specialist in international law, was not a political liberal, and Wilson intended that Lansing should perform the legal chores while he himself directed policy. Lansing set out to enforce strict neutrality to the letter of the law. Just as House relished secret talks, Lansing enjoyed bringing international offenders to heel by writing stern diplomatic notes. He put strong pressure on the German government to admit to the illegality of the sinking of *Lusitania*, and when, in November, a submarine flying the Austrian ensign sank the Italian liner *Ancona*, Wilson had to tone down the severity of Lansing's note of protest.

The autumn of 1915 also saw the beginning of negotiations which resulted in the House-Grey Memorandum. House had become convinced that, if the military deadlock continued, the advocates in Berlin of all-out submarine warfare would gain control, and the United States would be forced into the war. House wanted to use American belligerency for loftier objectives than mere retaliation.

[2] Speech in St. Louis, February 3, 1916, *PWW*, Vol. 36, p. 120.

The Colonel saw his opportunity when he received a suggestion from Sir Edward Grey that American mediation might be welcomed if the peace settlement provided for postwar disarmament and an association of nations to insure the peace. House was further stimulated by an angry remark about German brutality, which Wilson made after the sinking of *Arabic*. To establish world peace on the basis of an Anglo-American entente was the dream of House's life, and he warmed to his task.

Short of Philip Dru's achievement, House's plan for Anglo-American cooperation for peace was the most remarkable conception to have sprung from the Texas Colonel's imagination. At a time to be designated by the British and French governments—that is, if their military position became poor—the United States would issue a call for a peace based on the elimination of militarism and navalism. If both sides accepted, he would have accomplished a diplomatic master stroke. If Germany refused to attend the peace conference, the United States would break diplomatic relations and throw its whole force on the side of the Allies. Since the British and French would be privy to the purpose behind the President's offer, his language to them could be as severe as that to the Central Powers. The Germans would have no knowledge of the prior arrangement with the British and French governments, and House would encourage their acceptance by intimating that the British would reject the plan. In such fashion, House's yearnings for secrecy and intrigue would be gratified, and his intimacy with the President would be restored.

The Colonel presented his plan on October 8 during Wilson's visit to New York. Since Wilson and Mrs. Galt were engaged in a very social weekend,[3] House could talk with Wilson only briefly. According to the account in the House diary, Wilson was startled but said nothing. Usually House indicated his disapproval of Wilson's ideas by remaining silent, but, on this occasion, he took Wilson's silence for approval. How much of the detail House revealed is not stated, and one can only wonder about what passed through the President's mind as he listened to this decidedly unneutral proposal.

Wilson's enthusiasm was definitely aroused a week later when House showed him a letter from Grey in which the Foreign Secretary asked whether the United States would join a postwar league of nations whose member states would be bound to take action against any power

[3] They selected an engagement ring from a display of thirteen which House, knowing Wilson's lucky number, had requested a jeweler to bring to his apartment. The couple went for an automobile ride along the East River, and, with the Houses, attended the theater.

which broke a treaty or otherwise violated rules governing international relations. House, with Wilson's approval, responded affirma-
tively. A detailed account of House's mission is beyond the scope of
this chapter. He was cordially welcomed in London, Berlin, and Paris,
but received no support for his plan. Grey was, at best, lukewarm.
Yet the Colonel reported great success. Shortly after leaving France,
he wrote to Wilson: "A great opportunity is yours, my friend—the
greatest, perhaps, that has ever come to any man. The way out seems
clear to me and, when I can lay the facts before you, I believe it will
be clear to you also."[4] However, when House did spell out the "facts,"
he neglected to state that he had assured the British and French that
the United States would enter the war on their side by the autumn of
1916—in any event. Moreover, Wilson had charged his emissary to
emphasize urgently in London the grievances of American shippers.
However, when Grey suggested that the British might ease their blockade as a concession to the United States, House advised against such
a step.[5] The Colonel returned to Washington early in March with the
Memorandum in hand. Wilson congratulated him effusively: "It would
be impossible to imagine a more difficult task than the one placed in
your hands, but you have accomplished it in a way beyond my expectations." House responded modestly by stating that he would feel
pride enough if only Wilson could have an opportunity to carry out
the plan.[6] Wilson only inserted the word "probably" before the statement that the United States would become a belligerent.

Wilson was particularly gratified by House's apparent success because it promised a way out of mounting diplomatic difficulties. These
were at least partly of his own making. Perhaps because he had been
so occupied with his wedding, he had not coordinated the House plan
with the activities of the State Department. Lansing, with Wilson's
approval, had been pushing the Germans to the wall over a settlement
of the *Lusitania* incident. Moreover, the President and the Secretary
agreed that it was unfair to ask the German submarine commanders
to follows the rules of visit and search and provide for the safety of
crews, when the guns of an armed ship could destroy the surfaced
submarine in the act of giving warning.[7] Accordingly, they considered
imposing a *modus vivendi* whereby the Allies would agree not to arm
merchant ships in return for a German promise to follow the rules of
cruiser warfare in attacking them.

[4] House to WW, February 9, 1916, *PWW*, Vol. 36, MS.
[5] House diary, February 10, 1916.   [6] *Ibid.*, March 6, 1916.
[7] British armed ships were under orders to attack German submarines after warning
had been given.

Lansing sent his *modus vivendi* to the Allies on January 18, 1916. The British, not surprisingly, were puzzled and outraged by a scheme which would have left their merchantmen defenseless against enemy submarines. Lansing also implied, in a conversation with the Austrian Chargé d'Affaires, that the Central Powers would be justified in attacking armed merchantmen. This prompted the Germans to announce that armed Allied merchant ships would be treated as auxiliary cruisers. The President, on his return from his preparedness tour, moved swiftly to repair the damage. The demand for the disarming of Allied merchant ships was shelved, and the administration announced that it would defend the right of Americans to travel on ships that were defensively armed. Wilson did all this to smooth House's path in London.

Wilson's tactics in preparing the way for the House-Grey agreement were as confusing to Congress as they were to the British. Democratic leaders, who had not been informed of the reasons for his abrupt change in policy, came to the White House on February 21 to ask what would happen if a submarine sank an armed ship carrying Americans. Wilson's reply that he would hold Germany to strict account but not compel the Allies to disarm merchant vessels set off a panic. Representative Jeff McLemore of Texas introduced a resolution warning Americans not to travel on belligerent ships. This action directly threatened Wilson's leadership, and he reacted in typical fashion. He secluded himself, and, when Senator William J. Stone, chairman of the Foreign Relations Committee, a loyal follower, asked to see Wilson again, the President refused another personal confrontation. Instead, he replied to Stone in an open letter.

Wilson asserted that he had done everything in his power to keep the country out of war, but the honor and self-respect of the country were at stake, and he could not consent to any abridgement of American rights. If the government forbade its citizens to exercise their rights, including the right to travel on belligerent ships, it would be an explicit acquiescence in the violation of the rights of mankind everywhere. "Once accept a single abatement of right," he declared, "and many other humiliations would certainly follow, and the whole fine fabric of international law might crumble under our hands piece by piece."[8]

Wilson had substituted rhetoric for answers. He did not take up the specific issue of armed versus unarmed ships, which had so troubled

[8] WW to William J. Stone, February 24, 1916, *PWW*, Vol. 36, MS. The phrase was Tumulty's. Wilson merely inserted "fine." Link, *Wilson*, IV, 173. Tumulty was adept at imitating Wilson's style and, to Mrs. Wilson's annoyance, his signature.

Stone. The letter also indicated his disregard of the legalities of the matter. No "fine fabric" of international law existed in respect to the new submarine weapon. Moreover, the United States had acquiesced frequently in British violations of maritime law. Wilson's words expressed his feelings vividly and succeeded in repelling the challenge to his leadership. However, on the record, his message was the most sweeping and dogmatic pronouncement of American rights that he had yet made.

That Wilson's language was more experiential than referential is shown by his reaction to the next crisis—the torpedoing on March 24 of the French channel steamer *Sussex*. Colonel House came down to Washington to urge him to break diplomatic relations with Germany; Lansing proposed the same action. Wilson, however, kept his own counsel, and House returned to New York without being told what he intended to do.

The Colonel confided his bitter disappointment to his diary: "Grayson thinks the President is a man of unusually narrow prejudices and is intolerant of advice. I did not argue the matter with him as I feel that while the President is not unwilling to accept advice from me, Grayson's general characterization of him is correct. Grayson says if one urges Wilson to do something contrary to his own conviction, he ceases to have any liking for that person.[9] He does not like to meet people and isolates himself as much as anyone I have ever known. . . . His immediate entourage, from the Secretary of State down, are having an unhappy time just now. He is consulting none of them and they are as ignorant of his intentions as the man in the street."[10]

Wilson, who had strong hopes for the implementation of the House-Grey Memorandum, did not sever relations with Germany. Instead, he issued another warning that violations of the rules of cruiser warfare would result in a diplomatic break. The advocates of a moderate submarine policy were still in control in Berlin, and the Germans yielded. They promised to spare passenger ships and agreed to follow cruiser rules in respect to merchant vessels. However, they reserved the right to resume attacks without warning if the British did not cease their illegal blockade practices.

Throughout the spring and early summer of 1916, Wilson and House unsuccessfully pressed Grey to ask for American mediation under the House-Grey Memorandum. As before, the British were reluctant to attend a conference at which the Germans would hold the

[9] One wonders whether the discreet Grayson would ever have said any such thing to House.

[10] House diary, April 2, 1916.

territorial bargaining chips. They knew that Wilson would insist, generally, upon a peace settlement based on the status quo antebellum. Grey's moderating influence had ebbed, and the more militant members of the government were determined to win the war on the battlefield. They were dealing more sternly than ever with the neutrals. They published a "blacklist" of American and Latin American firms trading with the Central Powers to which Wilson responded by obtaining retaliatory legislation from Congress. There was also a heightening of anti-British sentiment throughout the country because of the ruthless suppression of the Irish rebellion and the execution, despite a Senate appeal for clemency, of Sir Roger Casement.[11]

Wilson was also occupied by troubles with Mexico. He had given *de facto* recognition to the Carranza regime in October 1915 and thereby had incurred the wrath of American investors and the Roman Catholic hierarchy. His action also incited the defeated, but far from subdued, Pancho Villa to launch a campaign to provoke American military intervention. In January a band of *Villistas* robbed and killed a group of American mining engineers in northern Mexico. Despite the clamor for war, Wilson insisted that the Mexican Revolution be permitted to run its course without outside interference. He pointed out that the murdered men had disregarded State Department warnings not to travel in the particular area and said that, while the United States would do its best to protect its citizens in northern Mexico, such efforts were limited by the unstable condition of that area. No sooner had the excitement subsided when Villa, in person, led a raid on Columbus, New Mexico, which resulted in the death of nineteen American soldiers and civilians. Wilson did not act precipitately as he had done after the far less serious Tampico incident of 1914. He secured agreement among his cabinet and Democratic congressional leaders, and sought the cooperation of the Carranza government before deciding to send troops into Mexico for the express purpose of capturing Villa.[12] The history of the Punitive Expedition is well known. Not only did it fail to catch Villa, but it clashed with regular Mexican troops. War was narrowly averted by mutual accommodation, but the question of withdrawal of the American force remained. The Punitive Expedition was recalled in January 1917, and *de facto* recognition of a new constitutional Mexican government followed shortly afterward.

---

[11] Casement was convicted of treason for organizing Irish prisoners of war in Germany into an invasion force. His alleged homosexuality may have been a factor in the refusal of the British government to commute his sentence.

[12] Although the United States gained the approval of the Mexican Minister of War and Navy, General Álvaro Obregón, and the Secretary of Foreign Relations, Cándido Aguilar, it did not obtain Carranza's consent.

The episode shows Wilson at his best as a statesman. He had learned a great deal about Mexico and revolution in the two years since he had tried to coerce Huerta into saluting the American flag. Another factor was that Wilson did not bear the passionate personal hatred for Carranza—or for that matter for Villa—that he had had for Huerta. Also, Wilson was in far better emotional shape than he had been in 1914.

We have relatively little specific information about Wilson's health during 1916. Since he and his wife were rarely apart, they did not correspond, and he no longer wrote to Mary Hulbert. Dr. de Schweinitz came to Washington in July, but there is no record of what he told the President. Wilson looked exceedingly well on his return from his honeymoon in January, and reporters noted that he was in fine physical form after his preparedness tour. Dr. Grayson commented that making speeches was as good for him as a game of golf.[13] Wilson was not well while he was working on the *Sussex* note. He left for a cruise on *Mayflower* on the morning of Friday, April 7, but returned the following day and spent the remainder of the weekend in his quarters. He canceled his Monday appointments, went for a ride in the afternoon, and completed his draft late that night. House, who had breakfast with Wilson the next morning, noted that his voice was weak after his four-day illness.[14] After Ray Stannard Baker interviewed Wilson in May, he reported that, while the President looked well, he complained that he grew very tired.[15] Two weeks later, House noted that Wilson showed signs of fatigue while he was in New York for the Grayson-Gordon wedding.[16] On July 23, 1916, Wilson wrote to Colonel House: "I have not been very well for the past week or two,—since I came back from Detroit. My digestion has been upset in some way. But I am slowly getting it in shape again, I believe, the undeniable truth being that a rest, a real rest, has been now a long time overdue. I wish I were in better trim for the campaign."[17] The President was compelled to remain in Washington through August because of the threat of a railroad strike. He spent the months of September and October at Shadow Lawn on the Jersey shore, where, soon after his arrival, he experienced a sick headache which kept him in bed all of one morning.[18]

Wilson faithfully carried out Dr. Grayson's program of sufficient

[13] Link, *Wilson*, IV, 48-49.
[14] House diary, April 11, 1916.
[15] Interview with WW, May 12, 1916, Baker Papers.
[16] House diary, May 24, 1916.
[17] WW to House, July 23, 1916, *PWW*, Vol. 37, MS.
[18] Edith Bolling Wilson, *My Memoir*, p. 105.

rest and recreation. He rose at six and, after breakfast and golf, went to his office at ten. He returned for lunch at one, and, after office appointments in the early afternoon, usually went for an automobile ride. He had dinner with his family, and in the evening he and Mrs. Wilson read, played pool, and decoded cables. They attended the theater once or twice a week and took frequent cruises on *Mayflower*.[19] Only rarely did Wilson work in the evening or on weekends.

The Democrats, with Wilson firmly in control, had prepared for the election of 1916 by passing significant social legislation, including a child labor act—which Wilson had previously failed to support—and legislation favorable to organized labor and farmers. In January Wilson appointed Louis D. Brandeis to the Supreme Court over strong conservative opposition.[20] Wilson ran against Charles Evans Hughes on a platform of progressivism and peace. The moderate Republicans were also for peace, but Hughes, less adept than Wilson in evading embarrassing questions, intimated that he would have broken relations with Germany after the sinking of *Lusitania*. Roosevelt and Lodge called for more aggressive policies toward Germany and Mexico, and the latter charged that Wilson, in an unsent postscript to the *Lusitania* note, had sought to soften its effect, and had proposed arbitration. It will be recalled that Wilson had indeed written a press release, at Bryan's request, but had decided not to send it. In response to Lodge's charge, however, he denied that he had ever written or contemplated any "postscript." It was a case of his use of literal language to hide the truth. Wilson retaliated by not inviting Lodge to a dinner for the Allied diplomatic corps, although Republican members of the Senate Foreign Relations Committee and the House Foreign Affairs Committee had been asked.

The election contest was further embittered by the intrusion of religious and ethnic issues, and the Republicans spread slanderous stories about Wilson's personal life. Throughout, Wilson preserved his calm. When a Hughes triumph appeared likely, he acted on a suggestion of House's and decided that, if he was defeated, he would resign in order to avoid a lame-duck regime. On the night of the election, after the *New York Times* and New York *World* had conceded to Hughes, Wilson rose above the surrounding gloom, drank a glass of milk, and went to bed.[21] Returns from the West over the next two days, although favorable to Wilson, were not conclusive,

[19] The Head Usher's Diary, *passim*, Wilson Papers; hereinafter cited as Head Usher's Diary.

[20] House was appalled by the nomination. Link, *Wilson*, IV, 325.

[21] Edith Bolling Wilson, *My Memoir*, p. 115.

and he was on his way to Williamstown to attend the baptism of his new granddaughter, Eleanor Axson Sayre, when, in the morning of November 10, he finally received the news of his victory.

Although the election results vindicated Wilson's policies, he was profoundly disturbed over the prospects of war with Germany. During the campaign, he had stated that the position of neutrals had become "intolerable," and that a "society of nations" to keep the peace was necessary.[22] The conflict in Europe was still a bloody standoff. The Germans had been stopped at Verdun; by November the British offensive on the Somme had come to a halt. Although the Germans had, by and large, observed the *Sussex* pledge, their submarines had exacted a high toll, and the British had maintained their pressure on the neutrals. When the armed British merchantmen *Marina* and *Arabia* were sunk, Wilson told House and Vance McCormick, chairman of the Democratic National Committee, that he did not believe that the American people would support war no matter how many lives were lost at sea. He also made the amazing misstatement that the *Sussex* pledge covered only passenger vessels.[23]

Wilson did not make issues over the *Marina* and *Arabia* sinkings because he had for some months been formulating a peace plan of his own. His opportunity came when the Imperial German Chancellor, Theobald von Bethmann Hollweg, concluded that, should the deadlock continue, Wilson's mediation offered the only alternative to unrestricted submarine warfare. Wilson welcomed the Chancellor's overture, and not even the deportation of Belgian civilians to work in Germany deterred him. At the same time, he put pressure on the financially embarrassed British by tightening credit restrictions. Wilson told House of his plan to intervene on November 14, but he fell ill before he could prepare a draft of a peace note. He described his condition in a letter to House on November 25: "I have had a really overwhelming cold during nearly the whole of the week, and it has sadly thrown my plans out. The paper I had intended to write needed the clearest thinking I could do, and not until to-night have I ventured to begin it. Even now I have gone no further than a skeleton outline. . . . I am so sorry I am not to see you to-morrow, but it would be folly for me to risk the exposure at the present stage of my cold."[24]

The nature of Wilson's illness is not clear. As we know, he was apt to attribute a variety of ailments to a "cold." Mrs. Wilson made no

[22] Speech in Cincinnati, Ohio, October 26, 1910, in Baker and Dodd, eds., *Public Papers of Woodrow Wilson*, IV, 381.
[23] House diary, November 2, 1916.
[24] WW to House, November 24, 1916, Wilson Papers.

mention of a cold and stated that he was weary and unwell—a reaction against the strain of the campaign.[25] Colonel House commented that, on the morning of Wednesday, November 15, Wilson was unusually late for breakfast and looked as if he had had a bad night.[26] Mrs. Wilson was sufficiently alarmed to summon Dr. Grayson. However, the patient was better on the following day. For the next twelve days he spent most of his time in his quarters. He was evidently not confined to bed continuously because he went to his office for cabinet meetings, saw a few official visitors, and played golf several times. On Thursday, November 23, he took a turn for the worse. He went out to the golf course in the morning but did not play and remained in his bedroom all day after canceling his appointments. Despite his indisposition, Wilson worked on a draft of a peace note, which, he told his wife, might prove to be "the greatest piece of work" of his life.[27] The illness was disturbing enough for Wilson to lighten his schedule. Throughout the remainder of 1916, and during 1917 and 1918, he no longer went to his office in the forenoon, but remained in his private quarters in the morning with time out for golf.[28]

Wilson read his draft to House on November 27. The opening paragraph, with its emphasis on "life," indicates the intensity of his feelings. It ran: "The war is disturbing the whole life of the world, making it hard everywhere for governments to serve and safeguard the life of the nations they serve, and all but impossible for the poor to live at all." He deplored the ravages of a war, the causes of which, he said, were obscure. None of the belligerents, he pointed out, had ever stated their war aims. He demanded that the fighting stop and offered his mediation. The foundations of peace, equality of rights among nations, and international good will, he asserted, could not be built on a triumph in which one side would be overwhelmed and humiliated. The belligerents had a right to name the terms of the peace, but the establishment of a league of nations was necessary to preserve it. Wilson emphasized that haste was necessary lest "attrition and ultimate exhaustion" intervene.[29] Possibly, as at Princeton after his stroke of 1906, the quickening of feelings of mortality during his illness added to his sense of urgency.

From the first, Colonel House was distressed by Wilson's plan to intervene. The entire shift from secret diplomacy was contrary to his

[25] Edith Bolling Wilson, *My Memoir*, p. 120.
[26] House diary, November 15, 1916.
[27] Edith Bolling Wilson, *My Memoir*, p. 121.
[28] Head Usher's Diary, *passim*.
[29] Baker, *Wilson*, VI, 380-86.

convictions, and he still wanted to carry out his arrangement with Grey. The Colonel did all that he could to delay and dilute the note; he was especially upset by Wilson's statement that the causes of the war were obscure, and he told the President that the British would regard American intervention to be in Germany's interest. He raised the specter of the Yellow Peril; if the British won, they could destroy the American navy and land Japanese troops. After Wilson suggested that he go to London to press the urgency of the situation, House confided to his diary that he would prefer Hades.[30] On December 20, two days after Wilson sent a revised note, House wrote: "I find the President has nearly destroyed all the work I have done in Europe."[31] When it seemed that a conference might be held, the Colonel lent his best efforts; but for the first time he had openly opposed Wilson and placed his political judgment above his loyalty to the President.

Wilson's effort for peace brought out some negative features of his relationship with Lansing. Despite the latter's high office and technical abilities, Wilson began to regard Lansing as a mere functionary and did not treat him with the same respect that he had accorded Bryan. At the same time, he gave Lansing wide latitude and did not discourage some of his more aggressive policies until some crisis had developed. The Secretary's ego suffered as a consequence, and the severity of his diplomatic notes to London, as well as to Berlin, may have served to salve his wounded pride. Actually, Lansing was pro-British, and his fear that Wilson's plan would endanger Anglo-American relations caused him, as Link has shown, to attempt to sabotage Wilson's peace move. He had no faith in the kind of league of nations which the President envisaged and, while he sent peremptory notes to the Allies, he privately assured British and French diplomats that the United States was on their side. On December 21, the day on which the text of the peace note appeared in the newspapers, Lansing, without consulting Wilson, told reporters that the country was on the "verge of war." The President forced him to retract his statement, and Wilson later told House that he almost decided to demand his resignation.[32] Over the next three years Wilson complained repeatedly about Lansing's failings but did not dismiss him.

House and Lansing's objections apparently had some effect on Wilson because by the time that he issued his peace note, it had undergone radical alterations—House said he had never seen the President make as many changes.[33] It had lost a good deal of its forcefulness

---

[30] House diary, November 14, 1916.
[32] Link, *Wilson*, V, 221-25.

[31] *Ibid.*, December 20, 1916.
[33] House diary, December 20, 1916.

in that the demand for a conference of belligerents had been replaced by a request for a statement of war aims. There was considerable sentiment for peace in all the belligerent countries, but, no matter what language Wilson might have used, his endeavor would probably have failed. Neither the German nor Allied governments were prepared for a peace on any basis other than one calling for large territorial acquisitions and payment of harsh indemnities. The Allies responded to the note with a statement of aims which called for the evacuation of invaded territories with "just reparation," the return to France of Alsace-Lorraine, the liberation of Italians, Roumanians, and Czechoslovaks from foreign domination, the freeing of the subject populations of the Turkish Empire, and the independence of Poland. The Germans agreed to a conference of belligerents but would not reveal terms despite a personal plea by Wilson that their conditions be imparted to him in confidence. Wilson supplemented his diplomatic efforts with his famous "Peace without Victory" speech to the Senate on January 22, 1917. By then, however, time in Berlin had run out for Bethmann. The Imperial government declared that, after February 1, all ships, belligerent and neutral, armed and unarmed, found in specific war zones would be sunk without warning.[34]

Wilson was deeply discouraged by what he regarded as his failure. House noted: "The President was sad and depressed and I did not succeed at any time during the day in lifting him into a better frame of mind. He was deeply disappointed at the sudden unwarranted action of the German Government. We had every reason to believe that within a month the belligerents would be talking peace. . . . The President said he felt as if the world had suddenly reversed itself; that after going from east to west, it had begun to go from west to east and that he could not get his balance."[35]

There was no outward change in the House-Wilson relationship, and the President continued to express affection for his friend. However, the episode caused a further loosening of emotional ties. Wilson suggested that the Colonel might replace Page in London—earlier, he would have been uncomfortable with his counselor so far away—and Mrs. Wilson repeated the offer when House visited the White House for the second inaugural. House declined in each instance. Probably the most significant indication of the change was the substitution in the salutation of Wilson's letters of "My dear House" for "Dearest Friend."

[34] There was one exception. One American passenger ship, painted with red and white stripes and carrying no contraband, would be permitted to sail each week between New York and Falmouth.

[35] House diary, February 1, 1917.

The announcement of unrestricted submarine warfare left Wilson with no option other than to break relations with Germany. (Link suggests that if the Germans had restricted their operation to armed vessels and belligerent merchantmen, he would have avoided a break.) After consulting with House, Lansing, the full cabinet, Stone, and a group of Democratic senators, he ordered that Count von Bernstorff be given his passports. Even then, Wilson continued to hope for a peaceful solution. The Germans granted a month of grace, and continued to observe cruiser rules, while the President refused to arm American merchant vessels as he was constitutionally empowered to do. On February 26, however, a few days before Congress was due to adjourn, he went before that body to request legislation to permit him to arm ships and "to employ any other instrumentalities or methods that may be necessary and adequate to protect our ships and our people in their legitimate and peaceful pursuits on the seas." He was not contemplating, he concluded, only material interests, but "more fundamental things"—the right to life, the rights of humanity, and the righteous passion for justice that was the foundation of all law and liberty and America's existence as a nation. He could not imagine any man with American principles in his heart hesitating to defend these things.[36]

This virtual request to carry out an undeclared naval war, unhampered by congressional control, met with strong resistance. Most senators were not disposed to give the President a free hand. The advocates of intervention, led by Senator Lodge, feared that Wilson would not pursue a strong enough policy, while antiwar senators believed that a naval incident would lead to a full-scale war. Wilson then sought to bring public pressure on Congress by exploiting two events. He decided to release the Zimmermann telegram,[37] the text of which he had been given on February 25, and to make an issue of the sinking, without warning, of the armed British liner *Laconia*, in which several Americans, including two friends of Mrs. Wilson, perished. Waves of indignation and calls for war swept the country, but, after a filibuster by eleven antiwar Democrats and progressive Republicans in the Senate, the session of Congress expired on March 4 without the passage of the armed-ship bill.

Wilson's fury mounted as he followed the debate. Not only had

[36] Link, *Wilson*, V, 301, 346-49.

[37] A telegram from the Foreign Secretary in Berlin to the German Minister to Mexico, Heinrich von Eckhardt, which proposed a German-Mexican alliance in the event of war with the United States. The Mexicans were to seek the aid of Japan, and were promised the lost territories of Texas, Arizona, and New Mexico. The message had been intercepted and decoded by the British. *Ibid.*, pp. 342-45.

some Democratic senators defied his authority but they had shown, in his view, a lack of trust and loyalty. On the afternoon of March 4—since March 4 was a Sunday, the Inaugural had been moved forward to Monday—Wilson denounced his opponents privately to a group of his advisers and complained that he could not put his remarks into his Inaugural Address. House then suggested that he give out his remarks to the newspapers. After gaining the approval of Tumulty, McAdoo, Burleson, and McCormick, Wilson issued the following statement:

"The termination of the last session of the Sixty-fourth Congress by constitutional limitation disclosed a situation unparalleled in the history of the country, perhaps unparalleled in the history of any modern Government." Congress, in the midst of the gravest international crisis in the nation's history, had been "unable to act either to safeguard the country or to vindicate the elementary rights of its citizens." A little "group of eleven Senators" had determined that it should not act. They had prevented adoption, not only of the armed-ship bill, but also of other measures vital to the country's welfare. It would not cure the difficulty, the President went on, to call the Sixty-fifth Congress into extraordinary session. "The paralysis of the Senate would remain," even though Congress was more united in purpose and spirit than it had been within the memory of living man. But the Senate could not act unless its leaders could obtain almost unanimous consent. Its majority was "powerless, helpless." "In the midst of a crisis of extraordinary peril, when only definite and decided action can make the nation safe or shield it from war itself by the aggression of others, action is impossible." And the worst of it was that governments abroad would conclude that they could act as they pleased because the American government could do nothing. "A little group of willful men, representing no opinion but their own, have rendered the great Government of the United States helpless and contemptible."[38]

The language of Wilson's main statement was not only hyperbolic and self-referential but, as Link points out, it grossly misrepresented the facts and cruelly impugned the patriotism of his opponents. It ignored the fact that Wilson's own delay in asking Congress for special authority had been partly responsible for the debâcle. The statement was inaccurate in stating that the filibusterers had been responsible for the failure of other legislation. The Republicans had already indicated that they would force Wilson to call a special session. The

[38] Address to the country, March 4, 1917, in Baker and Dodd, eds., *Public Papers of Woodrow Wilson*, IV, 433-35.

great majority of the senators believed that armed neutrality would lead to war, and those who opposed the bill believed they were being true to the country's tradition in not permitting the President to wage an undeclared war without the express knowledge and consent of Congress.

Wilson may have already fallen ill when he issued his intemperate and ill-conceived remarks. On March 7, Dr. Grayson ordered him to bed for what was officially termed a cold—presumably contracted at the inaugural ceremonies,[39] which had taken place on a cold, blustery day. Wilson remained in his private quarters for another ten days and saw only a few visitors. He canceled a cabinet session scheduled for March 13, but against the Doctor's advice he held a brief meeting three days later. On March 20, he was well enough to play golf with Grayson and met with his cabinet as usual in the afternoon. For reasons already given, it is unlikely that Wilson had a cold, or at least one which necessitated so long a confinement. House, in his diary entry of March 27, speaks of a headache. Ike Hoover reportedly said on March 31: "I never knew him to be more peevish. He's out of sorts, doesn't feel well, and has a headache."[40] Mrs. Wilson, in her not always chronologically accurate memoir, states that her husband suffered from frequent and severe headaches throughout the war years.[41] It is likely that Wilson had experienced the same symptoms during the *Sussex* crisis and when he was writing his peace note. Each episode seems to have been precipitated by emotional tension, and probably Dr. Grayson ordered him to bed because of elevated blood pressure. There is no evidence that Wilson had had another stroke, although his reference to the "paralysis of the Senate" suggests that the fear of one may have been on his mind. It certainly could have been on Dr. Grayson's.

Wilson made the decision for war during this period of illness,

---

[39] Anticipating violence, Colonel House had summoned "Bill" McDonald and had his own automatic ready. However, neither teacher nor pupil had an opportunity to demonstrate the quick draw. House diary, March 5, 1917.

[40] Link, *Wilson*, V, 419-21.

[41] Mrs. Wilson's dramatic description reads: "In the coming years [from 1916] when every nerve was tense with anxiety during the War, and burdens on his shoulders enough to crush the vitality of a giant, there would come days when he was incapacitated by blinding headaches that no medicine could relieve. He would have to give up everything, and the only cure seemed to be sleep. We would make the room cool and dark, and when at last the merciful sleep would come, he would lie for hours in this way, apparently not even breathing. Many a time I have stolen in and leaned over him to listen—to see if he were really alive. Sometimes this sleep would last for five, six, or even eight hours. He would awaken refreshed and able at once to take up work and go on with renewed energy." Edith Bolling Wilson, *My Memoir*, p. 116.

shortly after he received word that German submarines had sunk three American ships, in two cases without warning, and with the loss of fifteen crewmen, on March 18. He came to his conclusion with great misgivings which he expressed in an interview with Frank I. Cobb, editor of the New York *World*. A declaration of war, he told Cobb, would mean that Germany would be beaten so badly that there would be a dictated peace. He predicted, also, that free speech and tolerance would disappear, and that the spirit of reckless brutality would enter into the fiber of national life. It would be impossible, he feared, to fight Germany and maintain the ideals of government that all thinking men shared. However, in the face of Germany's determination to wage all-out submarine warfare he could see no alternative.[42]

The President closed his war message to Congress on April 2 with the following peroration:

"It is a fearful thing to lead this great peaceful people into war, into the most terrible and disastrous of all wars, civilization itself seeming to be in the balance. But the right is more precious than the peace, and we shall fight for the things which we have always carried nearest our hearts—for democracy, for the right of those who submit to authority to have a voice in their own Governments, for the rights and liberties of small nations, for a universal dominion of right by such a concert of free peoples as shall bring peace and safety to all nations and make the world itself at last free. To such a task we can dedicate our lives and our fortunes, everything that we are and everything that we have, with the pride of those who know that the day has come when America is privileged to spend her blood and her might for the principles that gave her birth and happiness and the peace which she has treasured. God helping her, she can do no other."

Could Wilson's emphasis on the word "right" have indicated his own doubts about whether he had done the right thing? He said over and over again that he was struggling for the right policy and was unsure of his ground.[43]

It is Link's opinion that the most important factor in Wilson's decision was "his conviction that American belligerency now offered the surest hope for early peace and the reconstruction of the international community." As a neutral he would continue to be frustrated by both sides, but as a belligerent he would have a place at the peace table and be in a position to insure the establishment of a league of nations.

[42] John L. Heaton, comp., *Cobb of "The World": A Leader in Liberalism* (New York, 1924), pp. 268-70.

[43] War Message to Congress, April 2, 1917, in Baker and Dodd, eds., *Public Papers of Woodrow Wilson*, V, 16.

Wilson was further influenced by the news of the Russian revolution and the announced intention of the new liberal government to carry on the war for democratic aims. Also, he hoped that liberal forces in Germany would gain control and refuse to fight for imperialistic ends.[44]

Consideration may also be given to certain aspects of Wilson's personality, especially his modes of adaptation to stress, and his ability to reconceptualize reality in new cognitive and symbolic patterns. Throughout Wilson's career, themes which, in one context, had been catastrophic, became positive achievements in another. We have seen how he adapted to his lexical difficulties by learning shorthand, and how he had formulated a theory of history which dispensed with the accumulating of detailed facts. He had retrieved his failure as a lawyer by a brilliant conception of the teaching of the law. The very language which had contributed so heavily to his defeats at Princeton helped to launch him on a successful political career. The concepts which he had used to expiate the sin of his extramarital relationship had led to the new morality. After the failure of his peace plan, the symbols of humanity and justice, which had justified the cause of American neutrality, became the moral justification for America's entry into the war.

[44] Link, *Wilson*, V, 426.

CHAPTER XIX

Prelude to Paris

ONE OF WILSON'S great misgivings in asking for a declaration of war was his knowledge of the Allies' intention to impose a conqueror's peace. His apprehensions were confirmed in April, when Arthur Balfour, Grey's successor at the Foreign Office, came to the United States in order, among other reasons, to acquaint Wilson with the details of the secret treaties. These were the clandestine arrangements in which the Allies divided the spoils of victory. One of these arrangements, the Treaty of London, signed in 1915, went far beyond the liberation of oppressed minorities—a war goal which the Allies had proclaimed in their answer to Wilson's peace note of 1916. The Treaty of London provided that Italy, in return for entering the war on the side of the Allies, would receive territories containing large German and Slavic populations.[1] The pact, of course, was a gross violation of Wilson's principle of self-determination.

These treaties had become known even before Balfour revealed them in detail to Wilson and House.[2] The American ambassadors to London, Rome, and Paris had learned about the Treaty of London shortly after it was signed, and had cabled the information to the State Department. The terms were published in the *New York Times*. Senator La Follette had called attention to them in his resolution of August 11, 1917, to the effect that the United States disavowed any intention to continue the war for the territorial aggrandizement of any power.[3] Wilson,

---

[1] The Treaty of London promised Italy the South Tyrol, the Trentino, a strip of the Dalmatian coast, including offshore islands, formal recognition of Italy's possession of the Dodecanese Islands seized from Turkey in 1912, parts of Anatolia, and possible acquisitions in Africa. Along with the Treaty of London, a secret treaty gave Constantinople to Russia; the Sykes-Picot Agreement between the British and French provided for the dismemberment of the Ottoman Empire; and the Treaty of Bucharest promised Hungarian and Bulgarian territory to Rumania.

[2] House diary, April 28 and 30, 1917. Balfour sent a copy of the treaties to Wilson shortly after his return to England. The documents and Wilson's acknowledgement of their receipt are in the Wilson Papers. The absence of any annotation, underlinings, or marginal markings, contrary to Wilson's custom, suggests that he did not read them or, at the most, merely scanned them, since he was already unhappily familiar with most of their contents.

[3] Lawrence E. Gelfand, *The Inquiry: American Preparation for Peace, 1917-1919* (New Haven, Conn., and London, 1963), p. 20.

however, decided to ignore the secret treaties. He evidently accepted House's opinion that any objection would interfere with the unity of the war effort. Wilson hoped that a league of nations would annul any prior secret agreements among its members. At the end of the war, he told House, the Allies would be so exhausted materially that he could force them to accept his program over their treaty obligations.[4]

Although Wilson did not recognize the secret treaties, his awareness of them added to his burden of guilt and dominated his thinking throughout the war. He designated the United States as an associated power rather than as an ally in order to symbolize the difference between his liberal aims and the selfish ambitions of the Entente powers. He insisted on a separate American military command and further dissociated the United States by refusing to appoint a permanent civilian representative to the Supreme War Council. Late in October 1917, Wilson sent House to London to press the Allies to cooperate in the issuance of a liberal statement of war aims. While House was still abroad, the Bolsheviks overthrew the provisional Russian government and called for a "democratic" peace based on self-determination and evacuation of occupied territories. When the Allies refused, the Bolsheviks opened peace negotiations with the Germans and published many of the secret treaties. Wilson, in response, issued the Fourteen Points on January 8, 1918. The first of these reads: "Open covenants of peace, openly arrived at, after which there shall be no private international understandings of any kind but diplomacy shall proceed always frankly and in the public view."[5]

The conflicting roles of war leader and prospective mediator of a just peace posed great problems for Wilson. On the one hand, he had to gain popular support for an all-out war effort. On the other hand, he had to prepare the American people for a settlement in which a liberalized and not too badly defeated Germany would be a partner. He accordingly, over and over again, distinguished the German people from their rulers, the "military masters of Germany." For example, in his war message he had said: "We have no quarrel with the German people. We have no feeling towards them but one of sympathy and friendship. It was not upon their impulse that their government acted in entering this war." Or, again, "We know now . . . that we are not the enemies of the German people and that they are not our enemies."[6]

[4] WW to House, July 21, 1917, House Papers.

[5] The text of Wilson's Fourteen Points Speech can be found in Baker and Dodd, eds., *Public Papers of Woodrow Wilson*, V, 155-62.

[6] War Address, April 2, 1917; Flag Day Address, Washington, D. C., June 14, 1917, *ibid.*, pp. 11, 60-67.

However, Wilson's rhetoric was so stirring, and the administration's propaganda so effective, that Americans had difficulty in differentiating the German people from their Prussian masters. Civil rights, as Wilson had predicted, suffered as a result.

Possibly the most striking example of Wilson's ambivalence toward the war comes from William C. Bullitt, a young official in the State Department, whose admiration for Wilson at the time later turned to hatred. Bullitt reports that, after Wilson had delivered his Annual Message to Congress in December 1917 (in which he denounced German militarism and called for a scrutiny of war aims), the President, with tears in his eyes, turned and said: "Yes, and wasn't it horrible? All those Congressmen and Senators applauding every wretched little warlike thing I had to say, ignoring all the things for which I really care. I hate this war! I hate all war, and the only thing I care about on earth is the peace I am going to make at the end of it."[7]

Wilson of course came under mounting and tremendous pressures as the war progressed. War production had to be built up virtually from scratch. A number of Democratic legislators opposed the draft, and Wilson needed Republican votes to get a selective service bill through Congress. Although the associated governments came to agreement on matters of matériel and strategy, they disagreed about the use of American troops. Above all, fundamental political differences existed. Wilson spoke about the emancipation of the German people, while the Allied governments were far more interested in territorial arrangements, economic concessions, and reparations than in the kind of government in Berlin. Wilson was also fearful that British and French dealings with Japan would work to the detriment of China. The Allies favored a league of nations, but the French wanted either an innocuous debating society or what would in effect be a military alliance against a permanently weakened Germany. The British insisted on maintaining their traditional naval supremacy and hoped to eliminate Germany as a trade rival in the postwar world.

Of all of Wilson's problems, the most baffling was the Russian question. During 1917 the western powers tried to keep the Russians in the war, and Wilson sought the establishment of a democratic government. However, the Bolshevik takeover and the signing of the peace of Brest-Litovsk in March 1918 dashed these hopes. The Allies supported the Whites, or anti-Bolsheviks, in the Russian Civil War, and for months Wilson resisted strong pressure by the British and French to send American divisions to Siberia. Wilson viewed the Rus-

---

[7] Freud and Bullitt, *Thomas Woodrow Wilson*, pp. 200-201.

sian Revolution much as he saw the struggle in Mexico, and he believed that the introduction of foreign troops would only strengthen the forces of reaction and work against the interests of the Russian people. In July 1918 he yielded to Allied pleas of military necessity; he sent small forces to guard military stores at Murmansk and dispatched some 7,000 men to Vladivostok to protect the Czech Legion, stationed along the Trans-Siberian Railway, from the Bolsheviks.[8] In the view of Betty Unterberger, Wilson's actual motive, when he sent troops to Siberia, was to counter Japanese ambitions there.[9] Wilson, in acting independently, expressed the suspicion that the Allies had tried to trick him into a full-scale military intervention.[10] It was in reference to the Russian question that Wilson remarked to House, "It goes to pieces like quicksilver under my touch."[11]

House continued to be Wilson's principal adviser on foreign affairs throughout the war; the two men worked together closely on the preparation of the Fourteen Points address and on the draft of a constitution for the proposed league of nations. Wilson asked his friend to take responsibility for assembling historical, political, geographical, economic, and demographic data for the peace conference by a group of experts subsequently known as The Inquiry.[12] House kept Wilson in touch with liberal and socialist opinion abroad and became an intimate friend of Sir William Wiseman, a British intelligence agent in close touch with the Foreign Office. Wiseman, who had House's qualities of urbanity, inconspicuousness, and persuasiveness, gained great influence over the Colonel and provided him with the kind of entrée into British governmental circles which he had previously enjoyed through Grey. In return, House's influence gave Wise-

[8] The Czechs were former Austro-Hungarian prisoners of war who had been recruited into the Russian army. Following the Treaty of Brest-Litovsk, they retained their identity under a French commander. They formed the most effective fighting force in Russia and were actually in no danger of attack by the disorganized Bolsheviks. Wilson was the victim of misinformation concerning the military stores. According to George Kennan, most of the stores had been removed from Murmansk, and the remainder were at Archangel. George F. Kennan, *Russia and the West Under Lenin and Stalin* (Boston, 1960), pp. 75-79.

[9] Betty Miller Unterberger, *America's Siberian Expedition, 1918-1920: A Study of National Policy* (Durham, N. C., 1956), pp. 231-32.

[10] Wilton B. Fowler, *British-American Relations, 1917-1918: The Role of Sir William Wiseman* (Princeton, N. J., 1969), pp. 193-94.

[11] WW to House, July 8, 1918, House Papers.

[12] House appointed his brother-in-law Sidney E. Mezes, President of the College of the City of New York, as head of The Inquiry. The project was begun in secrecy, but its purpose soon became known.

man personal access to Wilson, who became very fond of the Englishman.[13]

Wilson entrusted House with important diplomatic negotiations, but the Colonel did not have the same voice in overall policy and domestic affairs that he had once enjoyed. Wilson turned down House's suggestion that he, House, take charge of the war mobilization effort[14] and rejected a number of his choices for office. Wilson worked efficiently with a war cabinet which consisted of Secretary of War Newton D. Baker, Secretary of the Navy Daniels, Harry A. Garfield, his old Princeton friend, Herbert Hoover, Vance C. McCormick, chairman of the Democratic National Committee, and Bernard M. Baruch. Despite some disagreements on policy, notably over the nature of the reply to the Pope's mediation offer of August 1917,[15] Wilson and House remained good friends. The Wilsons took summer cruises to visit the Houses at Magnolia, Massachusetts, and House won favor with Mrs. Wilson. The latter two were united in their opposition to Tumulty and they persuaded Wilson to promote Cary Grayson to the rank of rear admiral over more than one hundred more experienced officers. House felt very close to his chief when, prior to departing on a mission to England and France in November 1917, he wrote: "The friendship and affection shown me by the President . . . touches me deeply. There is no subject too intimate to be discussed before me."[16]

There is little specific information about Wilson's health for reasons already mentioned. He seems to have been relatively well through 1917, but, in 1918, there are more references to his fatigue and to his spending most of the day in his private quarters.[17] However, Wilson maintained his routine of golf and motoring and rarely had other appointments on the Tuesdays and Fridays on which he met with his

[13] Wiseman served virtually as British ambassador. Wilson and House found it difficult to work with Sir Cecil Spring Rice, who was not recalled until January 1918. Spring Rice suffered from Graves disease, a condition often associated with marked emotional instability. Wilson called him "a highly excitable invalid." House diary, November 28, 1915, PWW, Vol. 35, p. 260. Moreover, Spring Rice was a close friend of Roosevelt and Lodge. Wilson found Wiseman far more congenial than Spring Rice's successor, Lord Reading. For fascinating studies of Wiseman, see Fowler, British-American Relations, and Arthur Willert, The Road to Safety: A Study in Anglo-American Relations (New York, 1952).

[14] House diary, July 4, 1917.

[15] House complained in his diary that Wilson's mind was not running parallel with his own. Ibid., August 18, 1917.

[16] Ibid., October 24, 1917.

[17] Ibid., December 30, 1917, February 24, 27, March 4, 1918; Head Usher's diary, January 24, 25, and 26, February 15, 16, and 19, March 8, May 2, 9, and 23, 1918.

cabinet. He worked on his correspondence in the evenings and attended the theater several times a week. Wilson tended to joke about his weariness. At a theatrical performance in May, in which he was impersonated, he acknowledged the applause of the audience and told them that they were laboring under a delusion; they were not seeing the President of the United States, but really a tired man having a good time.[18] He wrote to House in July: "I am very tired, for there never were so many problems per diem it seems to me, as there are now. But I am well. *We* are well."[19] When the worried House asked Dr. Grayson if Wilson could stand another term in office, the Doctor gave the oracular answer that he might go on for another ten years "if nothing untoward happened."[20]

Wilson also showed changes in his behavioral responses to stress, and several episodes occurred in which outbursts of anger almost led to embarrassing international consequences. After the breakthrough by the Germans on the Somme during the Second Battle of the Marne in 1918, in which the British suffered enormous losses, Lord Reading, in a speech at the Lotos Club, appealed for more American troops. Upset by the implications that American aid had been insufficient, Wilson wanted to ask for the Ambassador's recall.[21] When Prime Minister William Hughes of Australia, a strong advocate of commercial punishment of Germany, proposed to come to the United States on a speaking tour, Wilson ordered the London embassy to deny him a visa, but was persuaded to act more diplomatically.[22] Wiseman observed that Wilson had a "one-track mind."[23] Louis D. Brandeis told Ray Stannard Baker that, before August 1918, Wilson had been a bold and independent leader, but that, after that time, Wilson's judgment was not as good as it had been before, and that he did things which were "unnatural" to him.[24]

Edmund Starling, one of the Secret Service agents assigned to protect the President, wrote that the first episode of unusual behavior occurred in December 1917. The presidential car went through a stop sign, and Wilson spoke coldly to the watchman for having scolded the driver.[25] Wilson's behavior, trivial in itself, was in sharp contrast to his habitual

[18] House diary, May 17, 1918.
[19] WW to House, July 8, 1918, House Papers.
[20] House diary, August 18, 1918.
[21] *Ibid.*, March 28, 1918.
[22] Fowler, *British-American Relations*, pp. 213-14.
[23] *Ibid.*, p. 207.
[24] Memorandum of interview with Louis D. Brandeis, March 23, 1929, Baker Papers.
[25] Thomas W. Sugrue and Edmund W. Starling, *Starling of the White House* (New York, 1946), pp. 97-98.

courtesy toward subordinates. He had reacted quite differently in an almost identical situation earlier.[26] Psychologically, the incident was significant because motoring was a rite with Wilson. It relaxed him and drove the cares of the world away, its metaphors dramatized political issues, and his insistence on set and numbered car routes gave him a sense of control of his environment. Starling commented that the incident was a forecast of things to come.

Wilson also became more defensive, suspicious, and secretive. He refused to let his Fourteen Points address be known in advance to the press, because, he said, the newspapers invariably speculated on what he would say, and such forecasts were often taken for what he actually said.[27] He expressed the idea that the crank letters he received were connected with his difficulties with Congress.[28] While the Chamberlain Senate Committee on Military Affairs was carrying on an investigation of alleged inefficiency in the War Department,[29] Wilson and House attended a service at the Washington Cathedral. It seemed to Wilson— and House agreed—that the minister was about to preach about the alleged deficiencies, but changed his mind when he saw Wilson in the congregation.[30] Wilson became less discreet in his personal criticisms: he told several senators that he could not consult with Hitchcock[31] because he could no longer trust him with information.[32]

There is also evidence, particularly in the latter part of 1918, that

[26] Dr. Grayson relates that, one evening, a bicycle policeman stopped the President's car on 16th Street. A brief exchange ensued between the policeman and the Secret Service agent in the front seat. However, once the policeman recognized the car, he recoiled in embarrassment. Meanwhile, Wilson had awakened from a nap and asked what had happened. When the policeman apologized, he answered, "Tell me what is the matter. If we are disobeying any law I must know it. I am not exempt from the law. On the contrary, I of all people must observe the laws." Grayson, *An Intimate Memoir*, p. 48.

[27] House diary, January 9, 1918.

[28] The author's experience with crank letters to various Presidents is that writers are too preoccupied with their own problems to follow the workings of Congress. Edwin A. Weinstein and Olga G. Lyerly, "Symbolic Aspects of Presidential Assassination," *Psychiatry*, XXXII (1969), 1-11.

[29] Democratic Senator George E. Chamberlain of Oregon. Wilson, in a public statement, called Chamberlain's charges "astonishing and absolutely unjustified distortions of the truth," but he did admit that there had been "delays and disappointments and partial miscarriages of plans." See Wilson's statement, January 21, 1918, in Baker and Dodd, eds., *Public Papers of Woodrow Wilson*, V, 167.

[30] House diary, February 24, 1918.

[31] Senator Gilbert M. Hitchcock of Nebraska had succeeded William J. Stone of Missouri as chairman of the Foreign Relations Committee after Stone had sustained an incapacitating stroke.

[32] House diary, May 17, 1918.

Wilson's memory was not as good as it had been. In August 1917 he had commented to Newton D. Baker that he was growing absent-minded.[33] A year later, after telling House that he could not remember what conclusion he had come to after a meeting with Paul S. Reinsch, Minister to China, he commented that his mind was becoming "leaky." He adopted the practice of having a memorandum written by persons with whom he had spoken.[34] In the hectic days surrounding his departure for the peace conference, he made decisions which he later forgot.[35] These incidents also reflected Wilson's lack of a personal staff that could help to keep him abreast of details.

Diminished emotional control, greater egocentricity, increased suspiciousness and secrecy, and lapses in judgment and memory are common manifestations of cerebral arteriosclerosis. In Wilson's case, the symptoms seem to have been brought on by a combination of his vascular disease and the extraordinary degree of external stress to which he was subjected. In 1918 events were growing more complex and unpredictable, and much of Wilson's behavior seems to have been a defense against feelings of incapacity and a sense that he was no longer in control of his environment.

The history of Wilson's attitude toward the constitution of the proposed league of nations indicates his growing egocentricity. Before the war, he had been quite open about his ideas, and, in a speech in May 1916, he had virtually endorsed the purposes of the League to Enforce Peace.[36] In March 1917 he called in the French Ambassador, Jean Jules Jusserand, and expounded his plan of a universal entente with a mutual obligation to submit disputes to a conference of non-involved countries, out of which a league would gradually evolve. At about the same time, he outlined a "Bases of Peace" for the guidance of the State Department. These were mutual guarantees of political independence,

[33] WW to Newton D. Baker, August 17, 1917, Wilson Papers.

[34] House diary, August 19, 1918.

[35] One was the appointment of two men whom he disliked to the secretariat of the Peace Commission; another was the authorization of the appointment of John Foster Dulles, a young State Department officer, to be the exclusive channel of statistical information at the Paris Peace Conference. *Ibid.*, December 14, 1919; Freud and Bullitt, *Thomas Woodrow Wilson*, p. 205; Gelfand, *The Inquiry*, pp. 177-78.

[36] The League to Enforce Peace was founded in June 1915, with former President Taft as its president. It called for submission of international disputes to an international court, while nonlegal disputes would be subjected to arbitration. It envisaged the use of force against aggressors in certain circumstances. Many of the leaders of the League to Enforce Peace were Republicans. Lodge had been a member but withdrew after Wilson, in his "Peace Without Victory" speech of January 1917, conjoined the league plan with the liberal peace program. Ruhl J. Bartlett, *The League to Enforce Peace* (Chapel Hill, N. C., 1944), *passim.*

territorial integrity, equal opportunities of trade, and limitation of armaments. Probably with reference to the program of the League to Enforce Peace, he suggested that it would not be necessary to set up a permanent tribunal or administrative agency, but only to maintain an office of correspondence to act as a clearing house for information.[37]

From early 1918 onward, however, Wilson became progressively more proprietary about the league and consulted directly with no one except House. When A. Lawrence Lowell, on behalf of the League to Enforce Peace, suggested that he be permitted to establish contact with interested groups abroad, Wilson replied, "I should consider it very embarrassing to have a private organization like the League to Enforce Peace take this matter up, since the immediate establishment of a league of nations is a question of government policy not only, but constitutes part of the intricate web now being woven between the associated governments."[38] Actually, no web was being woven between the governments: House had been carrying on informal conversations, but Wilson refused to appoint a commission to confer with the official British committee on a league of nations.[39] Moreover, Wilson discouraged the publication of the committee findings, which were known as the Phillimore report. He wrote to House in a more personal vein: "The thing I wanted particularly to see you about when I sent the message through Gordon[40] was the folly of these League to Enforce Peace butters-in. We must head them off one way or another. Bain-

[37] Arthur S. Link, *Woodrow Wilson: Revolution, War, and Peace* (Arlington Heights, Ill., 1979), pp. 75-77. One year later, Wilson, in a letter to House, expressed these ideas in more metaphorical fashion: "My own conviction, as you know, is that the administrative constitution of the League must *grow* and not be made; that we must *begin* with solemn covenants, covering mutual guarantees of political independence and territorial integrity (if the final territorial agreements of the peace conference are fair and satisfactory and *ought* to be perpetuated), but that the method of carrying those mutual pledges out should be left to develop of itself, case by case. Any attempt to begin by putting executive authority in the hands of any particular group of powers would be to sow a harvest of jealousy and distrust which would spring up at once and choke the whole thing. To take one thing, and only one, but quite sufficient in itself: The United States Senate would never ratify any treaty which put the force of the United States at the disposal of any such group or body. Why begin at the impossible end when there is a possible end and it is feasible to plant a system which will slowly but surely ripen into fruition?" WW to House, March 2, 1918, House Papers.

[38] A. Lawrence Lowell to WW, July 10, 1918; Wilson to A. L. Lowell, July 11, 1918, Wilson Papers.

[39] A group of experts in international law headed by Lord Phillimore, appointed by Balfour, had drawn up an interim report which included a draft of a constitution for a league.

[40] Gordon Auchincloss, House's son-in-law, for whom House had obtained a position in the State Department.

bridge Colby[41] is on rather cordial terms with Mr. Taft and he saw Mr. T. for me and thinks he has prevented the particular thing I feared, that they would insist upon a discussion now of the *constitution* of the league of nations: but Mr. T. never stays put. I had before that written to Mr. Marburg of Baltimore,[42] one of the principal wool-gatherers, stating my position very flatly."[43]

Wilson feared that, if his peace plans became known, they would be attacked by Republicans and isolationists. He adopted the strategy of avoiding any specific statements before the peace conference. He expected that the league would be made an integral part of the peace settlement and that the Senate would have no choice but to accept it. Despite the urging of Stockton Axson and House, Wilson refused to discuss his program with congressional leaders of either party. He continued to evade consultations with the British, although the draft of a constitution for a league, which he and House prepared, was based on the Phillimore report. He further justified his action by telling Wiseman that to arrange for a league before the peace conference convened would be to construct a sort of Holy Alliance against Germany.[44]

The British and French, less dependent on American aid as the war drew to an end, now asserted their claims more vigorously. There was still no agreement on peace terms, and Wilson coped with the problem by a method by which he had solved many political crises. On September 27, 1918, he delivered in New York one of the most dramatic speeches of his career. He asked rhetorically:

"Shall the military power of any nation or group of nations be suffered to determine the fortunes of peoples over whom they have no right to rule except the right of force?

"Shall strong nations be free to wrong weak nations and make them subject to their purpose and interest?

"Shall peoples be ruled and dominated, even in their own internal affairs, by arbitrary and irresponsible force or by their own will and choice?

"Shall there be a common standard of right and privilege for all peoples and nations, or shall the strong do as they will and the weak suffer without redress?

---

[41] A New York lawyer and former Progressive party leader, who had supported Wilson in 1916. After Wilson dismissed Lansing in 1920, he appointed Colby as Secretary of State.

[42] Theodore Marburg, one of the leaders of the League to Enforce Peace.

[43] WW to House, March 20, 1918, House Papers.

[44] Fowler, *British-American Relations*, p. 215.

"Shall the assertion of right be haphazard and by casual alliance, or shall there be a common concert to oblige the observation of common rights?"

He then, in somewhat repetitive fashion, explained that the constitution of the league would have to wait until Germany had redeemed her character:

"And, as I see it, the constitution of that League of Nations and the clear definitions of its objects must be a part, is in a sense the most essential part, of the peace settlement itself. It cannot be formed now. If formed now, it would merely be a new alliance confined to the nations associated against a common enemy. It is not likely that it could be formed after the settlement. It is necessary to guarantee the peace; and the peace cannot be guaranteed as an afterthought. The reason, to speak in plain terms again, why it must be guaranteed is that there will be parties to the peace whose promises have proved untrustworthy, and means must be found in connection with the peace settlement itself to remove that source of insecurity. It would be folly to leave the guarantee to the subsequent voluntary action of the governments we have seen destroy Russia and deceive Rumania."

Wilson went on to denounce secret alliances, understandings, and treaties, and—in an obvious reference to British intentions—condemned postwar economic boycotts. He did not doubt, he said, that the leaders of the Associated Powers entertained a like purpose. However, he added: "Because the air every now and again gets darkened by mists and groundless doubtings and mischievous perversions of counsel," it was necessary once again to sweep aside all "irresponsible talk about peace intrigues and weakening morale and doubtful purpose on the part of those in authority utterly, and if need be unceremoniously, and say things in the plainest words that can be found, even when it is only to say over again what has been said before, quite as plainly if in less varnished terms."

Then, in a manner similar to the way in which he had once inspired his audiences in Princeton and New Jersey, he declared:

"And the forces that fight for them [the issues of the war] draw into closer and closer array, organize their millions in more and more unconquerable might, as they become more and more distinct to the thought and purpose of the peoples engaged. It is the peculiarity of this great war that, while statesmen have seemed to cast about for definitions of their purpose and have sometimes seemed to shift their ground and point of view, the thought of the mass of men whom statesmen are supposed to instruct and lead has grown more and more unclouded; more and more certain of what it is that they are fighting for. National purposes have fallen more and more into the background, and the common purpose of enlightened mankind has taken their place. The counsels of plain men have become on all hands more simple and straightforward and more unified than the counsels of sophisticated men of affairs, who still retain the impression that they are playing a game of power and playing for high stakes. That is why I have said that this is a peoples' war, not a statesmen's. Statesmen must follow the clarified common thought or be broken."[45]

Wilson's address heartened masses of people around the world and may have hastened the overthrow of the German military government, but it did nothing to hasten agreement with the Allies. On October 6 the Kaiser's new government, headed by Prince Max of Baden, asked for an armistice and the summoning of a conference of belligerents to discuss a peace based on the Fourteen Points and Wilson's subsequent war addresses. A series of notes between Wilson and the Germans drew the acceptance from the Germans of the military supremacy of the Associated and Allied Powers and made it certain that Germany could not resume offensive operations. Reasonable terms, Wilson also indicated, would depend on the establishment of a representative democratic government in Germany. Assured that such a German government now existed, Wilson transmitted the correspondence to the Allies for their approval. He opposed occupation of German territory and wanted to preserve enough German military power to serve as a counterweight to the French.[46] The French and British, who had never officially recognized the Fourteen Points as the basis of the peace, had meanwhile prepared harsher armistice terms. Marshal Ferdinand Foch demanded unconditional surrender and the occupation of the Rhineland, and the British called for the surrender to them of the entire German battle fleet. After some reluctance to send an envoy to the Supreme War Council,[47] Wilson dispatched House to Paris. After threatening that the United States would negotiate a separate peace, the Colonel persuaded the Allies to accept the Fourteen Points as the basis of the settlement. The agreement, however, was amended to include a British reservation concerning the freedom of the seas, and

[45] Fourth Liberty Loan Address, September 27, 1918, Baker and Dodd, eds., *Public Papers of Woodrow Wilson*, V, 253-61.

[46] WW to House, October 28, 1918, House Papers. Unfortunately for secrecy, the code in which Wilson and House communicated was known to the British.

[47] Wilson reportedly told the French Ambassador that an agent might be too influenced by alien surroundings to be able to speak as an American. J. J. Jusserand to the Foreign Ministry, October 11 and 12, 1918, cited in Arthur Walworth, *America's Moment, 1918: American Diplomacy at the End of World War I* (New York, 1977), p. 24.

a French elucidation that Germany be required to pay for civilian damages caused by her aggressions. House also agreed to the occupation of the Rhineland and the surrender of the German battle fleet. Nevertheless, House cabled the President that they had won a great diplomatic victory.[48]

Historians agree that one of Wilson's greatest mistakes was to issue, on October 25, an appeal for the election of a Democratic Congress in 1918. Since the issue here concerns mainly Wilson's language, it is presented in full. It reads:

"The congressional elections are at hand. They occur in the most critical period our country has ever faced or is likely to face in our time. If you have approved of my leadership and wish me to continue to be your unembarrassed spokesman in affairs at home and abroad, I earnestly beg that you will express yourselves unmistakably to that effect by returning a Democratic majority to both the Senate and the House of Representatives. I am your servant and will accept your judgment without cavil, but my power to administer the great trust assigned me by the Constitution would be seriously impaired should your judgment be adverse, and I must frankly tell you so because so many critical issues depend upon your verdict. No scruple of taste must in grim times like these be allowed to stand in the way of speaking the plain truth.

"I have no thought of suggesting that any political party is paramount in matters of patriotism. I feel too keenly the sacrifices which have been made in this war by all our citizens, irrespective of party affiliations, to harbor such an idea. I mean only that the difficulties and delicacies of our present task are of a sort that makes it imperatively necessary that the nation should give its undivided support to the government under a unified leadership, and that a Republican Congress would divide the leadership.

"The leaders of the minority in the present Congress have unquestionably been pro-war, but they have been anti-administration. At almost every turn, since we entered the war they have sought to take the choice of policy and the conduct of the war out of my hands and put it under the control of instrumentalities of their own choosing. This is no time either for divided counsel or for divided leadership. Unity of command is as necessary now in civil action as it is upon the field of battle. If the control of the House and Senate should be taken

---

[48] As Inga Floto points out, it was a victory for England and France, particularly the latter. French occupation of the Rhineland added heavily to Wilson's problems at Paris. Inga Floto, *Colonel House in Paris: A Study of American Policy at the Paris Peace Conference 1919* (Aarhaus, Denmark, 1973), p. 45.

away from the party now in power, an opposing majority could assume control of legislation and oblige all action to be taken amidst contest and obstruction.

"The return of a Republic majority to either house of the Congress would, moreover, certainly be interpreted on the other side of the water as a repudiation of my leadership. Spokesmen of the Republican party are urging you to elect a Republican Congress in order to back up and support the President, but even if they should in this way impose upon some credulous voters on this side of the water, they would impose on no one on the other side. It is well understood there as well as here that the Republican leaders desire not so much to support the President as to control him. The peoples of the allied countries with whom we are associated against Germany are quite familiar with the significance of elections. They would find it very difficult to believe that the voters of the United States had chosen to support their President by electing to the Congress a majority controlled by those who are not in fact in sympathy with the attitude and action of the administration.

"I need not tell you, my fellow countrymen, that I am asking your support not for my own sake or for the sake of a political party, but for the sake of the nation itself, in order that its inward unity of purpose may be evident to all the world. In ordinary times, I would not feel at liberty to make such an appeal to you. In ordinary times, divided counsels can be endured without permanent hurt to the country. But these are not ordinary times. If in these critical days it is your wish to sustain me with undivided minds, I beg that you will say so in a way which it will not be possible to misunderstand either here at home or among our associates on the other side of the sea. I submit my difficulties and my hopes to you."[49]

The reader will note the emphasis on "control," the frequent use of the first syntactical person,[50] and Wilson's favorite "other side of the water."

Much of what Wilson said was true. The Republicans had supported the war—more enthusiastically in fact than many Democrats—and they were determined to have a say in the peace. They had been waging a vigorous campaign to win control of Congress. They had attacked the Fourteen Points, particularly the one relating to the removal of trade barriers; and the Republican press accused Wilson of leading the

[49] Baker and Dodd, eds., *Public Papers of Woodrow Wilson*, V, 286-88.

[50] Wilson used the personal pronouns "I," "my," and "me" eight times more frequently than he had in his first Inaugural Address. The usage may indicate increased anxiety.

country toward socialism. Senator Miles Poindexter of Washington claimed that Wilson had no constitutional authority to negotiate, and he introduced a resolution forbidding peace talks until Germany had surrendered and making it illegal for any governmental official to answer a German note. Even the moderate Taft criticized Wilson for not having consulted immediately with Prime Minister David Lloyd George and Premier Georges Clemenceau. Lodge and Roosevelt demanded unconditional surrender and a peace, the latter declared, to be dictated "by the hammering of guns" and not to "the clicking of typewriters."[51]

Wilson issued his statement in response to pleas from Democratic congressmen and senators up for reelection and on the advice of some of his principal domestic advisers.[52] He arrived at the final working draft only after considerable hesitation and indecision. At first he thought that he would make his appeal in the form of a letter to a prominent Democrat, who would then publish it. Then he prepared a draft with some caustic references to Lodge and other Republican super-patriots, but was persuaded to alter it. On October 22 he wrote to Senator Hitchcock that it would be safer to "leave the matter to the good sense" of voters who could "read English" than to respond to "perversions and misrepresentations."[53] Roosevelt's taunt, which appeared in the newspapers on the morning of October 25, may have been the precipitating factor. That evening, Wilson personally typed out his final draft.

The Republicans won majorities in both houses of Congress, by a margin of two votes in the Senate, and Lodge would become the chairman of the Foreign Relations Committee in the next Congress. Ironically, the election did not prove to be a clear test of the President's leadership. In Livermore's opinion, the deciding factor was the resentment of midwestern farmers over grain ceilings while southern cotton went uncontrolled.[54] Wilson, however, blamed his defeat on the insufficient loyalty of Democratic congressmen.

Wilson had planned originally to have Colonel House represent him at the peace conference but, after House's difficulties in Paris, he

[51] Seward W. Livermore, *Politics Is Adjourned: Woodrow Wilson and the War Congress, 1916-18* (Middletown, Conn., 1966), *passim*; Arno J. Mayer, *Politics and Diplomacy of Peace Making: Containment and Counterrevolution at Versailles, 1918-1919* (New York, 1967), *passim*.

[52] Tumulty, Burleson, Homer S. Cummings, vice-chairman of the Democratic National Committee, and Edward W. Pou, chairman of the House Rules Committee.

[53] WW to Hitchcock, October 22, 1918, Wilson Papers.

[54] S. W. Livermore, "The Sectional Issue in the 1918 Congressional Elections," *Mississippi Valley Historical Review*, XXV (June 1948), 29-60.

decided to go in person. "I . . . assume that the Allies cannot honorably turn the present discussions into a peace conference without me," he cabled House.[55] He appointed House, Lansing, and two able, but politically obscure, Republicans[56] as the other members of the commission.

The language in which Wilson justified his rejection of prominent Republicans indicates the degree to which the bitterness of the election campaign had affected him. He vehemently turned down House's suggestion that he appoint Root and Taft, even though he had not voiced any serious objection when Mrs. Wilson had raised the question during the previous January.[57] Wilson thought that Root was a hopeless reactionary and that, at the age of seventy-three, his mind was narrowing and was losing its resiliency.[58] Wilson wrote to Richard Hooker, editor of the *Springfield Republican*, a newspaper friendly to the administration: "I would not dare take Mr. Taft. I have lost all confidence in his character. And the other prominent Republicans whom one would naturally choose are already committed to do everything possible to prevent the Peace Conference from acting upon the peace terms which they have already agreed to.[59] It is a distressing situation indeed, but one which they themselves have created."[60]

The President and Mrs. Wilson sailed for France aboard *U.S.S. George Washington* on December 4. The trip is very well documented by the diary entries of Dr. Grayson, "Ike" Hoover, and Mrs. Wilson's secretary, Edith Benham, and notes of a talk to members of The Inquiry. After spending the first forty-eight hours resting in his cabin—on account of a "husky" voice suggestive of a cold, Grayson recorded[61]—Wilson appeared brisk and genial and took a two-mile walk about the deck. He gave his views to reporters over the next few days. He told them that the Allies were determined to get as much out of Germany as they could, even though they knew that she was down and out. What the Allies should get would be determined by what they were entitled to, and by what Germany could afford. Italy, he said, had an entirely different idea of what she should get than his

---

[55] WW to House, October 29, 1918, House Papers.

[56] General Tasker H. Bliss, a nominal Republican and the American military member of the Supreme War Council, and Henry White, a veteran diplomat, who had been Roosevelt's representative at the Algeciras Conference of 1906.

[57] House diary, January 27, 1918.

[58] *Ibid.*, December 1, 1918.

[59] Congress had never officially endorsed the Fourteen Points.

[60] WW to Richard Hooker, November 29, 1918, Wilson Papers.

[61] Grayson diary, December 4, 1918.

advisers had, but he would deal with the Italians generously.[62] More than ever, he affirmed, a peace without victory was essential. England had infringed on American neutral rights on the same grounds of necessity which had prompted Germany to invade Belgium. Wilson said that he was in favor of admitting Germany to the league but, in view of her present chaotic state,[63] she should go through a period of probation. Wilson did not think that the Kaiser was entirely responsible for the war—there was evidence that he had been coerced—and he, Wilson, believed that the war was the product of the German General Staff system.[64]

Wilson also discussed his aims with the experts of The Inquiry. He knew that absolute justice could not be obtained in each case, but he promised to do his best. On a more belligerent note, he charged that the United States would be the only disinterested party at the peace conference, and that the peoples of Europe were being betrayed by leaders who did not truly represent them.[65] Wilson told the scholars that, although he expected them to work through the American commissioners, he wanted them to feel free to come straight to him with anything that affected a critical decision. "Tell me what is right and I'll fight for it," he said.[66] With her most distinguished passenger in a sanguine mood, *George Washington* entered the harbor of Brest on December 13.

[62] When Wilson was approached by the Italian Ambassador, Count Macchi di Cellere, he put him off with a pleasant comment. *Ibid.*, December 7, 1918.

[63] Food was short, and the provisional government was threatened with a Bolshevik revolution.

[64] Grayson diary, December 11, 1918.

[65] Wilson, still smarting from his defeat by the Republicans, was obviously self-referential. Lloyd George, running on a platform calling for a punitive peace, soon won a smashing electoral victory, and Clemenceau gained an overwhelming vote of confidence in the Chamber of Deputies.

[66] Ray Stannard Baker, *Woodrow Wilson and World Settlement,* 3 vols. (Garden City, N. Y., 1923), I, 10.

CHAPTER XX

The Paris Peace Conference

THE PARIS PEACE CONFERENCE opened on January 18, 1919, after the President and Mrs. Wilson had returned from triumphal tours of England and Italy. The first matters taken up were the preparation of a constitution for a league of nations and the chaotic conditions in eastern Europe, particularly in Russia. The long-standing differences among the victors soon surfaced. Foch advocated an invasion of Russia to overthrow the Bolshevik regime, while Wilson favored sending food to relieve widespread starvation and worked for a conference among the contending factions. The French wanted strong Polish and Czechoslovakian states—containing large German minorities—and an independent Rhenish republic under French control, but Wilson believed that such a policy would only lead to new irredenta. The British opposed the French because they did not want French military domination of the Continent. Quarrels and minor wars occurred among the successor states of the Central Empires, and Italy and Yugoslavia were at odds over Dalmatia. The question of reparations was still unanswered. Wilson thought that the figures which the British and French put forth were absurd; when Lloyd George proposed the formation of a committee for "reparations and indemnities," Wilson asked that the latter term be stricken. The Covenant of the League of Nations was adopted by the Plenary Session on February 14. The only other major issue which had been settled when Wilson left for the United States on the following day was the creation of a system of mandates for the former German colonies.

Wilson returned to Washington to attend to accumulated domestic business and to cope with Republican opposition to the League.[1] He followed House's suggestion and gave a dinner for the members of the congressional committees concerned with foreign affairs. At the

---

[1] Ray Stannard Baker, Wilson's press relations chief, was aboard *George Washington* on its way back to the United States. Wilson rested a good deal and went to the movies so frequently that Baker wondered how he could stand such trash. Wilson attended a minstrel show put on by the crew and was not amused when the "leading lady" put "her" arms around him and chucked him under the chin. Franklin D. Roosevelt never forgot the look on Wilson's face. Baker diary, March 8, 1919; Franklin D. Roosevelt to RSB, October 3, 1939, Baker Papers.

dinner, he discussed the Covenant at length, but Lodge remained un-
convinced. Two days before the Wilsons were to sail for France, Lodge
read in the Senate a round robin signed by thirty-seven Republican
senators—more than enough to defeat approval of a treaty—which
declared that the Covenant of the League of Nations, in its present
form, was unacceptable.

Wilson replied to Lodge in a speech at the Metropolitan Opera
House on March 4. He claimed that an overwhelming majority of
Americans favored the League[2] and praised the support of Taft, who
had preceded him. Wilson said that, even if the League should prove
to be merely a debating society, prior discussions among the belligerents for a single week would have prevented the outbreak of war
in 1914. Wilson promised that, when he came back with the treaty,
the "gentlemen on this side will find . . . so many threads of the treaty
tied to the covenant that you cannot dissect the covenant from the
treaty without destroying the whole vital structure." "The structure
of peace," he declared, "will not be vital without the League of Nations, and no man is going to bring back a cadaver with him." He
said that the average American was often selfish, but he was also
willing to die for an ideal. American soldiers had crossed the sea, not
only to defeat Germany, but to show "that the United States . . . would
go anywhere where the rights of mankind were threatened."[3] Despite
his defiant words, Wilson accepted suggestions for modification of the
Covenant in order to attract more Republican and isolationist support.
The changes provided for the right of withdrawal from the League,
the right of member nations to refuse a mandate, the exclusion of
domestic matters, such as the tariff and control of immigration, from
the jurisdiction of the League, and the approval of "regional agreements" such as the Monroe Doctrine.

Wilson was dismayed, on his arrival at Brest, to find that House,
despite explicit instructions to the contrary, had agreed to a preliminary treaty without the Covenant and had acquiesced in the establishment of a Rhenish Republic under French control. Wilson immediately announced his opposition and fought the French vigorously
in the Council of Four. The Paris newspapers ridiculed Wilson and
accused him of trying to rob France of the fruits of her victory. The
French attacks on the Covenant were so bitter that Wilson wondered

[2] A *Literary Digest* newspaper poll of April 5, 1919, showed that almost 10,000,000
Americans supported the League and that more than 4,000,000 persons opposed it.
The main opposition came from the Hearst press. Thomas A. Bailey, *Woodrow Wilson
and the Lost Peace* (New York, 1944), p. 354.

[3] Baker and Dodd, eds., *Public Papers of Woodrow Wilson*, V, 444-55.

privately if the French wanted to renew the war.[4] Clemenceau presented a new demand (which he had discussed previously with House) for the Saar Valley for which, Wilson pointed out, there was not even a valid historical basis. As other nations pressed their claims, Wilson reminded the Council that all of the ancient injustices of Europe could not be corrected.[5] Wilson continued to oppose military action against the Bolshevik regime and voiced strong objections to French and Italian proposals that Vienna, Budapest, and Lemberg be occupied against the threat of revolution.[6] While the French and British wrangled over their shares of reparations, Wilson stated that, even though he was aware of the ways in which the Germans might seek to evade their obligations, they should be invited to discuss the matter.[7] He was incredulous when Clemenceau proposed that the French occupy German territories as a guarantee that the indemnity would be paid.[8] The conferees were not only apart on major issues, but they spent hours discussing the ethnic makeup of obscure towns and the courses of railroads and rivers.

Tempers flared under the strain. After one particularly stormy session on reparations, Clemenceau accused Wilson of being pro-German and of ignoring the sufferings of the French. The conference came close to disruption when, on March 28, each man threatened to resign. Wilson persevered in his efforts for a just peace. He changed habits of many years: he gave up the games of golf he had been able to play occasionally, went motoring only on Sundays, and on some days worked as long as ten hours. Unlike other men, he did not find relaxation in discussing matters with his colleagues. Another problem was that he did not have an adequate administrative staff.[9] By the beginning of April, Wilson seemed to Baker to be completely fagged out. "Sometimes . . . I went up to see him in the evening after the meetings of the Four, he looked utterly beaten, worn out, his face quite haggard and one side of it and the eye twitching painfully;[10] but the next morning he would appear refreshed and eager to go on with the fight."[11] On March 28 Wilson replied to Baker's suggestion that he

[4] Grayson diary, March 22, 1919.

[5] Paul Mantoux, *Paris Peace Conference, 1919; Proceedings of the Council of Four, March 24-April 18*, John B. Whitton, trans. (Geneva, 1964), p. 45.

[6] *Ibid.*, pp. 32-35.   [7] *Ibid.*, p. 39.

[8] *Ibid.*, p. 63.

[9] House had assured him that his own large staff would handle communications and other administrative matters. House diary, December 14, 1918.

[10] Wilson's long-standing tic was not accompanied by pain. Rather, it may have been painful for Baker to watch him.

[11] Baker, *Woodrow Wilson and World Settlement*, II, 43.

issue a public statement: "If I were to tell the truth, I should have to put the blame exactly where it belongs—upon the French."[12] Edith Benham comments that she had never seen Wilson so angry as he was on April 2, after he had learned, among other things, that the French were not permitting the German delegates to communicate directly with Berlin.[13]

Until early April 1919 Wilson had been fairly well. He had several "colds," which responded to what Dr. Grayson called "heroic" treatment—probably a nasal spray.[14] Wilson appeared fatigued in Washington but, according to Grayson's report, Wilson's blood pressure, blood, and urine were "unusually good for a man of his years."[15] On the return voyage, Wilson developed an elevated temperature and a chill after dental work, and he commented to the Doctor: "You made an error in my diagnosis. It is true I had a headache, neuralgia, sore-throat, tooth-ache, fever and a chill, and my equatorial zone has been on a strike. . . . My trouble is . . . I am suffering from a retention of gases generated by the Republican Senators—and that's enough to poison any man."[16]

Wilson had another opportunity to represent both a transient ailment and feelings of resentment in self-referential language. While he was touring the devastated regions of France on March 23, his car hit a shell hole, and he sustained a scalp contusion followed by severe headache. A few days later, in a conversation with Lloyd George, the Prime Minister explained to Wilson that if he (Lloyd George) did not support high reparations, he would lose a vote of confidence, and his government would fall. Wilson replied that he did not regard that as a catastrophe, since nothing could be finer than to be put out of office for doing what was right. Wilson predicted that, when Lloyd George's successor discovered that he had assumed a task which could not be accomplished, the roof of the temple would fall on his head, and history would give Lloyd George the fine distinction of standing for what was right and for not being awed by the opinion of the majority who were in the wrong. "I could not wish a more magnificent place in history," Wilson added.[17]

Wilson became violently ill on Thursday, April 3, with vomiting, diarrhea, and severe generalized pains. He described the onset to Dr.

[12] *Ibid.,* p. 37.

[13] The diary of Edith Benham (Helm), April 2, 1919, the Papers of Edith Benham Helm, Library of Congress; hereinafter cited as the Benham diary.

[14] Grayson diary, January 18 and 19, February 20, 1919.

[15] *Ibid.,* March 4, 1919.   [16] *Ibid.,* March 11, 1919.

[17] *Ibid.,* March 26, 1919.

Grayson: "I am feeling terribly bad. My equatorial zone was considerably upset soon after lunch but I was anxious to proceed with the afternoon conference, which I was barely able to d͟c owing to intense pains in my back and stomach and head. It has now turned into a severe coughing spell . . . which is very distressing and harassing."[18] Grayson soon made a diagnosis of influenza.[19] Wilson did not think he had a fever, but Grayson found that he had a temperature of 103. The patient passed a restless night with severe paroxysms of coughing, and the next morning his fever was 101. Dr. Grayson regarded his condition as "distinctly serious," but he told reporters that Wilson was suffering from a cold. Wilson had another bad night during the course of which Mrs. Wilson summoned Grayson several times.[20]

On Saturday morning, April 5, Wilson had a temperature of 101, and he had difficulty in breathing because his respiratory passages had filled up with mucus. Dr. Grayson administered an expectorant and, after a thorough examination, assured him that his lungs were not involved. Wilson then called Grayson's attention to the great benefit that he had received from the deep breathing exercises that Grayson had instituted six years previously: "I notice the difference, not only in the fact that my chest has increased in size, but when I speak I never get out of breath. . . . Don't you think that these deep-breathing exercises have helped me perhaps from suffering from bronchial troubles or influenza or possibly an attack of pneumonia?" When the Doctor agreed, Wilson went on to say: "I think it is remarkable . . . since I have followed out the line of treatment you have given me, this is the first *real* [author's emphasis] cold I have had in three years. Before I came to Washington, and the first winter I was in Washington, I would have sometimes as many as two colds a month."[21] On Sunday, April 6, Wilson's temperature was only one degree above normal, and he was expectorating freely. That evening, he had dinner at a bedside table with Mrs. Wilson and Grayson.[22] On Tuesday afternoon, Wilson, with his temperature now subnormal and still wobbly on his feet,[23] held a session of the Council of Four in his bedroom.[24]

[18] *Ibid.*, April 3, 1919.

[19] Grayson, *An Intimate Memoir*, p. 85.

[20] Grayson diary, April 3 and 4, 1919.

[21] *Ibid.*, April 5, 1919. Wilson's statement is indeed remarkable because it confirms the fact that his many "colds" were euphemistic designations for other conditions or convenient excuses to take a rest.

[22] *Ibid.*, April 6, 1919.   [23] *Ibid.*, April 8, 1919.

[24] Mrs. Wilson's dramatic account of this meeting indicates once more that, on matters relating to her husband's health, the chronology of her recollections is apt to be garbled. She relates that the men talked in the bedroom "while Dr. Grayson and I sat outside

Wilson's history of cerebral vascular disease and the severe behavioral sequelae of his illness has suggested that he may have had another stroke.[25] However, the evidence of the Grayson diary shows his acute symptoms to have been typical of influenza. The great pandemics of 1917, 1918, and 1919 occurred in the winter and early spring. The influenza viruses attack not only the gastrointestinal and pulmonary systems but other organs,[26] including the heart and brain. Wilson's heart was involved. He developed enduring nocturnal dyspnea—difficulty in breathing from a reclining position at night—and episodes of "asthmatic coughing."[27] Wilson's brain involvement—the manifestation of which will be described presently—was the effect of either the influenza virus or the frequently associated virus of encephalitis lethargica,—an agent known to cause personality changes. In either case, the sequelae were more severe because of the preexistence of cerebral vascular disease.

So-called postgrippal asthenia is a usual sequel of influenza. It usually lasts a week or two, but in Wilson's case it seems to have persisted throughout most of the remainder of his stay in Paris. He developed a disinclination to walk despite the pleasant spring weather. Edith Benham noted that Mrs. Wilson would have to drag him out, and that she would never leave the house if there was a chance that he would want to go for a walk.[28] Starling observed that, during the final return voyage to the United States, Wilson repeatedly stumbled over an iron ring set in the deck.[29] Grayson attributed Wilson's difficulty to overwork and worry, but, by the end of April, most of the difficult issues had been resolved, and Wilson's schedule had become much less arduous.

Euphoria and disregard of his incapacity were striking features of Wilson's illness. Despite Grayson's advice and his wife's protests, he continued to work. In the evening of April 3, the day on which he

---

fuming, for the President was sapping every drop of vitality left. Then came a night of burning fever." *My Memoir*, p. 249.

[25] Edwin A. Weinstein, "Woodrow Wilson's Neurological Illness," *Journal of American History*, LVII (September 1970), 324-51.

[26] Wilson's prostate may have been affected. Dr. Albert Richard Lamb, one of Dr. Grayson's associates, who did not see the patient, reports that Grayson asked him to obtain urotropin, a urinary antiseptic. A. R. Lamb to "Dear Johnny," July 4, 1957, MS. in the Wilson Collection, Princeton University Library.

[27] Grayson, *An Intimate Memoir*, p. 85. These symptoms indicate that, because of heart failure, Wilson's lungs were congested. The condition may have been superimposed on previous hypertensive heart disease.

[28] Edith Benham Helm, *The Captains and the Kings* (New York, 1954), pp. 108, 122.

[29] Sugrue and Starling, *Starling of the White House*, p. 145.

was stricken, he received Vance McCormick and Norman Davis, an economic adviser. McCormick noted that the President looked "tired and discouraged."[30] Wilson sent Colonel House to take his place at the Council sessions of April 4, but on April 5 he insisted that the meeting be held in the sitting room adjoining his bedroom, and House shuttled back and forth to keep him informed of the proceedings.[31] On Sunday, April 6, although he was still in bed with a sore throat and fever, Wilson called in the American peace commissioners to discuss matters at home and the Russian situation.[32] That evening, at the height of his deadlock with Clemenceau, Wilson issued an order for *George Washington* to repair to Brest, ready to sail for the United States. On the evening of the next day, April 7, he met with Baker and assured him that he would stand firm against the French and Italian demands.

Patients with influenza usually are lethargic and feel debilitated, but Wilson was in high spirits. Grayson noted on April 6 that he looked as if he did not have a "care in the world."[33] The next day Wilson announced that he was feeling really "first-rate."[34] The experience of increased mental activity was another feature of Wilson's hypomanic state. He told Grayson that there were so many things in his mind that he had difficulty sleeping.[35]

Some of the most important decisions of the Paris Peace Conference were made during Wilson's acute illness and the period immediately following. At the Council session of April 5, the President, with House as his intermediary, yielded to the British and French demand that no monetary or time limit be placed on German reparations. He also agreed to a clause, first drafted by John Foster Dulles, which attributed the damage suffered by the Allies to German aggression. Over the week of April 7, Wilson and Clemenceau, in the face of Lloyd George's opposition, reached agreement on the Rhineland and the Saar. France was to occupy the Rhineland for fifteen years, after which the area would be demilitarized. The French obtained economic concessions in the Saar (in return for German wanton destruction of French mines and factories) for fifteen years under League administration; at the expiration of such time, a plebiscite would be held to determine whether the Saar would be French or German. The German army was limited to 100,000 men, and Wilson and Lloyd George signed a se-

[30] The diary of Vance McCormick, April 3, 1919, Yale University Library.
[31] House diary, April 5, 1919.
[32] Mayer, *Politics and Diplomacy of Peacemaking*, pp. 480-81.
[33] Grayson diary, April 6, 1919.
[34] *Ibid.*, April 7, 1919.   [35] *Ibid.*, April 6, 1919.

curity treaty with Clemenceau which provided for American and British assistance in the event of a German invasion during the next ten years.

Although Wilson had given in on the reparations issue and had achieved no better than a compromise in respect to the Rhineland and the Saar, he reacted as if he had won a victory. He was convinced that his threat to go home had brought the French around, and he reported enthusiastically to Grayson and Baker that, through his own efforts, great progress was being made.[36] Wilson also became more outgoing socially; despite his tendency toward fatigue, he engaged in many ceremonial activities which he could easily have avoided. On April 11 he received two Galician goatherds in native costume, who had walked all the way to Paris to ask the President to give Galicia to Poland. Wilson had eighteen appointments on April 17, including meetings with the Patriarch of Constantinople, the Assyrian-Chaldean delegate, and the Chargé d'Affaires of San Marino. He also had two interesting conversations with Queen Marie of Rumania. She told him that the Bolsheviks had made women the property of the state, and that they could sleep with their husbands only twice a week.[37] Wilson may have been even more startled when, in the course of pleading for more territory for Rumania, the Queen showed him and Mrs. Wilson a photograph of her "dark and passionate" love child.[38] The Queen, Wilson commented to Grayson, traveled in "high gear."[39]

Wilson's euphoric mood was mixed with irritability and suspiciousness. While still in bed, he became irascible with the servants—an attitude which Dr. Grayson took as a good sign, because it showed that he was paying attention to the daily routine.[40] On Saturday, April 5, Gilbert Close and Charles L. Swem, Wilson's secretaries, drove out to Versailles after ascertaining that they would not be needed. Wilson, however, sent for them and Hoover, and, on learning of the absence of all three, issued an order which forbade members of his party to use cars for other than official business. This action struck Hoover as very strange because, prior to his illness, Wilson had been extremely solicitous in urging the staff to take as much recreation as they could.[41]

---

[36] *Ibid.*, April 9, 1919; Baker diary, April 11, 1919.

[37] Grayson diary, April 10, 1919.

[38] As quoted by Edith Wilson in *My Memoir*, p. 258.

[39] Grayson diary, April 10, 1919.

[40] *Ibid.*, April 5, 1919.

[41] I. H. Hoover, "The Facts about President Wilson's Illness," MS. in the Papers of I. H. Hoover, Library of Congress; G. F. Close to Arthur Walworth, May 7, 1951, letter in Walworth's possession. Close adds that Wilson, on the next day, sent for him and did not mention the incident and gave Close the impression that all was forgiven.

When Wilson got out of bed, he became obsessed with the idea that the French cooks, maids, waiters, and porters all spoke perfect English, overheard everything he said, and reported his words back to the French government. Hoover and the Secret Service men investigated but found only one servant who could speak more than a few words of English. Nothing they could say, however, made Wilson change his mind.[42] Despite the negative report, the President had one of the agents sit in his room when he went out, and he got a strong box for papers which he had previously kept in his desk.[43] Hoover also noted that Wilson took personal responsibility for all of the property in the house. When he saw that several articles had been moved—they had actually been taken by the caretaker with the owner's permission—he demanded that everything be itemized.[44]

Wilson had brought up the question of espionage even before his illness. He had explained to Lady Northcliffe at luncheon on March 29 that he could not answer some of her questions because he had discovered that one of the servants spoke English "perfectly" although he addressed the Americans in French only.[45] The French used espionage or were reputed to do so,[46] but it is highly unlikely that *all* of the French help spoke perfect English and overheard everything that Wilson said. Although most biographers have ignored or rejected Hoover's testimony, he was a reliable witness and devoted to Wilson. Perhaps the best evidence for the validity of his observations is that the themes of automobiles and "perfect English" were very important features of Wilson's identity system and symbols through which he expressed his strongest feelings.[47] We have seen that Wilson habitually

[42] Hoover, "The Facts about President Wilson's Illness."

[43] Benham diary, April 21, 1919.

[44] Hoover, "The Facts about President Wilson's Illness."

[45] Grayson diary, March 29, 1919.

[46] The British delegation had brought their own servants to Paris because of fear of espionage and disease, yet they kept their papers in a hotel that had French help. Lloyd George told Frances Stevenson, his secretary, mistress, and later his wife, that Clemenceau had the police give him a report each morning of where each member of his government had been the night before. Colonel House had his telephone line to Wilson "covered" to make sure that it was not tapped. Harold Nicolson, *Peacemaking 1919* (Boston and New York, 1933), p. 44; Frances Stevenson, *Lloyd George* (New York, 1971), p. 286; House diary, January 7, 1919.

[47] Such misconceptions are not simply distortions of reality, but are highly condensed metaphorical representations of motives and problems. They provide a sense of social and emotional reality by the way in which they give unity and order to disparate and uncontrollable events, and because the themes form significant elements of patterns of social relatedness. Edwin A. Weinstein, *Cultural Aspects of Delusion: A Psychiatric Study of the Virgin Islands* (New York, 1962); Weinstein *et al.*, "Confabulation as a Social Process."

indicated his determination by stating that he would talk in "plain language" and "the plainest words." Even before his illness Wilson had criticized the French because they talked interminably.[48] His belief about the French servants seems to have symbolized the feeling—not otherwise represented in consciousness—that he had been bested by Clemenceau, who, incidentally, spoke excellent English.

As clinical improvement occurs in cases of brain injury, delusions may be succeeded by other symbolic patterns which represent the same motivations and problems.[49] These include clichés, puns, and "ludic" behavior.[50] The meaning of Wilson's concern about the furniture's having been moved became apparent on May 1. After lunch, the President, Mrs. Wilson, and Grayson moved into the big parlor adjoining the dining room, and Wilson remarked: "I don't like the way the colors of this furniture fight each other. The greens and the reds are all mixed up here and there is no harmony. Here is a big purple, high-backed covered chair, which is like the Purple Cow, strayed off to itself, and it is placed where the light shines on it too brightly. If you will give me a lift, we will move this next to the wall where the light from the window will give it a subdued effect. And here are two chairs, one green and the other red. This will never do. . . . Over in the right-hand corner at our meetings are the British together; in the left hand corner the Americans; in the middle the French are seated. When we meet every day it would amuse you to see us walk to our respective corners just as if we were school children occupying our regular seats. Now, we will put all the reds over here in the American corner, next to the red sofa; the greens we will put over here for the Britishers; the odds and ends we will put here in the center for the French, and we will harmonize them as much as possible. The other chairs that do not harmonize we will put on the edge where the experts can occupy them when they are called in before the Big Three." Dr. Grayson noted how pleased and relaxed his patient became after they had rearranged the furniture.[51]

Probably the most startling political expression of the changes in Wilson's behavior was the reversal of his attitudes on German war guilt and the trial of the ex-Kaiser. On April 2, the day before Wilson

[48] Baker diary, March 3, 1919; Grayson diary, March 22 and 27, 1919.

[49] Edwin A. Weinstein and Olga G. Lyerly, "Confabulation Following Brain Injury: Its Analogs and Sequelae," *Archives of Neurology and Psychiatry*, XVIII (1968), 349-54.

[50] A term introduced by Jean Piaget to indicate the play and imitative and dramatic aspects of behavior in young children. Dr. Wilson might have pointed out that "ludic" and "delusion" derive from the same Latin root.

[51] Grayson diary, May 1, 1919.

was stricken, Lloyd George and Clemenceau introduced a resolution to try the former German Emperor. Wilson replied that a dangerous precedent would be set if the victors in a war were also the judges. He pointed out that, up to the present time, responsibility for collective crimes had been solely a collective one, and that to construe an act of this nature as an individual crime would—contrary to all juridical tradition—give a retroactive force to the principles now formulated. When Lloyd George suggested that the Americans were fearful of creating a precedent which could be used against a President, just as the Japanese did not want a precedent which might affect their Emperor, Wilson replied that it was the Congress, not the President, that declared war. He acknowledged, however, that he, as President, had the real, if not the legal, responsibility for having brought the United States into the war. He thought that the Kaiser would be execrated by history, but he did not want history to reproach the peace conference for arranging to try the former Emperor before having established the juridical basis for such a trial.[52]

On Wilson's return to the conference on April 8, he again objected to flouting the principles of the law and said that the worst of punishments would come from public opinion. (Clemenceau advised him not to count on it.) However, in a discussion about a tribunal, Wilson began to weaken. He asked who would establish the tribunal and said that, if each great power had three representatives, the body would be too large. He wondered if Serbia should be one of the prosecutors and asked if the verdict would have to be unanimous. He also raised the practical question of whether Holland could be made to give up the Kaiser. His last word on the subject was that he would have to consult with his Secretary of State.

Whether or not Wilson consulted with Lansing is not clear, but the next day he opened the meeting by reading a text providing for a trial which he had prepared overnight. The ex-Emperor was to be brought to judgment, not for "an offence against criminal law, but as a supreme offence against international morality and the sanctity of treaties." Wilson stated that the tribunal would be guided by the "highest motives of international policy, with a view to vindicating the solemn obligations of international undertakings and the validity of international morality." Wilson said that he was mindful of the objections of the Japanese, but that these were not relevant to the case.[53] At the afternoon session Wilson rejected suggestions that the signing be delayed until the Japanese were present, and he personally passed the

---

[52] Mantoux, pp. 91-93.   [53] *Ibid.*, pp. 144-51, 153.

papers around for the others to sign.[54] After the meeting Wilson took an automobile drive and exulted to Grayson, "We made progress today, not through the match of wits, but simply through my hammering and forcing them to decisions."[55]

Before his illness Wilson had been considerate of the German delegates; afterward he manifested a personal dislike for them. He told Edith Benham that the sight of the arrogant Germans aroused in him all the hatreds and animosities which had lain dormant in the past,[56] and he remarked to Grayson that the Germans were such a "job lot"[57] that it was difficult for him to take any interest in them.[58] Count Ulrich von Brockdorff-Rantzau, chief German delegate, replied to the terms of the peace on May 7. He admitted the wrong done by his country to Belgium, acknowledged Germany's obligation for certain war damages, and asked for a committee of experts to determine the amount. On the other hand, he denied that Germany bore sole guilt for the war and stated that the conflict had its background in the imperialistic and expansionistic policies of the European powers. Brockdorff not only recited Wilson's formerly expressed views of the origins of the war, but also read the Fourteen Points. Wilson called the German's speech "stupid"[59] and remarked to Grayson that Brockdorff, although whipped, had failed to show the "slightest sporting disposition."[60]

Several lay observers noted that the President's behavior had changed as a result of his illness. Lloyd George said that Wilson had had something like a stroke, after which he fell completely under the influence of Clemenceau.[61] Herbert Hoover stated that, prior to his illness, Wilson had been incisive, quick to grasp essentials, unhesitating in his conclusions, and willing to listen to advice. Afterward, he "groped for ideas," and his mind constantly strove for precedents.[62] Dr. E. P. Davis thought that Wilson's breakdown in October 1919 had begun with the Paris illness. Wilson's memory also appeared affected. Following the morning session of the Council on May 3, he told Grayson and Baker that he was so fatigued that he had difficulty

[54] Grayson diary, April 9, 1919.   [55] Ibid.

[56] Helm, The Captains and the Kings, p. 107.

[57] Max Weber was a delegate. Wilson was probably unaware of his presence; The Protestant Ethic and the Spirit of Capitalism did not appear in English until 1930.

[58] Grayson diary, May 7, 1919.

[59] Baker diary, May 7, 1919.

[60] Grayson diary, May 7, 1919.

[61] Diaries and Letters of Harold Nicolson, 1930-1939, Nigel Nicolson, ed. (New York, 1966), p. 123.

[62] Herbert Hoover, The Memoirs of Herbert Hoover, 2 vols. (New York, 1951-57), I, 468.

in remembering what had happened.[63] In a classic "third person" representation of problems, Wilson observed that Clemenceau's memory seemed to be affected, as the Frenchman would avoid decisions with the excuse that he must consult with his experts.[64]

The effects of Wilson's illness on his behavior can be compared to the effect of electroshock therapy, another form of stress to the nervous system. A series of electrically induced convulsions produces changes in brain function, in which problems to which the patient had previously reacted with depression and a sense of guilt and failure may be denied, forgotten, or formulated in new language patterns. The depressive mood is replaced by euphoric and sometimes paranoid attitudes. There are shifts in the syntactic use of person (from first person to third person) and tense (from present to past). More self-references are noted. These changes in patients without prior brain damage generally last for about three weeks.[65] Wilson's illness "cured" him of his depression and furnished a neural milieu for a new relationship to events. Formerly, Wilson had expressed the hope that the Fourteen Points might be carried out. Now he believed that they had indeed been fulfilled. His reversal of attitude toward Germany's responsibility for the war relieved him of the moral guilt which he probably felt because he had not vindicated all of the Fourteen Points.

Wilson used much self-referential representation of his problems with his health during the discussions with his colleagues over the treaty. The British, in response to a change in public opinion at home and fear of French military dominance and that the Germans would not sign the treaty, proposed that the terms be softened. They asked that Germany become a member of the League at an early date, and that she be permitted to make a cash offer of reparations. Clemenceau was strongly opposed to any changes, and Wilson, disinclined to reopen the fight with the French and eager to get the treaty out of the way and begin the fight for ratification, agreed with Clemenceau.

Bernard Baruch gives an account of a meeting between Lloyd George and Wilson, which the former had asked him to arrange. When the Prime Minister said that neither the British fleet nor the army would compel Germany to sign, Wilson's "jaws clenched and he showed that flinty eye I had seen when the battle was aroused within him." " 'Mr.

[63] Grayson diary, May 3, 1919; Baker diary, May 3, 1919.

[64] Grayson diary, April 14, 1919.

[65] Robert L. Kahn, Max Fink, and Edwin A. Weinstein, "Relation of Amobarbital Test to Clinical Improvement in Electroshock Therapy," *Archives of Neurology and Psychiatry*, LXXVI (1956), 23-29; Max Fink, *Convulsive Therapy: Theory and Practice* (New York, 1979), pp. 132-38.

Prime Minister,' he replied, 'you make me sick! For months we have been struggling to make the terms of the Treaty exactly along the lines you now speak of, and never got the support of the English. Now, after we have finally come to agreement, and when we have to face the Germans and we need unanimity, you want to rewrite the Treaty.' "[66]

The British suggestions, however, found strong support among the American delegation. In an effort to have Wilson reconsider, Herbert Hoover persuaded him to call a meeting for June 3. After General Bliss expressed opposition to French occupation of the Rhineland, Colonel House proposed the appointment of a committee of experts. Wilson agreed and stated that such a group might, "without having any of the usual round-about expressions of international intercourse, learn each others' minds, real minds."[67] "Meeting of the minds" and "matching of minds" were among Wilson's favorite expressions, but the injection at this point suggests that he was unconsciously referring to his own mind.

Wilson went on to dismiss fears that the Germans would not sign the treaty: "It makes me a little tired for people to come and say now that they are afraid the Germans won't sign, and their fear is based on things they insisted upon at the time of the writing of the treaty; that makes me very sick.

"And that is the thing that happened. These people that over-rode our judgment and wrote things into the treaty that are now the stumbling blocks, are falling over themselves to remove these stumbling blocks. Now, if they ought not to have been there I say, remove them, but I say do not remove them merely for the fact of having the treaty signed."[68]

The most vivid symbolic representation of Wilson's illness came during the discussion of reparations. Thomas W. Lamont said that the difficulties with Germany would fade away if Wilson, Lloyd George, and Clemenceau would only instruct their experts to come up with a fixed sum within twenty-four hours rather than two years. Wilson replied, "We instructed them once to find a definite sum. And then we got Klotz on the brain."[69] (Louis Lucien Klotz was the French Finance Minister and one of those who "talked interminably.")[70] Wilson's pun suggests the possibility that he believed that he had had a stroke.

[66] Bernard M. Baruch, *Baruch*, 2 vols. (New York, 1960), II, 120-21.

[67] Stenographic report of meeting, June 3, 1919, printed in Baker, *Woodrow Wilson and World Settlement*, III, 493.

[68] *Ibid.*, p. 503.   [69] *Ibid.*, p. 480.

[70] Wilson had made a similar pun on April 15 when he told Grayson: "I had thought

Wilson's illness was one of the factors which led to his break with Colonel House. The basic reasons were the personalities of the men, the assumption by House of a new role in the partnership, growing divergence in political views, and, as shown by Inga Floto,[71] an attempt by House to carry out a policy at odds with Wilson's position. Some of these features antedated the peace conference. As we have seen, Wilson and House had differed on occasion during the war, but Wilson had continued to trust his friend. When the Colonel asked for instructions prior to going to France for the armistice talks, Wilson told him: "I have not given you any instructions because I feel you will know what to do."[72] However, the men no longer engaged in intimate, far-ranging discussions. At the peace conference, although the commissioners were familiar with Wilson's goals, none, including House, was privy to his thinking.

In Paris the Colonel saw many diplomats and reporters, who found him far more accessible and informative than his chief. The French and some English newspapers hailed House as a great diplomat and as the power behind the throne—impressions which neither he nor his admiring son-in-law, Gordon Auchincloss, did anything to discourage. Mrs. Wilson, in particular, became disturbed by the Colonel's growing prominence and by some of Auchincloss's remarks. The praise reinforced House's great confidence in his abilities, and he gradually took on the role of mediator. He advised not only Wilson but also Lloyd George and Clemenceau, and he tried to play one off against the other. He noted with satisfaction that Lloyd George referred to him as a prime minister.[73] In another diary entry, which attested to his belief in his influence over the French leader, House recorded that he "convinced" Clemenceau of the need for a League of Nations and pointed out that England would oppose a powerful France. His quoting of Clemenceau's statement that he loved House as a brother[74] suggests that he was more closely in the Tiger's embrace than he realized.

The President and his adviser differed fundamentally in outlook. Wilson believed literally in the Fourteen Points and saw negotiations as a way of fulfilling them. House saw the Fourteen Points as a means of justifying certain tactics. The Colonel, who regarded himself as far superior to Wilson as a negotiator, saw his opportunity to break the

several times I would have to send for you to treat me for 'clots on the brain.' " Clemenceau told Wilson that Klotz was the only Jew he had ever known who did not know anything about finance. Grayson diary, April 15, 1919.

[71] Floto, *Colonel House in Paris, passim.*

[72] House diary, October 15, 1918.

[73] *Ibid.,* March 7, 1919.   [74] *Ibid.,* January 7, 1919.

impasse while Wilson was in the United States. Wilson expressed his anger and disappointment to his wife on his return, but he did not reprimand House. He followed the same course with House as he had with Page and Lansing.[75] Relations were outwardly the same over the next three weeks, but they changed suddenly during Wilson's illness. In his state of disturbed consciousness, his suppressed feelings toward House emerged as a kind of dream image. On the evening of April 7 he asked Grayson whether he did not think the Colonel looked strange, as if he had "something on his conscience."[76] Wilson's euphoria may have dissolved any immediate regrets over the loss of a long and close friendship. From this point on, the relationship between Wilson and House was strictly formal. After House bade Wilson farewell upon his embarkation for the United States, the two men never saw each other again.

[75] General Pershing can be added to the list. During the negotiations over the Armistice, Wilson told Pershing that he should feel entirely free to consult with House and himself. Instead, the General—who had presidential ambitions—took the opportunity to urge the Supreme War Council to demand unconditional surrender. Secretary of War Baker and Chief of Staff Peyton C. March were outraged, and Baker prepared a letter of reprimand for the President's signature. Wilson, however, instructed Baker to leave the matter to House. Wilson's suppressed anger over the incident surfaced a month later in a private conversation aboard *George Washington*. The war, he said, would have been over a month earlier had not Pershing been "glory mad" and, contrary to Foch's advice, insisted on attacking near Metz. Baker, *Wilson*, VIII, 515-16, 520-22; WW to Newton D. Baker, November 1, 1918, Wilson Papers; Benham diary, December 5, 1918.

[76] Grayson diary, April 7, 1919. This may have been impressionistic on Wilson's part. House rarely, if ever, had things on his conscience.

CHAPTER XXI

A Massive Stroke and the Politics of Denial

WILSON'S CAPACITIES were below par when he returned home to work for the ratification of the Treaty. Dr. Grayson noted that, aboard ship, Wilson had difficulty in arranging his thoughts for his presentation to the Senate. It was the first time in his life, the Doctor commented, that the President had not been satisfied with a draft. Wilson "said that he had made a false start" because he had so "little respect for the audience to which he would deliver" his message. He quoted his father's maxim that "it was impossible to reason out of a man something that had not been reasoned into him."[1]

Wilson's contempt for the Senate contributed to the tone of the address in which he presented the Treaty. He indicated his willingness to confer with the Foreign Relations Committee and implied that he had kept the senators informed of events in Paris. He had, in fact, virtually ignored them. As Link comments, he did not refer to the senators, as he often had, as "colleagues," nor did he speak of seeking "common counsel" with them. He did not so much ask for their views as to inform them that a world settlement had been made. He did not speak of the difficulties of making a fair settlement at the peace conference or state that the Treaty was the best bargain he could obtain in the circumstances. Rather, he portrayed the accomplishments of the peace conference in glowing terms—of people who had lived in utter darkness and who had been brought into the light. He closed with a dramatic peroration:

"The stage is set, the destiny disclosed. It has come about by no plan of our conceiving, but by the hand of God who led us into this way. We cannot turn back. We can only go forward, with lifted eyes and freshened spirit, to follow the vision. It was of this that we dreamed at our birth. America shall in truth show the way. The light streams upon the path ahead, and nowhere else."[2]

Forty-four of the forty-seven Democratic senators supported the

[1] Grayson diary, July 1, 1919.
[2] Link, *Revolution, War, and Peace*, p. 107.

Treaty while the Republicans were divided. Fourteen isolationists, or irreconcilables, notably William E. Borah of Idaho and Hiram W. Johnson of California, were against a league in any form. Henry Cabot Lodge, with Elihu Root's guidance, led a group of twenty-three senators who would accept the League only with strong reservations to protect national sovereignty. Lodge was also motivated by his hatred and jealousy of Wilson, and by his determination to assert the power of the legislative branch in foreign affairs. The so-called strong reservationists insisted that one reservation state specifically that the United States was the sole judge of its duties under the Covenant and that the United States assumed no obligation—as stipulated in Article 10—to preserve the territorial integrity and political independence of member states. A third group of Republicans allegedly favored the Treaty with mild reservations in the nature of the interpretation of its provisions; actually, most of them favored the Root-Lodge reservation to Article 10. Wilson consulted with most of the mild reservationist Republicans, mainly in individual interviews, without notable success, and on August 19 he met with the Foreign Relations Committee at the White House.

Wilson opened the meeting by reading a prepared statement. He emphasized that the nation's economic and military planning depended on early ratification of the Treaty. There was no objection, he said, to making the right to withdraw explicit. It had not been done so, he explained, because the peace conference had recognized that the "question must be left . . . [to] the conscience of the nation proposing to withdraw." He knew, he told the senators, that the United States would never propose to withdraw if its conscience was not entirely clear. Article 10, he declared, was the "very backbone" of the Treaty. It constituted a solemn obligation for the United States, but it was "a moral, not a legal, obligation." It was binding in conscience only, and it left Congress "absolutely free to put its own interpretations upon it." Wilson said that he had no objection to such interpretations, but he warned that they would cause long delays, inasmuch as all nations would have to accept what would be in effect a change in the language of the Treaty. He asserted that, if the document was qualified in any way, other nations, including Germany, would follow with reservations, and the meaning and operative force of the Treaty would be clouded from beginning to end.

Wilson reiterated these views in the three hours of interrogation which followed. Borah asked whether the right to withdraw from the League, once notice was given, was unconditional. Wilson replied that it depended upon the faith and conscience of the withdrawing nation.

Philander C. Knox of Pennsylvania, another irreconcilable, asked whether, in case of obvious aggression, the United States would be under a legal obligation to participate in action against the aggressor. Wilson said that, while there was no legal obligation, there was an "absolutely compelling moral obligation." He later distinguished between being "bound" and "morally bound." Warren G. Harding of Ohio asked why Articles 10 and 11—the sections which authorized the League to take action in case of war or a threat of war—had been included if they were only moral obligations. Wilson replied that there was such a thing as a national conscience, and that a moral obligation was superior to a legal one. A person might escape an obligation through legal technicalities, he told Harding, but he could not escape his own conscience. Porter J. McCumber of South Dakota, a Republican who approved the Treaty, suggested a reservation that Congress might use its own judgment in respect to following the recommendations of the Council. Wilson said that, while he did not differ with the Senator, it would be a serious practical mistake to put his statement in the form of a reservation.[3]

The Democrats thought that Wilson had been high-minded and eloquent, while the Republicans regarded him as vague and evasive. Wilson's language reflected his belief that, although he had not been legally responsible for America's entry into the war, he bore the moral responsibility for it. The compromises which he had been forced to make at Paris may have contributed to his feeling of guilt. When he spoke of the conscience of the nation and its moral obligations, he referred particularly to his own conscience. The Treaty, especially Article 10, was a sacred pledge by which he could redeem himself. Any change in its language would, in Wilson's opinion, not give it the same significance. Wilson's thought was closely connected with his imagery, and, as he had said in presenting the Covenant of the League to the peace conference, the League was a living thing; hence any tampering would destroy its organic integrity.[4] These facts, among others, help to explain why Wilson was so reluctant to have reservations accompany American ratification of the Treaty.

At the meeting with the Senate Foreign Relations Committee, Wilson

[3] Report of the conference between the Senate Foreign Relations Committee and Wilson, August 19, 1919, in *66th Congress, 1st Session, May 19-November 19, 1919, Senate Documents* (Washington, 1919), XIII, Document No. 76, pp. 3-6, 11, 14-15, 19, 11-12.

[4] "A living thing is born, and we must see to it what clothes we put upon it," Wilson declared. See his address, February 14, 1919, Baker and Dodd, eds., *Public Papers of Woodrow Wilson*, V, 426.

insisted that he had not known of the secret treaties before he went to Paris. Under grilling by Borah and Johnson, Wilson claimed that he had not been informed of the treaties, officially or unofficially. When Johnson asked if the Fourteen Points had not been laid down to counter the war aims embodied in the treaties, Wilson denied that this had been the case. His negative answers were not qualified or accompanied by any explanation. On the other hand, he readily answered questions about the Shantung settlement, which was based on secret arrangements—previously unknown to Wilson—between the Allies and the Japanese.[5]

Wilson's denial emphasizes the importance of the psychological factors which motivated his behavior. There is no question that Wilson had been familiar with the contents of the secret treaties among the European powers before he went to Paris. He stood to win no political advantage by not saying that he knew about the treaties. As Link suggests, he might even have gained credit had he admitted his prior knowledge and pointed out that the treaties had added greatly to his difficulties at Paris.[6] His guilt and anger—he was confronted by two of the bitterest opponents of the League—made him relatively inarticulate. He may have felt justified in uttering a diplomatic lie in his belief that the welfare of the country and the fate of mankind were at stake.

The meeting did not change any votes, and Lodge and his allies intensified their fight against the Treaty. Wilson countered with a decision to appeal directly to the people. He had contemplated a speaking tour for some time but had postponed it in hopes of coming to an agreement. Before Wilson left, he entrusted Senator Hitchcock with four acceptable reservations which, at some opportune time, Hitchcock was to put forward as his, the Senator's, own. The reservations covered the major Republican objections, and, in Wilson's opinion, did not violate the spirit of the Treaty and did not require renegotiation.[7] Wilson took the trip against the advice of his closest associates. Hitchcock opposed it, and Herman H. Kohlsaat, a journalist whom Wilson trusted, told the President that, while he could

[5] Report of the conference between the Senate Foreign Relations Committee and Wilson, August 19, 1919, *Senate Documents*, XIII, Document No. 76, pp. 22, 28-30, 30-31.

[6] Link, *Revolution, War, and Peace*, p. 78.

[7] For the text of the Hitchcock reservations, see Thomas A. Bailey, *The Great Betrayal* (New York, 1945), pp. 393-94. See also Kurt Wimer, "Woodrow Wilson Tries Conciliation: An Effort That Failed," *The Historian*, XXV (August 1963), 419-38, and "Senator Hitchcock and the League of Nations," *Nebraska History*, XLIV (September 1963), 189-204.

not change the vote of a strong reservationist like Reed Smoot by going to Utah, he might influence the Senator's vote by talking with him in Washington.[8] When Dr. Grayson and Mrs. Wilson pleaded with Wilson not to go, he replied that he had played his last card and lost and that he could not put his personal safety above his duty.[9] Wilson's mood varied from hopeful anticipation to despair. On the eve of his departure, he seemed "blithe and happy," according to Josephus Daniels, but he told Kohlsaat that he did not care if he died the minute after the Treaty was ratified.[10]

Wilson's health had not been good over the summer. He had resumed his routine of golf, motoring, and weekend cruises, but he held interviews in the White House rather than in the Executive Office so that he could rest between appointments.[11] Sir William Wiseman, who had lunch with him on July 18, noted that he looked gray and tired and that his face twitched a great deal. At Mrs. Wilson's suggestion, Wiseman stayed away from topics which might upset the President.[12] That weekend Wilson became indisposed on a cruise and spent two days in bed on his return.[13] He set out on his journey on September 3 and, over a period of twenty-two days, he gave thirty-two major addresses, made numerous rear platform appearances, and participated in various ceremonies. His health deteriorated further. He suffered from severe headaches even before he left, and he developed double vision, indicative of a stroke involving the ocular centers of the brain. A week out of Washington, he showed signs of cardiac decompensation: he had episodes of coughing at night, difficulty in breathing, and was forced to sleep in a sitting position.[14] Dr. Grayson and Mrs. Wilson urged him to rest, but he insisted on carrying on.[15] His condition grew steadily worse, and the tour ended on September 25, when he sustained a stroke which paralyzed his left side.

Wilson's addresses were extemporaneous, and the more emotional sections contained metaphorical representations of the problems which threatened his physical health and personal integrity. In Des Moines

[8] H. H. Kohlsaat to WW, July 25, 1919, Wilson Papers.

[9] Edith Wilson, My Memoir, pp. 273-74; Grayson, An Intimate Memoir, p. 95.

[10] Josephus Daniels, The Life of Woodrow Wilson, 1856-1924 (Philadelphia, 1924), p. 327; Herman H. Kohlsaat, From McKinley to Harding: Personal Recollections of Our Presidents (New York, 1923), p. 219.

[11] Head Usher's diary, passim.

[12] Walworth, Wilson, II, 344.

[13] Head Usher's diary, July 19-21, 1919.

[14] Grayson diary, September 25, 1919; Grayson, An Intimate Memoir, pp. 96-97.

[15] Wilson visited his two old loves: he saw Mrs. Hulbert in Los Angeles and Harriet Woodrow Welles in Denver.

he declared that American soldiers had fought with "no curtain in front" of their "eyes."[16] A week later he exclaimed: "The truth is the regnant and triumphant thing in this world. You may trample it under foot, you may blind its eyes with blood, but you cannot kill it."[17] Wilson made vivid use of metaphors of the respiratory and cardio-vascular systems: "The world cannot breathe in the atmosphere of negations," he declared in Omaha.[18] Commenting on German-Amer-ican opposition to the Treaty, he charged that the pro-German element had "air in its lungs" again.[19] The following day Wilson told an au-dience in Minneapolis that he had had to guard his "breathing ap-paratus" at the peace conference against the "miasma" that arose from some of the secret treaties.[20] On the day on which Dr. Grayson re-corded signs of cardiac failure—September 11—Wilson said of Article 10: "Without that clause the heart of the recent war is not cut out. The heart of the recent war was an absolute disregard of the territorial integrity and political independence of the smaller nations. If you do not cut the heart of the war out, that heart is going to live and beat and grow stronger, and we will have the cataclysm again."[21]

Wilson identified himself with the American soldiers who had died for the redemption of their country and the salvation of mankind; and, as the trip progressed, he made frequent references to his re-sponsibility for their deaths. He told an audience in Pueblo on Sep-tember 25:

"Again and again, my fellow citizens, mothers who lost their sons in France have come to me and, taking my hand, have shed tears upon it not only, but they have added, 'God bless you, Mr. President!' Why, my fellow citizens, should they pray God to bless me? I advised the Congress of the United States to create the situation that led to the death of their sons. I ordered their sons oversea. I consented to their sons being put in the most difficult parts of the battle line, where death was certain. . . . They believe, and they rightly believe, that their sons saved the liberty of the world. They believe that wrapped up with the liberty of the world is the continuous protection of that liberty by the concerted powers of all civilized people. They believe that this sacrifice

[16] Address at Des Moines, Ia., September 6, 1919, in Baker and Dodd, eds., *Public Papers of Woodrow Wilson*, VI, 21.

[17] Address at Helena, Mont., September 11, 1919, *ibid.*, p. 136.

[18] Address at Omaha, Neb., September 8, 1919, *ibid.*, p. 42.

[19] Address at Sioux Falls, S. D., September 8, 1919, *ibid.*, p. 47.

[20] Address at Minneapolis, Minn., September 9, 1919, *ibid.*, p. 74.

[21] Address at Helena, Mont., September 11, 1919, *ibid.*, p. 129.

was made in order that other sons should not be called upon for a similar gift—the gift of life, the gift of all that died."[22]

The first signs of the stroke appeared as Wilson mounted the speaker's platform in Pueblo. He stumbled and, uncharacteristically, permitted Starling to assist him. His voice was weak, he mumbled at times, and there were long pauses as if he was having difficulty following a train of thought.[23] He also complained of a headache, and the train was stopped so that he and Mrs. Wilson could go for a walk before dinner. That evening, as Mrs. Wilson was getting ready for bed, Wilson knocked on her door, and she noted that his left arm was drawn up in an unnatural position. Tumulty, who saw him several hours later, recognized that the whole left side of his body was paralyzed.[24] The next morning, although his left side was still weak and his speech indistinct, Wilson shaved and dressed and insisted on finishing his schedule. Otherwise, he said, his friends and Senator Lodge would say that he was a quitter, and the Treaty would be lost.[25] Dr. Grayson, Tumulty, and Edith dissuaded him, and the remainder of his schedule was canceled. As the train sped toward Washington, Edith Wilson vowed to herself that neither the public nor her husband must ever know how ill he was.[26] By the time that the party reached Union Station, Wilson's condition had improved, and he was able to walk unassisted to his automobile.

The improvement was transitory. Edith awoke on the morning of October 2 to find her husband on the edge of his bed: his left arm hung limply, and he complained of a lack of feeling in his hand. According to her account, she helped him to the bathroom and went to her room to telephone Dr. Grayson. Then she heard a noise and returned to find Wilson sitting on the bathroom floor unconscious. He recovered immediately and asked for a glass of water. She brought him the water, placed a pillow under his head, and awaited the arrival of the Doctor, who assisted her in getting him to bed.[27]

One gets a different version of the onset of Wilson's stroke from Irwin Hoover. According to the head usher, it was exactly ten minutes before nine when Mrs. Wilson telephoned him to summon Dr. Gray-

---

[22] Address at Pueblo, Colo., September 25, 1919, *ibid.*, pp. 413-14.

[23] Sugrue and Starling, *Starling of the White House*, p. 152; Lawrence, *The True Story of Woodrow Wilson*, p. 279.

[24] Edith Wilson, *My Memoir*, pp. 283-84; Tumulty, *Woodrow Wilson as I Know Him*, pp. 447-48.

[25] Tumulty, *Woodrow Wilson as I Know Him*, p. 447.

[26] Edith Wilson, *My Memoir*, p. 284.   [27] *Ibid.*, pp. 287-88.

son. She did not call from the bedroom but from a phone at the other end of the hall which did not connect with the White House switchboard. Hoover immediately sent a car and the Doctor arrived a few minutes after nine. The men went upstairs, but when Dr. Grayson tried to enter the bedroom he found the door locked. Mrs. Wilson responded to his knock and, after ten minutes, the Doctor emerged with his arms raised and exclaimed, "My God, the President is paralyzed!" Hoover entered the bedroom in the late afternoon and saw the President lying in the Lincoln bed, unconscious—"he looked as if he were dead"—and noticed two long fresh cuts over Wilson's temple and nose. After making discreet inquiries over the next two days, Hoover concluded that Wilson had fallen from the toilet seat and struck his head on the protruding bathtub fixtures.

Hoover's account suggests that Mrs. Wilson washed the blood from her husband's face and carried him into bed herself.[28] Her behavior was not unusual: a patient (and his relatives) often postpones calling a doctor until he is presentable. Mrs. Wilson's reaction and later account of it were also motivated by her determination to keep her husband's condition secret and to minimize it. Although she states that Wilson had only a momentary lapse of consciousness, Hoover indicates that his state of alertness was impaired during the three weeks that he lay immobile in bed.[29] Dr. Grayson's diary does not cover this period, but his published memoir notes that Wilson could swallow with difficulty at the end of a week but could not speak above a whisper.[30]

Wilson's condition was complicated by a urinary obstruction, presumably caused by his immobile position and his enlarged prostate. Dr. Hugh H. Young, chief of urology at the Johns Hopkins Medical School, and another urologist, Dr. Harry A. Fowler of Washington, were called in. There was some discussion of an operation[31] to relieve the obstruction, but Dr. Young advised against it on the ground that

[28] Edith Wilson was a strong woman, capable of a ten-mile hike through the Maine woods with a pack on her back. *Ibid.*, p. 51.

[29] Hoover, "The Facts about President Wilson's Illness."

[30] Wilson whispered the limerick:

> A wonderful bird is the pelican
> His bill will hold more than his bellican
> He can take in his beak enough food for a week
> I wonder how in hell-he-can.

Grayson, *An Intimate Memoir*, p. 108.

[31] The proposed operation would have been a median line abdominal incision to open the bladder and insert a catheter.

Wilson might not survive it and that he probably would void naturally. Dr. Young's decision was vindicated a few hours later.[32] Mrs. Wilson, however, relates that Dr. Young advised an operation but that Grayson told her that Wilson could not stand the procedure and that *she* refused consent.[33]

The symptoms indicate that Wilson suffered an occlusion of the right middle cerebral artery, which resulted in a complete paralysis of the left side of his body, a loss of sensation on that side, and a left homonymous hemianopia—a loss of vision in the left half fields of both eyes.[34] Because he had already lost central vision in his left eye from his stroke in 1906, he had clear vision only in the temporal (outer) half field of his right eye. The weakness of the muscles of the left side of his face, tongue, jaw and pharynx accounted for his difficulty in swallowing and the impairment of his speech. His voice was weak and dysarthric, and his speech never regained its modulation, resonance, fluency, and melody.[35] It was especially affected by emotion. At the end of October, he was taken out of bed and placed in a chair; he could not support himself, however, and a large rolling chair equipped with braces was obtained. Power in his left arm never returned, and it was not until after Christmas that he could stand and walk a few steps with the assistance of a cane. When he tried to smile or speak, the weakness of his left face became more apparent. It was evidently for this reason that Wilson grew a beard and a mustache. His visual loss made it difficult for him to read, and the tendency of patients with large right-hemisphere lesions to ignore visual (and auditory) stimuli on the left side, a condition known as hemi-inattention, added to his problems.[36]

Wilson had no visitors for four weeks and received his first callers when the King and Queen of the Belgians came to see him on October 31. Hoover describes the technique used for such occasions. Wilson was put to bed, propped up, and his body covered, except for the head and right arm. The curtains were drawn, the room dimly lit, and the visitor placed on his right. This was done to conceal Wilson's paralysis and to insure that he would not ignore people on his left side. Mrs.

[32] Hugh H. Young, *Hugh Young, A Surgeon's Autobiography* (New York, 1940), pp. 399-401.

[33] Edith Wilson, *My Memoir*, p. 291.

[34] There is no evidence that his condition was due to syphilis, as was rumored. Serological tests were negative.

[35] Perry, *And Gladly Teach*, p. 283.

[36] See Weinstein and Friedland, eds., *Hemi-inattention and Hemisphere Specialization*.

Wilson stood at the foot of the bed and Dr. Grayson at the doorway, ready to interrupt if necessary. The royal couple may have been startled by the President's white beard, but the interview went well. When they were questioned by reporters afterward about his condition, they observed protocol and replied that he was fine.[37]

The stroke also resulted in changes in Wilson's behavior. He developed manifestations of anosognosia—literally, lack of knowledge of disease—a condition in which the patient denies that he is paralyzed, or has lost his vision, or even that he is ill in any way. Anosognosia is commonly associated with hemi-inattention as a consequence of large right-hemisphere lesions. (It occurs less frequently with pathology of the left hemisphere.) Although the anosognosic subject is not conscious of his incapacities, he shows knowledge of them in a number of ways. He may transfer his incapacity to another person: a hemiplegic patient may say that someone else is weak and paralyzed. Although the subject may admit to some deficiency, he tells of activities which are obviously incompatible with his impairment. For example, a patient of the author's with articulatory and praxic difficulties said that he had written a speech to be delivered by President Eisenhower. The anosognosic patient frequently represents the situation of illness metaphorically or humorously.[38] A man who had undergone a brain operation called his head bandage a "turban," and a woman referred to her hospital bed as a "chaise lounge." Mood is inappropriate: despite severe incapacities patients seem calm and unconcerned. Some have periods of euphoria, while others express paranoid reactions such as attributing a paralyzed limb to mistreatment by doctors and nurses. Certain areas of language and cognition remain unaffected; on tests of general intelligence the patient may achieve the score expected from his educational background. In casual conversation, the anosognosic patient may appear quite normal, even bright and witty.

The form and intensity of anosognosia depends not only on the location, extent, and rapidity of onset of the brain lesion, but also on the social milieu in which the behavior occurs, and on the patient's premorbid personality. Verbal denial is prominent in persons such as Wilson, who have habitually minimized illness, for whom illness has meant a loss of status and personal integrity, and who have regarded its manifestations as outside the self. Also, like Wilson, they have

[37] Hoover, "The Facts about President Wilson's Illness"; Edith Wilson, *My Memoir*, pp. 292-95.

[38] Some patients nickname an affected part of the body. MacDonald Critchley, "Misoplegia, or Hatred of Hemiplegia," *The Mount Sinai Journal of Medicine*, XLI (1974), 82-87.

tended to consider these manifestations in the context of principles and values.[39]

Wilson did not deny that he was physically ill, and he realized that the functioning of his left limbs was impaired—he referred to himself euphemistically as "lame." He did not believe that his illness prevented him from properly carrying on his duties, and he did not declare himself disabled. On the contrary, as we will see, he sought a third term. Nor did Wilson recognize the extreme self-referential character of his language and the degree to which his judgment of men and events was determined by his felt inadequacies. His judgment was far better in matters which did not threaten his integrity. Formerly, Wilson had used images and figures of speech to present well-thought-out ideas more vividly; however, after his brain lesion, his metaphors often controlled his thinking. He maintained his principles of morality, honor, and duty: these categories, however, contained what others interpreted as unrelated and contradictory elements. In his classification, Wilson reduced complex issues to all-or-none questions of right or wrong, and of morality or immorality. Thus, under the conditions of brain dysfunction, the language which had enabled Wilson to adapt to stress and to shape the behavior of people became maladaptive and self-isolating.

Wilson's wife and doctor reinforced his denial. Mrs. Wilson believed that it would be therapeutic to conceal the seriousness of his illness from him, and that his recovery would be hindered if he was presented with matters which might tax his capacities. She and Dr. Grayson were also concerned that, if the nature of Wilson's illness was known, his authority would be impaired. Accordingly, during the first months of his illness, Wilson saw neither Tumulty nor any members of his cabinet. Mrs. Wilson consulted with them, took their messages, and reported what her husband had said. She sometimes answered in a handwritten note, or wrote Wilson's instructions on the margin of the document. A number of letters went unopened. When Wilson's general condition improved so that he could receive visitors, they were screened to insure that they would not upset him and would make favorable comments on his health.[40]

Mrs. Wilson states in her *Memoir* that she did nothing in political matters except to follow doctors' orders. She relates that, as soon as Wilson was out of danger, she inquired about his prognosis and was told that he would recover only if he was removed from every dis-

[39] For a discussion of phenomenological, neurophysiological, sociocultural, and personality dimensions of anosognosia, see Weinstein and Kahn, *Denial of Illness.*

[40] Hoover, "The Facts about President Wilson's Illness."

turbing influence. When she asked Dr. Dercum how she could do so when the country looked to him for leadership, the Doctor reportedly told her: "Madam, it is a grave situation, but I think you can solve it. Have everything come to you; weigh the importance of each matter, and see if it is possible by consultation with the respective heads of Departments to solve them without the guidance of your husband. In this way you can save him a great deal. But always keep in mind that every time you take him a new anxiety or problem or excite him, you are turning a knife in an open wound. His nerves are crying out for rest, and any excitement is torture to him." When Mrs. Wilson asked if it would be better if the President resigned, the Doctor allegedly told her: "No, not if you feel up to what I have suggested. For Mr. Wilson to resign would have a bad effect on the country, and a serious effect on our patient. He has staked his life and made his promise to the world to do all in his power to get the Treaty ratified and make the League of Nations complete. If he resigns, the greatest incentive to recovery is gone; and as his mind is clear as crystal he can still do more with even a maimed body than any one else. He has the utmost confidence in you. Dr. Grayson tells me he has always discussed public affairs with you; so you will not come to them uninformed."[41] It is extremely unlikely that Dr. Dercum would have assumed such responsibility or would have used language so much like Mrs. Wilson's. By the time her book was published, the Doctor was dead.

On October 6, four days after the onset of the incapacitating stroke, Lansing called a meeting of cabinet members at which Dr. Grayson was asked for a diagnosis of the President's condition. The Doctor replied that Wilson was suffering from "a nervous breakdown, indigestion, and a depleted nervous system." Grayson warned that the patient should be bothered as little as possible, since any excitement might kill him. At the end of the meeting, Daniels suggested to Grayson that, if the truth of the President's illness was known, there might be a great wave of sympathy for Wilson.[42] Grayson agreed, but said that he had been forbidden—presumably by Mrs. Wilson—to speak of Wilson's illness.[43] Lansing cited the section of the Constitution which provided for the Vice-President to assume the office of the President during the period of the latter's incapacity, but Dr. Grayson refused to sign any certificate of disability. The Doctor also told the group that Wilson had expressed irritation over the report of the meeting and had wanted to know by whose authority it had been

[41] Edith Wilson, *My Memoir*, pp. 288-89.
[42] Houston, *Eight Years with Wilson's Cabinet*, II, 38.
[43] Daniels, *The Wilson Era*, II, 512.

called.[44] The following day Grayson gave more information to his friend, Breckinridge Long, Third Assistant Secretary of State. Long's diary for October 7 reads: "This afternoon I talked to Admiral Grayson at the White House and he said the President is still in grave danger and will be for some days, possibly weeks, to come and that by the date of the intended arrival of the Prince [of Wales] [in November] he will probably not be well enough to have him at the White House as a guest and may not be able even to see him. His blood pressure is getting back to normal but he is very weak and some of his veins are very thin and Grayson fears even the least irritation or worry. He has even taken the newspapers from him and is keeping him absolutely quiet and fears it may be two months before he will be well again tho' he feels he can soon decide official business of a routine nature if it is put to him in writing."[45] In view of Wilson's medical condition, it is highly unlikely that his wife or Dr. Grayson would have told Wilson about the cabinet meeting.

In November, Senator Lodge introduced the Treaty with fourteen reservations, and Senator Hitchcock called on Wilson to discuss Democratic strategy. He asked Wilson if he had read the Lodge reservations and if he had anything to suggest concerning them. Wilson, according to Grayson, who was present at the interview, immediately replied, "I consider it a nullification of the Treaty and utterly impossible." Wilson then drew the dubious analogy between the resolution and South Carolina's nullification of the Tariff Act of 1832. When Hitchcock called his attention to the reservation to Article 10, Wilson replied, "That cuts the very heart out of the Treaty; I could not stand for those changes for a moment because it would humiliate the United States before all of the allied countries." When Hitchcock commented upon the effect of the defeat of the Treaty, Wilson spoke of the humiliation of having to ask Germany to accept reservations. He then declared: "If the opponents are bent on defeating this Treaty, I want the vote of each Republican and Democrat recorded, because they will have to answer to the country in the future for their acts. They must answer to the people. I am a sick man, lying in this bed, but I am going to debate the issue with these gentlemen in their respective states whenever they come up for reelection if I have breath enough in my body to carry on this fight. I shall do this even if I have to give my life for it. And I will get their political scalps when the truth is known to the people. They have got to account to their constituents for their

[44] Houston, II, 69; E. David Cronon, ed., *The Cabinet Diaries of Josephus Daniels, 1913-1921* (Lincoln, Neb., 1963), p. 445.
[45] Long diary, October 7, 1919.

actions in this matter. I have no doubt what the verdict of the people will be when they know the facts."[46]

Hitchcock recalled the exchange which closed the interview:

"Mr. President," I said, "it might be wise to compromise with Lodge on this point."

"Let Lodge compromise," he replied.

"Well, of course," I added, "he must compromise also, but we might well hold out the olive branch."

"Let Lodge hold out the olive branch," Wilson concluded.

"And that ended it for the day," Hitchcock said, "for he was too sick a man to argue in the presence of his anxious doctor and his more anxious wife."[47]

Wilson's combative words posed a sad contrast to his physical helplessness. Although he vowed to bring his opponents to account, he did not have the strength and balance to stand erect, and he was otherwise totally unable to make a speech. In his isolated state, he did not recognize that for most Americans and their representatives in Congress it did not matter vitally if the reservations were adopted. Indeed, probably a majority of Americans favored reservations in some form. Wilson's language, however, controlled his behavior; he saw no middle ground, and he directed Hitchcock to instruct the Democrats to vote against ratification with the Lodge reservations.

Mrs. Wilson pleaded in vain with her husband to yield. She recalled: "He turned his head on the pillow and stretching out his hand to take mine answered in a voice I shall never forget: 'Little girl, don't you desert me; that I cannot stand. Can't you see that I have no moral right to accept any change in a paper I have signed without giving to every other signatory, even the Germans, the right to do the same thing? It is not *I* that will not accept; it is the Nation's honour that is at stake. . . . Better a thousand times to go down fighting than to dip your colours to dishonourable compromise.' "[48] Hitchcock suggested that he draft a letter which the President might send to him. Most of the corrections in the letter are in Mrs. Wilson's handwriting. Wilson's errors, confined to the extreme left side of the page, indicate his hemi-inattention.

The Democrats followed the President's bidding and joined with the irreconcilables to defeat the Lodge resolution by a vote of fifty-five to

[46] Grayson, *An Intimate Memoir*, pp. 102-103.

[47] "Brief View of the Late War and the Struggle for Peace Aims," an address made by Hitchcock before the Nebraska Historical Society, Lincoln, Nebraska, January 13, 1925, p. 21, the Papers of Gilbert M. Hitchcock, Library of Congress.

[48] Edith Wilson, *My Memoir*, pp. 296-97.

thirty-nine. It is the author's opinion that the cerebral dysfunction which resulted from Wilson's devastating strokes prevented the ratification of the Treaty. It is almost certain that had Wilson not been so afflicted, his political skills and his facility with language would have bridged the gap between the Hitchcock and Lodge resolutions, much as he had reconciled opposing views of the Federal Reserve bill in 1913, for example, or had accepted the modifications of the Treaty suggested in February, 1919.

Questions of Wilson's mental competence arose in the Senate, and diagnoses of his condition were determined by party affiliation. Senator George H. Moses, Republican of New Hampshire, charged that Wilson had a brain lesion, and Dr. Grayson replied that his mind was clear as a bell. After the kidnapping of an American consular agent, William O. Jenkins, in Puebla, Mexico, Senator Albert B. Fall of New Mexico introduced a resolution for the appointment of a committee to visit the President, ostensibly to discuss Mexican affairs, but in fact to determine his mental status. Fall and Hitchcock were selected and came to the White House on the afternoon of December 5. Wilson was in bed in a shaded room, and Mrs. Wilson stood on his left side, holding a pad and pencil—in order, she said, to avoid shaking hands with Fall. Dr. Grayson explained that the President was in bed because he had been up much of the morning. Fall greeted Wilson by saying, "Well, Mr. President, we have all been praying for you." "Which way, Senator?" Wilson countered. His wit was not altogether spontaneous, as his father had often made the same quip to well-wishing parishioners. The interview went well: Fall did most of the talking and Wilson listened attentively. His speech slightly thick, he told Fall that he would read his memorandum, go over the facts, and let the Senator know his decision. Wilson also commented on Senator Moses's statement. Moses, Wilson said, would be reassured by the result of the conference although he might be disappointed. After the meeting Fall and Hitchcock informed reporters that Wilson was in fine trim mentally and physically. They were so impressed that Hitchcock reported that Wilson had used *both* hands freely in picking up and laying down a copy of Fall's resolution.[49]

Wilson handled the Mexican situation effectively. The Carranza government's policy of expropriating large foreign agricultural properties and oil holdings had created pressure for intervention, and the Jenkins kidnapping incited demands for war. Even though Jenkins was released, Lansing recommended a break in relations. Wilson directed

---

[49] *Ibid.*, p. 299; *New York Times*, Dec. 6, 1919.

that negotiations be continued and informed the Senate that, although its consent was necessary for the ratification of international treaties, the present situation did not require its advice on relations with Mexico.[50] The Mexican affair did not contain the elements of personal stress that were involved in the ratification of the Treaty. Wilson, over the years, had avoided war with Mexico, despite provocations, and had no reason to feel guilty over his actions. Accordingly, he was under no compulsion to vindicate himself.

Wilson conceived the singular idea of having his Republican opponents in the Senate resign and seek reelection on the sole issue of the League. If a sufficient number of them were returned to office, he would appoint a Republican as Secretary of State. He and his Vice-President would then resign and, in accordance with the existing order of succession, the Secretary of State would assume the presidency. To expect that the Republicans would consent to the plan was, of course, unrealistic, and he was persuaded to pigeonhole the proposals. He returned to the subject in a message read at the annual Jackson Day Dinner in Washington on January 8, 1920. Wilson's original letter, edited by members of the cabinet, contained so many errors that Houston found it hard to believe that Wilson had had anything to do with its preparation.[51] Wilson stated that his western tour had confirmed his belief that the great majority of the American people favored the Treaty without reservations, and he proposed that the next election should take the form of a "great and solemn referendum" on the Treaty. The message had disastrous consequences. It opened a new breach with Bryan, who was willing to accept the Lodge reservations, and discouraged moderates who still hoped for some compromise. In Link's opinion, it destroyed Wilson's leadership among religious leaders, educators, editors, and publicists, who now all regarded Wilson as sick and petulant.[52]

The Jackson Day message indicated that Wilson might seek a third term, and the White House began a campaign to convince the public that he was physically fit. On February 10 the Baltimore *Sun* reported an interview with Dr. Young, who stated that the President had improved in all respects: "The slight impairment of his left arm and leg have improved more slowly. . . . At no time was his brain power or the extreme vigor and lucidity of his mental processes in the slightest degree abated. . . . The President walks sturdily now, without assistance and without fatigue. . . . As to his mental vigor, it is simply prodigious.

---

[50] Daniel M. Smith, *Aftermath of War: Bainbridge Colby and Wilsonian Diplomacy* (Philadelphia, 1970), pp. 102-103 and *passim*.

[51] Houston, II, 47.   [52] Link, *Revolution, War, and Peace*, p. 126.

Indeed, I think in many ways the President is in better shape than before the illness came. . . . His frame of mind is bright and tranquil and he worries not at all. . . . You can say that the President is able-minded and able-bodied, and that he is giving splendid attention to the affairs of state."[53] On the following day the *New York Times* printed an editorial which praised Dr. Young for rendering such "a service to common sense and truth by his temperate and exact statement."[54] A week later the White House announced that the President was at his desk every morning at 9:30; on March 19 the press was notified that he had taken his first automobile trip.

These statements did not accord with the facts. Wilson's left arm was useless; he could not rise unaided from a sitting position; and he could walk across a room only with the assistance of his cane, which he christened his "third leg." A visitor who saw him on February 25 found him sitting in his wheel chair wrapped in blankets and was shocked by his feeble appearance.[55] Wilson was incapable of working at a desk; his signature was distorted, probably because he wrote from bed or a wheel chair. His usual routine was for him to be taken from bed at about ten in the morning, placed in his chair and rolled to the South Portico or, weather permitting, outdoors. His automobile rides were discontinued because he could not sit erect against the motion of the car and pitched forward. The trips were resumed when he could be braced into the front seat.[56]

Wilson's dismissal of Lansing in February was a dramatic gesture of leadership. It was likewise an indication of Wilson's disbelief that he had been so desperately ill that he could not meet with his cabinet. Lansing had opposed Wilson's policies for years, and Wilson had ample justification for dismissing him. Wilson, however, did not cite these reasonable grounds but dismissed Lansing because he had learned that he had held cabinet meetings in his absence and without his permission. Wilson disregarded Tumulty's argument that, while the decision was right, the timing was wrong, since it would aggravate dissensions in the party. Mrs. Wilson asked him to document the real evidence against Lansing, but he refused because, he said, it would hurt Mrs. Lansing's feelings.[57] Wilson's publication of the correspondence between himself and Lansing indicates further how poor his judgment could be when denial of illness was a major motive.

[53] *Baltimore Sun*, February 10, 1920.
[54] *New York Times*, February 12, 1920.
[55] The visitor was Bainbridge Colby. Smith, *Aftermath of War*, p. 10.
[56] Hoover, "The Facts about President Wilson's Illness."
[57] Edith Wilson, *My Memoir*, pp. 300-301.

Wilson chose Bainbridge Colby to succeed Lansing. Colby was a New York lawyer who had been a Progressive in 1912 and had supported Wilson in 1916 when Roosevelt failed to receive the Republican nomination. Colby had won Wilson's trust with the aid of flattering letters, and Wilson had appointed him to the Shipping Board. Colby's qualifications for the post of Secretary of State were minimal. He was, however, an excellent orator and writer, and Wilson hoped that he would compensate for his own deficiencies. Under normal conditions, Wilson probably would have appointed Newton D. Baker, whom he had long considered as a successor to Lansing.

The extent of Wilson's disability was revealed in his first cabinet meeting held on April 13. Hoover wheeled him into the room and, as the members entered, they were announced by name—a procedure necessitated by Wilson's poor vision. His jaw drooped, but he appeared bright and cheerful at the outset, and began the session, as he often did, by telling a joke. It was about the Chicago aldermen who had got their heads together to form a solid surface. There was then a silence when Wilson did not follow up on his initiative. He said little throughout the rest of the session and, when the critical railroad situation was brought up, he had difficulty in fixing his mind on the topic. Dr. Grayson looked in several times as if to warn against tiring the President, and, at the end of an hour, Mrs. Wilson suggested that the members leave.[58]

Wilson began to suspect that Tumulty and members of his cabinet were trying to deprive him of the nomination. Actually, with the exception of Colby, they dreaded the prospect, but none dared to tell him so directly. Just as Dr. Grayson had been unable to tell his chief in 1914 that Ellen Wilson was fatally ill, the Doctor could not bring himself to inform him that his physical condition would not permit him to run.[59] There were demands over the country for Wilson to declare himself or indicate what candidates were acceptable to him, but the White House remained silent. McAdoo, a leading aspirant, sought a number of times to sound out his father-in-law but was denied an audience. Wilson also refused to speak with another prospective candidate, Attorney General A. Mitchell Palmer. He remarked to Grayson that it showed a lack of character in a cabinet officer to

[58] Hoover, "The Facts about President Wilson's Illness"; Houston, *Eight Years with Wilson's Cabinet*, II, 69-70.

[59] When it appeared that Wilson was actually planning to have his name placed in nomination, Dr. Grayson begged Senator Carter Glass of Virginia to talk him out of it. Rixey Smith and Norman Beasley, *Carter Glass: A Biography* (New York, 1939), pp. 205-206.

want to supersede his chief.[60] He indicated his intention to run when he told the members: "I cannot retreat from conscientious duty. I may not talk as well but I can still use the English language and if the people do not see the issue clear, I will put it so plain they must see it."[61]

On June 13, two weeks before the opening of the Democratic convention, Dr. Grayson presented the facts of Wilson's condition to Robert W. Woolley, an influential party leader. The President, Grayson told Woolley, was "permanently ill physically," was gradually weakening mentally, and could not recover. At times, the Doctor said, Wilson by grit and determination seemed to show a slight improvement. He was in good spirits for several days, even for a week or ten days, and would transact business with Tumulty. Then he would suffer a relapse and become so morose that it was distressing to be in the same room with him. No one, Grayson confided, could possibly appreciate what his wife and he, Grayson, had had to endure.[62]

Two days later Wilson summoned Louis Seibold, Washington correspondent of the New York *World*, to the White House. Seibold reported that Wilson was in fine shape and that his complete restoration to health seemed assured. According to the interview, Wilson made decisions unwaveringly and signed documents decisively, and, although he walked with a limp, he did not drag his leg as badly as General Wood.[63] Wilson's gait had improved slightly, but Seibold's appraisal was grossly misleading. There appeared, at the same time, pictures of Wilson, in right profile, seated at a desk with a pen in his hand, with Mrs. Wilson standing by holding papers for him to sign. On the eve of the convention, the White House released the news that Wilson had taken a long automobile ride.

Colby wired Wilson from San Francisco that the convention was prepared to nominate him and that he would put his name in nomination unless otherwise instructed. "The outstanding characteristic of the convention has been the unanimity and fervor of feeling for you."[64]

[60] The diary of Charles L. Swem, May 17, 1920, Charles L. Swem Collection, Princeton University Library; hereinafter cited as the Swem Diary.

[61] Cronon, ed., *The Cabinet Diaries of Josephus Daniels, 1913-1921*, p. 520.

[62] Robert W. Woolley, "Politics Is Hell," MS. in the Papers of Robert W. Woolley, Library of Congress.

[63] Bailey, *The Great Betrayal*, p. 310. General Leonard Wood had been a leading Republican candidate. He had a meningioma, a benign brain tumor, which had been operated on successfully by Dr. Harvey Cushing. Wood limped, but, unlike Wilson, other functions were unaffected. William C. Procter, Wilson's old protagonist in the fight over the graduate college at Princeton, had been Wood's campaign manager.

[64] Bainbridge Colby to WW, July 2, 1920, Wilson Papers.

Colby's plan was that, in the event of a deadlock, he would move for a suspension of the rules and call for Wilson's nomination by acclamation. Although the delegates expressed great sentiment for Wilson, they gave him no support and, to spare him humiliation, the leaders forced Colby to send a message of retraction.[65] Governor James M. Cox of Ohio was nominated on the forty-fourth ballot after a close fight with McAdoo. Wilson was displeased; when he heard that Cox had been chosen, he reportedly exclaimed, "They've picked the weakest one."[66]

Cox and his running mate, Franklin D. Roosevelt, called at the White House to announce their support for the League and were graciously received. Wilson's infirmities, however, prevented him from playing more than a minimal role in the campaign. He was active only sporadically amid periods of lethargy and depression. In contrast to his former punctuality, he often filed letters which he did not wish to read and did not reply until he was reminded by his wife. He did not acknowledge messages from his old friend, Frederick Jackson Turner.[67] One of the consequences of his stroke was a loss of sustained initiative. He would dictate a few letters and then lapse into "a sort of coma" from which he would rouse when Edith urged him to say what was on his mind.[68] However, he had periods when he functioned efficiently. At cabinet meetings, he appeared inactive until a discussion was begun, and then he would become alert and take part.[69] Stockton Axson recalled to Ray Stannard Baker: "I have seen Mrs. Wilson bring in to him some message that required some decision; and I have seen him immediately, just as quiet as you are now—just gather himself together without any marked physical effort,—and he would word the answer as clearly as he ever did anything in his life."[70]

Swem reported an incident which suggests that Wilson had impaired visuo-constructive skills, another sign of brain damage, particularly of the right cerebral hemisphere. Wilson complained that his letters, which were folded lengthwise by Mrs. Wilson, did not fit in the long Number 9 envelopes. Swem showed him how the page could be folded

[65] Daniels, *The Wilson Era*, II, 555-56.

[66] Hatch, *Edith Bolling Wilson*, p. 243. For accounts of Wilson's quest for a third term, see Kurt Wimer, "Woodrow Wilson and a Third Term Nomination," *Pennsylvania History*, XXIX (1962), 193-211, and Wesley M. Bagby, *The Road to Normalcy: The Presidential Campaign and Election of 1920* (Baltimore, 1962), pp. 54-62, 117-19.

[67] Swem diary, July 26, 1920.

[68] *Ibid.*, July 26, 1920.

[69] Houston, II, 91-92.

[70] Memorandum of interview with Stockton Axson, September 2, 1931, Baker Papers.

in three folds beginning at the bottom. Wilson did not seem to understand how it could be done and ordered special size envelopes.[71]

As brain disease becomes more chronic, displays of loss of emotional control are common. Wilson had frequent temper outbursts directed even against Dr. Grayson.[72] Axson observed: "I would read to him a great deal, back there in the autumn of 1920. I would read to him every morning and every afternoon. I would be reading to him, and he would be in a rather abject state, and occasionally would be seized with what, to a normal person, would seem to be inexplicable outbursts of emotion (he would begin sobbing, when there didn't seem to be anything particular in the text to call for it)."[73] Axson's observation is a classic description of so-called forced crying, a manifestation of chronic brain disease.

As the campaign drew to a close, it became evident that the Democrats would be badly defeated. Since Wilson seemed oblivious to the signs, Daniels tried to prepare him for the shock. Wilson, however, assured Daniels that the people could not possibly elect Harding.[74] He told Axson that the people always rose to "a moral occasion" and that Harding would be "deluged." Axson recalled: "Up to the last day I could make no impression on him. The day after the election I was so nervous about him that I called up the White House early and was told he was all right. As soon as I knew I could see him I went over. He was as serene as in the moments of his own preceding victories (and the matter can't be stated stronger than that). His first words, after greetings, were (and I remember them verbatim) 'I have not lost faith in the American people. They have merely been temporarily deceived. They will realize their error in a little while.' " With great insight, Axson wondered whether Wilson's attitude might not be a symptom of his disease.[75]

Wilson manifested less denial during his remaining months in office and continued to show signs of loss of initiative and emotional instability. It was necessary for Colby to draft his Thanksgiving proclamation for him. Wilson was often petulant and unreasonable. He would not sign a nomination until he asked the Attorney General which senator was behind the man, and if a senator of whom Wilson dis-

[71] Swem diary, August 13, 1920.

[72] Ishbel Ross, *Power with Grace: The Life of Mrs. Woodrow Wilson* (New York, 1975), p. 216.

[73] Memorandum of interview with Stockton Axson, September 2, 1931, Baker Papers.

[74] Daniels, *The Wilson Era*, II, 561.

[75] Memorandum of interview with Stockton Axson, September 2, 1931.

approved had written even a routine letter of support, the man would not be approved. Wilson took great delight in repeatedly watching a film of his trip abroad, and Mrs. Wilson surrounded him with symbols of his greatness—illuminated presentations from English cities, plaster of Paris casts of him, and cartoons showing him in a crusader's garb, holding a sword aloft and looking into the sun.[76] Wilson held his last cabinet meeting on March 1, 1921. After Colby and Houston had expressed their love and admiration and offered their wishes for his recovery, Wilson, with tears in his eyes and trembling lips, replied, "Gentlemen, it is one of the handicaps of my physical condition that I cannot control myself as I have been accustomed to do. God bless you all."[77]

[76] Swem diary, *passim*.
[77] Houston, II, 147-49.

CHAPTER XXII

Last Years

FOR FOUR YEARS after his retirement, Wilson lived in a house on S Street in northwestern Washington. The other occupants of the three-storeyed building were his wife, her brother, John Randolph Bolling, who acted as Wilson's secretary, and the servants, Isaac and Mary Scott. Dr. Grayson was detailed to duty in Washington by President Harding's order so that he could look in on Wilson, and a day nurse and a male night nurse completed the medical staff. The log kept by Bolling, Edith Wilson's *Memoir*, and notes made by visitors give us a picture of the daily routine.

Wilson rose early and had breakfast in bed, while his wife read the newspapers to him. He went downstairs in the electric elevator to the library, where he attended to his mail. The letters, which had been sorted by Bolling and gone over by Mrs. Wilson, were read to him or their contents summarized, and he either dictated a reply or gave instructions as to how the letters should be answered.[1] The mail finished, he took his daily walk back and forth across the hall. He then rested and went back upstairs, where he shaved himself. He usually had lunch in his bedroom with Mrs. Wilson's assistance. Sometimes an intimate friend, such as Bernard Baruch or Norman Davis, came to visit. Baruch noted on one visit that Edith wiped off a bit of rice which had stuck to Wilson's lip.[2] (The ignoring of utensils on one side of a setting or of food left on one side of a patient's cheek is a common feature of hemi-inattention.) Wilson might see another visitor before he went for his automobile ride in the afternoon. He usually had his dinner in front of the fireplace in the library with his wife in attendance. Only rarely did he take his meals with the family or with guests in the dining room.[3]

Mrs. Wilson read to him in the evenings—detective stories, the novels of Scott, Dickens, and Stevenson, and articles from *The Atlantic Monthly* and *The Forum*. He liked to look at the pictures in architectural and movie magazines: a rack beside him contained his reading glasses, a magnifying glass, and a flashlight. Some evenings he and his

---

[1] Edith Wilson, *My Memoir*, p. 322. [2] *Baruch*, II, 145.
[3] Edith Wilson, *My Memoir*, pp. 324-25.

wife played Canfield, and they watched movies about once a month. Wilson did not care for the radio, but he and Mrs. Wilson often attended the theater. They went to Keith's for vaudeville regularly on Saturday nights, and to plays at the National Theater less frequently.[4] In the baseball season, Wilson went to games at Griffith Stadium occasionally, where he watched the play from his car parked in the outfield.[5]

Wilson retained his passion for motoring. He purchased from the government the Pierce Arrow which he had used in the White House. His initials replaced the presidential seal and a miniature Princeton tiger sat on the radiator cap. The car was equipped with a closed body for the autumn and winter and an open one for the spring and summer so that Wilson could go out in all kinds of weather. As always, motoring had a high symbolic valence. Wilson insisted that his chauffeur, George B. Howard, keep within the speed limit of eighteen miles an hour, and, to avoid being conspicuous, he preferred that Howard not wear his uniform.[6] Wilson was also concerned that others abide by the law. While still in office he had written to the Attorney General to ask if the President did not have the powers of a magistrate so that he could "hold up some scoffing automobilist and fine him about a thousand dollars."[7] Starling commented that when Wilson's car was passed by another vehicle he would demand that the offending motorist be arrested for speeding.[8] On trips, Wilson never failed to salute a soldier or raise his cap to the flag. Sometimes he would order the car stopped so that he could talk with a disabled veteran.[9] Appropriately, on his last birthday he received the gift of a Rolls Royce from his friends.

Wilson found the transition from the presidency to private life difficult. He had long planned to write a book on government, but could not get past the dedication to his wife.[10] When Bainbridge Colby told him that he was going back into private law practice, Wilson suggested that they go into partnership. Mrs. Wilson was of two minds: she recognized that her husband could participate only minimally, but she wanted him to keep busy. Thus the partnership of Wilson and Colby, with offices in New York and at 1315 F Street, N.W., Washington, was formed. The plan was for Wilson to spend an hour a day in the Washington office, but he never made an appearance. Corporations

[4] *Ibid.,* pp. 324, 346-47.
[5] Interview with George B. Howard, June 27, 1976, author's possession.
[6] *Ibid.*   [7] Swem diary, September 9, 1920.
[8] Sugrue and Starling, *Starling of the White House,* p. 157.
[9] Grayson, *An Intimate Memoir,* p. 128.
[10] Edith Wilson, *My Memoir,* pp. 309-10.

and foreign governments sought the firm's services, but Wilson turned them down on the ground that he, as a former President, could not be a party to any action which involved the United States Government. (He took the fees of the single case which he accepted to buy his wife an electric car.)[11] After a year, Colby issued a statement to the newspapers that, in view of Mr. Wilson's continued progress toward good health, he, Colby, was withdrawing from the firm so that Wilson could turn his energies to greater things. Wilson's powers as a lawyer, Colby said, had been a revelation. Wilson replied, "I wish that it were all true."[12] Otherwise, Wilson recognized his limitations. He turned down contracts and many offers to write articles and columns, and he refused all offers to speak.

The first few months of retirement were depressing for Wilson. Homer S. Cummings, who visited him in April 1921, noted that he was still in bed and looked more depressed than Cummings had ever seen him. (Baruch told Cummings that he had a similar impression.) Wilson did not open the conversation, as he usually had, with a joke or an anecdote. He denounced the Democrats who had not stood by him and, in a self-referential vein, spoke of the helplessness of the United States in international affairs. He gloomily—and perhaps accurately—predicted that the French occupation of the Ruhr, if it went on for a lengthy period, would lead to the economic collapse of Europe and sow the seeds of a second world war. When Cummings remarked that it had taken all of his philosophy to overcome his disappointment over the defeat of the Versailles Treaty, Wilson replied, "If I had nothing but philosophy to comfort me, I should go mad." His eyes "filled with tears" and he seemed to Cummings "on the verge of a breakdown." The matter, Wilson said, was in the hands of Providence, and he and Cummings were only His humble instruments. At the conclusion of the meeting, Mrs. Wilson joined them, and her conversation at lunch did much to relieve the solemnity of the occasion.[13]

Although Wilson's neurological status did not improve during 1921 and 1922, and although his vision gradually declined because of progressive retinal vascular damage, he looked better and his spirits brightened. He had moods in which he was irritable and petulant, but he enjoyed visits from former associates. They took care not to tire him, but when they suggested leaving he often urged them to remain. Some

[11] *Ibid.*, pp. 326-29.

[12] Gene Smith, *When the Cheering Stopped: The Last Years of Woodrow Wilson* (New York, 1964), p. 209.

[13] The diary of Homer S. Cummings, April 25, 1921, in the Papers of Homer S. Cummings, University of Virginia Library; hereinafter cited as the Cummings Papers.

consulted with Mrs. Wilson about their meetings so that they would not say anything that might upset him.[14] Wilson sought the help of Baker, Baruch, Davis, Brandeis, and Cobb in composing the "Document," a statement of principles which would serve as a platform in 1924 and revitalize the party. Wilson also received visits from men with whom he had worked in Paris: Clemenceau, Lord Robert Cecil, Eleutherios Venizelos of Greece, and Philip Kerr (later Lord Lothian and British Ambassador to the United States). There were also visits from old Princeton friends and students: his classmates Cleveland H. Dodge, William Brewster Lee, and Dr. Edward P. Davis, and Bliss Perry, Lawrence C. Woods, and Roland S. Morris, whom Wilson had appointed Ambassador to Japan.

Cummings, who called on his old chief again in June 1922, saw a great change from the spring of the previous year. Wilson, he thought, looked better than "at any time since his illness began." He was in the library sitting in a straight chair, fully dressed and his handshake was "firm." Cummings noted that his host motioned him to a chair directly in front of him, evidently because of his poor vision. Wilson remarked that he had used the chair when he was President of Princeton and gave some pleasant reminiscenses of that period. The talk drifted into politics, and Wilson praised the work of Cordell Hull, who had succeeded Cummings as chairman of the Democratic National Committee. Wilson criticized the current administration for its lack of leadership. It was better, he told Cummings, for the country to have a strong leader like Theodore Roosevelt or himself who made mistakes than to have a President who did nothing. He made no direct personal references to Harding except to comment on his "mixed English." Wilson became emotionally upset only when the subject of the League came up but he quickly recovered himself.[15]

Wilson regained his sense of humor and his interest in language. He typed a constitution for a Pure English Club to remind his family to speak properly. He also began the study of Greek with his old friend Professor Williamson U. Vreeland of Princeton. He told Franklin D. Roosevelt that it was a race between them to see which of them would play golf first.[16] Wilson had become upset at any mention of death, but when Dr. Grayson told him that the Senate had passed a resolution congratulating him on his supposed return to health, he recited the limerick:

[14] Memorandum of interview of William G. Rice with WW, November 17, 1923, Baker Papers.
[15] Memorandum of interview with WW, June 28, 1922, Cummings Papers.
[16] Interview of William G. Rice with WW, May 2, 1922, Baker Papers.

There was an old man from Khartoum,
Who kept two black sheep in his room,
To remind him, he said, of two friends who were dead,
But he never would specify whom.[17]

A story reported by David Lawrence is a striking representation of
Wilson's left-sided loss of function, and perhaps of his dependence on
his wife. It was prompted by a visitor's remark that he must leave
because his wife was taking him on an errand. The story ran: A
monarch called together all of his male subjects and ordered those
who obeyed their wives to stand on his right side. All present—except
for one "puny" fellow, who did not look as if "he had spunk enough
to blow out a candle"—walked over to the king's right. "Do you not
obey your wife?" asked the monarch. "Oh, yes, sire." "Then why do
you not cross to my right side?" "Because my wife always told me to
avoid crowds," he replied.[18]

Wilson may have had a temporary exacerbation of his neurological
condition, perhaps transient strokes, in September 1922. Dr. Grayson,
who had seen him only occasionally since he left the White House,
saw him frequently, and Dr. Dercum was summoned from Philadelphia.[19] In 1923 Wilson's health grew steadily worse. His vision deteriorated so much that he became almost blind in both eyes.[20] Dr. de
Schweinitz was called into consultation,[21] but he could do nothing
except confirm his earlier diagnosis.

Upset by his declining health, Wilson became extremely anxious
about the state of the world and decided to call the public's attention
to the dangers. The task was agonizing; he could neither read nor
write and, often when his wife and Scott thought that he was asleep,
he would call out from bed to ask one of them to take down a sentence
or two.[22] Stockton Axson aided him in the preparation of the article,
and it was printed in *The Atlantic Monthly* in August 1923. It was
entitled "The Road Away from Revolution," and it began: "In these
doubtful and anxious days, when all the world is at unrest and, look
which way you will, the road ahead seems darkened by shadows which
portend dangers of many kinds, it is only common prudence that we
should look about us and attempt to assess the causes of distress and
the most likely means of removing them."[23] He spoke of the great

[17] Grayson, *An Intimate Memoir*, p. 135.   [18] Lawrence, p. 353.
[19] Bolling log, September 5, 7, 16, 20, 1922, Wilson Papers.
[20] Edith Wilson, *My Memoir*, p. 358; Grayson, *An Intimate Memoir*, p. 138.
[21] Bolling log, October 18, 1923.   [22] Edith Wilson, *My Memoir*, p. 347.
[23] "The Road Away From Revolution," in Baker and Dodd, eds., *Public Papers of Woodrow Wilson*, VI, 536.

mass of the Russian people whose lives, before the Revolution, were hemmed in by "barriers against which they were constantly flinging their spirits, only to fall back bruised and dispirited." The world, he said, had been made safe for democracy but not against "irrational revolution," and he appealed to churches, political organizations, and capitalists to follow the teachings of Christ.[24]

Wilson's slowly progressive brain pathology did not permit the gross denial which had followed his acute massive stroke. He was extremely depressed and obsessed with fears of abandonment. When Scott went on holiday in the summer, he could not sleep and was "frightfully nervous."[25] Scott may have sensed the situation from afar, for he returned on the fifth day of a two-week vacation. Dr. Grayson stayed in the house when the exhausted Mrs. Wilson took a week's vacation in August. With the single exception of a trip to New York to attend Lord Robert Cecil's address to the Woodrow Wilson Foundation, it was the only time that she had been away overnight. Wilson became severely depressed in her absence.[26]

Bernard Baruch's daughter, Belle, tried to cheer Wilson by inviting him to deliver an Armistice Day address on the radio. Edith, mindful of the torture he had endured in preparing his article for *The Atlantic Monthly*, sought to dissuade him, but he would not turn back. On the evening of November 10 he stood before a microphone in his library, supported by his cane. He could not read the page in front of him, nor had he been able to memorize it; his voice was forced and halting; he gasped audibly, and it was necessary for his wife to prompt him.[27] In his speech, Wilson poured out the accumulated bitterness of years of disappointment and suffering. The first paragraph of his brief address reads:

"The anniversary of Armistice Day should stir us to great exaltation of spirit because of the proud recollection that it was our day, a day above those early days of that never-to-be-forgotten November which lifted the world to the high levels of vision and achievement upon which the great war for democracy and right was fought and won, although the stimulating memories of that happy triumph are forever marred and embittered for us by the shameful fact that when the victory was won—won, be it remembered, chiefly by the indomitable spirit and ungrudging sacrifices of our own incomparable soldiers— we turned our backs upon our associates and refused to bear any

[24] *Ibid.*, pp. 536-39.
[25] Edith Wilson, *My Memoir*, pp. 349-50.   [26] *Ibid.*, pp. 351-52.
[27] *Ibid.*, p. 352; Smith, *When the Cheering Stopped*, pp. 228-29.

responsible part in the administration of peace, or the firm and permanent establishment of the results of the war—won at so terrible a cost of life and treasure—and withdrew into a sullen and selfish isolation, which is deeply ignoble because manifestly cowardly and dishonorable."[28]

Wilson left the library "utterly discouraged" over his performance.[29] However, many of the three million people who heard his voice were thrilled, and the next day a large crowd gathered in front of his home. After Carter Glass delivered a brief address, Wilson spoke: "Senator Glass, ladies and gentlemen: I am indeed deeply touched and honored by this extraordinary exhibition of your friendship and confidence; and yet I can say without affectation that I wish you would transfer your homage from me to the men who made the Armistice possible. It was possible because our boys had beaten the enemy to a standstill. You know—if you will allow me to be didactic for a moment—'Armistice' means 'standstill of arms.' Our late enemies, the Germans, call an Armistice 'Waffenstillstand,' an armed standstill; and it was the boys who made them stand still. If they had not, they would not have listened to proposals of armistice. I am proud to remember that I had the honor of being the commander in chief." When someone in the crowd shouted "The best on earth," Wilson's voice broke and he apologized for his emotion. He finished, however, and, as he started back into the house on the arm of an old Princeton student, he whispered to him for the crowd to be silent. Then in a strong voice he said: "Just one word more; I cannot refrain from saying it. I am not one of those that have the least anxiety about the triumph of the principles I have stood for. I have seen fools resist Providence before, and I have seen their destruction, as will come upon these again, utter destruction and contempt. That we shall prevail is as sure as that God reigns. Thank you."[30] Wilson had indeed come to a standstill; his words were the last he was to utter in public.

Over the last two or three months of his life, Wilson relived the past, sometimes in fantasy. "I owe everything to your mother," he told his daughter, Nell; as he dozed in the evenings, he had visions of Ellen reading poetry to him at Muskoka.[31] He hoped that he could obtain the presidency of a university so that he could continue the work

---

[28] "High Significance of Armistice Day," November 10, 1923, in Baker and Dodd, eds., *Public Papers of Woodrow Wilson*, VI, 540.

[29] Edith Wilson, *My Memoir*, p. 355.

[30] Smith, *When the Cheering Stopped*, pp. 230-32.

[31] McAdoo, *The Woodrow Wilsons*, p. 300.

which he had left unfinished at Princeton.[32] He commented to James Kerney that the liberals of the world still looked to him for leadership.[33]

Woodrow Wilson faced the end with courage and equanimity and, like his father, with humor. When Fosdick asked him how he felt, Wilson quoted one of his predecessors, "John Quincy Adams is all right, but the house he lives in is dilapidated, and it looks as if he would soon have to move out."[34] On January 27, Wilson did not appear noticeably worse to Dr. Grayson, and the Doctor left for a vacation at Bernard Baruch's estate in South Carolina. The next day, however, Wilson weakened badly, and Grayson returned to find him in extremis. As the consultants, Dr. Fowler and Dr. Sterling Ruffin, were about to enter, Wilson whispered, "Be careful. Too many cooks spoil the broth."[35] It was Wilson's last jest; he died at 11:15 on the morning of February 3, 1924.

[32] Raymond B. Fosdick, *Chronicle of a Generation: An Autobiography* (New York, 1958), pp. 230-31.

[33] Kerney, *The Political Education of Woodrow Wilson*, p. 466.

[34] Fosdick, *Autobiography*, p. 231.

[35] Grayson, *An Intimate Memoir*, p. 110.

SOURCES AND WORKS CITED

MANUSCRIPTS

Stockton Axson, Memoir of Woodrow Wilson, in the possession of Arthur S. Link.

Papers of Ray Stannard Baker, Library of Congress.

Bolling Log, Wilson Papers, Library of Congress.

Henry Wilkinson Bragdon Collection, Library of Princeton University.

Admission Records of the Central State Hospital, Milledgeville, Ga., Georgia State Archives.

The Diary of Homer S. Cummings, Papers of Homer S. Cummings, Library of the University of Virginia.

The Diary of Cary T. Grayson (December 3, 1918 to September 27, 1919), in the possession of Cary T. Grayson, Jr.

The Head Usher's Diary, Wilson Papers, Library of Congress.

The Diary of Edith Benham (Helm), Papers of Edith Benham Helm, Library of Congress.

Papers of Gilbert M. Hitchcock, Library of Congress.

The Diary and Papers of Edward M. House, Library of Yale University.

Interview with George B. Howard, in the possession of Edwin A. Weinstein, Bethesda, Md.

Papers of Breckinridge Long, Library of Congress.

The Diary of Vance McCormick, Library of Yale University.

"Princeton University. Minutes of the Standing Committee of the Board of Trustees on the Graduate School, from 1901 to 1946," bound minutebook, Archives of Princeton University.

The Diary of Charles L. Swem, Charles L. Swem Collection, Library of Princeton University.

Andrew F. West, "A Narrative of the Graduate College of Princeton University . . . ," Archives of Princeton University.

Papers of Woodrow Wilson, Library of Congress.

Woodrow Wilson Collection, Library of Princeton University.

Robert W. Woolley, "Politics is Hell," MS. in the Papers of Robert W. Woolley, Library of Congress.

PUBLIC DOCUMENTS

Publications of the United States Government

66th Congress, 1st Session, May 19-November 19, 1919, Senate Documents. Washington, 1919.

CORRESPONDENCE AND COLLECTED WORKS

Baker, Ray Stannard, and William E. Dodd, eds., *The Public Papers of Woodrow Wilson*. 6 vols., New York and London, 1925-1927.

Hirst, David W., ed., *Woodrow Wilson: Reform Governor: A Documentary Narrative*. Princeton, N.J., 1965.

Link, Arthur S., David W. Hirst, John E. Little *et al*., eds., *The Papers of Woodrow Wilson*, 38 vols. to date. Princeton, N.J., 1966-   .

McAdoo, Eleanor Wilson. *The Priceless Gift: The Love Letters of Woodrow Wilson and Ellen Axson Wilson*. New York, 1962.

Seymour, Charles, ed. *The Intimate Papers of Colonel House*. 4 vols., Boston and New York, 1926-1928.

AUTOBIOGRAPHIES AND MEMOIRS

Baruch, Bernard M. *Baruch*. 2 vols., New York, 1960.

Bernstorff, Count Johann H. von, *My Three Years in America*. New York, 1920.

Cronon, E. David, ed. *The Cabinet Diaries of Josephus Daniels, 1913-1921*. Lincoln, Neb., 1963.

Daniels, Josephus. *The Life of Woodrow Wilson, 1856-1924*. Philadelphia, 1924.

————. *The Wilson Era: Years of Peace*. Chapel Hill, N.C., 1944.

Elliott, Margaret Axson. *My Aunt Louisa and Woodrow Wilson*. Chapel Hill, N.C., 1944.

Ely, Richard T. *Ground Under My Feet: An Autobiography*. New York, 1938.

Finney, John M. T. *A Surgeon's Life: The Autobiography of J.M.T. Finney*. New York, 1940.

Fosdick, Raymond B. *Chronicle of a Generation: An Autobiography*. New York, 1958.

Grayson, Cary T. *Woodrow Wilson: An Intimate Memoir*. New York, 1960.

Grey, Sir Edward. *Twenty-Five Years, 1892-1916*. 2 vols., New York, 1925.

Helm, Edith Benham. *The Captains and the Kings*. New York, 1954.

Hoover, Herbert. *The Memoirs of Herbert Hoover*. 2 vols., New York, 1951-1957.

Hoover, Irwin H. "The Facts about President Wilson's Illness," MS. in the Papers of I. H. Hoover, Library of Congress.

————. *Forty-Two Years in the White House*. Boston, 1934.

House, Edward M. "Reminiscences of Edward M. House, 1858-1912," Papers of Edward M. House, Library of Yale University.

Houston, David F. *Eight Years with Wilson's Cabinet, 1913-1920.* 2 vols., Garden City, N.Y., 1926.

Hulbert, Mary Allen. *The Story of Mrs. Peck: An Autobiography.* New York, 1933.

Kohlsaat, Herman H. *From McKinley to Harding: Personal Recollections of Our Presidents.* New York, 1923.

Lawrence, David. *The True Story of Woodrow Wilson.* New York, 1924.

McAdoo, Eleanor Wilson. *The Woodrow Wilsons.* New York, 1937.

Nicolson, Nigel, ed. *Diaries and Letters of Harold Nicolson, 1930-1939.* New York, 1966.

Perry, Bliss. *And Gladly Teach.* New York, 1935.

Reid, Edith Gittings. *Woodrow Wilson: The Caricature, the Myth, and the Man.* London and New York, 1934.

Scott, William B. *Some Memories of a Paleontologist.* Princeton, N.J., 1939.

Sugrue, Thomas W., and Edmund W. Starling. *Starling of the White House.* New York, 1946.

Tumulty, Joseph P. *Woodrow Wilson as I Know Him.* Garden City, N.Y., 1921.

Wilson, Edith Bolling. *My Memoir.* New York, 1938.

Young, Hugh H. *Hugh Young, A Surgeon's Autobiography.* New York, 1940.

MISCELLANEOUS CONTEMPORARY WORKS

Collins, Varnum Lansing. *Princeton.* New York, 1914.

Hale, William Bayard. *Woodrow Wilson.* New York, 1912.

[House, Edward M.] *Philip Dru, Administrator: A Story of Tomorrow.* New York, 1911.

Mantoux, Paul. *Paris Peace Conference, 1919: Proceedings of the Council of Four, March 24 to April 18.* John B. Whitton, trans. Geneva, 1964.

McCosh, James. *The New Departure in College Education: Being a Reply to President Eliot's Defense of It in New York, February 24, 1885.* New York, 1885.

Nicolson, Harold. *Peacemaking 1919.* Boston and New York, 1933.

Norris, Edwin M. *The Story of Princeton.* Boston, 1917.

Presbrey, Frank B., and James Hugh Moffatt, eds. *Athletics at Princeton.* New York, 1901.

Smith, Arthur D. Howden. *The Real Colonel House.* New York, 1918.

West, Andrew F. *The Proposed Graduate College at Princeton University.* Princeton, N.J., 1903.

White, William Allen. *Woodrow Wilson: The Man, His Times, and His Task.* Boston and New York, 1924.

Williams, Charles Richard. *The Cliosophic Society of Princeton University.* Princeton, N.J., 1916.

Wilson, Joseph R. *Mutual Relation of Masters and Slaves as Taught in the Bible. . . .* Augusta, Ga., 1861.

WORKS BY WOODROW WILSON

George Washington. New York, 1897.

Mere Literature and Other Essays. Boston and New York, 1896.

NEWSPAPERS CITED

Baltimore *Sun.*
Daily Princetonian.
New York Times.

PERIODICALS CITED FOR EDITORIAL OPINION

Nassau Literary Magazine, XL (November 1904).
Olla Podrida '91, Middletown, Conn., 1890.

CONTEMPORARY ARTICLES

Butler, Howard Russell, "The History of the Lake," *Princeton Alumni Weekly,* V (April 29, 1905), 489-92.

Hulbert, Mary Allen, "The Woodrow Wilson I Knew," *Liberty: A Weekly for Everybody,* I (December 20, 1924), 8.

Lawrence, David, "The Inauguration of President Wilson," *Princeton Alumni Weekly,* XIII (March 5, 1913), 421.

"A Neutral." "Woodrow Wilson: The President's Policies Analyzed in the Light of His Natural Inhibitions and His Past Record," *The Nation,* CIII (September 14, 1916), 256-58.

"President Wilson's Address to the Board of Trustees," *Princeton Alumni Weekly,* VIII (June 12, 1907), 606-15.

Price, Carl F., "Woodrow Wilson at Wesleyan," *Wesleyan University Alumnus,* VIII (March, 1924), 3-7.

SECONDARY WORKS

Aristotle's *Poetics, Oxford Dictionary of Quotations.* 2nd ed., London, 1953.

Bagby, Wesley M. *The Road to Normalcy: The Presidential Campaign and Election of 1920.* Baltimore, 1962.

Bailey, Thomas A. *Woodrow Wilson and the Great Betrayal.* New York, 1945.

———. *Woodrow Wilson and the Lost Peace.* New York, 1944.

Baker, Ray Stannard. *Woodrow Wilson: Life and Letters.* 8 vols., Garden City, N.Y., 1927-1939.

———. *Woodrow Wilson and World Settlement.* 3 vols., Garden City, N.Y., 1923.

Bartlett, Ruhl J. *The League to Enforce Peace.* Chapel Hill, N.C., 1944.

Beam, Jacob N. *The American Whig Society of Princeton University.* Princeton, N.J., 1933.

Bragdon, Henry W. *Woodrow Wilson: The Academic Years.* Cambridge, Mass., 1967.

Burns, James McGregor. *Roosevelt: The Lion and the Fox.* New York, 1956.

Clements, S. D. *Brain Dysfunction in Children.* Washington, 1966.

Condit, Kenneth H. *A History of the Engineering School of Princeton University, 1875-1955.* Princeton, N.J., 1962.

Devlin, Patrick. *Too Proud to Fight: Woodrow Wilson's Neutrality.* Oxford, 1974.

Finch, Edith. *Carey Thomas of Bryn Mawr.* New York, 1947.

Fink, Max. *Convulsive Therapy: Theory and Practice.* New York, 1979.

Floto, Inga. *Colonel House in Paris: A Study of American Policy at the Paris Peace Conference 1919.* Aarhaus, Denmark, 1973.

Fowler, Wilton B. *The British-American Relations, 1917-1918: The Role of Sir William Wiseman.* Princeton, N.J., 1969.

Freud, Sigmund, and William C. Bullitt. *Thomas Woodrow Wilson: A Psychological Study.* Boston, 1967.

Gelfand, Lawrence E. *The Inquiry: American Preparation for Peace, 1917-1919.* New Haven and London, 1963.

George, Alexander, and Juliette George. *Woodrow Wilson and Colonel House: A Personality Study.* New York, 1956.

Gunther, John. *Roosevelt in Retrospect: A Profile in History.* New York, 1950.

Hale, William B. *The Story of a Style.* New York, 1920.

Hatch, Alden. *Edith Bolling Wilson: First Lady Extraordinary.* New York, 1961.

Heaton, John L., comp. *Cobb of "The World": A Leader in Liberalism.* New York, 1924.

Kennan, George F. *Russia and the West Under Lenin and Stalin.* Boston, 1960.

Kerney, James. *The Political Education of Woodrow Wilson.* New York and London, 1926.

King, Charles E. *From the Landing to Modern Port Arthur.* Port Arthur, Ont., 1927.

Link, Arthur S. *Wilson.* 5 vols. to date, Princeton, N.J., 1947- .

———. *Woodrow Wilson: Revolution, War, and Peace.* Arlington Heights, Ill., 1979.

Loetscher, Lefferts A. *The Broadening Church: A Study of Theological Issues in the Presbyterian Church Since 1869.* Philadelphia, 1954.

Livermore, Seward W. *Politics Is Adjourned: Woodrow Wilson and the War Congress, 1916-18.* Middletown, Conn., 1966.

Mayer, Arno J. *Politics and Diplomacy of Peace Making: Containment and Counterrevolution at Versailles, 1918-1919.* New York, 1967.

Mowry, George F. *The Era of Theodore Roosevelt, 1900-1912.* New York, 1958.

Mulder, John. *Woodrow Wilson: The Years of Preparation.* Princeton, N.J., 1978.

Noble, Ransom E., Jr. *New Jersey Progressivism Before Wilson.* Princeton, N.J., 1946.

Prescott, Samuel C. *When M.I.T. was "Boston Tech."* Cambridge, Mass., 1954.

Richardson, Robert N. *Colonel Edward M. House: The Texas Years, 1858-1912.* Abilene, Tex., 1964.

Rixey, Marion Presley. *The Life Story of Presley Marion Rixey: Surgeon General, U.S. Navy 1902-1910.* Strasburg, Va., 1930.

Ross, Ishbel. *Power with Grace: The Life of Mrs. Woodrow Wilson.* New York, 1975.

Rudolph, Frederic. *The American College and University.* New York, 1962.

Smith, Daniel M. *Aftermath of War: Bainbridge Colby and Wilsonian Diplomacy.* Philadelphia, 1970.

Smith, Gene. *When the Cheering Stopped: The Last Years of Woodrow Wilson.* New York, 1964.

Smith, Rixey, and Norman Beasley. *Carter Glass: A Biography.* New York, 1939.

Stevenson, Frances. *Lloyd George.* New York, 1971.

Strode, Hudson. *The Story of Bermuda.* New York, 1932.

Unterberger, Betty Miller. *America's Siberian Expedition, 1918-1920: A Study of National Policy.* Durham, N.C., 1956.

Viereck, George S. *The Strangest Friendship in History: Woodrow Wilson and Colonel House.* New York, 1932.

Walworth, Arthur. *America's Moment, 1918: American Diplomacy at the End of World War I.* New York, 1977.

———. *Woodrow Wilson.* 2nd ed., Cambridge, Mass., 1965.

Weinstein, Edwin A. *Cultural Aspects of Delusion: A Psychiatric Study of the Virgin Islands.* New York, 1962.

———, and Robert P. Friedland, eds., *Hemi-inattention and Hemisphere Specialization.* New York, 1977.

———, and Robert L. Kahn. *Denial of Illness: Symbolic and Physiological Aspects.* Springfield, Ill., 1955.

Wertenbaker, Thomas Jefferson. *Princeton, 1746-1896.* Princeton, N.J., 1946.

Willert, Arthur. *The Road to Safety: A Study in Anglo-American Relations.* New York, 1952.

SECONDARY ARTICLES

Ainsworth, Mary D. S., and S. M. Bell. "Mother-Infant Interaction and the Development of Competence," in K. J. Connolly and Jerome Bruner, eds., *The Growth of Competence.* London and New York, 1974.

Batten, George M., Jr. "Cary Travers Grayson," *National Cyclopædia of American Biography.* 58 vols., New York, 1940, XXVIII, 132-33.

Challener, Richard D. "William Jennings Bryan," in Norman A. Graebner, ed., *An Uncertain Tradition.* New York, 1961.

Critchley, MacDonald. "Misoplegia, or Hatred of Hemiplegia," *The Mount Sinai Journal of Medicine,* XLI (1974), 82-87.

Cutler, Charles C., Jr. "Dear Mrs. Peck," *American History Illustrated,* VI (1971-72), 5-9, 46-48.

Davies, J. D. "The Lost World of Andrew Fleming West," *Princeton Alumni Weekly,* LX (Jan. 15, 1960), 10-14.

Fromm-Reichmann, Frieda. "Loneliness," *Psychiatry,* XXII (1959), 1-15.

Geschwind, Norman. "The Apraxias: Neural Mechanisms of Disorders of Learned Movement," *American Scientist,* LXIII (March-April 1975), 188-95.

Hirst, David W. "Francis Landey Patton," in Alexander Leitch, ed., *A Princeton Companion.* Princeton, N.J., 1978.

Hutchison, William R. "Disapproval of Chicago: The Symbolic Trial of David Swing," *Journal of American History,* LIX (June 1972), 30-47.

Kahn, Robert L., Max Fink, and Edwin A. Weinstein. "Relation of Amobarbital Test to Clinical Improvement in Electroshock Therapy," *Archives of Psychiatry and Neurology*, LXXVI (1956), 23-29.

Link, Arthur S. "Woodrow Wilson and the Study of Administration," in Link, *The Higher Realism of Woodrow Wilson and Other Essays*. Nashville, Tenn., 1971.

Livermore, S. W. "The Sectional Issue in the 1918 Congressional Elections," *Mississippi Valley Historical Review*, XXV (June 1948), 29-60.

Mijuskovic, Ben. "Loneliness: An Interdisciplinary Approach," *Psychiatry*, XL (1977), 113-32.

Root, Robert K. "Wilson and the Preceptors," in William Starr Myers, ed., *Woodrow Wilson: Some Princeton Memories*. Princeton, N.J., 1946.

Stroufe, L. Alan. "Attachment and the Roots of Competence," *Human Nature*, I (1978), 50-57.

Weinstein, Edwin A. "Woodrow Wilson's Neurological Illness," *Journal of American History*, LVII (September 1970), 324-51.

———, and R. P. Friedland. "Behavioral Disorders Associated with Hemi-inattention," in Weinstein and Friedland, eds., *Hemi-inattention and Hemisphere Specialization*. New York, 1977.

———, and Olga G. Lyerly. "Confabulation Following Brain Injury: Its Analogs and Sequelae," *Archives of Neurology and General Psychiatry*, XVIII (1968), 349-54.

———, and Olga G. Lyerly. "Symbolic Aspects of Presidential Assassination," *Psychiatry*, XXXII (1969), 1-11.

Weisenburger, Francis P. "The Middle Western Antecedents of Woodrow Wilson," *Mississippi Valley Historical Review*, XXIII (December 1936), 375-90.

Wimer, Kurt. "Senator Hitchcock and the League of Nations," *Nebraska History*, XLIV (September 1963), 189-204.

———. "Woodrow Wilson and a Third Term Nomination," *Pennsylvania History*, XXIX (1962), 193-211.

———. "Woodrow Wilson Tries Conciliation: An Effort That Failed," *The Historian*, XXV (August 1963), 419-38.

Zaidel, Eran. "Lexical Organization in the Right Hemisphere," in Pierre A. Buser and Arlette Rougeu-Buser, eds., *Cerebral Correlates of Conscious Experience: Proceedings of an International Symposium on Cerebral Correlates of Conscious Experience, Held in Senanque Abbey, France on 2-8 August 1977*. Amsterdam, 1978.

INDEX

Publication of Supplementary Volumes to *The Papers of Woodrow Wilson* is assisted from time to time by the Woodrow Wilson Foundation in order to encourage scholarly work about Woodrow Wilson and his time. All volumes have passed the review procedures of the publishers and the Editor and the Editorial Advisory Committee of *The Papers of Woodrow Wilson*. Inquiries about the Series should be addressed to The Editor, Papers of Woodrow Wilson, Firestone Library, Princeton University, Princeton, N.J. 08544

Raymond B. Fosdick, *Letters on the League of Nations. From the Files of Raymond B. Fosdick* (Princeton University Press 1966)

Wilton B. Fowler, *British-American Relations, 1917-1918: The Role of Sir William Wiseman* (Princeton University Press 1969)

John M. Mulder, *Woodrow Wilson: The Years of Preparation* (Princeton University Press 1978)

George Egerton, *Great Britain and the Creation of the League of Nations* (University of North Carolina Press 1978)

Stephen L. Vaughn, *Holding Fast the Inner Lines: Democracy, Nationalism, and the Committee on Public Information* (University of North Carolina Press 1980)

Robert C. Hilderbrand, *Power and the People: Executive Management of Public Opinion in Foreign Affairs, 1897-1921* (University of North Carolina Press 1980)

Inga Floto, *Colonel House in Paris: A Study of American Policy at the Paris Peace Conference 1919* (Princeton University Press 1980)

Edwin A. Weinstein, *Woodrow Wilson: A Medical and Psychological Biography* (Princeton University Press 1981)

Library of Congress Cataloging in Publication Data

Weinstein, Edwin A., 1909-
  Woodrow Wilson, a medical and psychological biography.

  (Supplementary volumes to the papers of Woodrow
Wilson)
  Bibliography: p.
  Includes index.
  1. Wilson, Woodrow, 1856-1924.   2. Presidents—United
States—Biography.   I. Title.   II. Series. [DNLM: WZ 313
W754W]
E767.W42   973.91'3'0924 [B]   81-47162
ISBN 0-691-04683-2   AACR2